The Research University in a
Time of Discontent

The Research University in a Time of Discontent

Edited by Jonathan R. Cole,
Elinor G. Barber, and Stephen R. Graubard

The Johns Hopkins University Press
Baltimore and London

Portions of this book appeared in *The American Research University,* the Fall
1993 issue of *Dædalus,* volume 122, number 4, of the *Proceedings of the
American Academy of Arts and Sciences.* The Preface and chapters 5, 8, 9, 11, 12,
13, 16, 17, and 19 constitute new materials prepared expressly for publication in
this book.

The Johns Hopkins University Press
2715 North Charles Street
Baltimore, Maryland 21218-4319
The Johns Hopkins Press Ltd., London

Library of Congress Cataloging-in-Publication Data will be found at the end of
this book.
A catalog record for this book is available from the British Library.

ISBN 0-8018-4957-8
ISBN 0-8018-4958-6 (pbk.)

Contents

Preface   vii

1   Balancing Acts: Dilemmas of Choice Facing
Research Universities
Jonathan R. Cole   1

2   The Politics of Ambivalence: Diversity in the
Research Universities
Neil J. Smelser   37

3   Rationality and Realism, What Is at Stake?
John R. Searle   55

4   Making Choices in the Research University
Donald Kennedy   85

5   Presidential Leadership
Steven Muller   115

6   Competition and the Research Universities
Stephen M. Stigler   131

7   The Mission of the Research University
Nannerl O. Keohane   153

8   The Place of Teaching in the Research University
Frank H. T. Rhodes   179

9   Can the Research University Adapt to a
Changing Future?
Walter E. Massey   191

10   America's Research Universities under Public Scrutiny
Kenneth Prewitt   203

11 In Defense of the Research University
    Seymour Martin Lipset   219

12 The Research University as a Setting for
    Undergraduate Teaching
    Adrienne Jamieson and Nelson W. Polsby   225

13 Current Criticisms of Research Universities
    Harvey Brooks   231

14 The Appropriate Scale of the Health
    Sciences Enterprise
    William C. Richardson   253

15 Federal Science Policy and Universities:
    Consequences of Success
    Rodney W. Nichols   271

16 Governing the Modern University
    Robert M. Rosenzweig   299

17 The Distinction and Durability of American
    Research Universities
    Francis X. Sutton   309

18 Knowledge without Borders? Internationalization
    of the Research Universities
    Eugene B. Skolnikoff   333

19 The Research University: Notes toward a
    New History
    Stephen R. Graubard   361

    Index   391

Preface

P ERIODICALLY, IT BECOMES IMPERATIVE TO CONFRONT a growing concern about the state of higher education in the United States and today, particularly, about the American research university, the unique creation of the last century. The authors in this volume have different, if somewhat overlapping, perspectives on the current troubles. Some, choosing to look forward, are persuaded that the research university is basically sound and successful, despite the criticisms frequently heard, and that the central challenge is for these institutions to continue on their proven course. While no one denies that the environment for higher education is in certain respects less benign than it was, this may be seen as providing the opportunity to define and realize new broad objectives, in consonance with traditions of inquiry and scholarship which have become established.

To assess the consequences of diminished federal research support and to consider the advantages and perils of the larger international stage on which the American research university is today obliged to operate are among the major concerns of this volume. No such consideration can fail to take account of the major internal changes taking place, reflecting strains created by an increasing diversity of faculty and students and by the profound substantive controversies that threaten the traditional values of meritocracy and, indeed, of rationality itself. In these conditions problems of governance become preoccupying. The challenge is to reorganize and perhaps downscale university activities without encroaching on the necessary autonomy of faculties, without compromising the legitimate teaching and research functions of various of its component schools.

The "mission" of the research university in the United States waits to be redefined in ways likely to resonate for the various publics concerned that the service function is today being scanted, that teaching, particularly of undergraduates, is woefully neglected. A growing commitment to include many previously underrepresented minorities in teaching and research has to be integrated into the mission. To relate all these components, and indeed to make them cohere, requires some reconsideration of the reward systems that exist, the disciplinary boundaries that have grown up, the criticisms being leveled, and the critical importance of public approval and support. While it is possible to differ about the gravity of the "crisis" that exists in higher education today, it makes no sense to ignore the potential for change, to reflect on where the universities might profitably seek to move in the years ahead.

The Research University in a Time of Discontent represents a collaboration between the American Academy of Arts and Sciences and Columbia University. At all stages of this project the volume's three editors, Jonathan R. Cole, Elinor G. Barber, and Stephen R. Graubard, were centrally involved in the plans and decisions.

An initial meeting was held at the American Academy of Arts and Sciences on 28–29 May 1991 to ascertain from knowledgeable individuals whether, indeed, there was agreement with the diagnosis that excellence in higher education is at risk. The following individuals attended, along with the editors: David E. Apter, Daniel Bell, David Finn, Gerald Holton, Carl Kaysen, Morton Keller, Sally F. Moore, Joel Orlen, Diane Ravitch, Walter A. Rosenblith, Robert M. Rosenzweig, Gian-Carlo Rota, and Edward Said. The participants confirmed the validity of concern about the issue at hand. We are grateful for their time and effort.

In the planning phase, in a meeting held on 2–3 April 1992, at the Academy, the editors had valuable assistance from the following participants: John F. Ahearne, Bernard Bailyn, Felix Browder, W. Robert Connor, Howard Gardner, Philip Gossett, Gerald Holton, William Kelley, Elizabeth T. Kennan, Daniel J. Kevles, Lance Liebman, Martin Meyerson, Francis Oakley, Kenneth Prewitt, Maxine Singer, Neil J. Smelser, Michael Teitelbaum, Samuel Thier, and Marina von Neumann Whitman. The editors, who also participated, are much indebted to these participants.

As a consequence of this meeting and other discussions, an issue of *Dædalus* took shape: topics were specified and authors were selected. Pursuing the customary *Dædalus* practice, all the papers were circulated among all the authors, who met, again at the Academy, in June 1993. That meeting was attended also by Michael Teitelbaum and Harriet Zuckerman. Again, we appreciate the time and effort expended by all those attending the meeting, and we are grateful to the participating authors for providing and accepting criticism of the articles. The Fall 1993 issue of *Dædalus*, "The American Research University," contained articles by Jonathan R. Cole, Donald Kennedy, Nannerl O. Keohane, Rodney W. Nichols, Kenneth Prewitt, William C. Richardson, John R. Searle, Eugene B. Skolnikoff, Neil J. Smelser, and Stephen M. Stigler.

Following the appearance of the *Dædalus* issue, we began to transform it into the present book. To add further perspectives on the present state and future prospects of the American research university, the editors solicited comments from another set of informed observers of the higher education scene in the United States. On relatively short notice, the following individuals contributed their perceptions and insights: Harvey Brooks, Stephen R. Graubard, Adrienne Jamieson and Nelson W. Polsby, Seymour Martin Lipset, Walter E. Massey, Steven Muller, Frank H. T. Rhodes, Robert M. Rosenzweig, and Francis X. Sutton.

Finally, we gratefully acknowledge the support of this undertaking which we received from three foundations: the James S. McDonnell Foundation, the Andrew W. Mellon Foundation, and the Alfred P. Sloan Foundation.

The Research University in a
Time of Discontent

Balancing Acts: Dilemmas of Choice Facing Research Universities

P ROGNOSTICATIONS OF THE DECLINE of American higher education, and particularly of our research universities, are not
infrequent. Analyses of the "current crisis" by critics and
friends surface only somewhat less frequently than the seven year
locust.[1] The list of diseases and etiologies leading to the imminent
decline of these institutions is long and includes such familiar items
as: claims of administrative waste, fraud, and abuse, and of the
corruption of fundamental academic values and standards; a retreat
from the undergraduate classroom; the perversion of the academic
reward system; the end of meritocracy; the triumph of corporate,
bureaucratic models of governance over the more congenial ecclesi-
astical style of shared decision-making through consensus formation; the ceding by faculty of academic authority and responsibility
for producing a rigorous and sound curriculum that defines the
shape and scope of the educated person; the erosion of public trust;
and among many more, the absence of visionary academic leaders
who can articulate the mission of research universities, who can
write the brief for them, and who can argue the case persuasively
before critical attentive audiences—in short, the lamentable absence
of the voices that represented the academy from the time of Eliot
and Hutchins to Conant and on down until only a generation or
two ago. Yet, none of these perceived problems is particularly new.[2]
Simultaneously, many shrewd, knowledgeable veterans of higher
education point out that the American research university continues
to be the jewel in the higher education crown, that it remains the

*Jonathan R. Cole is Quetelet Professor of Social Science and Provost of Columbia
University.*

envy of the world, the set of universities with the highest prestige and distinction in the nation, the institutions that hold the most sought after positions for talented faculty and students, the continuing producer of more Nobel Prize quality science than any other type of educational or research institution in the world, and one of the few remaining American "industries" with a favorable balance of trade. None of these defenses has been recently copyrighted.

What is new in the current debates about the state of research universities? The problems in generic form are not particularly new. They have existed above or below the surface over an extended period of time quite simply because they are linked fundamentally to the basic social and organizational structure of research universities. When these complex social systems experience disequilibrium, the problems surface. They tend to become open to substantial discourse only periodically—usually when the economies of research universities are constrained or when the conflicts within the university echo broad and fundamental conflicts within American society. But when they do surface anew, they are more often than not brought forward by a new set of critics who are unfamiliar with the history of research universities and the earlier appearances of these problems. In short, problems of governance, leadership, the foci of faculty and student attention, and the relationship of universities to external social systems of government, industry, and the general culture always exist. Nonetheless, our concerns today with the state of research universities do reveal some important new substantive variations on older themes. These new variations are the foci of this volume.

The contemporary problems involve dilemmas of choice that have become more pressing over the past several decades. I want to outline a number of these dilemmas and suggest that while the research university as an institution is not about to disappear or to lose its fundamental character and basic strengths, those universities that successfully deal with the dilemmas of choice will have important strategic advantages over their peers in the decades to come. Before discussing a number of these dilemmas, I want to indicate how patterns of growth and change in higher education over the past fifty years have created tensions within the academy and between the academy and some of its traditional partners who support research.

PATTERNS OF GROWTH AND CHANGE

We tend today to think of the major research universities—Berkeley, Chicago, Columbia, Harvard, Stanford—much as we did in the past. In important respects, there are great similarities in the pasts and presents of these universities, perhaps most notably in their basic commitment to teaching and research at a very high level of excellence. They are, after all, elite institutions whose reputations have been largely intact for the better part of the century.

Moreover, there has been relatively little change over the past half century in the number of schools within the universities or in their basic organizational structure.[3] But in ways that are not entirely appreciated, the Harvard or Columbia of today is a very different institution from what it was in 1945. The fundamental difference is in its size and complexity and in its responses to the exponential rate of growth of knowledge. Research universities, our principal incubators of new discoveries and ideas, reflect the pattern of exponential growth first described by the historian and sociologist of science Derek J. de Solla Price.[4]

While Columbia, for example, is in many ways the same university that Nicholas Murray Butler left behind in the academic year 1944–1945 (his last as president), it is in basic ways an entirely different enterprise.

Even in 1944, Columbia was concerned about a balanced budget: it faced a $1.6 million deficit, which it adroitly turned into a $65,000 surplus by June of 1945. This was all on an operating budget that totaled about $11 million. Today, still struggling to balance our books, Columbia will have an operating budget in 1993–1994 that is estimated to be roughly $1.1 billion—a budget 100 times greater than at the point of Butler's departure. Even a cursory glance at the intervening decades reveals dramatic growth in the University's expenses, signaling growth in the number and size of academic programs: from $57 million in 1959–1960 to $170 million in 1969–1970, to $317 million by 1979–1980, to about $800 million in 1989–1990. We have witnessed at Columbia more than a doubling in budgetary size about every ten years, with our annual expenses increasing at a compound rate of close to 10 percent for the past forty-five years.[5] Even allowing for the substantial inflation in portions of that period, this is an enormous rate of real growth. The same pattern of growth has been sustained by most of the other major research universities.[6]

Patterns of budgetary growth simply reflect patterns of expanding research and teaching opportunities. These changes are the underlying causes of the dilemmas I will consider. Change has come as a consequence of the salience of relatively new concerns of these universities about such matters as equal access to education (which has led to need blind/full need admissions and financial aid policies), affirmative action, and greatly increased support services for students. The positive results of the civil rights movement have led to increased diversity of the university population, and with increased diversity have come new conflicts over the curriculum, university hiring and promotion policies, and admissions and financial aid standards and practices at university colleges. Now that research universities reflect more closely the socioeconomic composition of the larger society, it is inevitable that they will experience more conflicts that were avoided when they had too little of a good thing.

The increased dependence of research universities on federal government financing of research and student financial aid has changed academic and financial relationships within universities. This has led to the enormous growth of health science divisions at research universities, has altered the relative size of health science compared with the arts and sciences and other professional schools, and has produced uncertainty about the future of scientific research at universities dependent on continued government support.

Add to these changes the growth of claims for new scholarly disciplines, the expanded number of Ph.D. programs competing for resources, the emergence of philosophical relativism, the increasing imbalance between research and teaching, and the transformation produced by the information revolution. When this is mixed in with a set of externally imposed constraints caused by a national economy that is not expanding at a rate comparable to that experienced in the 1980s, you have the conditions for dynamic change that will require research universities to confront many difficult dilemmas of choice. When resources contract even as the legitimate demands for sustaining academic excellence expand, universities will face dilemmas of choice, as they do now.

Dilemma One: Governance

How do research universities define their priorities? Who decides what to build, what to favor, what to contract, and what to eliminate? What gives the process legitimacy?

Of critical importance to the research university is the exponential growth of knowledge during the postwar period. Much of this growth was fueled by a massive increase in the federal government's investment in scientific research at the major universities. As knowledge expanded at this pace, there emerged a plethora of new claims for resources to fund new areas of knowledge. Even the great research universities began to experience a gap between the expanding knowledge base and the capacity to offer programs of high quality in *all* of these new areas—while also retaining excellence in the programs that had been sustained for generations.

During periods of rapid expansion in resources—which occurred to a substantial degree through the 1950s, 1960s, and 1980s—the research universities were able to live with the illusion that they could remain "full service universities" without having to make many difficult choices about which new areas of knowledge would take programmatic form and would be supported at a level needed to achieve true distinction; which currently supported areas would have to be phased out; and which areas of knowledge would go uncovered, left for others to develop, thus creating a true division of intellectual labor in higher education.[7]

It is rapidly becoming accepted that the 1990s will not allow for the expansion of the research university at the rate achieved in the 1980s and before. We have seen, accordingly, a spate of articles, generally authored by university or college presidents, former presidents, or those who make it their business to monitor the economics of higher education, that call for "doing more with less," or "growing through substitution" or "making difficult choices between competing goods." There is widespread recognition that it is no longer possible for research universities to afford excellence in all areas of knowledge, including those supported currently and those required to cover the most important areas of new knowledge. Most leaders of America's great research universities recognize that they have to make choices and that failure to do so bespeaks implicit choice in any event. Nonetheless, there has been far more talk about the need to make critical choices than a willingness to engage directly the problems associated with choice: to make creative, strategic decisions, and then to implement them within a reasonable time.

The fundamental problem of choice at research universities has more to do with basic ambiguity over governance than with the ability to articulate alternatives. Who has the authority, beyond the formal authority registered in the statutes or the table of organization, to make such choices? Who has the power to "veto" the choices made? What are the processes by which the choices of the decisionmakers are legitimated within the university community? What is the role of faculty, students, administrative leaders, trustees, and alumni in making such choices? Traditional business organizations have little problem assigning responsibility for decisions, while universities have failed to do so. The structure of universities impedes decisions from being made, creates suspicion among schools and departments about the explicitness and fairness of criteria for dividing up scarce resources, and reduces the flexibility institutions require to respond imaginatively and reasonably to new academic needs and priorities.[8]

Of course, research universities are not, cannot, and should not be organized in imitation of corporations. The process of decision-making is going to take longer than in the hierarchical culture of the corporate world. The goal is not to imitate the business community, but to take some lessons from it (especially in the administrative and business side of research universities). We must recognize that the rhythms of the external world have changed and that these changes directly affect the internal life of universities. The faster pace and the rapid growth of the institution requires more rapid, year-round responses and initiatives. This new environment requires a clearer process of decision-making so that universities can make meaningful changes and adaptations in a timely way.

The problem that universities have in reaching difficult decisions is not simply a matter of speed, but of certain structural features that produce difficulty in reaching conclusions.[9] First, they tend to be organized around a "company of equals" pattern. Second, they rely heavily on peer judgments of academic quality, which has great value but is not noted for producing high levels of consensus or for unambiguous judgments. Third, there is a high level of motivated unwillingness of any academic unit to criticize any other—at least when the stakes are as high as reductions in size or possible program elimination. Fourth, the pattern of economic commitments and rigidities associated with tenure can place a significant drag on movements to create changes in the composition of academic units and subunits. Finally, since most academic deans anticipate rejoining the faculty, they are reluctant to burn bridges behind them—a likely outcome if they make difficult decisions that cannot possibly please everyone.

Given these constraints, should such matters of choice be left principally, if not entirely, in the hands of the faculty? Can faculties with highly diverse and often competing interests lead each other to consensus? Is it the mark of outstanding academic leaders that they define priorities and build coalitions within the faculty to support a strategic plan for change—one that involves elimination of some programs and expansion of others? Will popular academic leaders lose their luster at the precise moment that they propose substantial cuts in some academic programs in order to focus resources on other areas of comparative strength? Should presidents and provosts of universities articulate the academic mission and vision for the university and then consult with the faculty about proposed changes?[10] What forms of consultation are appropriate for decisions involving reallocation of resources? To what extent should a limited number of active faculty be permitted to forestall proposed change? Answers to these questions are hardly self-evident since research universities do not have constitutions to govern this decision-making process and the "common law" at universities remains quite ambiguous about how and where decision-making authority resides.

It is, after all, one thing to say that universities will thrive if they have leaders who can build faculty coalitions supportive of difficult choices; it is another matter to articulate how that gets done. The difficulty derives, in part, from the strong value placed on faculty governance, when the vast majority of faculty focus appropriately on their teaching and research and know little if anything about the economics of the university.[11] It is also far easier to argue that there should be "competition" for resources among academic programs—followed by faculty discussion of the relative merits of these programs, which in turn would lead to faculty consensus on choices—

than to operationalize a structure for this competition and achieve faculty consensus. Admirable efforts at consensus building have been known to break down at the first mention of eliminating a department, reallocating faculty billets from one department to another, or reassigning laboratory space from one research program to another.

Efforts at making difficult choices have led to tense times at research universities. Many faculty tend to be opposed to any significant program change—any shift in academic priorities that is accompanied by shifting resource allocations—because they believe it is the slippery slope that could end with reconsideration of their own department's allocations. History will likely show that where substantial changes have occurred as a result of "choices," they have been unsystematic in their development, have involved small units and large expenditures of effort, and have been only tangentially related to any well-defined effort to shape the future direction of the university.

My recent experience at Columbia provides three exquisite, if not entirely admirable, examples. Over the past seven years, while there was substantial growth of academic programs at the university, two departments were closed— Geography and Linguistics—and the School of Library Service. Each of these fields is important, but was deemed not to be central to the future mission of the university. In the case of the School of Library Service, it took two years of intensive work by faculty and administrative committees, senate reviews, and responses to hundreds of individual and many group protests before the decision was implemented. That is the success story. It took seventeen years between the decision and the actual closing of the Linguistics Department; it took nearly as long to do the same with the Geography Department.

The closing of the School of Library Service is particularly instructive because of the implicit criteria of choice that the faculty and administration articulated in the process and debated at some length before the final decision was made. The fact that it was a small unit (four tenured faculty) probably contributed to the eventual outcome, but it was not a central factor. The framework for choice included the following elements: 1) an effort to establish a balance between core activities of the University and those that are peripheral (if enriching) activities; 2) academic priorities that juxtaposed the cost of maintaining and enhancing a preeminent school against the resources required for higher priority arts and sciences needs and the necessity to invest in other new programs; *3)* an evaluation of whether the School was critical to the educational and research missions of *other* schools of the University; *4)* the opportunity costs associated with over 25,000 square feet of space (in a space-poor campus) that might otherwise be used for renovation and expansion of Columbia's main library; *5)* an evaluation of whether the School would move decisively into information science, a goal that had been set five years earlier; *6)* the possibility of students interested in traditional forms of library service obtaining a quality education in the discipline at other universities in the nation; and *7)* the impact on the University's larger reputation of closing a school in an area in which we had been pioneers.

These criteria were used, often without explicit articulation, throughout the discussion of the School's future. There was never any disagreement about the quality of the past contributions of the School or of several of its current programs. There was substantial disagreement, however, in evaluations on some of the criteria and the weight that individuals place on the various elements in the framework. In the end, the decision was not one that called for weighing dollars against academic purposes, but one which confronted academic priorities in weighing the merits of competing academic needs.

The resistance to closing such academic units highlights not only the disposition of faculty, students, staff, and loyal alumni to protect everyone's turf lest their own become vulnerable, but also the distorted conception of the "life cycle" of academic departments, specialties, institutes, and centers at research universities. We have a marvelous sense of fertilization; we are experts at gestation and early development; we know about maturation and full expansion; but we refuse to confront dying and death. The academic way of death is traditionally through atrophy at a Darwinian pace. We rarely consider the idea of a full life course— of what should be associated not only with a beginning but with an end. And this is so because we have neither the rules that permit for orderly governance of choice nor the conceptual frameworks to guide those choices. Moreover, without clear, agreed-upon criteria, many academic leaders, looking at the consequences of "boldness" among some of their brethren, see, quite accurately, that making significant changes in the face of limited faculty opposition often leads to larger-scale faculty opposition, and potentially to a loss of personal authority and legitimacy.

Establishing informal criteria of choice in the case of the Library School constituted the beginning of a framework to guide difficult choices of this type.[12] The point is simply that discussions of choices would best be held within an agreed-upon framework of evaluation. In fact, we have only rare examples of faculties and their leaders engaged in thoughtful discussion of principles to guide choice. Research universities must consider what internal processes will increase the chances that choices will be viewed as legitimate by the university community.

If research universities can no longer cover all areas of knowledge, then each university will have to determine those areas in which it has comparative advantages in developing and maintaining true distinction. It will also have to judge which are the "core" areas of knowledge, the areas of such importance to the future of knowledge that any great research university, to be defined as such, will have to demonstrate excellence in them.

Finally, research universities will have to develop mechanisms that will enable them, despite their substantial fixed costs, to gain greater control over the resources needed to support new areas of knowledge.[13] Perhaps the greatest limit on flexibility is the tendency to allocate "permanent" tenure billets to departments. Mechanisms need to be developed at many universities for redistributing faculty lines and for developing full resource models for departments that treat resources as more fungible assets that can be distributed to support faculty, student fellowships, scientific facilities, and support services of academic departments.

What, then, is in order? It is time that these universities articulate a division of primary responsibility and authority in decision-making. It has often been repeated that the university *is* the faculty. But in the contemporary world of universities, faculty governance must be shared in an effective way with administrative leaders. Administrative leaders are drawn almost always from the faculty and do not renounce their faculty citizenship when assuming the office of president, provost, or chancellor. The false dichotomy between the faculty and administration ought to be replaced by a more sociologically appropriate view that some members of the faculty change their roles and their role obligations during their tenure as administrators. As administrative leaders, their interests may no longer be entirely consistent with the interest of their "home" department or school, but they continue to embody the core values and interests of the faculty. Nonetheless, primary control and responsibility for curricular decisions, faculty appointments, and promotions should reside, as they do now, in the active teaching and research faculty. The development of academic priorities should be a collaborative enterprise, with the faculty working with academic leaders. The academic vision and institutional priorities should be articulated by the university's president, provost, and deans—with the president as the voice of the university. The business of translating goals into achievements must be delegated to the executive arm of the university, backed explicitly by the trustees.

Difficult decisions will be better understood within the community if they are consistent with a well-defined, visible set of academic priorities for the university. But ultimately, there must be clear, final authority over the allocation of resources and the changing foci of attention at the university that is vested in its academic leaders. Consultation with faculty, students, and alumni about the bases for choices is essential, but there cannot be inordinate delays in decisions to mollify everyone. Academic leaders should present the faculty and students with clear explanations for their decisions. And, once the choices have been made, there ought to be open reporting of the outcomes that will permit the university community to evaluate the academic and financial consequences of the actions taken.

Dilemma Two: Who Owns the Null?

Research universities are facing a set of challenges and choices of a wholly different kind from those associated with the allocation of scarce resources. One of these is represented by a significant attack on the prevailing organizational axioms, or presuppositions, on which research universities have been built. A second is represented by a fundamental challenge to what John Searle calls "the Western Rationalistic Tradition" in his essay in this volume. This attack is leveled against the presuppositions of rationality, of objectivity, of truth, of "there being a there out there," among other basic epistemological and metaphysical presuppositions that have guided discourse throughout most of Western history, and certainly since the seventeenth century. These challenges to the university's organizational principles and to its philosophical presuppositions are interrelated. They involve conflicting views of the basic principles and what is required to prove that one or another organizational principle is right or wrong.

I shall call this conflict, which involves fundamental choices, "a conflict over who owns the null."[14] As users of statistical analysis will know, hypothesis testing involves setting up a "null hypothesis" and trying to overturn it. The null hypothesis states the hypothesis of zero difference or equality. This can be contrasted with the research hypothesis which involves a statement of expected differences. For example, suppose that I believe that science treats women unfairly in hiring, promotions, salaries, and peer recognition. That belief can be framed as my research hypothesis. To test that hypothesis, I set up the null hypothesis: science treats women fairly, that is, there are no differences in these forms of recognition between men and women. As a researcher, in order to "prove" that there is unfair treatment, I try to overturn the null by collecting sufficient evidence to demonstrate that the null hypothesis of equality must be rejected, that it is not true. I can use various tests, but generally in order to make the research hypothesis credible, I must minimally show that the pattern of difference between men and women would not have occurred by chance more often than five out of one hundred times.

As any empirical social scientist can attest, it is extremely difficult to accumulate enough acceptable evidence to reject, or overturn, the null hypothesis, given the limited power of social science theory and our inability to identify adequate methods and techniques that can be applied to complex social situations. Therefore, whoever controls, or "owns," the definition of the null is apt to preserve it against attacks based on existing evidence. The formulation of the null also determines who bears the burden of proof. It makes a great deal of difference if the null hypothesis is: "University X is a meritocratic institution without racism," rather than "University X is fundamentally a racist institution." Since overturning the null is difficult, the individual or group that "owns" it has a good chance of controlling the conclusion reached. This is particularly true because owning the null gives the owner control over the standards and practices in establishing "truth." It gives the owner the power to establish the methodology that is acceptable in trying to overturn the null—and that is what can make it doubly hard to overturn.

Consider first the challenge to the basic core values of the research university: meritocracy, rationality, organized skepticism, which enjoins members of the community to test ideas against appropriate evidence, and an open society which supports a free marketplace of ideas. Universities have been organized particularly around the value of meritocracy, which defines and requires the use of universalistic rather than particularistic standards of judgment. This value holds that the admission of students, the hiring and promotion of faculty, and the allocation of other forms of rewards and recognition will be based upon the quality of performance, not on the personal, ascribed characteristics of the individual. To be sure, universities have too often not fully approximated this ideal, but the value has been deeply ingrained in the institution and its self-definition.[15] Those who have governed the elite research universities and who have taught at them strongly believed in these core values. They have thus far controlled the definition of the null hypothesis.

At colleges and research universities, there is a substantial political drama unfolding over who owns the null—who gets to define the "truth" that must be falsified. Interestingly, the current attack on the existing "null" comes from both the cultural Right and the Left. From the Left, in its crudest form, comes the attack that the research universities as institutions are basically repressive, corrupt, racist, sexist, homophobic, biased in favor of Western cultural history and its literary forms, particularistic and nonmeritocratic, and are organized to perpetuate these values. Part of this attack is associated with aspects of "political correctness": efforts to limit "offensive," hurtful speech on campus through the introduction of speech codes; to review teaching and course materials for their content; and to review the content of presentations in the classroom for their offensive character.

Somewhat more subtle are the claims that a reward system that depends upon peer-reviewed publications and peer-reviewed assessments of quality undermines opportunities for "outsiders" to become "insiders." Under the prevailing system, the defender of the old order (read "old null") purports to make evaluations and decisions about admissions, appointments, and tenure without regard for the personal characteristics of individuals. In fact, the claim is made that these personal characteristics have always been relevant, but not acknowledged, and should now be made an explicit part of the decision-making process. These personal characteristics are relevant in at least two ways— even if *all parties* to the transaction are entirely unaware of their relevance. First, the person or group that owns the null cannot help judging the world from that point of view; and second, there are intrinsic differences between the way in which men and women, blacks or whites, do their work and, accordingly, in the criteria by which their work should be judged.

The attack on the existing presuppositions from the cultural Right assumes that the transfer of control of the null has been all but completed. The presumption is that the cultural Left has won, that the leaders of research universities have capitulated and officially endorsed various forms of limitations on free speech, have supported the creation of academic programs for political rather than substantive reasons, have adopted quota systems in admissions, financial aid, and academic appointments (or at least have adopted a set of different standards that are applied to groups rather than individuals), and have failed to defend faculty and students against unfounded, stigmatizing attacks. Faculty now live with great apprehension that they can be labeled a "racist" or a "sexist" without substantial support from their colleagues or university leaders and the burden of proof now lies with faculty to demonstrate that such allegations are false. Universities are attacked for capitulating to pressure from the Left to increase diversity and multiculturalism, for adopting the principles of group justice while abandoning the concept of individual opportunities without guaranteed outcomes. It is further claimed that entitlement has replaced meritocracy and opportunity as the governing principle in university decision-making.

Whether and how to formulate the null hypothesis is not a trivial decision. On the one hand, if we hold to the presupposition that the university is meritocratic, and that the university defines what "meritocratic" means, the burden of proof remains on those who believe otherwise. If, on the other hand, the null is framed as: "the university is fundamentally racist, sexist, and homophobic," then the burden of proof lies with those who want to prove that this is not the case. Since disproving the null is difficult, the ownership of the null corresponds to a set of important consequences in the formation of university policy.

Because it is difficult to prove or disprove complex phenomena like discrimination or racism, especially when the conflict is in part over the methods of proof, it is not surprising that the conflict takes on an ad hominem character. Assertions and counterassertions substitute for evidence, in part because the methods of establishing facts are the heart of the dispute. In Neil J. Smelser's chapter in this volume, Smelser suggests that academic leaders and faculty at research universities today have an easier time defending themselves against attacks from the Right than from the Left. He notes that universities are traditionally liberal institutions and leaders have had more experience defending against the cultural Right— and they feel more comfortable doing so. But liberal academic administrators and members of the faculty are ambivalent about defending themselves against attacks from the cultural Left, since they share a commitment to many of the goals associated with the Left, such as increased diversity on campus. Nonetheless, they have substantial difficulty with the means used to achieve those goals, and do not share the basic goal of redefining the null hypothesis. Thus, administrators and faculty leaders tread lightly in turning back assertions from the Left that are not supported by evidence. Smelser poses the dilemma faced by these leaders:

> Liberal academic administrators and faculty generally applaud and welcome "diversity" if it is carried out within the confines of meritocracy and the preservation of the values of the academy. When those values themselves come under attack, however, and when the attacks on them appear to be made in the context of antimeritocratic demands for entitlement, liberals are cast in an uncomfortable role, in which they experience a dissociation of—indeed a conflict between— meritocracy and egalitarianism. Their role now becomes one of a conservative elite, jealously guarding those values of universalism that were invented and best suited to challenge conservative elites.[16]

Ironically, liberal administrators feel reluctant to take a liberal stand for fear of not appearing liberal enough. A good example of this reluctance can be found in the recent debates over free speech and speech codes on campus. The prevailing null is that the university campus should be a free marketplace of ideas, with no limits on speech except, perhaps, in those rare events when the physical safety of the community is at risk. But that position, which would be held by liberal advocates of first amendment protection, is under attack. The position to the Left suggests that the protection of disadvantaged groups and the creation of a civil society on campus call for some judicious limitation on speech when speech takes the form of hate speech or displays of "offensive" symbols, such as sexually explicit photographs, a Confederate flag, or a swastika on the outside of a dormitory wall or inside a student's room. This attack on the null is cautiously, and ambiguously, resisted— often because of apprehension that those who defend free speech will become its victims, a result of stigmatizing labels. The liberal administrator fails to use speech in defense of his position for fear of being labeled racist or sexist, and as a result suggests an absence of commitment to the null.

What makes the current dilemma particularly interesting at universities is that the conflict over who owns the null hypothesis is a struggle for political power between groups within departments, centers, student bodies, faculties, institutes, administrations, and professional associations, and is being influenced by the changing social and ideological composition of these groups. The ultimate "fate" of the null may not be the result of any single choice, but of a series of choices, each having only a limited effect on the final outcome. This is the way social change often comes about.

Control of the null is no less important in the contemporary debates over the content and methods of scholarly work within many of the humanities and social science disciplines. It is not clear that the debates are carried on in terms of standard criteria of scholarship — or should I say traditional forms of scholarly discourse—since in some sense the criteria themselves are the subject of the conflict.

With increasing frequency, scholars in the humanities and social sciences at research universities are extending the older attack on positivism, but often without much knowledge or understanding of the deep philosophical and sociological questions that are involved in the challenge. The challenge is for control of the content of scholarship, and in some cases basic intellectual control over the core journals, the disciplines, and departments. In its current form, this challenge asserts that the fundamental tenets of Western philosophy, those on which modern science and social science have been built, are misguided. The challenge is to the basic concept of rationality. The constructivist argument is that there is no objective reality, that scientific knowledge—indeed all knowledge—is subjective and socially constructed, and that facts cannot exist independently of the attributes of their producer.[17]

Many of the critics of rationality, reality, objectivity, and the correspondence theory of truth associate that epistemology and metaphysic with a repressive social organization of the research universities—if not larger communities. The critics and their followers have multiple objectives. For some members of the professoriate who have thought deeply on these issues, it is to overturn the cognitive null because they believe that the older Western metaphysic and epistemology is wrong or no longer has positive heuristic value. For some within the professoriate and student body, it is to further a political agenda that has little to do with philosophy or scholarship. In some departments at research universities, the critique of the principles of reality, rationality, and objectivity has become the "politically correct" position and those scholars who fail to accept the critique are apt to find promotion and peer recognition increasingly difficult to acquire. It is not clear that members of university communities are fully aware of the implications of the attack on the cognitive null. In the meantime, scholarship at universities is changing without many members of the scholarly community coming to grips with the implications of these trends. For better or worse, control of the null is being relinquished in many departments at research universities without a serious discussion of the consequences of the transformation for scholarship and the training of students.

The unwitting abandonment of ownership of the null involves verbal transactions that are interesting enough to have attracted the attention of playwright David Mamet.[18] His play, *Oleanna*, shows us three meetings between John, a professor, and Carol, his student, in which the ownership of the null passes progressively from his hands to hers. At their first meeting, Carol has come to see him because she has written an unsatisfactory paper and is failing his course. Carol is, as she states early on, from a lower social and economic class than the faculty and many of the other students. She has worked hard and sacrificed to come to college and is diligent and earnest. She finds that despite her hard work she does not understand most of what transpires in her classes: her determination to succeed makes her aggressive about her failure to understand. Mamet's audience laughs when John, in an attempt to show Carol that her paper is gibberish, reads it aloud: "'I think that the ideas contained in this work express the author's feelings in a way that he intended, based on his results.'" John then asks her, "What can that mean? Do you see?" Mamet's audience are also people who own the null and although they may find John a bit pompous, they share with him the judgment that Carol's words do not mean anything. Carol, although she does not understand why her words lack meaning to John, believes entirely in John's evaluation of her work and in the absolute and eternal correctness of the ideals and standards which give him the right to judge. John owns the null, the power to define the vocabulary and syntax of the classroom, to define the kinds of logic and reasoning that are legitimate, to define who will receive a college degree and go on to reap the social and financial rewards it confers and who will not. John is clearly the beneficiary of this system: he has just received word he will be granted tenure and he is preparing to buy a house for his wife and child.

Mamet begins the first interview by giving John an innocently pompous speech which gives nothing away to Carol but which shows the audience the way in which the routine speech of academic daily life contains within itself the seeds of its own destruction. Carol asks, "What is a 'term of art'?" John's answer is innocently filled with academic terms of art:

> What is a "term of art"? It seems to mean a *term*, which has come, through its use, to mean something *more specific* than the words would, to someone *not acquainted* with them. . .indicate. That, I believe, is what a "term of art" would mean.[19]

His definition of a "term of art" reveals to the audience if not to Carol that language is not a universally clear medium. At the same time, his use of the rhetorical question, the conditional tense, and the insincerely self-deprecating "seems to mean" and "I believe" which reveal him as an academic insider to the audience are taken literally by Carol who asks, "You don't know what it means?" The literalness of Carol's response confirms that she is not privy to these academic terms of art. The stock diffidence, self-examination, and self-deprecation of academic speech of which John is a master and which mark him as an insider will turn out to belie real diffidence, real introspection, and real self-deprecation. The desire to *sound* open-minded and thoughtful does indeed reveal an ambivalent and fatal desire to be open-minded.

In words that should be uncomfortably familiar to everyone in academics, John goes on in the remainder of their first meeting to give away both his ownership and his claim to ownership of the null. In the face of Carol's persistence and lack of understanding, John attempts to mollify her and end the endless interview by means of a series of partially hypocritical, partially truthful statements of self-deprecation. First, John tries to put Carol off by insincerely suggesting to her that she is very bright but angry. Then he almost saves himself by beginning to suggest to Carol that her failure is her own fault. When Carol protests, he does not finish his thought. Almost immediately, John makes one more pass at upholding his standards and then he flounders:

John: What do you want me to do? We are two people, all right?
       Both of whom have subscribed to. . .

Carol: No, no. . .

John: . . .certain arbitrary. . .[20]

He reminds Carol that she is failing according to criteria to which she subscribed in a disinterested manner before she could know the outcomes of her subscription, but then in a moment of honesty, doubt, and weakness, he characterizes these standards as "arbitrary." Contrary to John's intentions, this only upsets Carol further and she presses on, insisting that there are standards that he must teach her, that she must understand. Finally, John succumbs to Carol, to his own self-doubt, to the complexity of the issue, and to open-minded diffidence and self-scrutiny which his discipline has held up to him as good. He suggests to Carol that she did not understand his book because "perhaps it's not well written. . .," that the distinction between teacher and student is an "Artificial *Stricture*," that the tests which students take in school and in college are "nonsense," designed "for idiots. . .*by* idiots. . .," that he would not employ the people on his tenure committee to wax his car, that she will get an "A" in his course because they will "break the rules" and "start over," and that they can do this because "What is the Class but you and me?" Carol is, of course, shocked. She has been told that there is absolute meaning in the world and in words and that her professors will teach her to understand. She has been told, as John says, and holds it as "an article of faith, that higher education is an unassailable good." In this interview, John has revealed something that he does not entirely believe—that he owns the null by power rather than by right. The possibility that this is true will transform both of them and redefine the entire discourse of the world of the play.

At their second meeting, Carol has brought John up on charges of elitism, sexism, and sexual harassment. Carol has quoted him accurately to the committee, and he finds in their report his own words. As he realizes that he no longer controls the definition of the vocabulary, John begins to find it difficult to make sense—or to understand. On the contrary, Carol, whose speech has been rather minimal, begins to speak in longer, more sustained and impassioned phrases. Of the charges, she says:

> You think, you think you can deny that these things happened; or, if they *did*, if they *did*, that they meant what you *said* they meant. Don't you see? You drag me in here, you drag us, to listen to you "go on"; and "go on" about this, or that, or we don't "express" ourselves very well. We don't say what we mean. Don't we? Don't we? We *do* say what we mean. And you say that "I don't understand you."[21]

Now, the words and the charges mean what Carol says they mean and it is John who does not understand. When John tries to deny that he intended to harass or intimidate her, Carol eloquently tells him what his own words meant to her:

> How can you *deny it*, You did it to me. *Here*. You *did*. . .You *confess*. You love the Power. To *deviate*. To *invent*, to transgress. . .to *transgress* whatever norms have been established for us. And you think it's charming to "question" in yourself this taste to mock and destroy. But you should question it. Professor. And you pick those things which you feel *advance* you: publication, *tenure*, and the steps to get them you call "harmless rituals." And you perform those steps.

Although you say it is hypocrisy. But the aspirations of your students. Of *hardworking students*, who come here, who *slave* to come here—you have no idea what it cost me to come to this school—you *mock* us.[22]

At their third meeting, Carol, and her "group," has seized the null not only within the university, but in the society at large: John has been charged with rape, the statutory definition of which, according to the authorities, matches his actions. The audience knows that according to the statutes and definitions of the old null John neither intended nor committed attempted rape. To prevent their sympathies from going over to him and also to reveal the weakness of his unexamined principles, Mamet has John try to take refuge in his belief in "freedom of thought." Carol understands perfectly that from her point of view "freedom of thought" is the last refuge of professorial scoundrels:

Then why do you question, for one moment, the committee's decision refusing you tenure?. . .You believe in what *you call* freedom of thought. Then, fine. *You* believe in freedom-of-thought *and* a home, and, *and* prerogatives for your kid *and* tenure. And I'm going to tell you. You believe *not* in "freedom of thought," but in an elitist, in, in a protected hierarchy which rewards you. And for whom you are the clown. And you mock and exploit the system which pays your rent. You're wrong. I'm not wrong.[23]

Carol brings the point home both to John and to the audience that "any atmosphere of free discussion is impossible" when one of the discussants has power over the other. As long as there is a null, someone will own it, and as long as someone owns the null, speech can never be free. Mamet does not explore the implication that without the null, or with a uniformly and universally-held null, speech might be said to be free—except that it would be meaningless. Mamet does suggest that he sees no net gain or loss in the transferring of the null we have just witnessed, simply a transfer of power and a shift in terms.

Oleanna has created quite a bit of controversy and has been disliked particularly by people who feel that the play portrays Carol's feminist awakening unsympathetically. These audiences are, in fact, people who believe in John's version of the null so strongly that they cannot imagine it ever being justly changed. They, like

John, want to enlarge the ownership of the null without changing its content. History and Mamet both teach us that this is unlikely.

Why does the current struggle for ownership of the null pose a dilemma of choice for university faculty and administrators? Because our own ideal of free inquiry and our own pride of intellect requires us to acknowledge the ways in which universities are not meritocratic or open to free inquiry and speech. Simultaneously, many of us believe in the ideals of meritocracy, organized skepticism, rationality, objectivity, and truth and wish to preserve them. To agree that there have been violations of the basic principles does not require their abandonment. To agree, however, that such principles are unattainable ideals may perhaps reduce them to empty words which allow one group to exercise power over others. The dilemma that universities face is how to deal effectively with demonstrable abridgments of the principles of meritocracy, objectivity, and rationality without fatally undermining them. Unless it rests on these principles, control of the null at the university is simply another sort of political power and social coercion.

It is hardly a new idea that knowledge is in some measure situationally based. However, does accepting the fundamental idea that scientists and the sciences are affected by their social characteristics and location mean that we must abandon the idea that there is an objective reality that is being increasingly approximated with additional knowledge? If owners of the null acknowledge that knowledge is to some extent socially constructed, that there are limits to objectivity, must they give up the ideal of objectivity and the correspondence theory of truth?

When we examine social and intellectual changes in scholarly disciplines and in the character of the university itself, the seeds of the transformation may prove to be sowed by the groups that currently claim ownership of the null. Those who relinquish the null may contribute to their own loss because they see some "truth" in the criticism and because they are committed to rationality and objectivity. Ownership can change as an unanticipated consequence of a commitment to ideals that are under attack; ideals that will be abandoned. If leaders go further, as in Mamet's play, and agree that the basic principles are empty and that they represent nothing other than expressions of prevailing power relationships, the stage is set for the overturn of the null. The leaders of university administrations and departments are being challenged to defend the core principles on a philosophical and sociological basis. If they choose not to respond to the challenge, transformations or stability in the null is apt to hinge on the efficacy of local political maneuvering and tests of power.

Two propositions are worth considering. First, overturning the null comes easily when the owners are not deeply committed to the principles that underlie the ownership. Second, with the shift in ownership of the null comes a shift in control of moral authority. For these reasons, among others, the stakes of the challenge are high at the research universities.

Dilemma Three: Striking a Proper Balance between the Demands of Scientific and Scholarly Research and of Teaching

Research universities continue to face the dilemma of how to fulfill their dual mission of excellence in teaching as well as in research. Is it possible in the highly competitive world of research universities, where academic free agency flourishes, for universities to produce faculty members who are among the most distinguished in the world in terms of research productivity and who will devote sufficient time and energy to teaching, particularly of undergraduates?

The legitimacy of the research university is at stake in being able to demonstrate that the answer to this question is yes. The dilemma is how to maximize productivity on both fronts so that these universities can reinforce their claims to preeminence in research with those who support and evaluate it and demonstrate teaching excellence and commitment by senior faculty with a public that is beginning to demand it.

If academic leaders feel that there is currently an imbalance between the time allocated to research and to teaching, it is of their own making. The current state of affairs results from research universities being in a highly competitive environment where the goal is to be "the best" (among the top five to ten ranked departments or professional schools), and to be *perceived* as among the best. Such perceptions will not come from hiring and promoting those who have extraordinary track records as teachers without equivalent research records. To be recognized as the best, research universities try to monopolize the talent market. This is even more difficult today than fifty years ago, but that is the goal: to bring in as many truly distinguished faculty as budgets and persuasion will permit—both younger and more established eminences, whose research publications are envied by others and who have won recognition from institutions that confer recognition and rewards for research achievements. That is the script for legitimating the strength of a department, a school, or a research university. It is the basis on which universities make claims for their unique quality and preeminence. It is how research universities gain legitimacy and increased resources in the competitive world of research funding and in the competition for the best students and faculty. It is the principal basis for their reputational standing and prestige. Moreover, it is the basis for prestige for individual members of faculties—even those who gain recognition not for their own achievements but through their association with a distinguished department or school. Thus, personal and institutional legitimacy is obtained predominantly through research achievements. That is what academic leaders have coveted as much, if not more, than the faculty. Indeed, to a significant degree, enhancing research excellence is a measure of an academic leader's performance in office.

Thus, the dilemma is often incorrectly cast in terms of individual faculty members trying to avoid teaching while academic administrators seek to steer them back to the classroom. I know very few faculty who are not interested in teaching bright students and very few academic leaders who do not spend time recruiting scholars and scientists who are known for their research rather than for their teaching. In fact, academic leaders have consistently applied strong pressure and provided large incentives for faculty to pursue their research interests with almost singular devotion. And for good reason. This not only reinforces what most faculty find exciting and enjoy doing, and leads to a national and international reputation, but research excellence legitimates the university's claim to greatness. Greatness, as currently defined, depends almost exclusively on the quality and quantity of research produced by the faculty and on knowledge within important reference groups of that quality. Academic leaders recruit and support scientists and scholars who have made or are apt to make seminal discoveries—those who define fields and specialties.

The real puzzle is how to reshape a reward system, which has been created by the competition for quality and prestige in research and which has upset the balance between teaching and research, so that the scales are rebalanced and research is unimpaired. Is it possible to achieve very high levels of commitment to and excellence in teaching among the most prominent scholars at research universities without damaging the quality of the research enterprise? What price needs to be paid and will the outcome prove worthwhile?

Some years ago, former Yale University president A. Bartlett Giamatti, in one of his lyrical essays about the "real world of the university," enjoined research universities to increase their commitment to teaching. "All the research we want to do, all the obligations we must carry as faculty are in some sense nurtured by and are versions of that first calling, which is to teach our students. We want always to do more, but we can never do less."[24] Many university presidents have followed Giamatti in calling for increased attention to teaching, and particularly to undergraduates. There is, of course, much virtue in these statements of mission. As lyrical and appealing as Giamatti's prose may be, his rhetoric fails to capture the structural tension that exists at research universities between these two dimensions of the mission, and the language surely fails to recognize fully the set of fundamental cross pressures and structurally induced ambivalences felt by many faculty who aim simultaneously to be "the best" in the laboratory and in the classroom. The cross pressures result from being encouraged to apply for and to obtain as many research grants as possible; to support expensive research programs and laboratories, including support for graduate and postdoctoral students; and to publish research that brings renown to the university, while being pushed to devote time to graduate and undergraduate classroom teaching at a level of commitment and performance equal to that displayed in running a research program. Not only do these normative prescriptions create substantial time-budget problems, but they often lead to uncertainty among faculty about how they are expected to spend their time. Under these stressful conditions, most faculty members look to the reward system for guidance. Until the reward system changes and the incentive structures shift, there will continue to be a preponderance of effort directed toward research.

It is not impossible to address this dilemma and to make an effort to rebalance the scales. Academic leaders can do more to shift the balance through their actions than their rhetoric. Consider some of the things that could be done at research universities to gain greater support for undergraduate and graduate classroom teaching, and ultimately to place greater emphasis on the lasting contributions scholars can make through the achievements of their students. First, as former Harvard University president Derek Bok has suggested, research universities should not compete for faculty by negotiating reduced teaching loads or unusually generous paid leave arrangements.[25] During the 1980s, the bidding wars for academic stars often led renowned professors away from students. This created a "class" structure within the ranks of the professoriate; and reinforced the perceptions that classroom teaching was not prized. The legitimacy of these universities began to be undermined as the public became aware of escalating tuition costs coupled with the retreat from the classroom.

Second, research universities must try to create a culture that explicitly honors excellence in teaching as well as in research. We must not only insist on good teaching, but we must demonstrate that it will be rewarded. Again, Derek Bok, among others, has suggested that we create "teaching portfolios" that will not only be used in promotion and tenure decisions, but in helping young scholars become outstanding teachers.[26] We must not simply demand better teaching, as if the demand will be sufficient to create the supply of distinguished teachers. We should invest in programs that help young researchers become outstanding classroom teachers, and begin to develop better indices of the quality of their teaching performance—ones that measure different types of teaching in different types of settings.

Third, this desirable cultural change is more apt to happen if research university leaders insist that quality of research dominate quantity. Promotion and tenure decisions must focus on the best that a scholar or scientist is able to produce, not on the sheer volume. Limiting the number of publications that could be submitted for review by a candidate for tenure would reinforce the effort to limit output for its own sake. It might also permit greater concentration on teaching roles and the interaction between research and teaching.

Finally, we must clarify the problem itself. Complaints about undergraduate teaching at American universities have occurred regularly at least since Benjamin Franklin ridiculed the instruction offered to Harvard undergraduates in 1772. The problem today, as two hundred years ago, is not one of the quantity of teaching as much as of the content and the quality. The dilemmas associated with a rebalancing of the roles of teaching and research will not be solved even if we manage the difficult assignment of changing the reward system. It is not simply a matter of substituting full professors for advanced graduate students in undergraduate classrooms, or of faculty offering more courses. The absence of full professors from classrooms may be symptomatic of the problem, but it fails to confront the major issues of the quality of teaching, and the lack of coherence in the curriculum that we offer students—that is, unstructured curriculums that do not represent the books and materials that the faculty believes college students should engage, but a grab bag of courses that capitulate to market forces and current fashion. A serious examination of classroom teaching will undoubtedly reveal that some advanced graduate students are brilliant teachers who will become the great, full professor teachers of tomorrow, while some of the "giants" of today who are absent from the classroom were the poor teachers of the past. The problem is not really the professorial rank of instructors (although professors of all ranks should be active teachers of undergraduate and graduate students); it is the absence of institutional interest in understanding the bases for a productive advanced learning experience, and an unwillingness of many research universities to commit the resources necessary to improve teaching performance.

Until now, research universities have failed miserably in teaching young scholars and scientists about the art of teaching. We tend to scoff at pedagogy, are unwilling to take seriously the idea that young scholars can acquire skills as teachers, and we do not prepare them for one of their two fundamental roles as professors. This does not mean that universities foster poor teaching. They do not, but the quality of teaching that exists is a function of individual endowments and effort, largely made in isolation, and there is little being done to help young scholars become better teachers—and to have them consider new, nontraditional modes of acquiring and transmitting knowledge. We would never contemplate a similar approach to the research training of graduate students. This set of attitudes needs to be changed if we are to improve the quality of the teaching offered to both undergraduate and graduate students at research universities.

The real challenge then for research universities is not to lower research standards in appointment, promotion, and tenure decisions in order to accommodate "better teaching," but to recognize and facilitate demonstrated quality in teaching performance among brilliant researchers. The message sent by academic leaders to the faculty must be unambiguous; the actions that follow must demonstrate that the words in the message are not empty. It would be a significant mistake, and unnecessary, for research universities to lower the threshold on research quality required for recognition and tenure. Research universities need to increase expectations and rewards for teaching excellence—and to require that all members of the permanent faculty demonstrate their capability as teachers. They need to systematically evaluate teaching performance in every hiring and promotion decision; they need to increase the visibility of extraordinary teaching in the university community; and they need to initiate programs that will help brilliant young scientists and scholars become outstanding teachers. The research university should become the place where it is once and for all demonstrated that it is a myth that excellence in research and teaching performance are fundamentally incompatible.

Dilemma Four: The Partnership between Research Universities and the Federal Government

How can the partnership between research universities and the federal government be redefined and new sources of research support be acquired without entering into Faustian bargains? The 1940s Vannevar Bush paradigm, which defined the partnership between the federal government and the research university, is rapidly changing.[27] It is ironic, of course, that this is the case since this partnership has resulted in American preeminence in science in the postwar period. When all is said and done about changes in the Bush paradigm, the federal government must and will continue to be the principal supporter of basic research in the nation and at universities. But it is not apt to invest on the same terms that existed during the period of extraordinary growth in knowledge over the past fifty years.

Consequently, research universities face increasingly important dilemmas about the support of basic science and technology. *1)* What role should the research universities play (indeed what role can they play) in modifying or replacing the older Bush paradigm with a new framework that maintains American preeminence in science and preserves the research university's role as the principal incubator of scientific ideas and talent? *2)* How can research universities retain commitments from the federal government while simultaneously developing new sources of research support that do not exacerbate existing tensions between the government and the universities? *3)* Can and should university scientists redefine their scientific goals and reorient themselves toward new types of scientific and technological problems that have the potential for short-term practical results? *4)* Can research universities adapt successfully to changing research conditions by increasing the number of inter-university collaborations and consortial research efforts? *5)* Can research universities increasingly collaborate with international partners without undermining national economic interests and American support for their research efforts? *6)* How can research universities develop new research relationships with the industrial and corporate world without entering into a Faustian bargain?

The dilemmas facing research universities are nothing less than how to sustain the world's most creative science and technology enterprise without the rate of increases in federal support that would appear to be needed to do so. But these dilemmas are not simply about obtaining new research resources. They are about the types of changes that the university scientific community will have to undergo and the bargains it will have to strike in the effort to preserve and expand the research enterprise while ensuring its continued quality. The drama in the situation lies in the nature of the bargains: what is being given up, at what cost, to achieve what goals?

Within the past five years, it has become increasingly clear that the rate of increase in government investments in science and technology, which has been doubling every decade or so, and which marked most of the postwar period, will no longer be sustained. Given the nation's economic problems and the current efforts at deficit reduction, real growth during the 1990s is apt to diminish. Moreover, the increased cost of conducting pioneering scientific research will increase, intensifying still further the existing competition for federal dollars among research universities.

Unfortunately, the reduced rate of investment in science has exacerbated tensions between Congress and the research universities. The points of view in these recent debates between Congress and the research community have been extensively covered in the media. In the end, leaders of the research universities fear that the recent polemics and congressional actions have further undermined the special status that research universities have enjoyed in American society over the past half century: higher education has become just one more competitor for a piece of the federal budget.

In the post-Cold War era, the military rationale for government investments in science (which was in fact more central to the Bush paradigm than most observers acknowledge) will have to be replaced by a new rationale—one that builds on the social and economic benefits for the continued investments in American science and technology. As I have noted, there can be no substitute for federal support of science if American leadership in science and technology is to be maintained. But there are possibilities for new sources of substantial, supplemental capital that could fuel the next phase of scientific advance by releasing creative scientific energy that thus far has remained fettered.

One such source of financial and human capital can be found in a closer partnership between the federal government, American industry, and the research university—with the American public as potential beneficiaries. The building blocks for that partnership are, in fact, already in place. They have been developed as a direct consequence of the prescient Dole-Bayh Bill of 1981, which authorized universities to hold the patent and licensing rights to discoveries that were produced with federal funding. A new, expanding partnership with the industrial and corporate world holds great promise for new sources of capital that can produce important scientific and technological discoveries, but entering into that new partnership is fraught with its own dilemmas and difficult choices.

Recognizing the potential for support of biomedical and other scientific activities, university leaders have developed new offices of science and technology that examine research discoveries for their potential practical applications. While these offices are only in their blueprint phase of development, the patents and licenses that result from their work are linking the university research community with biotechnology incubator companies and with more established firms, as well as with new computer software businesses. Some universities are developing new high-technology "parks" that are introducing new industries into urban centers desperately in need of economic development. The income from the patents and licenses is bringing substantial new resources to the universities that can be used for internal reinvestments in their scientific and engineering activities. This new capital allows universities to seed innovative, high-risk, high-payoff programs; to invest in novel ideas that cannot initially obtain government funding. These investments can, however, be leveraged into research programs that are highly attractive in the longer run to government funding agencies.

The resources that could be made available for investments in new scientific efforts at the research universities are not trivial. At Columbia, for example, annual revenues from patents and licenses have risen from roughly $4 million to $24 million over the past five years. Other major research universities have experienced similar growth. It is noteworthy that this represents the annual return on an endowment of about $480 million, given a 5 percent spending rule. Moreover, it is widely believed that we are seeing just the tip of the iceberg. Over the next decade, we could see these figures grow to as much as $75 million a year.

But there is a potentially darker side to these bright possibilities. What price, if any, will have to be paid for these new partnerships, and therefore, what balancing acts must be considered by research universities? Consider six problems that already exist for those that have taken the lead in developing these new relationships.

First, industrial support has, of course, its own uncertainties. Motivated more by the bottom line than universities, businesses that invest in university-based research can and will make rapid decisions to cut support when and if they feel it lacks profitability. Reducing dependence on federal grants and contracts through partnerships with industry has its own set of built-in uncertainties that can affect university capital investments as well as hiring and promotion decisions. Second, universities will have to balance investments in high economic payoff research against sustained effort in more basic and intellectually challenging research. It is not, in fact, known whether or not these efforts truly compete with each other, or whether the efforts are additive or complementary. Third, research universities will have to examine increasingly the allocation of effort by the faculty when some patentable, but less significant, research may lead to large personal gains for the faculty. There is a real possibility that the normative code of scientific research will be modified as a result of the terms of the new partnership with industry. In the past, individual scientists sought recognition for their discoveries but eschewed direct economic gain. That has now changed. Many scientists with extraordinary capabilities are now direct beneficiaries of the patents and licenses produced by universities. This is a matter of university policy. An increasing number of university faculty members are stakeholders in incubator biotechnology or computer software companies. Indeed, many universities are becoming holders of equity in these new companies. These new relationships between economics and science pose a set of dilemmas for universities that are just beginning to be addressed. In fact, the possible changes in the normative structure of science is related to a fourth problem: universities must balance their dedication to a neutral position regarding the outcome of scientific experiments against their efforts to support the entrepreneurial efforts of their talented faculty. This may not seem like a thorny issue, but anyone who has served recently on internal science and technology review committees can tell you that universities are increasingly facing ethical and moral issues that previously they rarely had to confront. Conflict of interest policies are being redrafted with an eye toward maintaining the norm of organized skepticism while reinforcing creative faculty research energies. Fifth, universities must deal with new problems regarding the training of their graduate students. They will have to be concerned about how scientists who stand to gain from patented discoveries mentor students. When there is a potential conflict, do faculty continue to steer students toward the most intellectually interesting and challenging projects rather than to those with the greatest potential for personal profit? Finally, research universities will have to examine closely how their commitment to open science is affected by their relationships with both foreign and domestic businesses. Each of these problems represents new policy questions and choices to be made by universities as they seek to fulfill their research mission.

Some observers of research universities foresee major structural changes over the next decade. They envision the end of the nineteenth-century Germanic model of departmental and school boundaries. I doubt that we will see these types of structural reorganizations, and we surely will not see them artificially imposed on the current structure of departments, centers, and interdepartmental research institutes. The best of the research universities will continue to be sources of national pride—an American institution that remains superior to its counterparts around the world. Nonetheless, by the turn of the century, we will probably return to many of the same problems and dilemmas that we have discussed in this volume. The themes will be the same; the variations will have changed. When we think about which research universities during the 1990s made significant gains in their relative quality and reputational standing, we will, I believe, focus on those that dealt effectively with the dilemmas of choice discussed in this volume.

ACKNOWLEDGMENT

Special thanks to Dr. Elinor Barber for her critical role in developing this volume and for her insightful comments on this paper.

ENDNOTES

[1] Among other works, see, Martin Anderson, *Impostors in the Temple: American Intellectuals Are Destroying Our Universities and Cheating Our Students* (Englewood Cliffs, N.J.: Simon & Schuster, 1992); Jacques Barzun, "We Need Leaders Who Can Make Our Institutions Companies of Scholars, Not Corporations with Employees and Customers," *Chronicle of Higher Education*, 20 March 1991; Allan Bloom, *The Closing of the American Mind* (Englewood Cliffs, N.J.: Simon & Schuster, 1987); Derek Bok, *Universities and the Future of America* (Durham, N.C.: Duke University Press, 1990); David Bromwich, *Politics by other Means: Higher Education and Group Thinking* (New Haven, Conn.: Yale University Press, 1992); Dinesh D'Souza, *Liberal Education: The Politics of Race and Sex on Campus* (New York: The Free Press, 1991); A. Bartlett Giamatti, *A Free and Ordered Space: The Real World of the University* (New York: W.W. Norton, 1988); Roger Kimball, *Tenured Radicals: How Politics Has Corrupted Our Higher Education* (New York: Harper and Row, 1989); Henry Rosovsky, *The University: An Owner's Manual* (New York: W.W. Norton, 1990); John Searle, "The Storm Over the University," *The New York Review of Books* XVII (19) (6 December 1990): 34 – 42; and Charles J. Sykes, *ProfScam: Professors and the Demise of Higher Education* (Washington, D.C.: Regnery Gateway, 1988).

[2]See, for example, "American Higher Education: Toward an Uncertain Future," Volumes 1 and 2, *Dædalus* 103 (4) (Fall 1974) and 104 (1) (Winter 1975). Eliot and Conant were, of course, distinguished presidents of Harvard; Hutchins established the preeminence of the University of Chicago.

[3]I will not attempt to define "the research university" beyond the obvious: its core mission is both teaching and research in the form of contributions to new knowledge through original scientific and scholarly discoveries and interpretations. Such a broad definition takes us only so far. Clearly, even the universities classified as research universities by the Carnegie Commission differ in the number of their professional schools and in their coverage of liberal arts subjects. The question remains whether some components of the research university are essential to its identity while others are not.

[4]Derek J. de Solla Price, who charted exponential growth in science, noted, for example, that fully half of all the scientists who have lived since the seventeenth century are alive today, and that the intellectual half-life of the scientific literature is rapidly decreasing because of the exponential growth of those literatures. For example, in a specialty like high-energy particle physics, the half-life is a mere five years.

[5]During the same forty-five year period, gifts to the university have grown from $1.4 million in 1945 to over $120 million in 1989–1990; faculty size has grown less rapidly, from 362 full professors in 1945 to about 750 today. Perhaps the anomaly in the overall pattern is found in the growth in the student population. This has varied widely by school, with the college almost tripling in size, while the graduate faculty of arts and sciences has grown by less than 20 percent.

[6]While I do not have precisely parallel data, budget materials obtained for Harvard, for example, suggest a budget growth from about $217 million in 1972–1973 to $1.2 billion in 1991–1992; and growth from $174 million to $653 million between 1972–1992 at the University of Chicago. Faculty size and student populations have not grown nearly so rapidly at these universities.

[7]The problem of dealing with a gap between the bases of knowledge and the resources to cover an expanding area has been the subject of concern in earlier periods as well. It is noteworthy that a number of the great research universities, such as Princeton, MIT, and Cal Tech, never defined their mission in terms of "full service." Nonetheless, the great private and public research universities have tried, by and large, to sustain substantial, if not full, coverage.

[8]I have focused here almost entirely on choices involving academic programs. Although universities do not find it easy to reach agreement about administrative cuts, and they too often do not link these cuts with an ordering of academic priorities that require some services more than others, making administrative cuts is much easier than making hard choices about academic programs.

[9]Dr. Elinor Barber's comments were particularly helpful.

[10]In one of his first communications, President Richard Levin suggests one method, building on the work of a predecessor at Yale: "On July 1, 1978, A. Bartlett Giamatti issued the first memorandum of his Presidency: 'In order to repair what Milton called the ruin of our grand parents, I wish to announce that henceforth, as a matter of University policy, evil is abolished and paradise is restored. I trust all of us will do whatever possible to achieve this policy objective.' I have ap-

pointed a committee, chaired by the University Chaplain, to investigate why the Giamatti Proclamation failed to produce the intended result. I have asked the committee to study the feasibility of abolishing evil and to develop a strategic plan for the restoration of paradise. The committee will present its findings to the University Budget Committee, which will determine whether paradise can be restored without further cuts in academic programs and support services. Before any action is taken, I assure you that there will be opportunity for full discussion by the appropriate faculties, the Yale College Council, the Graduate and Professional Student Senate, the Association of Yale Alumni, Locals 34 and 35, and the New York Times. I expect to transmit recommendations to the Yale Corporation before the end of the millennium." E-mail communication from Richard Levin to members of the Yale community, 1 July 1993, 11:27 AM.

[11]The strong value placed on faculty governance today is often mistakenly believed to have originated with the inception of the research university. In fact, Edward Shils has argued that there has been a de facto shift in authority from presidents and trustees to faculties since the early part of this century. Before the turn of the century, presidents were autocrats with complete backing from their trustees. By 1940, the faculty had gained control over appointments, promotions, degree re- quirements, new courses of study, etc. See, W. Allen Wallis, "Unity in the University," *Dædalus* 104 (1) (Winter 1975): 72.

[12]A recent joint faculty and administration effort at Columbia attempted to identify some criteria that might be used in establishing academic priorities. Consider the nine criteria that we thought should be considered when making choices among "competing goods:" *1)* centrality of the field to the university's mission and goals; *2)* current state of the field, discipline, or specialty; *3)* current academic excellence of the field at the university—whether its organizational shape is department, school, institute, or center; *4)* projected vitality of the field over the next several decades; *5)* relevance and contribution of the field to the undergraduate curriculum and to the training of graduate and professional students; *6)* contribution to other fields, disciplines, and schools at the university; *7)* additional investment required to improve significantly the quality of the department, school, or organizational structure; *8)* sense in which work in the field meets important social needs; and *9)* reversibility of the required commitment, such that the investment can be terminated or redirected if it yields less advancement of knowledge than anticipated. A host of questions could be raised about any framework such as this. For instance, how do we define and determine "excellence" or the current or projected future state of a discipline? Who decides such matters? Plainly, this particular set of principles is not definitive; many others could be developed. The appropriateness of these or other values will vary, of course, at different universities. No one would be foolish enough to claim that we could, or should, strive at this time to develop an algorithm for choices.

[13]A high proportion of fixed costs are associated with commitments to tenured faculty and maintenance of a physical plant. While I emphasize here the lack of flexibility in resource allocation, there is some value in moving so slowly. Institutions are less apt to shift significant resources to currently fashionable cognitive areas that prove of little lasting educational value. This functional consequence of a dysfunctional structure should not be lost on us or minimized.

[14]I first encountered this usage of the null hypothesis concept in a review essay by Harrison White of Jonathan R. Cole, *Fair Science: Women in the Scientific Com-*

munity (New York: The Free Press, 1979), which appeared in the *American Sociological Review* 87 (4) (January 1982): 951–56.

[15]Limited opportunities for members of various religious, racial, and ethnic groups at research universities are well documented, along with limitations placed on women. Substantial changes have occurred in opportunities offered to minorities and women at these universities in the recent past.

[16]Neil J. Smelser, "The Politics of Ambivalence: Diversity in the Research Universities" *Dædalus* 122 (4) (Fall 1993): 40–41.

[17]Richard Rorty, among others, presents an alternative view to Searle's. See Rorty's, "Science as solidarity," in Richard Rorty, *Objectivity, Relativism, and Truth* (Cambridge: Cambridge University Press, 1991), 35–45. There is an extended debate on these issues in the recent literature in philosophy, history, and sociology of science. For an important presentation of the alternative positions, which suggests both the value and limitations to both the traditional positivist and recent social constructivist points of view, see Stephen Cole, *Making Science: Between Nature and Society* (Cambridge, Mass.: Harvard University Press, 1992), chaps. 1–3. Cole stakes out a middle ground that has potential for theoretical and empirical elaboration.

[18]David Mamet, *Oleanna* (New York: Vintage Books, 1992). All quotations from the play are drawn from this edition. This discussion of Mamet's play and its relationship to ownership of the null has benefited from extensive discussion with Joanna Lewis Cole.

[19]Ibid., 3.

[20]Ibid., 10. The quotations in the following paragraph are drawn from Ibid., 10 –33.

[21]Ibid., 48 – 49.

[22]Ibid., 52.

[23]Ibid., 67– 68.

[24]A. Bartlett Giamatti, *A Free and Ordered Space*, 56 –57.

[25]Derek Bok, "The Improvement of Teaching," *Teachers College Record* 93 (2) (Winter 1991): 236 –51.

[26]A number of universities have begun a more systematic study of teaching performance and effectiveness. Among the more interesting recent efforts is one at Harvard University led by Richard J. Light. See the reports beginning in 1990 of *The Harvard Assessment Seminars*. Richard J. Light, "Explorations with Students and Faculty about Teaching, Learning, and Student Life," Cambridge, Mass.: Harvard University, Graduate School of Education and Kennedy School of Government, First Report 1990.

[27]Vannevar Bush, *Science—The Endless Frontier* (Washington, D.C.: National Science Foundation, 1960). The Report was first published in 1945 and transmitted to President Harry Truman. The Bush Report has probably been more heavily cited in the past several years than in its first forty years.

Neil J. Smelser

2

The Politics of Ambivalence: Diversity in the Research Universities

D EBATES OVER CULTURAL DIVERSITY, MULTICULTURALISM, and the integrity of the community are perennial in American history. They extend back at least to colonial times, when religious heterogeneity posed major social and political problems for many of the colonies. They became chronic in the nineteenth and early twentieth centuries, as waves of immigrants diversified the population. The movement of the black population northward and westward, beginning in earnest in the early twentieth century, generated a new heterogeneity, racial tensions, and alarms about the integrity of affected communities.

The current debates are thus properly regarded as the latest episode in the long history of the cultural diversification of America. What is new about them is the historically-specific confluence of social forces from which they emanate: the civil rights movements of the 1950s and 1960s; the campus and antiwar turbulence of the 1960s; the women's movement; the "sexual preference revolution"; the increasing political self-consciousness of many ethnic groups, including "white ethnics"; and the extraordinary increase of immigration—mainly but not exclusively Latin and Asian—during the past several decades.

Conflicts involving cultural diversity are not new in American academic circles: the historic flood of children from farm families into the teaching profession via colleges and universities; the entry of Irish Catholic Americans into the professions, notably engineering, through colleges; the struggle over Jewish quotas in elite private

Neil J. Smelser is University Professor of Sociology at the University of California, Berkeley.

institutions; and the evolution of Eastern private institutions from regional/social-elite to national/intellectual-elite institutions. All are episodes that involved issues of cultural diversity in academia. At the same time, the contemporary situation has some novel elements, and is grounded in a distinctive cultural setting.

SOCIAL AND POLITICAL DIMENSIONS

The University Context

The national debates about diversity affect all research universities across the nation. Within research universities these debates are reproduced as microcosms of the national political arena, with some notable regional differences. The debates occur in the context of the culture of those universities, which imparts a special form and flavor. It is necessary, therefore, to remind ourselves of a few characteristics of that culture.

First, the major research universities in the United States constitute a national *elite* among institutions. This status is evident in all measures—prestige, quality of faculty, quality of students, occupational placement of graduating students, and, not least, cultural voice. They share this elite status with liberal arts colleges on some of these measures. One implication of elevated status for institutions is that the real and symbolic stakes associated with access to them are high. Those who enter as students secure both status and enhanced life opportunities; those who enter as faculty share in their prestige.

Second, the research universities' cultural traditions give the highest premium to the values of *competitive excellence* and *meritocracy*. They compete aggressively with one another for outstanding faculty and students. They assess both their faculty and their students primarily on meritocratic criteria—that is, universalistic standards of judgment. The successful application of these criteria is, indeed, one of the conditions that sustain the elite status of research universities.

Third, the culture of research universities is *liberal* in several senses of the term. They, along with the rest of the academy, are the seat and the defenders of that special class of civil liberties known as academic freedom. They are committed, above all, to standards of freedom of inquiry and expression. And, in the national political spectrum, both faculty and students at research institutions, while internally diverse, lean in a liberal direction.

Fourth, because of their unique intellectual missions, controversies and debates in universities—perhaps especially in elite universities—take on a special *symbolic intensity.* As institutions, universities do not house much power, but they specialize in and are good at cultural symbolism. Debates in universities tend to take on an intellectualized, back-to-square-one quality. Being shrouded in symbolic discourse, these debates are likely to confound and irritate outsiders.

The Peculiarities of the Current Debates

Viewed simply, the current debates about cultural diversity derive historically from the political pressure that built up in the 1960s and 1970s, as one categorical group after another began expressing a collective claim for increased access to and more equitable recognition in academic institutions. Universities reacted to these demands—and the demands of governmental and other pressures for affirmative action—with varying degrees of responsiveness and effectiveness. Now both the values of and procedures for affirmative action are in place, and the increased presence of most of these groups is visible. Recently, the debates have taken a more distinctively *cultural* turn—hence the salience of the terms "cultural diversity" and "multiculturalism."

The debates, as they have built up over the past decades, have generated a historically unique configuration of components:

1) The challenge has come from an unprecedented number and scope of sources—racial and ethnic minorities, women, and homosexuals—in many cases with the willing and active support of government and other public groups affecting the universities.

2) The challenge is not only to *gain access* to the dominant culture and opportunities of the university, but also to *question the legitimacy* of, and perhaps *unseat,* that culture—though, interestingly, not so much its associated opportunities. The traditional curriculum is challenged as being Eurocentric. Its language and assumptions are assaulted as being racist or sexist, and the world of heterosexual, older, white males is depicted as a bastion of illegitimate privilege and power.

3) The challenge is a *collective* one, involving the political efforts of identified groups. The logic of affirmative action should not conceal the fact that it is simultaneously an organized effort on the part of traditionally disadvantaged minority and gender groups aimed at the collective upgrading of those groups, as defined on the basis of ascribed *categories*, not simply at individual mobility for selected members of the groups.

4) Because the identifying (and self-identified) characteristics of the challenging groups are categorical, the challenge has overtones of *the entitlement of groups* to student, faculty, and administrative places in the university and to full citizenship and respect in these places. This feature arises simultaneously from three sources: the character of the demands of the claimants; the efforts of opponents of those demands to label them as illegitimate claims to entitlement; and the tendency of authorities (government officials and administrators) to acknowledge the entitlement aspect by responding to demands as *claims by categorical groups*.

Paradoxes and Vulnerabilities

These special features of the current debates pose a range of institutional dilemmas and anomalies that have not been encountered as such by universities in the past. Not the least of these is the dilemma posed for the dominant liberal culture of the current administrative/faculty "establishment." Historically the elements of liberalism, egalitarianism, and meritocracy have been comfortably fused, as nineteenth-century middle-class liberals challenged the entitlement claims of monarchy, aristocracy, and church in the names of democracy and meritocracy. In the contemporary scene, those components have become strangely disassociated from one another. Liberal academic administrators and faculty generally applaud and welcome "diversity" if it is carried out within the confines of meritocracy and the preservation of the values of the academy. When those values themselves come under attack, however, and when the attacks on them appear to be made in the context of antimeritocratic demands for entitlement, liberals are cast in an uncomfortable role, in which they experience a dissociation of—indeed a conflict between—meritocracy and egalitarianism. Their role now becomes one of a conservative elite, jealously guarding those values of universalism that were invented and best suited to challenge conservative elites.

A closely related feature of the contemporary struggles over diversity is the creation of new, improbable, and unstable combinations of bedfellows. Traditional struggles in academia have involved issues of academic freedom, in which liberal faculty stand up against bastions of power—usually coalitions of business-legal-political representatives of the Right—who are alarmed at the liberal/radical ideologies and teachings of academics. (The courts have usually acted as friends to academic freedom, and thus as countervailing forces to the external Right.) In these struggles, academic administrators sometimes have sided with the outside "Right," sometimes with the internal faculty "Left." Students have tended to be either indifferent or supportive of the faculty Left.

The contemporary political situation has torpedoed those comfortable political alliances and fashioned a new, unfamiliar political quilt. The challenge now comes from a new Left, made up of vocal representatives of different "minority" claimants—themselves standing in unstable coalition; of outside left political forces, often governmental, who are cognizant of their own dependence on minority constituencies in their political environments; of academic administrators who are directly in the line of fire from the external Left; of representatives of a generation of radical faculty—perhaps socialized in their student days in the 1960s; and of "new" minority members of the faculty and the administration. On the Right are liberal faculty (and sometimes administrators and students), cast in the role of conservatives, evoking universalistic values and meritocracy as a defense rather than a challenge, and eliciting arguments of academic freedom as a conservative defense against "political correctness," laws and rules against "hate speech," and other initiatives emanating from the Left. These liberal faculty are bolstered by their conservative colleagues and by other conservative groups, usually white, in the larger political community, who are alarmed at the challenge from various minority and other left sources.

If one translates these coalitions into the collective emotions that are typically associated with each, on the one side one finds a fusion of anger, guilt, uncertainty, and anxiety of minorities and liberal/radical white supporters. On the other, one finds the associated anger and guilt of the liberal/conservative forces. Furthermore, *both* of these affective mixes find support in a legitimate ideology—the ideology of egalitarianism, social justice, and past wrongfulness on the one side, and the ideology of universalism, meritocracy, and appeals to traditional liberal values of freedom on the other. In controversies in which such emotions fuse with ideologies based on such legitimate first principles, the resultant conflict produces high levels of righteousness and vindictiveness and low levels of self-insight on both sides.

The new battle lines are tenuous, however, because every sub-group in both major coalitions has its own particular agenda and its own particular ambivalence, which may surface at any time and occasion a subtle or open realignment. Liberal faculty are torn between their egalitarianism and their commitment to their cherished academic values of universalism. They are also often uncomfortable with being found in common cause with political conservatives. Asian Americans, like Jews in the past, are torn between the strategies of representing themselves with entitlement-like claims on the one hand, and "making it" within the context of meritocracy, in which they have been effective competitors, on the other. And Hispanic and black minorities, more drawn toward entitlement-like claims, forever wonder whether admission on an entitlement-like basis does not doom them to second-class citizenship in a world dominated by meritocratic values. All this makes for the greatest political fluidity, and for frustration on the part of observers and analysts who savor the neatness of political division.

To add to the confusion, the polity of the research university is not very well-equipped to handle controversies of the sort that have developed. That polity itself is a strange historical mélange, incorporating several different principles of maintaining order and community in the university. It contains historical residues of a *religious calling*, which combines self-imposed discipline and personal freedom, and elements of *collegiality*, a company of equals whose main political cement is civility and mutual influence (within this kind of polity, above all, resides the myth of the university as a unified community); elements of *formal bureaucracy*, superimposed over time by the exigencies of growing size and multifunctionality; and a system of dual governance that is simultaneously *hierarchical* (with administrators retaining final authority) and *democratic* (with administrators delegating widely to academic senates and consulting with faculty, and to a certain extent with staff, students, and alumni). Needless to say, these different principles of polity often stand in tension with one another.

Whatever the mix of these ingredients in any university, it is the case that representatives of that polity are peculiarly ill-equipped to handle *collective* struggles among categorical groups. Universities are institutionalized in large part in the name of values of individual achievement and are best-equipped to deal with individuals. They admit individuals, give instruction to and grade individuals, discipline individuals, graduate individuals, and prepare individuals for and place them in occupational positions. That institutional "tilt" also reveals a shortage of mechanisms to deal with group conflict. This deficit became evident during the turbulence experienced in higher education in the 1960s. Colleges and universities, reasonably able to handle traditional individual academic problems and individual disciplinary offenses, found themselves ill-equipped to deal with group phenomena such as mass demonstrations, protests, and violations of rules. They also discovered that they lacked—and had to invent—machinery to negotiate with such groups.

Two other factors contribute to the vulnerability of universities to group conflict. First, because they are generally liberal and tolerant, if not permissive—as institutions go — some political groups see them as especially inept at playing political hardball when confronted with protest and conflict. As such, universities are magnets for political action. Second, campus conflict is typically dramatized and magnified by the media, which gravitate toward conflict situations in any case, and perhaps take special glee in publicizing group conflict and disruption in institutions that have traditionally presented themselves as seats of collegiality, civility, and community.

Even with several decades of experience with group conflict, universities are still more comfortable in dealing with individuals than with groups. This constitutes a special vulnerability in the current conflict over diversity because so many of the groups involved define themselves in collective, if not primordial, ways— along gender, racial, ethnic, cultural, and life-style lines—and present themselves politically as groups, not as individuals. If one adds to these the "group" challenges from environmental, community action, animal rights, and other groups that impinge on the university's political environment, it becomes apparent that the university stands in a kind of political situation for which its history has not equipped it well.

Results of institutionalized ineptness in dealing with collective conflict are seen in the kinds of "impossible" political situations in which many universities find themselves. Two examples follow. First, the admissions policies of most universities have accepted the "numbers game" logic of admitting a percentage of different claimant groups, either by pointing with pride to achieved results or by vowing to do better in the future. The "impossible" aspect of this definition of the situation is that, in the end, the university is trapped in a zero-sum game. An increase in the percentage of *any* group means a decrease for another, which in the current atmosphere is politically unacceptable to the losing group. And even an increase does not silence the demands for greater increases. Second, in faculty hiring policies universities have likewise committed themselves to increase the numbers of women and minorities in an absolute sense. Particularly with respect to certain minorities— Native Americans, blacks, and Hispanics—this is currently a collectively impossible goal because of the small pool of doctoral candidates that appear in the market in any given year. The resultant situation is a heady competition for scarce minority candidates, including the practice of one institution pirating such candidates from another. Individual minority candidates may benefit from this process, but it does not seem to address the general problem of improving access for all minorities.

Prognosis

The upshot of the foregoing assessment is that the contemporary debates over diversity are particularly intractable and unclear. All sides find themselves successfully able to appeal to ideological and cultural arguments that still enjoy legitimacy, but which, by a turn of history, have become opposed to one another.

The special character of the present debates also defies those who would write simple scenarios for the future. Rather, it is more advisable to envision a separable set of ideal-type outcomes, all of which are plausible, given the special alignment of social forces at the present time. The following three scenarios can be imagined:

1) The program of assimilation of racially, ethnically, and culturally diverse groups to the existing values and roles of higher educa-

tion. This is the liberal view, and envisions continuing traditional patterns of liberal education and occupational and professional training, with students being socialized into these patterns, accommodating to them, and preparing themselves for participation in the institutions of the larger society.

2) The program of altering the traditional mission of higher liberal education—which, it is argued, is biased along racial/ethnic, class, and gender lines in any event—to some mission that gives greater recognition to nonmainstream groups. The recent episodes of pressure for curricular change are signs of this tendency, as are the recent debates on campus about "political correctness" and its possible threat to principles of academic freedom.

3) The program of converting campuses into a microcosm of the pluralistic polity, with racial, ethnic, cultural, gender, and other groups competing for the resources as well as the symbolic and real control of the institutional life of universities. This scenario, too, while not novel in the history of education, would mark a further change in the traditional, liberal mission of educational institutions. And, given the frail capacities of colleges and universities to manage group conflict, such a "political pluralism" model would prove difficult to stabilize.

Like the future of any complex social institution that is based on multiple values and principles, the future of research universities with respect to diversity will not reveal a clear victory for *any* of these scenarios. Some aspects of all will continue to be visible. Each one will persist, and each one will have its vicissitudes. With respect to the issue of diversity, then, the future will bring "process" rather than "product" as an outcome, with all involved parties struggling for but never finally gaining new and satisfactory definitions of the situation, institutional advantages, or political domination.

CULTURAL AND PSYCHOLOGICAL DIMENSIONS

Because so much of the contemporary discussion of the diversity debate is "externalized" into the social and political arenas, reference to psychological dimensions that might be involved in the experience of those who are "diversifying" and those who are being "diversified" is neglected. The reason for this neglect is at least in part ideological. If one ventures into the psychological arena, it is often regarded as a means (if not a ploy) to "psychologize the issues away" as expressions of individual problems and, therefore, not matters for political concern. I do not accept this implication. To explore the psychological dimensions of a social problem is not to ignore the problem, but, instead, to probe into ever-present aspects of any process of change in institutional and group life. The remainder of this essay will focus on these aspects.

Old and New Diversification

At the outset it is essential to note that the cultures of universities are *already* culturally heterogeneous and diversified. With regard to the cultures of undergraduate student bodies of these institutions, for example, the following subtypes manifest themselves in varying degrees of visibility, coherence, and self-consciousness:

• a *collegiate* culture, which is highly social, has close links to fraternities, sororities, athletics, and alumni, and manifests a kind of innocent anti-intellectualism;

• a *preprofessional* culture of serious, competitive students, who are academic but not always intellectual in orientation;

• a culture of *free, intellectual spirits* who identify with the faculty and treasure intellectualism and the life of the mind;

• a *politically active culture*, typically liberal/radical in political tone, and often manifesting a species of anti-intellectualism;

• a culture of *expressive protest,* manifested in personal appearance, drug use, sexual liberty, and countercultural values;

• various *niche* cultures, including functionally-based groups such as drama, band, and undergraduate and graduate academic clubs and associations.

Similarly, graduate student cultures in research universities have never been homogeneous. They vary first of all by disciplinary commitment—field by field in the sciences, social sciences, humanities, and professional schools. Within fields, they vary by level of professional commitment and identification with the field of study. They differ in the degree to which graduate students are politically active *within* the university context, and the degree to which they give priority to intellectual, political, or moral concerns. Faculty cultures are also diversified within the research university, both by academic fields and by rank/age cohorts. They vary according to the priority they accord to the major sub-missions of the university—for example, excellence and national recognition in research, commitment to undergraduate teaching, and public and professional service. Faculties also differ along lines of their level of loyalty to or suspicion of academic administrators, of their level of commitment to traditional academic values and their derived hierarchies of prestige, and, like graduate students, in the salience of intellectual, political, and moral concerns in their outlook.

Formal and informal groups based on particular racial and ethnic backgrounds, gender, and sexual preference have always been a feature of collegiate and university life, but with the increasing heterogeneity of undergraduate student bodies—and to a lesser extent, of graduate students and faculty—these groups have increased in size, visibility, and social and political salience. However, it must be underscored that the new groups are entering into an arena that is already culturally highly diversified, and in which distinct subcultures can be identified.

THE OMNIPRESENCE OF AMBIVALENCE IN THE DIVERSIFYING PROCESS

The preexisting subcultures in a university community *all* constitute opportunities for personal identification for their incoming members. They also extend implicit cultural invitations for any new member so interested or so inclined to join.

To point this out is not to ignore the barriers to participation in all the cultural and life-style opportunities that campuses hold. The most obvious barriers are found in the fraternity and sorority world—a special subculture of the "collegiate" alternative for students—which, even if legally and formally barred from discrimination, certainly continue to be formally segregated along gender lines, and informally along class and racial/ethnic lines. In addition, any distinct subculture develops its own mechanisms of closing ranks and of discouraging entry through informal social sanctions of ignoring, snubbing, and making life generally uncomfortable for those regarded as alien to their subculture.

At the same time, the university campus, as a liberal and voluntaristic arena, has a range of freedom of choice. Within some limits, an individual student can choose to be serious or flippant in his or her commitments to academic study, to become "intellectual" or "anti-intellectual," to take a vocational or a liberal route in the curriculum, to adopt a traditional "Joe College" or "coed" role, to become politically active, to become bohemian, to go out for different kinds of activities such as athletics, band, or drama if able and interested, to join clubs, or to go it alone. Similarly, a faculty member has an element of choice as to whether to be a scholarly loner, a conscientious teacher, a participating or nonparticipating citizen in the academic community, a faculty conformist, or a faculty protester.

These choices, moreover, inevitably become invitations to incoming members to become something culturally *different* from what they were before entering that community. This principle is most vividly seen in the case of entering undergraduates. They are typically leaving their family and community of residence, whereas graduate students and faculty have presumably already been more fully socialized into the university cultures of their choice. Let us now consider this process from the standpoint of the undergraduate student, with special reference to racial and ethnic diversity.

There are three reasons why the collegiate experience is destined to pull students away from the cultural values and attitudes of their family, their social class, and their community. The first is found in the still viable philosophy embodied in the idea of a liberal education. Such an education is meant to be broadening, indeed *liberating* in its essence. It exposes students to new ranges of factual information, new perspectives, different ways of looking at the world, and, above all, challenges to what they have previously been taught and learned. A liberal education is thus intended to "diversify" the student to make him or her more universal, more cosmopolitan. Put more dramatically, a liberal education is based on the premise that "the student is always wrong." The sense in which that declaration is true is that the conscientious teacher takes as his or her mission the idea that students' existing knowledge and perspectives are limited; they are meant to be broadened in the educational process. The other corollary of the idea of liberal education is that, in the process, teachers are not supposed to hold out some kind of final, correct worldview, personal philosophy, or set of cultural values to the student, but rather to equip that student better to choose his or her preferred combination of these. Needless to say, this is an ideal representation of a liberal education, which does not always work out according to the ideal; nonetheless, it is still a discernible ingredient of the collegiate experience. The diverse student subcultures—serious youth culture, political activism, and bohemianism—also provide opportunities to experiment and broaden, even though they do not constitute part of the philosophy of liberal education as such.

Second, these ingredients of the collegiate experience promise not only to make the student different from his or her parents, class, and community. They also provide an opportunity for that student to *reject* those origins—to break from them in a process of rebellion that may range from polite to violent. The history of undergraduate education in America is a history of "liberated" sophomores bringing home the "enlightened" perspectives of Darwinism, Freudianism, Marxism, philosophical relativism—and nowadays deconstructionism—during vacations and torturing their stodgy and unenlightened parents with those perspectives. They may also bring home new life-style commitments as well—dissolute carousing, countercultural values, political radicalism, arrest records—and inflict the same torture on parents, even those (or perhaps especially those) who regard themselves as liberal.

Third, the collegiate experience is culturally defined as an avenue for *social mobility*. This cultural ideal is a deeply American one, namely to use higher education as a means to improve one's social standing by advancing occupationally and by gaining status-endowing credentials. Parents themselves usually conspire to assist in this mobility, by saving and paying for college for their children. Sometimes the mobility is not upward but simply "different"—the lawyer's daughter does not become a lawyer, the doctor's son does not become a doctor—and parents may not necessarily approve, but it is a kind of mobility all the same.

Liberation, rejection, and mobility invariably have some features in common. They are integral parts of an individual's personal growth and self-realization. But equally important—and this is where ambivalence makes its entrance—they always involve feelings of guilt. Guilt is always there for the student; it appears *no matter how* he or she resolves the tension between the culture of origin and the cultures that invite one to forsake that culture of origin. If one rejects the invitations of collegiate life, one is guilty for not having seized the opportunities—and perhaps for having disappointed one's parents in the process. If one rejects the cultural values of origin, one is guilty for having rejected them—and thus for having disappointed one's parents in another way. If one tries to strike some kind of middle ground between the two, one is certain to feel guilty on both counts. With guilt, moreover, comes anger, and that anger is likely to be directed at any and all parties who have conspired to set up the conflict that has generated the guilt in the first place.

The developmental ambivalence I have described is more or less universal, no matter what the origin of the student. However, it is particularly salient when the student comes *from* a subculture that regards itself as distinct, homogeneous, and discriminated against as a minority. Ironically, such students are often incorporated into the "middle-class," "Anglo," or "mainstream" American culture. One of the most vivid accounts of this ambivalence was described by William Foote Whyte fifty years ago in *Street Corner Society*,[1] an ethnographic study of life in the Italian community of North Boston. The two protagonists of the study constitute the two faces of the ambivalence—"Doc," the successful local politician who never left the family values, congeniality, and loyalty to friends of the Italian community, and "Chick," the successful businessman who went to a private college and forsook all of those. Both suffered the characteristic regret and guilt associated with the distinctive route he took.

Because of the increasing numbers of racial/ethnic minorities that have entered the college and university scene in recent decades—numbers that promise only to increase in the decades to come—this phenomenon of ambivalence toward culture of origin and cultures of invitation is and will be correspondingly more widespread. The core psychological tension is between a real or imagined "home" culture of parents and community who stress continuity, loyalty to group, and perhaps endogamy on the one side, and between a real or imagined "campus" culture—an amalgam of the diverse opportunities which constitute an invitation to leave and reject the home culture and enter some real or imagined larger, cosmopolitan, and alternative world. The "home" pressure emanates not only from home; any campus with a sizable group of minority students will have an association of conscious spokespersons for that group who stress cultural identity, loyalty, and demands for respect and participation. The ambivalence is thus real and present, and constantly stirs that range of effects—including especially guilt and anger—generated by ambivalence.

As a psychological phenomenon, ambivalence is difficult to deal with and tends to be unstable; it is forever being resolved into simpler alternatives that are easier to live with. The following resolutions are identifiable on university campuses: *1)* Accepting—either silently or rebelliously—the invitation to leave the "home" culture and take on one of the available cultural alternatives of the campus; in this case the loyalty to the "home" culture is uneasily repressed or openly rejected. *2)* Affirming the "home" culture and repressing or rejecting the real or imagined "establishment" of the university, either by withdrawing from it or by actively assuming an alienated and critical stance toward it. *3)* Striking some compromise between the two sides of the ambivalence and thus trying to have it both ways; the student may be the loyal, conformist child when at home, while simultaneously exploring and adopting other cultural styles when on campus—hiding the two adaptations from one another; the student may be politically active in varying degrees on behalf of his or her group but remain in good standing with the academic culture of the university at the same time; or the student may major in something like ethnic studies, which is simultaneously a commitment to an academic path and an affirmation of group identification and loyalty. Some kind of compromise of this sort seems the most frequent resolution of cultural ambivalence in contemporary American campus life.

The common tendency of racial and ethnic groups to "ghettoize" on campuses is often ignored or regretted. When recognized, it is typically explained by a simple formula like "people being comfortable with their own kind." I believe the phenomenon is more than that, and can be interpreted consistently within the framework of the ambivalence that I have noted. Associating informally with one's "kind" is one—probably the most typical—mode of resolving that ambivalence. The campus ghetto is a kind of way station: a means of declaring one's loyalty to a real or imagined home community while participating in and presumably reaping the real or imagined benefits of the alternative cultures that university life has to offer.

The logic of ambivalence also applies to those who are part of the supposed "majority" on diversifying campuses—whether these are referred to as majority, white, Anglo, mainstream, or whatever. This group may, incidentally, include—psychologically—members of minority groups who have opted for the first-noted resolution of *their* ambivalence. On the one hand, they may experience the feeling that the dominant academic and collegiate cultures are historically "theirs" in some vague sense and that they are therefore being "invaded"; they are likely to interpret their own presence in the community as resulting from their having "made it" on traditional meritocratic grounds while others have not. On the other hand—many being liberal themselves and all being exposed to the traditionally liberal culture of the university—they welcome, or feel the pressure to welcome, historically less-privileged minority and other groups to that culture. This ambivalence of the majority group tends to be resolved in a number of different ways:

1) Asserting the traditional dominance of "their" historic university, whether this is expressed in the affirmation of meritocratic ideas which others have presumably not met, the conviction that the "diversifying" groups are aliens or less than first-class citizens, or, in some cases, outright racism.

2) Espousing egalitarian causes—liberal admissions policies, affirmative action, and multicultural curricular reform—and identifying with the incoming minority groups, their aspirations, their political positions, their social movements, and perhaps their social life.

3) Striking some compromise between the two sides, and thus having it both ways; perhaps to espouse liberal values but to associate informally with other "majority" students; periodically to espouse "causes," which, however, do not disturb the basic contours of traditional collegiate life. This kind of compromise is probably the most frequent among "majority" groups as well.

These are some of the manifestations of the complex process of personal and social adaptation to ambivalence. Let me end with two final observations. First, the analysis of ambivalence and its complications has been carried out mainly with reference to undergraduate students. The same dynamics and their resolutions, with different weights and in different contexts, apply equally well to graduate student bodies and faculties that are in the process of diversifying. Second, the politics emanating from the adaptations to multiple ambivalences generate an enormously complex mosaic. Not only does one find "minorities" and "majorities" opposed to one another—which is the relationship enunciated most frequently in public rhetoric—but one also finds these groups in common cause with one another, depending on the resolutions of the ambivalences on each side. Moreover, the politics of ambivalence means that many political subdivisions *within* both minorities and majorities emanate from the multiple resolutions of ambivalence. Finally, because these resolutions are superimposed on *other* divisions in the university— divisions among undergraduates, graduate students, faculty, administration, and staff—the possible permutations and combinations of political alliance and political division are even greater. These considerations carry us some distance toward understanding the special fluidity and volatility of politics on the campuses of research universities.

The conclusion to this psychological line of reasoning is similar to the conclusion emanating from the sociopolitical reasoning laid out in the first part of this essay. The political divisions that arise from the ambivalences of diversification are profound, multiple, and omnipresent, and the bases for these divisions are endemic. These politics show no signs either of abating or of yielding any simple social-psychological or political resolution. The political forces of the nation are such that the march of diversification in universities is becoming and will become an established historical fact. However, from the standpoint of the social psychology of diversification and its political manifestations, we must expect continuous process and flux, not a finished product.

ENDNOTE

[1]William Foote Whyte, *Street Corner Society: The Social Structure of an Italian Slum* (Chicago, Ill.: University of Chicago Press, 1955).

The "Idea of a University" was a village with its priests. The "Idea of a Modern University" was a town—a one-industry town—with its intellectual oligarchy. "The Idea of a Multiversity" is a city of infinite variety. Some get lost in the city; some rise to the top within it; most fashion their lives within one of its many subcultures. There is less sense of community than in the village but also less sense of confinement. There is less sense of purpose than within the town but there are more ways to excel. There are also more refuges of anonymity— both for the creative person and the drifter. As against the village and the town, the "city" is more like the totality of civilization as it has evolved and more an integral part of it; and movement to and from the surrounding society has been greatly accelerated. As in a city, there are many separate endeavors under a single rule of law.

Clark Kerr

From *The Uses of the University*
1963

Rationality and Realism, What Is at Stake?

D EBATES ABOUT THE NATURE OF HIGHER EDUCATION have been
going on in American research universities for decades.
There is nothing new about passionate controversies over
the curriculum, over academic requirements, and even over the aims
of higher education itself. But the current debates are in certain
respects unusual. Unlike earlier academic reformers, many of the
present challengers to the academic tradition have an explicitly
leftist political agenda, and they seek explicit political goals. Furthermore, and more interestingly, they often present a challenge not
just to the content of the curriculum but to the very conceptions of
rationality, truth, objectivity, and reality that have been taken for
granted in higher education, as they have been taken for granted in
our civilization at large. I would not wish to exaggerate this point.
The challengers of the tradition present a wide variety of different
viewpoints and arguments. They are by no means united. But there
has been a sea change in discussions of the aims of education in that
the ideals which were previously shared by nearly everyone in the
disputes—ideals of truth, rationality, and objectivity, for example—
are rejected by many of the challengers, *even as ideals*. This is new.

In some of the disciplines in the humanities and social sciences,
and even in some of the professional schools, there now are developing two more or less distinct faculty subcultures, one might
almost say two different universities. The distinction between the
two subcultures cuts across disciplinary boundaries, and it is not
sharp. But it is there. One is that of the traditional university

---

John R. Searle is Professor of Philosophy at the University of California, Berkeley.

dedicated to the discovery, extension, and dissemination of knowledge as traditionally conceived. The second expresses a much more diverse set of attitudes and projects, but just to have a label, I will describe it as the subculture of "postmodernism." I do not mean to imply that this concept is well-defined or even coherent, but when describing any intellectual movement it is best to use terms the adherents themselves would accept, and this one appears to be accepted as a self-description by many of the people I will be discussing.

I referred above to "debates," but that is not quite accurate. There really is not much in the way of explicit debate going on between these two cultures over the central philosophical issues concerning the mission of the university and its epistemic and ontological underpinnings. There are lots of debates about specific issues such as multiculturalism and affirmative action, but not much in the way of a debate about the presuppositions of the traditional university and the alternatives. In journalistic accounts, the distinction between the traditional university and the discourse of postmodernism is usually described in political terms: the traditional university claims to cherish knowledge for its own sake and for its practical applications, and it attempts to be apolitical or at least politically neutral. The university of postmodernism thinks that all discourse is political anyway, and it seeks to use the university for beneficial rather than repressive political ends. This characterization is partly correct, but I think the political dimensions of this dispute can only be understood against a deeper dispute about fundamental philosophical issues. The postmodernists are attempting to challenge certain traditional assumptions about the nature of truth, objectivity, rationality, reality, and intellectual quality.

In what follows, I will try to identify some of the elements of the Western conceptions of rationality and realism that are now under challenge. My aim is not so much to resolve the disputes but to identify (at least some of) what exactly is in dispute. I will also briefly discuss some of the consequences different conceptions of rationality and realism have for higher education. These are not the only issues underlying the disputes in current debates about higher education, nor are these the only theoretical and philosophical issues in higher education, but they are worth discussing and as far as I know have not been addressed in quite these terms before.[1]

THE WESTERN TRADITIONS: SOME PRELIMINARIES

There is a conception of reality, and of the relationships between reality on the one hand and thought and language on the other, that has a long history in the Western intellectual tradition. Indeed, this conception is so fundamental that to some extent it defines that tradition. It involves a very particular conception of truth, reason, reality, rationality, logic, knowledge, evidence, and proof. Without too much of an exaggeration one can describe this conception as "the Western Rationalistic Tradition." The Western Rationalistic Tradition takes different forms but it underlies the Western conception of science, for example. Most practicing scientists simply take it for granted. In the simplest conception of science, the aim of science is to get a set of true sentences, ideally in the form of precise theories, that are true because they correspond, at least approximately, to an independently existing reality. In some other areas, such as the law, the Western Rationalistic Tradition has undergone some interesting permutations and it is certainly no longer in its pure form. For example, there are rules of procedure and evidence in the law which are adhered to even in cases where it is obvious to all concerned that they do not produce the truth. Indeed, they are adhered to even in cases when it is obvious that they prevent arriving at the truth. The Western Rationalistic Tradition is not a unified tradition in either its history or in its present application.

Two forms of disunity need special emphasis. First, at any given time the most cherished assumptions of the Western Rationalistic Tradition have been subject to challenge. There has seldom been unanimity or even consensus within it. Second, over time those assumptions have evolved, typically in response to challenges. For example, the role of sacred texts such as Scriptures in validating claims to knowledge, the role of mystical insight as a source of knowledge, and the role of the supernatural generally have declined spectacularly with the demystification of the world that began, roughly speaking, with the advent of the modern era in the seventeenth century. Any attempt to characterize the Western Rationalistic Tradition, therefore, inevitably suffers from some degree of oversimplification or even distortion. Furthermore, any attempt such as I am about to make to describe its present form is inevitably from the point of view of a particular thinker at a particular time and place—how it seems to him or her, then and there. And, by the way, the recognition of this limitation—that accuracy and objectivity are difficult to attain because of the fact that all representation is *from a point of view* and *under some aspects and not others*—is one of the central epistemic principles of the Western Rationalistic Tradition in its current incarnation.

I believe a decisive step in the creation of the Western Rationalistic Tradition was the Greek creation of the idea of a *theory*. It is important to state this point precisely. Many features of the Western Rationalistic Tradition—the presupposition of an independently existing reality, and the presupposition that language, at least on occasion, conforms to that reality—are essential to any successful culture. You cannot survive if you are unable to cope with the real world, and the ways that human beings characteristically cope with the real world essentially involve representing it to themselves in language. But the introduction of the idea of a theory allowed the Western tradition to produce something quite unique, namely systematic intellectual constructions that were designed to describe and to explain large areas of reality in a way that was logically and mathematically accessible. Euclid's *Elements* provides a model for the kind of logical relationships that have been paradigmatic in the Western tradition. Indeed, the Greeks had almost everything necessary for theory in the modern sense. One essential thing they lacked and which Europe did not get until the Renaissance was the idea of systematic experiments. The Greeks had logic, mathematics, rationality, systematicity, and the notion of a theoretical construct. But the idea of matching theoretical constructs against an independently existing reality through systematic experimentation really did not come in until much later. However, I am getting ahead of my story.

Another feature of Western Rationalistic Tradition is its self-critical quality. Elements within it have always been under challenge; it was never a unified tradition. The idea of *critique* was always to subject any belief to the most rigorous standards of rationality, evidence, and truth. Socrates is the hero of the intellectual branch of the Western Rationalistic Traditional tradition in large part because he accepted nothing without argument and was relentlessly critical of any attempts at solving philosophical problems. Recently, however, the self-critical element in the Western Rationalistic Tradition has had a peculiar consequence. If the point of the criticisms is to subject all beliefs, claims, prejudices, and assumptions to the most rigorous scrutiny through the magnifying glass of rationality, logic, evidence, etc., then why should the criticisms eventually not be directed at rationality or logic or evidence themselves? The heroic age of the Western Rationalistic Tradition came during and after the Renaissance when the faiths and dogmas of the Middle Ages were subjected to ever more savage criticisms, until finally we reached the European Enlightenment and the skepticism of Hume and Voltaire, for example. But now, why should we not also be skeptical of rationality, logic, evidence, truth, reality, etc., themselves? If the uncritical acceptance of a belief in God can be demolished, then why not also demolish the uncritical acceptance of the belief in the external world, the belief in truth, the belief in rationality, indeed, the belief in belief? At this point, the Western Rationalistic Tradition becomes not merely self-critical, but self-destructive. Nietzsche, on one possible interpretation, can be regarded both as diagnosing and exemplifying this self-destructive element. Nietzsche is a philosopher of considerable variety, but at his worst he exhibits a distinct shortage of argument and a tendency to substitute rhetoric for reason. For the present discussion, the interesting point is that he has come back into fashion. I believe this is, in large part, because of his attacks on various aspects of the Western Rationalistic Tradition. It is not easy to locate any arguments, much less proofs, in his attacks.

THE WESTERN RATIONALISTIC TRADITION: SOME BASIC PRINCIPLES

Now I want to try to articulate some essential features of the Western Rationalistic Tradition in its contemporary incarnation. What is in dispute? What is under attack? What is presupposed by the intellectual tradition that stretches back to the Greeks? For example, the Western Rationalistic Tradition is sometimes accused of "logocentrism"; a few decades ago, the same style of objection was made to something called "linear thinking." What exactly does one accept when one is "logocentric," i.e., when one accepts the Greek ideal of "logos" or reason? What is one committed to when one engages in "linear thinking," i.e., when one tries to think straight? If we understand the answers to these questions, we will know at least something of what is at stake in the current debates in higher education.

It might seem impossible to make even the crudest summary of the Western Rationalistic Tradition because of the enormous variety I mentioned earlier, but there is a simple test for distinguishing the center from the periphery, namely what do the attackers of the tradition feel it necessary to attack, what do the challengers feel it necessary to challenge. For example, there are lots of theories of truth, but anyone who wants to challenge the tradition has to attack the correspondence theory of truth. The correspondence theory is the norm, the default position; other positions are defined in relation to it. Similarly, there are lots of versions of realism as well as of idealism, but anyone who wants to attack the accepted view in this domain has to attack the idea that there is a mind-independent reality, a real world that exists entirely independently of our thought and talk.

We cannot discover the essential elements of the Western Rationalistic Tradition just by studying the doctrines of the great philosophers. Often the important thing is not what the philosopher said but what he took for granted as too obvious to need saying. Some of the best known philosophers became famous for attacking central elements of the Western Rationalistic Tradition—the Irish philosopher George Berkeley, Hume, and Kant, for example.

For the sake of simplicity, I will state what I take to be some of the basic tenets of the Western Rationalistic Tradition as a set of propositions.

Reality exists independently of human representations. This view, called "realism," is the foundational principle of the Western Rationalistic Tradition. The idea is that though we have mental and linguistic representations of the world in the form of beliefs, experiences, statements, and theories, there is a world "out there" that is totally independent of these representations. This has the consequence, for example, that when we die, as we will, the world will in large part go on unaffected by our demise. It is consistent with realism to recognize that there are large areas of reality that are indeed social constructs. Such things as money, property, marriage, and governments are created and maintained by human cooperative behavior. Take away all of the human representations and you have taken away money, property, and marriage. But it is a foundational principle of the Western Rationalistic Tradition that there are also large sections of the world described by our representations that exist completely independently of those or any other possible representations. The elliptical orbit of the planets relative to the sun, the structure of the hydrogen atom, and the amount of snowfall in the Himalayas, for example, are totally independent of both the system and the actual instances of human representations of these phenomena.

This point needs to be stated carefully. The vocabulary or system of representation in which I can state these truths is a human creation, and the motivations that lead one to investigate such matters are contingent features of human psychology. Without a set of verbal categories I cannot make any statements about these matters or about anything else. Without a set of motivations, no one would bother. But the actual situations in the world that correspond to these statements are not human creations, nor are they dependent on human motivations. This conception of realism forms the basis of the natural sciences.

At least one of the functions of language is to communicate meanings from speakers to hearers, and sometimes those meanings enable the communication to refer to objects and states of affairs in the world that exist independently of language. The basic conception of language in the Western Rationalistic Tradition contains both the communicative and the referential character of language. The speaker can succeed in communicating thoughts, ideas, and meanings generally to a hearer; and language can be used by speakers to refer to objects and states of affairs that exist independently of the language and even of the speaker and the hearer. Understanding is possible because the speaker and the hearer can come to share the same thought, and that thought, on occasion at least, concerns a reality independent of both.

The philosophy of language has a curious history in the Western tradition. Though it is currently at or near the center of attention, especially in English-speaking countries, the forms of our present interests and preoccupations with language are fairly recent. The philosophy of language, in the contemporary sense of that expression, begins with the German mathematician and philosopher Gottlob

Frege in the nineteenth century. Previous philosophers often wrote philosophically about language, but none had a "philosophy of language" in the contemporary sense. Even such traditional topics on "the problem of universals" and "the nature of truth" were transformed by the post-Fregean movement.

I think part of the reason for this is that for many centuries most thinkers simply took it for granted that words communicate ideas, and they referred to objects by way of ideas. John Locke describes the accepted view, in contrast to his own, as follows:

> But though words, as they are used by men, can properly and immediately signify nothing but the ideas that are in the mind of the speaker, yet they in their thoughts give them a secret reference to two other things.
>
> *First, To the ideas in other men's minds.*—First, they suppose their words to be marks of the ideas in the minds also of other men, with whom they communicate: for else they should talk in vain, and could not be understood, if the sounds they applied to one idea were such as by the hearer were applied to another, usually to examine whether the idea they and those they discourse with have in their minds to be the same: but think it enough that they use the word, as they imagine, in the common acceptance of that language; which they suppose, that the idea they make it a sign of is precisely the same to which the understanding of men of that country apply that name.
>
> *Secondly, To the reality of things.*—Secondly, because men would not be thought to talk barely of their own imaginations, but of things as really they are; therefore they often suppose their words to stand also for the reality of things.[2]

With Frege the philosophical tradition did not abandon the two principles but rather came to see them as immensely problematic. How does it work? How is it possible that communication can take place? How is it possible that words and sentences relate? In the twentieth century, the philosophy of language became central to philosophy in general, both because of its own intrinsic interest and because it was central to other problems in philosophy such as the nature of knowledge and truth.

Truth is a matter of the accuracy of representation. In general, statements attempt to describe how things are in the world that exists independently of the statement, and the statement will be true or false depending on whether things in the world really are the way that the statement says they are.

So, for example, the statement that hydrogen atoms have one electron, or that the earth is 93 million miles from the sun, or that my dog is now in the kitchen are true or false depending on whether or not things in the hydrogen atom, solar system, and domestic canine line of business, respectively, are really the way these statements say that they are. Truth, so construed, admits of degrees. The statement about the sun, for example, is only *roughly true.*

In some versions, this idea is called the "correspondence theory of truth." It is often presented as a definition of "true" thus: *A statement is true if and only if the statement corresponds to the facts.*

In recent centuries, there has been a lot of debate among professional philosophers over the correspondence theory of truth. Much of this debate is about special problems concerning the notions of fact and correspondence. Does the notion of correspondence really *explain* anything? Are facts really independent of statements? Does every true statement really correspond to a fact? For example, are there moral facts? And if not, does that mean that there are no true statements in morals? I hold definite opinions on all these issues, but since I am now unveiling the Western Rationalistic Tradition and not expounding my own views, I will confine myself to the following.

The concept of truth as it has evolved over the centuries contains two separate strands, and the two strands do not always entwine together. Sometimes it seems we have two different conceptions of truth. Truth is an obsession of the Western Rationalistic Tradition, so this apparent ambiguity is important. The ambiguity is between truth as correspondence and truth as disquotation. On the correspondence theory, statement *p* is true if and only if *p* corresponds to a fact. For example, the statement that the dog is in the kitchen is true if and only if it corresponds to the fact that the dog is in the kitchen. On the disquotational theory, for any statement *s* that expresses a proposition *p, s* is true if and only if *p*. So, for example, the statement "the dog is in the kitchen" is true if and only if the dog is in the kitchen. This is called "disquotation" because the quotation marks on the left-hand side of "if and only if" are simply dropped on the right-hand side.

These two criteria for truth do not always appear to give the same result. The second makes it look as if the word "true" does not really add anything. Saying that it is true that the dog is in the kitchen is just another way of saying that the dog is in the kitchen, so it seems that the word "true" is redundant. For this reason, the disquotation criterion has inspired the "redundancy theory of truth." The first criterion, the correspondence criterion, makes it look as if there is a genuine relation between two independently identified entities—the statement and the fact. The difficulty, however, with this conception is that the two entities are not independently identifiable. You cannot answer the question, "which fact does the statement correspond to?," without stating a true statement. So, once I have identified the statement, "the dog is in the kitchen," and then I have identified the fact that the dog is in the kitchen, there is not anything else for me to do by way of comparing the statement to the fact to see if they really do correspond. The alleged correspondence relation has already been established by the very identification of the fact.

Is there any way to explain the correspondence theory which overcomes this difficulty, and is there any way to resolve the tension between the disquotation criterion and the correspondence criterion and overcome the apparent ambiguity in the concept of truth? I think that there is.

The word "fact" has evolved out of the Latin "facere" in such a way that it has come to mean that which corresponds to a true statement in virtue of which the statement is true. So the correspondence theory—a statement is true if and only if it corresponds to a fact—is a truism, a tautology, an analytic statement. But the grammar of the language then misleads us. We think that because "fact" is a noun, and nouns typically name things, and because "corresponds" typically names a relation between things, that therefore there must be a class of complicated objects, the facts, and a relation that true statements bear to these complicated objects, correspondence. But this picture does not work. It sounds plausible for the statement that the dog is in the kitchen but what about the true statement that the dog is not in the kitchen? Or the true statement that three-headed dogs have never existed? What complicated objects do they correspond to?

The mistake is to think that facts are a class of complicated objects, and that to find the truth we must first find the object and then compare it with a statement to see if they really do correspond. But that is not how language works in this area. The fact that the dog is not in the kitchen, or the fact that three-headed dogs have never existed are as much facts as any other, simply because the corresponding statements are true, and "fact" is *defined as* whatever it is that makes a statement true.

For this reason, because of the definitional connection between fact and true statement, there could not be an inconsistency between the correspondence criterion of truth and the disquotational criterion. The disquotational criterion tells us that the statement, "the dog is in the kitchen," is true if and only if the dog is in the kitchen. The correspondence criterion tells us that the dog is in the kitchen is true if and only if it corresponds to a fact. But which fact? The only fact it could correspond to, if true, is the fact that the dog is in the kitchen. But that is precisely the result given by the disquotational criterion, because that is the fact stated by the right-hand side of the equation: the statement, "the dog is in the kitchen," is true if and only if the dog is in the kitchen. So both the correspondence theory and the disquotational theory are true and they are not inconsistent. The correspondence theory is trivially true and thus misleads us because we think correspondence must name some very general relation between language and reality, whereas in fact, I am suggesting, it is just a shorthand for all of the enormous variety of ways in which statements can accurately represent how things are. Statements are typically true in virtue of, or because of, features of the world that exist independently of the statement.

The upshot of this discussion, as far as the Western Rationalistic Tradition is concerned, is this: for the most part the world exists independently of language and one of the functions of language is to represent how things are in the world. One crucial point at which reality and language make contact is marked by the notion of truth. In general, statements are true to the extent that they accurately represent some feature of reality that exists independently of the statement.[3]

There are various important philosophical problems about correspondence and disquotation, but if we mind our p's and q's we can see that none of these problems threatens our basic conception of truth as the accuracy of representation.

Knowledge is objective. Because the content of what is known is always a true proposition, and because truth is in general a matter of accurate representation of an independently existing reality, knowledge does not depend on nor derive from the subjective attitudes and feelings of particular investigators. All representation is, as I said earlier, from a point of view and under certain aspects and not others. Furthermore, representations are made by particular investigators, subject to all the usual limitations of prejudice, ignorance, stupidity, venality, and dishonesty; they are made for all sorts of motives on the parts of the makers, some benign, some reprehensible, including desires to get rich, to oppress the oppressed, or even to get tenure. But if the theories put forward accurately describe an independently existing reality, none of this matters in the least. The point is that the objective truth or falsity of the claims made is totally independent of the motives, the morality, or even the gender, the race, or the ethnicity of the maker.

It is worth pausing to state the significance of this principle to some of the present debates. A standard argumentative strategy of those who reject the Western Rationalistic Tradition is to challenge some claim they find objectionable, by challenging the maker of the claim in question. Thus, the claim and its maker are said to be racist, sexist, phono-phallo-logocentric, and so forth. To those who hold the traditional conception of rationality, these challenges do not impress. They are, at best, beside the point. To those within the Western Rationalistic Tradition, these types of challenge have names. They are commonly called argumentum ad hominem and the genetic fallacy. Argumentum ad hominem is an argument against the person who presents a view rather than against the view itself, and the genetic fallacy is the fallacy of supposing that because a theory or claim has a reprehensible origin, the theory or claim itself is discredited. I hope it is obvious why anyone who accepts the idea of objective truth and therefore of objective knowledge thinks this is a fallacy and that an argumentum ad hominem is an invalid argument. If someone makes a claim to truth and can give that claim the right kind of support, and if that claim is indeed true, then that person genuinely knows something. The fact that the whole enterprise of claiming and validating may have been carried out by someone who is racist or sexist is just irrelevant to the truth of the claim. That is part of what is meant by saying that knowledge is objective. It is less obvious, but I hope still apparent, why anyone who denies the possibility of objective truth and knowledge might find *these* sorts of arguments appealing. If there is no such thing as objective truth, then the criteria for assessing claims have no essential connection with truth or falsity, and may as well be concerned with the maker of the argument, his or her motives, the consequences of making the claim, or other such issues.

Logic and rationality are formal. In the Western Rationalistic Tradition, there are traditionally supposed to be two kinds of reason: theoretical reason, which aims at what is reasonable to believe, and practical reason, which aims at what is reasonable to do. But it is, I believe, an essential part of the Western conception of rationality, reason, logic, evidence, and proof that they do not *by themselves* tell you what to believe or what to do. According to the Western conception, rationality provides one with a set of procedures, methods, standards, and canons that enables one to assess various claims in light of competing claims. Central to this view is the Western conception of logic. Logic does not by itself tell you what to believe. It only tells you what must be the case, given that your assumptions are true, and hence what you are committed to believing, given that you believe those assumptions. Logic and rationality provide standards of proof, validity, and reasonableness but the standards only operate on a previously given set of axioms, assumptions, goals, and objectives. Rationality as such makes no substantive claims.

Where practical reason is concerned, this point is sometimes made by saying that reasoning is always about means not about ends. This is not quite right, given the Western conception, because one can reason about whether or not one's ends are proper, appropriate or rational, but only in the light of other ends and other considerations such as consistency. The formal character of rationality has the important consequence that rationality as such cannot be "refuted" because it does not make any claim to refute.

On a natural interpretation, the previous five principles have the following consequence.

Intellectual standards are not up for grabs. There are both objectively and intersubjectively valid criteria of intellectual achievement and excellence. The previous five principles imply, in a fairly obvious way, a set of criteria for assessing intellectual products. Given a real world, a public language for talking about it, and the conceptions of truth, knowledge, and rationality that are implicit in the Western Rationalistic Tradition, there will be a complex, but not arbitrary, set of criteria for judging the relative merits of statements, theories, explanations, interpretations, and other sorts of accounts. Some of these criteria are "objective" in the sense that they are independent of the sensibilities of the people applying the criteria; others are "intersubjective" in the sense that they appeal to widely shared features of human sensibility. An example of objectivity in this sense is the criterion for assessing validity in propositional calculus. An example of intersubjectivity is the sort of criteria appealed to in debating rival historical interpretations of the American Civil War. There is no sharp dividing line between the two, and in those disciplines where interpretation is crucial, such as history and literary criticism, intersubjectivity is correspondingly central to the intellectual enterprise.

There are endless debates in the history of Western philosophy about these issues. In my own view, for example, even objectivity only functions relative to a shared "background" of cognitive capacities and hence is, in a sense, a form of intersubjectivity. However, for the present discussion what matters is that according to the Western Rationalistic Tradition there are rational standards for assessing intellectual quality. Except in a few areas, there is no algorithm that determines the standards and they are not algorithmic in their application. But all the same they are neither arbitrarily selected nor arbitrarily applied. Some disputes may be unsettleable—but that does not mean that anything goes.

For the traditional conception of the university this principle is crucial. For example, in the traditional university, the professor assigns Shakespeare and not randomly selected comic strips, and she does so in the belief that she could demonstrate that Shakespeare is better. No principle of the Western Rationalistic Tradition is more repulsive to the culture of postmodernism than this one, as we will soon see.

SOME CONSEQUENCES OF HIGHER EDUCATION

One could continue this list of the essential claims of the Western Rationalistic Tradition for a long time. But even these six theses express a massive and powerful conception. Together they form a coherent picture of some of the relations between knowledge, truth, meaning, rationality, reality, and the criteria for assessing intellectual productions. They fit together. Knowledge is typically of a mind-independent reality. It is expressed in a public language, it contains true propositions—these propositions are true because they accurately represent that reality—and knowledge is arrived at by applying, and is subject to, constraints of rationality and logic. The merits and demerits of theories are largely a matter of meeting or failing to meet the criteria implicit in this conception.

All six of these principles are currently under attack in different forms, and I now want to explore some of the consequences, both of the principles and of the attacks. It is no exaggeration to say that our intellectual and educational tradition, especially in the research universities, is based on the Western Rationalistic Tradition. The scholarly ideal of the tradition is that of the *disinterested* inquirer engaged in the quest for *objective* knowledge that will have *universal* validity. Precisely this ideal is now under attack. In a pamphlet issued by the American Council of Learned Societies, authored by six heads of prominent humanities institutes and designed to defend the humanities against charges that they have abandoned their educational mission, we read: "As the most powerful modern philosophies and theories have been demonstrating, claims of disinterest, objectivity and universality are not to be trusted, and themselves tend to reflect local historical conditions." They go on to argue that claims to objectivity are usually disguised forms of power seeking.[4]

In most academic disciplines it is fairly obvious how acceptance of the Western Rationalistic Tradition shapes both the content and the methods of higher education. As professors in research universities, we traditionally take ourselves as trying to advance and disseminate human knowledge and understanding, whether it be in physical chemistry, microeconomics, or medieval history. It is less obvious, but still intelligible, how standards of rationality, knowledge, and truth are supposed to apply to the study of fictional literature or the visual arts. Even in these areas the traditional assumptions by which they were studied and taught were of a piece with the rest of the Western Rationalistic Tradition. There were supposed to be intersubjective standards by which one could judge the quality of literary and artistic works, and the study of these works was supposed to give us knowledge not only of the history of literature and art but of the reality beyond to which they refer, if only indirectly. Thus, for example, it was commonly believed, at least until quite recently, that the study of the great classics of literature gave the reader insights into human nature and the human condition in general. It was, in short, something of a cliché that you could learn more about human beings from reading great novels than you could from most psychology courses. Nowadays, one does not hear much talk about "great classics of literature," and the idea of intersubjective standards of aesthetic quality is very much in dispute.

If the relation of the Western Rationalistic Tradition to the traditional ideals of the university is—more or less—obvious, the relation between attacks on the Western Rationalistic Tradition and proposals for educational reform is much less obvious. It is simply a fact that, in recent history, rejection of the Western Rationalistic Tradition has gone hand in hand with the proposals for politically motivated changes in the curriculum. So, what is the connection? I think the relationships are very complex, and I do not know of any simple answer to the question. But underlying all the complexity there is, I believe, this simple structure: those who want to use the universities, especially the humanities, for leftist political transformation correctly perceive that the Western Rationalistic Tradition is an obstacle in their path. In spite of their variety, most of the challengers to the traditional conception of education correctly perceive that if they are forced to conduct academic life according to a set of rules determined by constraints of truth, objectivity, clarity, rationality, logic, and the brute existence of the real world, their task is made more difficult, perhaps impossible. For example, if you think that the purpose of teaching the history of the past is to achieve social and political transformation of the present, then the traditional canons of historical scholarship — the canons of objectivity, evidence, close attention to the facts, and above all, truth— can sometimes seem an unnecessary and oppressive regime that stands in the way of achieving more important social objectives.

In my experience at least, the present multiculturalist reformers of higher education did not come to a revised conception of education from a refutation of the Western Rationalistic Tradition; rather they sought a refutation of the Western Rationalistic Tradition that would justify a revised conception of education that they already found appealing. For example, the remarkable interest in the work of Thomas Kuhn on the part of literary critics did not derive from a sudden passion in English departments to understand the transition from Newtonian Mechanics to Relativity Theory. Rather, Kuhn was seen as discrediting the idea that there is any such reality. If all of "reality" is just a text anyway, then the role of the textual specialist, the literary critic, is totally transformed. And if, as Nietzsche says, "There are not facts, but only interpretations," then what makes one interpretation better than another cannot be that one is true and the other false, but, for example, that one interpretation might help overcome existing hegemonic, patriarchal structures and empower previously underrepresented minorities.

I think in fact that the arguments against the Western Rationalistic Tradition used by a Nietzscheanized Left[5] are rather weak, but this does not matter as much as one might suppose because the refutation of the Western Rationalistic Tradition is not the primary goal. It is only necessary that the refutation have enough respectability to enable one to get on with the primary social and political goal. Historically, part of what happened is that in the late 1960s and 1970s a number of young people went into academic life because they thought that social and political transformation could be achieved through educational and cultural transformation, and that the political ideals of the 1960s could be achieved through education. In many disciplines, for example, analytic philosophy, they found the way blocked by a solid and self-confident professorial establishment committed to traditional intellectual values. But in some disciplines, primarily those humanities disciplines concerned with literary studies—English, French, and Comparative Literature especially—the existing academic norms were fragile, and the way was opened intellectually for a new academic agenda by the liberating impact of the works of authors such as Jacques Derrida, Thomas Kuhn, and Richard Rorty, and to a lesser extent by Michel Foucault and the rediscovery of Nietzsche. Notice that the postmodernist-cultural Left differs from the traditional left-wing movements such as Marxism in that it makes no claims to being "scientific." Indeed it is, if anything, antiscientific, and Marxist-inspired philosophers who accept the Western Rationalistic Tradition, such as Jurgen Habermas, are much less influential in postmodernist subculture than, say, Derrida or Rorty.

There are now departments in some research universities that are ideologically dominated by antirealist and antirationalist conceptions, and these conceptions are beginning to affect both the content and the style of higher education. In cases where the objective is to use higher education as a device for political transformation, the usual justification given for this is that higher education has always been political anyway, and since the claim of the universities to impart to their students a set of objective truths about an independently existing reality is a sham hiding political motives, we should convert higher education into a device for achieving beneficial rather than harmful social and political goals.

So far I have argued that the biggest single consequence of the rejection of the Western Rationalistic Tradition is that it makes possible an abandonment of traditional standards of objectivity, truth, and rationality, and opens the way for an educational agenda, one of whose primary purposes is to achieve social and political transformation. I now want to explore the specific forms that this transformation is supposed to take. Most visibly in the humanities, it is now widely accepted that the race, gender, class, and ethnicity of the student defines his or her identity. On this view it is no longer one of the purposes of education, as it previously had been, to enable the student to develop an identity as a member of a larger universal human intellectual culture. Rather, the new purpose is to reinforce his or her pride in and self-identification with a particular subgroup. For this reason, *representativeness* in the structure of the curriculum, the assigned readings, and the composition of the faculty becomes crucial. If one abandons the commitment to truth and intellectual excellence that is the very core of the Western Rationalistic Tradition, then it seems arbitrary and elitist to think that some books are intellectually superior to others, that some theories are simply true and others false, and that some cultures have produced more important cultural products than others. On the contrary, it seems natural and inevitable to think that all cultures are created intellectually equal. In literary studies some of these features are indicated by a change in the vocabulary. One does not hear much about "the classics," "great works of literature," or even "works"; rather the talk nowadays is usually of "texts" with its leveling implication that one text is as much of a text as any other text.

Another form of transformation is this: we now commonly hear in the research universities that we must accept new and different conceptions of academic "excellence." We are urged to adopt different criteria of academic achievement. An argument sometimes given in favor of altering the traditional conception of academic excellence is that changes in the university brought about by changes in the larger society require new standards of excellence. A number of new faculty members were not recruited according to the traditional standards and did not enter the university with the idea of succeeding by those standards. Often they have been recruited for various social, political, or affirmative action needs. For these new interests and needs, new criteria of excellence have to be designed. However, the Western Rationalistic Tradition does not give you much room to maneuver where intellectual excellence is concerned. Intellectual excellence is already determined by a set of preexisting standards. In order to redefine excellence, you have to abandon certain features of the Western Rationalistic Tradition.

The connection between the attack on rationality and realism and curricular reform is not always obvious, but it is there to be found if you are willing to look closely enough. For example, many of the multiculturalist proposals for curricular reform involve a subtle redefinition of the idea of an academic subject from that of a *domain to be studied* to that of a *cause to be advanced*. Thus, for example, when Women's Studies departments were created some years ago, many people thought these new departments were engaged in the ("objective," "scientific") investigation of a domain, the history and present condition of women, in the same way that they thought that the new departments of Molecular Biology were investigating a domain, the molecular basis of biological phenomena. But in the case of Women's Studies, and several other such new disciplines, that is not always what happened. The new departments often thought of their purpose, at least in part, as advancing certain moral and political causes such as that of feminism.

And this shift from the territorial conception of an academic department to the moral conception in turn has further consequences down the line. Thus, traditionally the commitment to objectivity and truth was supposed to enable the scholar to teach a domain, whatever his or her moral attitudes about the domain. For example, you do not have to be a Platonist to do a good scholarly job of teaching Plato or a Marxist to do a good job of teaching Marx. But once the belief in objectivity and truth are abandoned and political transformation is accepted as a goal, then it seems that the appropriate person to teach Women's Studies would be a politically active feminist woman. On the traditional conception, there is no reason why Women's Studies should not be taught by a scholar who is male, even by a male who is unsympathetic with contemporary feminist doctrines; but in most Women's Studies departments in the United States that would now be out of the question. I hope it is obvious that analogous points could be made about Chicano Studies, Gay and Lesbian Studies, African American Studies, and other elements of the recent attempts at curricular reform.

Furthermore, the shift from domain-to-be-investigated to moral-cause-to-be-advanced is often not made explicit. When making the case to the general academic public for multiculturalist curriculum, the advocates often cite the uncharted academic territories that need to be investigated and taught, and the educational needs of a changing student population. Among themselves, however, they tend to emphasize the political transformations to be achieved, and these transformations include undermining certain traditional conceptions of the academic enterprise. Traditional "liberal" scholars are easily persuaded that new domains need to be investigated and new sorts of students need to be taught; they are often unaware that the main purpose is to advance a political cause.

I realize that the introduction of curricular reforms and even new academic departments to satisfy political demands is nothing new in the history of American universities. However, there is a difference between the traditional reforms and the new conception of education. Traditionally, the idea was that a new *science* of a particular area would help to solve some pressing political or social problem. For example, the development of political economy as a discipline was built in part around the conception of developing a scientific theory of economy and society that would help solve social problems. Part of the difference that I am pointing to is this: On the new conception, the very idea of "science" is itself regarded as repressive. The idea of developing a rigorous science to investigate, for example, gender and racial differences, is precisely the sort of thing that is under attack. In short, the idea is not to build a new policy on the basis of new scientific theory. Rather, the policy is given in advance and the idea is to develop a departmental and curricular base where that policy can be implemented in the university and extended to the society at large.

I do not wish these remarks to be misunderstood. There are many hard-working men and women engaged in solid traditional scholarship in these new disciplines, and they are committed to the highest standards of truth and objectivity as traditionally conceived. My point here is that they have a significant number of colleagues who do not share these values, and their rejection of these values is connected to their rejection of the Western Rationalistic Tradition.

The introduction of new academic departments is a visible sign of change. Less visible, but much more pervasive, is the change in the self-definition of the individual scholar. I mentioned earlier that there was an increase in the use of ad hominem arguments and genetic fallacies. If there is no such thing as objective truth and validity, than you might as well discuss the person making the argument and his motives for making it, as discuss its claims to validity and the alleged "truth" of its conclusions. But this is only the tip of the iceberg of a much larger shift in sensibility. The new sensibility is usually described (and excoriated) as "relativism," but I think a better term for it might be "politically motivated subjectivism." Previous scholars tried to overcome the limitations of their own prejudices and points of view. Now these are celebrated. For example, funding agencies such as the National Endowment for the Humanities (NEH) receive an increasing number of applications in which it is obvious that the scholar wants to write a book about his or her *politically motivated subjective reactions to, feelings about, and general "take on"* the Renaissance, the plight of women in the Middle Ages, minority novelists of the Pacific Northwest, transvestites in the eighteenth century.

Another scarcely noticed consequence of the rejection of the Western Rationalistic Tradition is the blurring of the distinction between high culture and popular culture in the teaching of the humanities. Traditionally, the humanities thought of themselves as conserving, transmitting, and interpreting the highest achievements of human civilization in general and Western civilization in particular. This view is now regarded as elitist, and there has now been a general abandonment of the idea that some works are qualitatively better than others. There is, rather, the assumption that all works are simply texts and can be treated as such.

On the traditional conception, the distinction between high culture and popular culture manifested itself in the fact that works of high culture were celebrated whereas works of popular culture were, if studied at all, treated as objects of sociological study or investigation. They were treated as symptomatic or expressive, but not themselves as achievements of the highest order. In the subtle shift that has been taking place, no works are celebrated as such. Rather, some works are regarded as important, significant, or valuable because of a political or social message that they convey.

SOME ATTACKS ON THE WESTERN RATIONALISTIC TRADITION

There are really too many kinds of attacks on the Western Rationalistic Tradition, and I am too unfamiliar with many of them, so I can only offer the briefest of surveys. There are deconstructionists, such as Derrida, inspired by Nietzsche and the later works of the German philosopher Martin Heidegger, who think that they can "deconstruct" the entire Western Rationalistic Tradition. There are some feminists who think that the tradition of rationality, realism, truth, and correspondence is essentially a kind of a masculinist device for oppression. There are some philosophers who think that we should stop thinking of science as corresponding to an independently existing reality. Rather, we should think that science in particular, and language in general, just gives us a set of devices for coping. On this view, language is for "coping," as opposed to "matching" or "corresponding." Thus according to Richard Rorty, the pragmatist "drops the notion of truth as correspondence with reality altogether, and says that modern science does not enable us to cope because it corresponds, it just plain enables us to cope."[6]

These attacks on the Western Rationalistic Tradition are peculiar in several respects. First, the movement in question is for the most part confined to various disciplines in the humanities, as well as some social sciences departments and certain law schools. The antirationalist component of the contemporary scene has—so far— had very little influence in philosophy, the natural sciences, economics, engineering, or mathematics. Though some of its heroes are philosophers, it has, in fact, little influence in American Philosophy departments. One might think that since the points at issue are in a very deep sense philosophical, the debates about the curriculum that are connected to the desire to overthrow the Western Rationalistic Tradition must be raging in philosophy departments. But at least in the major American research universities, this, as far as I can tell, is not so. Professional philosophers spend a lot of time fussing around the edges of the Western Rationalistic Tradition. They are obsessed by such questions as: "What is the correct analysis of truth?," "How do words refer to objects in the world?," and "Do the unobservable entities postulated by scientific theories actually exist?" Like the rest of us, they tend to take the core of the Western Rationalistic Tradition for granted even when they are arguing about truth, reference, or the philosophy of science. The philosophers who make an explicit point of rejecting the Western Rationalistic Tradition, such as Richard Rorty or Jacques Derrida, are much more influential in departments of literature than they are in philosophy departments.

A second, and perhaps more puzzling, feature is that it is very hard to find any clear, rigorous, and explicit arguments against the core elements of the Western Rationalistic Tradition. Actually, this is not so puzzling when one reflects that part of what is under attack is the whole idea of "clear, rigorous, and explicit arguments." Rorty has attacked the correspondence theory of truth, and Derrida has claimed that meanings are undecidable, but neither in their works, nor in the works of other favorites of the postmodernist subculture, will you find much by way of rigorous arguments that you can really sharpen your wits on. Somehow or other, there is the feeling that the Western Rationalistic Tradition has become superseded or obsolete, but actual attempts at refutations are rare. Sometimes we are said to be in a postmodern era, and have thus gone beyond the modern era that began in the seventeenth century; but this alleged change is often treated as if it were like a change in the weather, something that just happened without need of argument or proof. Sometimes the "arguments" are more in the nature of slogans and battlecries. But the general air of vaguely literary frivolity that pervades the Nietzscheanized Left is not regarded as a defect. Many of them think that is the way you are supposed to conduct intellectual life.

Two of the most commonly cited authors by those who reject the Western Rationalistic Tradition are Thomas Kuhn and Richard Rorty. I will digress briefly to say a little about them. Kuhn, in *The Structure of Scientific Revolutions*, is supposed to have shown that the claims of science to describe an independently existing reality are false, and that, in fact, scientists are more governed by crowd psychology than by rationality, and tend to flock from one "paradigm" to another in periodic scientific revolutions. There is no such thing as a real world to be described by science; rather each new paradigm creates its own world, so that, for example, as Kuhn says, "after a revolution scientists work in a different world."[7]

I think this interpretation is something of a caricature of Kuhn. But even if it were a correct interpretation, the argument would not show that there is no real world independent of our representations, nor would it show that science is not a series of systematic attempts, in varying degrees successful, to give a description of that reality. Even if we accept the most naive interpretation of Kuhn's account of scientific revolutions, it does not have any such spectacular ontological consequences. On the contrary, even the most pessimistic conception of the history of science is perfectly consistent with the view that there is an independently existing real world and the objective of science is to characterize it.

Rorty has many discussions of truth and correspondence and I could not attempt to do them justice here, but I will pick up on only one or two crucial aspects. He says repeatedly that "true" is just a term of commendation that we use to praise those beliefs that we think it is good to believe, and that truth is made and not discovered.[8] The difficulty with the first of these views is that in the ordinary sense of the word, there are lots of things that for one reason or another one thinks it is good to believe that are not true, and lots of things that are true but it would be better if they were not generally believed. I think, for example, that it is good that mothers believe the best of their children even though such beliefs often turn out false. Likewise, the persistence of religious beliefs is on balance a good thing, though most such beliefs are probably false. Rorty's claim suffers from the usual difficulty of such philosophical reductions: it is either circular or obviously false. On the one hand, the criterion of goodness can be defined as truth or correspondence to reality, in which case the analysis is circular. On the other hand, if one does not redefine "truth," there are lots of counterexamples, lots of propositions that it is good for one reason or another for people to believe but which are not true in the ordinary sense of the word; and there are propositions that for one reason or another it would be bad to believe but which are nonetheless true.

There is an ambiguity in Rorty's claim that truth is made and not discovered. Since truth is always in the form of true *statements* and true theories, then indeed true statements and true theories have to be made and formulated by human beings. But it does not follow from this fact that there is no independently existing reality to which their statements and theories correspond. So there is a sense in which truth is made—namely true statements are made. But there is also a sense, consistent with this, in which truth is discovered. What one discovers is that which makes the statements true (or false, as the case might be). In a word, true *statements* are made, but the truth of statements is not made, it is *discovered*.

Rorty's argument is typical of these discussions in that more is *insinuated* than is actually argued for. What is claimed, I guess, is that true statements, like all statements, are made by human beings. What is insinuated is much more serious: there are no facts in the real world that make our statements true, and perhaps the "real world" is just our creation.

THE STATUS OF THE WESTERN RATIONALISTIC TRADITION

I have not found any attacks on the Western Rationalistic Tradition—not in Rorty or Kuhn, much less in Derrida or Nietzsche—that seem to me at all convincing or even damaging to any of the basic principles I have enunciated. But the question naturally arises: is there anything to be said in *defense* of the Western Rationalistic Tradition? Is there any proof or argument that this is one possible right way to think and act? Certainly, alternative visions are possible, so why accept this one?

There is something puzzling about demanding an argument in favor of, or a proof of, the validity of a whole mode of sensibility and framework of presuppositions in which what we count as a proof and as an argument take place. The situation is a bit like the common occurrence of the 1960s in which one was asked to justify rationality: "What is your argument for rationality?" The notion of an argument already presupposes standards of validity and hence rationality. Something only counts as an argument given that it is subject to the canons of rationality. Another way to put this same point is: You cannot justify or argue for rationality, because there is no content to rationality as such, in a way that there is a content to particular claims made within a framework of rationality. You might show that certain canons of rationality are self-defeating or inconsistent, but there is no way to "prove" rationality.

It might seem that with realism the situation is different. Surely, one might say, the claim that reality exists independently of human representations is a factual claim and, as such, can be true or false. I want to suggest that in the actual operation of our linguistic, cultural, and scientific practices, all six principles function quite differently from ordinary empirical or scientific theses. Since realism is the foundation of the entire system, I will say a few words about it. I have presented the Western Rationalistic Tradition as if it consisted of a series of theoretical principles, as if it were simply one theory we might hold along with a number of others. Those of us brought up in our intellectual tradition find this mode of exposition almost inevitable, because our model of knowledge, as I remarked earlier, comes from the presentation of well-defined theses in systematic theoretical structures. But in order that we should be able to construct theories at all, we require a set of background presuppositions that are prior to any theorizing. For those of us brought up in our civilization, especially the scientific portions of our civilization, the principles that I have just presented as those of the Western Rationalistic Tradition do not function as *a theory*. Rather, they function as part of the taken-for-granted background of our practices. The conditions of intelligibility of our practices, linguistic and otherwise, cannot themselves be demonstrated as truths within those practices. To suppose they could was the endemic mistake of foundationalist metaphysics.

In "defense" of realism, the only thing that one can say is that it forms the presupposition of our linguistic and other sorts of practices. You cannot coherently deny realism and engage in ordinary linguistic practices, because realism is a condition of the normal intelligibility of those practices. You can see this if you consider any sort of ordinary communication. For example, suppose I call my car mechanic to find out if the carburetor is fixed; or I call the doctor to get the report of my recent medical examination. Now, suppose I have reached a deconstructionist car mechanic and he tries to explain to me that a carburetor is just a text anyway, and that there is nothing to talk about except the textuality of the text. Or suppose I have reached a postmodernist doctor who explains to me that disease is essentially a metaphorical construct. Whatever else one can say about such situations, one thing is clear: communication has broken down. The normal presuppositions behind our practical everyday communications, and a fortiori, behind our theoretical communications, require the presupposition of a preexisting reality for their normal intelligibility. Give me the assumption that these sorts of communication are even possible between human beings and you will see that you require the assumption of an independently existing reality. A public language presupposes a public world.

Realism does not function as a thesis, hypothesis, or supposition. It is, rather, the condition of the possibility of a certain set of practices, particularly linguistic practices. The challenge, then, to those who would like to reject realism is to try to explain the intelligibility of our practices in light of that rejection. Philosophers in the past who cared seriously about these matters, and who rejected realism, actually tried to do that. Berkeley, for example, tries to explain how it is possible that we can communicate with each other, given that on his view there are no independently existing material objects, but only ideas in minds. His answer is that God intervenes to guarantee the possibility of human communication. One interesting thing about the present theorists who claim to have shown that reality is a social construct, or that there is no independently existing reality, or that everything is really a text, is that they have denied one of the conditions of intelligibility of our ordinary linguistic practices without providing an alternative conception of that intelligibility.

CONCLUSION

There are many debates going on in the research universities today and many proposals for educational change. I have not tried to explain or even describe most of what is going on. I have been concerned with only one issue: the philosophical presuppositions of the traditional conception of higher education and the educational consequences of accepting or denying those presuppositions. I have claimed that a deeper understanding of at least some of the headline issues can be gained by seeing them in their philosophical content.

However, there is one danger endemic to any such presentation. You are almost forced to present the issues as clearer and simpler than they really are. In order to describe the phenomena at all, you have to state them as more or less clear theses on each side: the subculture of the traditional university and the subculture of postmodernism. However, in real life people on both sides tend to be ambivalent and even confused. They are often not quite sure what they actually think. In light of this ambivalence, it is perhaps best to think of the present account not so much as a characterization of the thought processes of the participants in the current debates but as a description of what is at stake.

ACKNOWLEDGMENTS

I have benefited from discussion of these issues with various colleagues and friends. I would especially like to express my gratitude to my fellow authors in this volume who participated with me in the *Dædalus* authors' conference in Cambridge and made valuable suggestions for improving the article. I have also been helped by Hubert Dreyfus, Jennifer Hudin, Dagmar Searle, and Charles Spinosa.

ENDNOTES

[1] I have discussed some related issues in two other articles. See John R. Searle, "The Storm Over The University," *New York Review of Books* XXVII (19) (6 December 1990): 34– 42, and John R. Searle, "Is There a Crisis in American Higher Education?," *The Bulletin of the American Academy of Arts and Sciences* XLVI (4) (January 1993): 24– 47.

[2] John Locke, *Locke on Human Understanding* (London: Routledge and Sons, 1909), 324–25.

[3]I say "in general" because, for example, sometimes statements are self-referential; for example, "This sentence is in English."

[4]The American Council of Learned Societies, *Speaking for the Humanities*, ACLS Occasional Paper, No. 7, 1989, 18.

[5]I believe this expression was coined by Allan Bloom.

[6]Richard Rorty, *Consequences of Pragmatism* (Minneapolis, Minn.: University of Minnesota Press, 1982).

[7]Thomas S. Kuhn, *The Structure of Scientific Revolutions,* 2d ed. (Chicago, Ill.: University of Chicago Press, 1970), 135.

[8]See especially Richard Rorty, *Objectivity, Relativism and Truth,* Philosophical Papers Vol. 1 (Cambridge and New York: Cambridge University Press, 1991.)

A more vexatious worry among us than the supply of teachers has to do with the kind of education we are to provide. The basic difficulty here seems always to turn on whether we are to think in terms of an educational program designed to be manageable by everyone in an age group or whether we are to try to maintain one that will test and stir the ablest and most enterprising of our young people. Arguments can be and are advanced on both sides of this question interminably. Unfortunately it is not a particularly fruitful discussion, for in fact we have always to do both things, and both things are worth doing. Our educational system must provide educational opportunity and experience, as the reports so frequently say, for all American youth; but we cannot stop there or rest too quickly, for it cannot be permitted to do this in terms only of a mass and so at the expense of its other function, which is a perpetual requirement to discover and develop talent, and this not only for the happiness of the individuals involved but also, of course, for the common good.

Nathan M. Pusey

From *The Age of the Scholar*
1963

Donald Kennedy

4

Making Choices in the Research University

U NIVERSITIES, LIKE OTHER ORGANIZATIONS, must make choices, and now the choices are becoming painful. On the one hand, the business of the research university is the expanding universe of knowledge, so the domain of opportunity is huge — and growing exponentially. On the other hand, resources have suddenly become more constrained. How, under such circumstances, can universities keep what matters most, and discard other things that matter less? And who decides what matters?

The second question is particularly important. In responding to the dilemma of growing opportunity accompanied by contracting means, governance becomes absolutely critical, and it is the governance of universities—the organizational context that directs how choices are made, and who makes them—that I shall discuss.

Much of what I say centers on a perpetual tension between centralized (usually "administrative") decision-making and peripheral or distributed (usually "faculty") decision-making. Major changes in direction will be required of the research universities, and sharp differences in quality and prestige will develop between the institutions that respond well and those that fail to make the turn.

Most social scientists would predict that during periods of resource constraint, systems will be driven inexorably toward centralization. In the present situation, I do not believe that axiom will yield a successful result, neither will a continued reliance on the present democratic but stubbornly conservative modes of peripheral

---

Donald Kennedy is President Emeritus and Bing Professor of Environmental Studies at Stanford University.

decision-making. Instead, the successes will be marked by a special kind of institutional leadership — one that forces administrations to form new alliances with faculties in order to achieve major shifts of direction, away from traditional academic norms.

GOVERNANCE, CHOICE, AND PLANNING

An account of this kind naturally begins with planning, because institutions need a systematic framework for establishing priorities and then for making choices. That is not an easy subject for universities and their leaderships to address. Indeed, planning is a source of persistent conflict between presidents and trustees or regents, especially those board members who bring with them substantial experience in the commercial sector. New members regularly ask for the Strategic Plan, or the Five-year or the Ten-year Plan, or at the very least the Mission Statement. The reaction of presidents to these requests varies. One colleague, who had a long and distinguished tenure at a noted institution, was a model of tact and patience in all matters save this one. When asked for his strategic plan, his response was to "go away and fall asleep somewhere, immediately." My own response was to inquire what the strategic plan for the future of the life sciences at Cambridge University was, circa 1857.

The research universities—being, as one of my Stanford colleagues put it, the "incubators of unlabeled eggs"— can lay special claim to a need for freedom and flexibility in planning the future. They must be able to respond to new opportunity, such as the revolution in scientific thinking that would have overtaken Cambridge's plan a couple of years after its formulation. To that end they need to maintain organizational arrangements that allow them to reallocate resources to fill suddenly arising needs. At the same time, it is difficult and perhaps even impossible to predict which domains of human knowledge will suddenly generate new requirements for curricular revision, or new opportunities for research breakthroughs.

Accordingly, it is frequently argued that adequate strength must be maintained in all. These two features—the stochastic character of intellectual opportunity and the need for a critical presence in all the disciplines—are often invoked in explaining why academic institutions are conservative and inhospitable to planning processes that set new priorities. It is not difficult to read, out of this argument, a formula for gridlock whenever resources are constrained.

The tension created as the flowering of new and often unexpected opportunity confronts static organization and dwindling resources has reached what some have described as a crescendo in the research universities. But, has it really? Or will it rise still further, to new levels of stress, and challenge the very structure of those institutions? I think it will, partly because our recent history has so profoundly conditioned our expectations.

RECENT GROWTH AND NEW LIMITS

The intellectual enterprise in the United States has grown at an extraordinary rate during the post-World War II era, partly because of rather special economic circumstances and partly because that is its nature.

There is an inherent reason why the acquisition of knowledge—surely the first and possibly the only element in the university's mission—becomes inexorably more expensive. That is equally true for both of the vital functions of knowledge acquisition: research and teaching. It was Planck who first observed that each new increment of knowing costs more than the last. Not only do we answer the easier questions first, but from answering them, we learn how to ask even more challenging and expensive ones. Moreover, we develop technologies and instrumentation to apply at each point, and these then open up new areas for exploration and instruction.

To that must be added the cost of managing our new knowledge and then transferring it. The rate of growth of the scientific literature has been analyzed in the work of the historian and sociologist of science Derek J. de Solla Price: in the twentieth century, Price estimates that the number of publications has increased an average of 6 to 7 percent per year—a doubling time of only a little more than a decade.[1] This is much faster, of course, than the rate of population growth in the industrial nations that produce that literature. It is small wonder that libraries, along with research instrumentation and computing, are among the fastest-growing items in university budgets.

Knowledge, therefore, becomes more expensive per unit over time, and the number of units increases exponentially. For short periods, fortunate societies may be able to keep pace with the challenge of such synergistic growth; our society has been one of the fortunate ones in recent times. During the interval from 1960 to 1967, federal support for American basic science (about two-thirds of which is done in the research universities) grew from about $2 billion to just over $5 billion in constant 1982 dollars. This is equivalent to a compound annual growth rate of about 15 percent. The growth rate then slowed significantly, and basic research support after inflation was at almost exactly the same level at the beginning of the 1980s as it had been in 1967.[2] This thirteen-year plateau was followed by more modest growth over the next decade—during which the federal deficit experienced its dramatic expansion. The size of that deficit, repeatedly revised upward during the transition in 1992 and 1993, is now the prime mover in our domestic political economy; the new administration and the Congress are plainly determined to reduce it dramatically, under substantial political pressure. It is inconceivable that our societal commitment to the support of knowledge acquisition will be maintained at historical levels.

That circumstance alone signifies that university leaders are facing a period of resource constraint unlike any they—or their faculties—have ever experienced. But that circumstance is *not* alone. The problem has been made much worse by a gradually developing, and now chronic, deterioration of institutional infrastructure. After the "science boom" was over, most federal research agencies responded, as political entities often will, to the demands of their constituencies. Support for buildings and major instrumentation was drastically curtailed in order to conserve funding for direct program support. To satisfy the demands of the researchers, political "targets" were established in order to fund a minimum number of grants. Inevitably, the targets were met by underfunding each award, forcing the scientists who were managing those grants and contracts to choose between people, on the one hand, and facilities and equipment, on the other. Naturally, they chose the people. The consequences are described, painfully but accurately, in the following passage from a statement by the president of the Association of

American Universities to the President's Council of Advisers on Science and Technology in 1992:

> Absent any large, new infusion of resources, the future of the other basic sciences may well come to resemble the present in the biomedical sciences: The number of applicants for grants grows faster than the available resources, the success ratio declines, unrealistic demands for university matching accompany reduced grant support, good research goes unfunded, good researchers become frustrated, young researchers leave the field, infrastructure problems are deferred, and the price for it all will be paid in the future by people who are not around now to assert their interests.[3]

Most recently, the system of indirect cost reimbursement has been brought under intense political attack, nominally for alleged abuses at Stanford University and elsewhere. A result of this scrutiny and the accompanying rhetoric has been to strengthen the public's perception that the "real" costs are program costs, and buildings, equipment, and the administrative maintenance of the system are simply "extras." As a consequence, science laboratories and libraries are in bad shape, and are steadily getting worse.

Nor is that the end of the difficulty. Twelve years of New Federalism, combined with local taxpayer revolts, sharply reduced the revenue stream many great public research universities had counted on from their states. Local economic difficulties during the recessionary years exacerbated that problem. On the private side, incentives for giving and access to tax-exempt debt for independent universities suffered grievously in the 1986 tax law revision. Thus, not only research support but the funding base for all university programs has been under increasing pressure.

At the same time, public expectations have been increasing. The failure of higher education to play a major role in addressing the crisis in grades K-12 has been noticed; we are also being urged to pay more attention to the quality of the education being offered to our undergraduates. All this is taking place against a background of heightened regulatory intervention from government at all levels— a distracting, costly, and often unwelcome addition to the university's other burdens.

This growing disparity between what we want to do and what we are given to do it with seems, to many of us in the universities, new, unfamiliar, and unpleasant. What we forget is the unprecedented character of the circumstances that we grew up in. As I write, the California newspapers are announcing "the end of a drought." What they should be saying is that we are being temporarily returned to that false sense of security we Westerners always get in a wet year. For the research universities, the period from 1952 to 1968 was like that. An unprecedented convergence of events— Sputnik, the baby boom, a postwar economic surge — created a unique set of social conditions and a remarkable period of growth. Thirty years later, the world has changed, but my generation of faculty, like the politicians who developed the Colorado River Basin allocations in the 1920s, can remember only the wet years.

All of this means that the research universities face a time not merely of choices, but of *hard* choices: hard in the sense that they require departures from cultural conditioning, and hard in the sense of tight finances. A growing literature already hints at one major direction of the response. "Productivity improvement" in higher education has become a buzzword, and the last several years have seen the development of large, foundation-sponsored studies of higher education management.[4] Doubtless there is room for improvement in this area—given that the "management" environment in universities is a mixture of academic and administrative cultures—it seems unlikely that such changes, however necessary, will be a sufficient source of relief.

So the working hypothesis of this paper is that the research universities will be forced to choose, in a much more disciplined way than ever before, not just among attractive new possibilities or program alternatives, but among traditional, well-established fields and disciplines.

HOW THE CHOICES ARE MADE: THE REALITIES OF LOCAL CONTROL

Universities are complicated places. To many observers—some disaffected faculty members and students and more than a few trustees—they look like other kinds of corporations: there is a chief executive officer, a group of fiduciaries (who try, on occasion, to be managers), a chief operating officer (the provost), and a group of divisions each with its own relatively independent leadership. Certain services are needed by all the divisions, and these are often managed centrally—development, some version of public affairs, legal services, human resources, and the like.

But there are terribly important differences. Perhaps the most significant in our present context is that the intellectual direction and even the leadership of the divisions is not controlled by the center. Nor is it really *managed* at the local level, where the putative "line managers" scarcely want to manage at all. Indeed, the equivalents of what would be called product and service lines in a corporation—the teaching and the knowledge-gathering missions of the institution—depend entirely on local divisions within which there is little or no management culture of the traditional corporate kind.

In more hierarchical organizational settings, changes in the direction of major units are achieved by two means: the ability to bring in new people to replace others, and the ability to make people accountable to central authority for their performance. In universities, neither of these opportunities comes readily to hand. The institution of tenure prohibits rapid changes in the composition of departments (and the removal of a mandatory retirement age has added to this stasis). At the same time, the powerful traditions of academic freedom and of peer review concentrate the power of appointment with local faculties. Lest these observations be interpreted as frustration-venting by a president emeritus, it must be noted that important institutional purposes are served by the principles that underlie local academic control and limit the authority of the center. We should not fail to recognize, however, that their undeniable benefits carry with them some important costs.

These costs—to flexibility and the capacity to respond to opportunity—might be mitigated by an ability on the part of the institution to make changes in divisional leadership. To be sure, that ability does exist in a technical sense, but it is difficult to exercise. Schools and departments, especially strong (i.e., prestigious) ones, regularly insist on and get an influential voice in the selection of their own leadership. Moreover, the positions themselves are transient, and are becoming more so: a three-year term is typical for a department chair, five or six years for a dean. Often those willing to take such posts, surrendering much of their scholarly opportunity to do so, are not among the division's most influential or distinguished members. Even the best department chairs are more likely to be agents of their colleagues' consensus than to be agents of change in some larger institutional interest.

It is within these units that the institution's strategy for academic development is formulated in practice. The departmental curriculum committee, the search committee for the vacant billet in Biology, the School appointment and promotion committee — are the critical organs of choice for the modern research university. Occasionally, the center can veto, or can induce change by financial incentive; in extremis, it can even invoke receivership. But these influences fall far short of realistic direction-setting.

The regular patterns of departmental choice suggest a powerful force in favor of incrementalism and against directed change. Collegiality is important in departmental function, especially where — as is often the case — unanimous consent is a practical requirement for major decisions like new faculty appointments. This often leads to a situation where the several subdisciplines are treated "equitably"—that is, in a way that tends to maintain current representation. The search committee in Biology will be looking for a mathematical ecologist or a molecular geneticist as the result of some earlier decisions, in which serious projections of opportunity and analyses of need may have been important. But it is also the result of some considerations that are essentially political: whether the population group or the molecular group received the last appointment; who is most distressed about other resource decisions; and which influential faculty members have other offers. In such environments, it is difficult to stray far from present conditions and historical assumptions.

Something is working at a deeper level here, as well. Faculty members are heavily invested in their own disciplines. Not only are they acculturated by belonging to an invisible legion that exists outside the institution and commands its own loyalty, but they also know or sense that robust survival of their discipline in the university is a form of insurance for their own well-being.

The strength of local custom and choice can be illustrated by looking at other kinds of appointment objectives. For example, it has been recognized for a dozen years that minority representation in the Ph.D.-granting academic disciplines has been falling gradually following its increase in the period from 1968 to 1976. Various incentives have been put in place, at Stanford and elsewhere, to remedy this distressing situation. These have included grants for minority undergraduate students for summer support, special forms of fellowship assistance, and active central encouragement for the enrollment of minority students at the graduate level. But here, as with the faculty recruitment of women and minorities, we have found that *the* criterion for success is the presence in a department of a small number of faculty members who are personally committed to the objective. Centrally-mediated persuasion, even when backed by significant financial incentives, has much less impact on outcomes than a special local interest in the matter.

CHOICES AT THE CENTER

Even though the critical matters of faculty appointment and the direction of the disciplines are determined at the level of the department or school, purposeful central control can surely be exerted through the devices of budget allocation, curriculum decisions, and the development of academic initiative. Can't it? Well, yes and no.

Leadership *can* be exercised, but it has significant limitations. Nowhere are these limitations more apparent than in central efforts to launch new academic ventures. At Stanford we felt ourselves relatively fortunate in having an institutional culture that favored interdisciplinary research and teaching, and that was hospitable to all sorts of ventures that crossed departments and schools. There was also an encouraging track record. On the research side, there was a cluster of flourishing interdisciplinary centers ranging from one on language and information to one on international security and arms control. On the teaching side, the justly popular and widely praised Program in Human Biology was an available reminder of what new initiative could accomplish. Yet, when efforts have been made to strengthen such programs by giving them limited authority of academic appointment, they have encountered a level of local resistance that, I have discovered in conversations with other presidents and provosts, is quite characteristic.

What are its sources? I can perceive at least two. Interdisciplinary programs have always been subject to departmental criticism on the ground that they are less "rigorous" than the source disciplines. There is a certain inevitability to this. How can a course that yields some time to biology that might have been given to economics possibly seem as rigorous to an economist as the offerings in the home department? An additional problem arises in the case of those interdisciplinary programs that include policy studies. A form of endemic resistance still exists in the academy with respect to worldly application. Time after time, the appointments needed in fields like language and area studies, international security, and the like are forestalled by departmental fears that they have been contaminated by practice.

These reservations, of course, stem from a desire to conserve the quality of the institution's faculty and programs that is both sensible and sincere. But it is also inflexible and turf-conscious, and it acts as a barrier to innovation. Some would argue that conservatism of this kind is necessary because everything in a university becomes permanent: an unwise or premature adoption will inevitably reify into an embarrassing landmark. But then one must ask whether the real problem is the university's reluctance to give things up, and inquire as to the source of that reluctance.

PROGRAM CHOICES: WHY UNIVERSITIES KEEP EVERYTHING

The answer one is likely to hear from a thoughtful academic in response to the question, "Why isn't this inactive field of study discarded?," will go something like this: "Its subject matter is important to teach, because it is basic to other things; besides, even disciplines that seem to be languishing may become revitalized by an unexpected new discovery."

Reasonable as it sounds, that simply cannot be right. As to the first clause, we have ten times as much important material to teach as we did when I began teaching; choices simply have to be made, and valuable things are left out of the best curricula. The most important residue of good education in a discipline, after all, is good analysis—not a catalog of facts. The argument, then, that we retain specialties for reasons of "coverage" is contradicted by our actual practices.

As to the second, senescence is not really very hard to detect, and is rarely reversed. High-voltage transmission reserved a place in engineering long after it had become relatively inactive; departments or schools of industrial relations, formed when labor-management disputes were an innovative terrain for the applied social sciences, are still around in a state of diminished usefulness. The reformulation of the basic biomedical sciences was deferred by a belief in anatomy and physiology that far outlasted their utility as separate departmental entities. It is, in any event, very difficult to justify holding the place of a tired discipline against hale and hearty claimants for admission—merely on the basis that it might one day recover. Hope does sometimes triumph over experience, but not very often.

One explanation for disciplinary conservatism may be more realistic than the rationale just given, though it is perhaps less respectable. University faculties have unwritten understandings, and one of them is that they usually criticize one another's disciplines only in private. In a recent round of harsh budget cuts at Stanford, we involved a group of distinguished faculty from all fields. They worked hard and faithfully with us on all aspects of the process, and in almost all respects their judgments were thoughtful and fair. In one regard, however, they demonstrated the point that I am making. They frequently worried that we were cutting too much "across-the-board," and not singling out whole programs for elimination; yet, they could not develop a consensus on which programs should go. There was private advice to us, of course, on what victim "the administration" might select—and in nearly every case the recommended deletion was a discipline far from the domain of the recommenders.

The problem of choosing among disciplines has been on recent and dramatic public display in the sciences. Sharp limitations on the federal funding of research have produced deep stresses in the scientific community. The distinguished physicist Leon Lederman, in assuming the presidency of the American Association for the Advancement of Science in 1991, conducted an informal survey of the academic state of mind. Though sharply criticized as an exercise in social science, it yielded a rich haul of angst in the form of discouraged comments by science faculty members. Lederman described it as having demonstrated ". . .a depth of despair and discouragement that I have not experienced in my forty years in science."[5] Yet, the pressure on the funding agencies from this constituency is to spread support widely, rather than to make priority judgments about fields. When the president of the National Academy of Sciences announced in 1988 that the scientific community would have to make hard priority choices among projects, there was instant resistance.[6] Two years later that position was replaced by a call for the doubling of federal support for scientific research.

At a more local level, I experienced the same sort of reluctance about hard choices. Stanford's provost and I had a series of luncheons with members of the science faculty in order to discuss a range of subjects over which they had expressed concerns. At one of these luncheons, the conversation turned to the cost of doing science, which has risen so rapidly in some disciplines that much of the work must be done in national or regional facilities. Other disciplines are nearing that point, and I suggested that perhaps as we looked at the prospects for developing one or another scientific field we might have to consider cost. It was as though I had proposed to abolish the institution of tenure during the dessert course; I was accused of advocating "cheap science"!

Resistance to the establishment of priorities is understandable. Choices among competing goods are by definition hard choices, and no one wants to be placed toward the bottom of the list. The result is a kind of logrolling, in which each claimant supports equity for all. The continued existence of the coalition depends upon loyalty to that custom, and in public the participants are highly resistant to proposals that would divide them. In private, they will lobby vigorously for the need to favor their own enterprises and to disfavor others.

In order to deal with this difficulty, universities often rely on the more objective evaluations of outside "visiting committees." Valuable though this practice may be in many respects, it seldom leads to hard-minded priority setting. I suppose that in nearly forty years as an academic, I have either served on or been advised by dozens of these bodies—nearly all of them composed of first-rate, thoughtful people. In all that time, I have *never* heard one propose significant reductions in the discipline it was called upon to visit. Instead, the visitors usually become advocates for their colleagues, helping them lobby the administration for more resources and more moral support for what they are convinced is an area of unique potential—in the words of one overenthusiastic colleague, "a virgin field, pregnant with possibilities."

In those rare cases where radical restructuring or elimination is actually proposed, it has never been difficult for advocates to marshal support and even to develop a national sense of outrage over the demise of whatever disciplinary landmark is about to disappear. Archaeology at Princeton, Architecture at Stanford, Demography at Berkeley, Library Science at Columbia, Organization and Management at Yale — each of these threats produced major stories in the national news, with sympathetic attention to the handwringing of the mavens in each discipline.

Lest it seem that all of the inertia-yielding impulse is lodged in the faculty, let me hasten to spread some blame on my own kind. Presidents (and, to a degree, provosts and deans) hold what have become political offices. It is difficult to occupy one of these positions without some sense that you are running for it every day. There is a powerful temptation to engage in the politics of self-preservation, which most often turn out to be the politics of caution. In hard times, this is likely to encourage pseudoequitable budget reductions across-the-board, rather than bold assaults on weak programs; in good times, it yields a form of bland opportunism, in which almost any plausible plan for growth is rewarded if it is offered under the right credentials. It is too easy to argue that these things are done "to please the faculty." In truth, they are often done in a form of isolation from well-formulated faculty views. Presidents, in particular, can find themselves badly out of touch if they do not take special care to engage faculty actively in the decision-making process. My own experience with that process is entirely positive —but it requires extraordinary efforts. It is not surprising that presidents often do not make them, and as a result find themselves increasingly distanced from the academic reality. The outcome is sure to be a form of central incrementalism at least as immobilizing as the inherent conservatism of the disciplinary units.

Thus there are many reasons why, in universities, sunset is an hour that almost never arrives. And that is not the only respect in which faculty preferences and administrative habits make what are called "product life cycles" elsewhere unusually long in universities. It is difficult to build modular, generic laboratory space that is constructed to last only for a few decades, even though this is clearly the most cost-effective solution for most research programs.

Such plans run up against the preference of the academic clients, as well as monument-loving administrators and trustees, for solidly-built, specially-designed buildings that have the look and feel of permanence. And, of course, the institution of tenure, the irresistible temptation to fill vacancies with senior appointments, and the uncapping of mandatory retirement have combined to make faculties older in both age and length of service.

There is a deeper explanation, I think, for the stubborn survival of academic programs, one that goes beyond the relative stability of facilities and of people. In universities, very careful planning goes into the making of programs, whether these are curricula, research centers, or entire departments or schools. In nature, the parts of organisms or ecosystems have complex relationships to one another because they have evolved together, often from beginnings very different from their present form. Darwin pondered (and contemporary creationists still use it against him) how a complex organ could ever have been developed by gradual change. What use is part of an eye? We now have an explanation: structures often assume entirely new functions as the organism undergoes evolutionary change, finding utility in a foreign context.

The parts of universities, however, are not like that at all. We insist that each added part be perfected at the workbench before it is made a part of the whole; it is a product of our insistence on excellence. Not much evolution in place is allowed because that would require a large investment— of time and of human loyalty— on behalf of each new addition. Small wonder, then, that there is so much reluctance to give one of them up.

Together, these forces—tenure, disciplinary loyalty, the structure of academic politics, monumental physical arrangements, and investment patterns that create huge regret functions—favor a stability that may be very useful in some ways, but makes it difficult for the university to take new directions nimbly. It enhances a distribution of decision-making power in which the periphery has a clear advantage over the center.

What is needed is a view of academic programs that goes far beyond "what is hot and what is not." Although matters of intellectual vigor and senescence have been at the center of much of the foregoing discussion, there is no reason for all research universities to make the same choices among fields. On the contrary, the pluralism of American higher education has always been one of its great strengths. I will return to this point later.

POLICY CHOICES: WHO SPEAKS FOR THE UNIVERSITY?

What I have said thus far applies primarily to those core aspects of the academic enterprise that we might call *program*: faculty appointments, balance among disciplines, research emphasis, curricula, and the like. But there are also *policies*: decisions about what the institution should do about enrollment, fellowship stipends, land use, community relations, retirement, faculty housing, making representations to the government, fund-raising objectives, and more. Surely in these areas, central initiative and choice play an important role, and may even overcome the decentralized damping that I have been describing.

By deciding on particular needs and making adroit use of its authority in making these kinds of decisions, the central administration can create directed change. But it is difficult to do, and even more difficult to do regularly. Two different versions of the university are blended, or sometimes confused, as these decisions are formulated. One is the university as a community of scholars; the other is the university as a legal entity.

Whether state or private, universities are public trusts, and their fiduciaries have duties they are legally bound to perform. Trustees see themselves as, and they *are*, spokespersons for the faculty that have not been appointed yet, the experiments that have not been thought of yet, and the students who have not been born yet. This gives a certain bite to central governance: no responsible trustee or regent is likely to approve an action that would significantly compromise the capacity of the institution to serve the next generation. But it is difficult for boards to focus on these issues. Too often their role is anything but fiduciary: they become absorbed in facilities decisions or in activities that cross the line from policy oversight into administrative intervention. Thus, their vital role in insuring intergenerational equity is often obscured and their central claim to authority weakened.

Let us suppose a situation in which trustees and their administrative appointees are acting, as they should, in the interest of the successor generation. Members of the present community, particularly the faculty, have substantial political power to push things in the other direction—to favor the present. Choices and conflicts of this sort are, fortunately, not common, but when they occur, they squarely pit the university community of the present against the fiduciary notion of the institution in perpetuity.

Perhaps a brief case study will illustrate the difficulty. At the time Congress was considering the full uncapping of mandatory retirement, a number of universities and their associations made representations about the special difficulties imposed by academic tenure. It was argued that the extension from age sixty-five to age seventy had already had significant effects on the average age of faculties, and that complete uncapping would leave us little choice but to consider modification of tenure policies. Like other university presidents, I reported the position we (by which I really mean the provost and I, after consultation with deans and elected faculty groups) were taking. There were strong objections—not from the majority of faculty, but certainly from an influential and vocal minority—to the effect that this was not only the wrong policy but that the administration had no right to make it without broad faculty consultation followed by the equivalent of legislative endorsement.

I cite this case not to promote our policy, though I continue to believe that the impact of uncapping will be a serious problem for the research universities. I cite it because it illustrates one of the ambiguities that confront academic decision-making. There is a strong sense of entitlement on the part of the community of scholars not only to make those decisions that are plainly "academic," that is, delegated powers in the constitutional sense, but to participate fully also in those that involve the university as a legal entity.

That is a problem because it often pits present against future interests, as it did in this case. In straightforward matters of faculty welfare— compensation, benefits, housing, teaching loads, and the like—these conflicts are usually obvious and are settled simply by a constitutional reservation of power to the board and its administrative appointees. There is usually no confusion about which version of the institution (communitarian or fiduciary) will be active in deciding them.

However, there are some signs of serious future danger even in this area. There was a time when universities provided faculty members with the briefest of descriptions of their duties, a salary figure, and little else. Now there is a complex panoply of benefits: retirement programs with multiple investment vehicles, health insurance plans, tuition benefits for children, and housing. Institutions blessed with a good deal of land have created large on-campus developments in which the university assumes the role of landlord and banker. These arrangements are complex enough to require financial counseling, and that is often provided as well. The result is a growing sense of both dependency and entitlement. There is a strong desire to participate in land-use decisions that "might affect the neighborhood," and the university becomes a looming paternal figure, subject to all the resentment that fathers sometimes get.

I have been talking about two areas of institutional decision-making that lie outside, or at least beyond, the standard "academic" decisions—which are heavily weighted away from the center and toward the periphery. The first is the usual realm of institutional policy decisions, in which there is clear central authority but sometimes a conflict between the university as a legal entity and the university as a "community." The second is an area we might call "faculty welfare." Here, central authority is unmistakable, but it may become more difficult to exercise because the university has entangled itself so deeply into the lives of its faculty.

CENTRAL INITIATIVES: TWO EXAMPLES

There is a third class of major decisions, and, for lack of a better word, they can be called central initiatives. How can big nonprogram changes in the institution be installed—changes, for example, like altering the relative rewards for undergraduate teaching and research, or changing the institution's role with respect to important external constituencies or activities? Such initiatives, though sweeping, seem to invade no particular local prerogatives, and ought to be the natural stuff of strong central leadership. Indeed they are, but they are also naturally suspect, and if they are demanded frequently, the academic body politic will develop strong antibodies against them.

My first example is an initiative that grew out of a continuing concern with the freedom of researchers to pursue their own interests without interference, particularly of prior restraint. In the early 1980s, Stanford took a leading role in opposing efforts by some in the Department of Defense to apply restrictions intended for devices and technology to basic research data.[7] We succeeded in making our case, but nearly a decade later, the National Heart, Lung and Blood Institute attempted to impose prior publication restraints on scientists doing controlled clinical trials of a new medical device.[8] Stanford sued and won. We also took strong, even politically risky public positions against research interference and intimidation by the animal rights movement.

Other challenges came from inside the institution. Faculty and student groups urged us to make the source of funds, or the prospect that socially harmful uses might be made of the results of research, criteria for rejecting outside funding for faculty-initiated investigations. Despite strong pressures to do so in particular cases, we rejected all these invitations.

These policies were not difficult to establish and maintain. They did worry some faculty members because, variously, they might bring to Stanford threats of reprisal, generate unfavorable publicity, carry a risk of government disapproval, or exacerbate tensions within the community. It was not unnoticed, either, that in the case of our disagreements with the government, Stanford was required to commit more than its fair financial share (of, for example, legal costs) in achieving what many regarded as consortial objectives. But in the main, these policies enjoyed strong support from faculty, staff, and trustees because 1) they were faithful to important academic principles; 2) they did not require significant changes in the responsibilities of any major constituency; and 3) they were directed primarily at problems of external origin.

When the central initiative is aimed entirely at policies and practices within the institution, and especially if it involves faculty responsibilities, the degree of difficulty is much higher—as illustrated by a second example. Partly as a result of an institutional planning process we had begun at Stanford in 1987, I decided it was necessary to reemphasize the importance of undergraduate teaching. Some of the reasoning is embedded in earlier parts of this account. A combination of pressures—many of them not of their own making—have forced faculty members to reallocate some time and attention from instruction to research. The activities that have suffered most are probably those rather personal, time-consuming interactions that seem least cost-effective but may be among the most valuable.

In 1991, I devoted my annual report to the faculty to this subject. I had to do it again in the following year because the level of consternation (and misunderstanding) was so high.[9] For much of that, I was to blame. The timing was unfortunate. The announcement came at a difficult time in Stanford's controversy with the government over indirect costs. And the press' treatment of the report made it sound significantly more radical than it was: "Teach or Perish" was the headline in one Bay area newspaper.

I thought my analysis of the problem was restrained, but it did contain an implied criticism. There were three kinds of reactions from the faculty, which I shall try to describe briefly without caricaturing them. The first, from a minority, was that this was an overdue and welcome change of emphasis. The second was that while the point might be a legitimate one, it opened the university to unfair criticism and therefore should not have been made in a public way. The third held that the diagnosis was wrong and that the patient was perfectly healthy. (A fourth—perhaps really only an element of the second and third—was that such a program would require evaluation efforts that would prove overly intrusive).

In a communication the next fall, I attempted to deal with these reactions and offered some concrete proposals. Two were particularly important: we made entirely new resources available for salary improvements for outstanding teachers, and established some new prizes; and we began a careful study of criteria for evaluating teaching and research in the appointment and promotion process.

The malaise has now attenuated, and because the problem is receiving more attention nationally our faculty feels less heat from the spotlight. Some commentators have responded favorably to the institutional lead Stanford took in what is now seen as a national problem, and that has helped. But there remains some residue of resentment that the faculty was unfairly pushed on the issue. Oddly, that is worsened by the support this initiative has received from students, trustees, and alumni, who are like the rest of the outside world in the priority they attach to teaching. Thus, this has been an object lesson in the deployment of central decision-making, one that emphasizes the need for caution and the diligent recruitment of stakeholders.

I have used this as an example of the difficulties that confront far-reaching new initiatives. But it is much more than an example; it is at the very core of a new and growing public dissatisfaction with the course of higher education.

It has to do with the changing attitudes of faculty members with regard to their own perceived welfare. Nearly every university president or provost with whom I have talked will testify privately that there is an increasing preoccupation with rights rather than responsibilities—though in almost the same breath we all wax ecstatic about the counterexamples. I think the problem has much to do with the way we treat the tenure process. Appointment without limit of time is viewed as an enormous hurdle — and, of course, it is one that is getting higher all the time. Those who clear it successfully have understandably high expectations about the quality of life on the other side. These feelings may be exacerbated by the generational disappointment felt by today's cohort of junior faculty. They belong, after all, to the first generation of American society that faces an economic future less hopeful than the one before — in a nation whose motif is continuous betterment.

Furthermore, the institution sends few signals about its expectations regarding faculty citizenship. A striking example of this is to be found in the way universities prepare their own doctoral candidates for academic careers. In the schools of law, medicine, and even business, one now sees well-taught, required courses with names like "Ethics for . . ." or "Professional Responsibility." Yet, one finds almost no systematic instruction of this kind for dissertation-level Ph.D. candidates. In this way, we broadcast the view that some form of civic education is in order for every profession *except* our own. And in our stress on research productivity and our eagerness to appoint scholars with star quality, we offer relief from many of the important tasks of institutional citizenship. Is it any wonder that faculty members display—as they sometimes do in letting self-interest influence their position on institutional change — an enlarged sense of entitlement? In his farewell report as Dean of the Faculty of Arts and Sciences at Harvard University, Henry Rosovsky made explicit what so many of us have noticed: "It is my distinct impression—'firm belief' would perhaps be a better expression—that there has been a secular decline of professorial civic virtue in the Faculty of Arts and Sciences."[10] When he wrote that,

Rosovsky was concluding a brief second term as dean—one separated by six or seven years from an earlier, much longer tenure; thus, he had an unusual position from which to view the change. The rest of us would surely concur in his observation that teaching loads have grown lighter, absences from campus more frequent, and commitments to outside activities more substantial—although we would want to stipulate that administrative demands and the institution's own reward structure bear some of the responsibility.

Clearly, these changes in professorial commitment and attitude form an important dimension of the university's capacity for change. Much of the power to make the needed choices resides, as we have seen, in the faculty. But if the faculty's commitment to the institution (as opposed to the discipline, or to the self) is diminished— or if the professoriate simply likes things as they are — then they are obviously less likely to change.

CENTRAL INITIATIVES: THE PATHS NOT TAKEN

If central initiatives sometimes falter because they encounter either peripheral inertia or faculty self-interest, there are surely others that *should* have been started, but were not because administrators were too cautious or lacked vision.

A particularly troublesome illustration of failed central planning in the past decade has been the management of institutional size and scope. At Stanford, as in other research universities, the 1980s saw significant growth in the size of staff compared with that of faculty or student body. Some of this was a response to increased transaction volume: more applications, more gifts to process, more regulatory requirements of all kinds. But the lion's share was "opportunistic growth" in areas not supported by the operating budget, like sponsored research. This growth in turn caused expansion of all the service elements of the institution: personnel, benefits, procurement, faculty/staff housing, and the like. As this infrastructure grew in complexity, two things became clear. First, it became less efficient, and service levels declined. Despite a high level of dedication on the part of individual staff members, faculty complaints about the quality of help they were getting increased even as the number of helpers was growing larger. Second, we began to recognize that the external costs of an enlarged staff rose in a nonlinear fashion—they were no longer met by the indirect cost revenues associated with the additional appointments.

These staff increases bear a major share of the responsibility for the "cost disease" that emerged for the universities in the 1980s. In a growth economy, such problems are masked; when external sources of support are on a plateau, however, they become severe. It is important to recognize that they are also responses to real needs: research growth, both in size and complexity; higher expectations on the part of everyone with regard to service levels; and increased burdens imposed by governments, foundations, utilities, and a long list of other external entities.

But we failed to recognize the seriousness of this problem. Some universities—and Stanford was at the front of the pack—identified the cost disease and began to deal with it at the very end of the decade. But we missed the vital linkage that coupled staff growth outside the primary academic budget to growth inside it, and we did not take preventive steps that might have saved the situation. In effect, we permitted restricted funds to tax the general fund. Nor did we perceive the revolution in personnel management that was beginning to take place in the profit sector—a revolution that might have allowed us to do more with less.

Second, we failed to recognize that our heavy dependence upon federal funding would encourage significant inroads by the government against the institution's autonomy. The list of these, for the decade of the 1980s alone, is alarmingly long: efforts to restrict the access of foreign nationals not only to data but to academic seminars; attempts to limit freedom of scholarly publication; civil investigative demands against nearly sixty colleges and universities, costing in the aggregate more than $20 million, to produce a consent decree among eight of them limiting consultation about financial aid; new certification requirements regarding drug and alcohol use on campus; and threatening inquiries from government officials about statements on these matters by individual faculty members. Perhaps the most alarming has been the replacement of an informal, occasionally flawed system for justifying the recovery of research costs with a set of requirements borrowed directly from the for-profit defense procurement sector—at great institutional cost.[11] None of these incursions, perhaps, would have been prevented by a more astute awareness of the liability of this degree of dependence. But had we had better foresight, we might have minimized their impact.

Our most important failure, however—and here I plainly cannot and should not implicate all institutions or all leaders—has been a general failure to create sharply individualized, recognizable identities for our own institutions. We say that we treasure the pluralism in American higher education. Yet, it sometimes seems as if we do everything possible to deny it—creating, instead, entities that look as though they came off the shelf labeled "generic." Presidents and chancellors move from one place to another without apparent discomfort, as though they were interchangeable parts. Brochures and catalogs look alike, and often stress the same values. *U. S. News & World Report,* presumably seduced by the sameness of it all, blithely ranks Cal Tech and the University of Michigan in the same set. Little, in short, is done to emphasize the differentiating characteristics and the particular strengths of each institution.

Perhaps that is because academic leaders have been so reluctant to create what Jonathan Cole, Provost of Columbia University, has called the "cognitive map" for their universities. It is part of the process of setting priorities, the difficulty of which I discussed earlier. Despite the inherent reluctance of the academic decision-making apparatus to make these choices, good leadership can point the way. Defining the institution's comparative advantage, working with faculty to identify the key locations on the cognitive map, and then returning again and again to reemphasize and support these few essentials is something presidents, provosts, and trustees can and should do. An institution might decide, for example, to develop a restricted graduate faculty, strong in the physical and engineering sciences and in several humanities and social science disciplines; to emphasize undergraduate education through a unique set of upper-division seminar and thesis requirements; and to eschew, despite some temptation, professional schools in business, law, and medicine, and thus retain manageable scope. It is easy to recognize Princeton in this quick vision, partly because so few other places have thought through their own destiny with such clarity and pursued it with such focus.

My point is simply that there is much to gain from a process in which faculty and administration together construct such a vision— deciding where to venture not simply on the basis of what is timely and seems important, but what can be done especially well and what forms a fit with existing programs. This exercise could potentially be inspiring and reinvigorating for the entire institution. It will be part of what successful responders do during this period of constraint. But it will not come easily or naturally.

THE NEXT GENERATION OF BIG CHANGES

I have been describing resource constraints, resistance to change, and altered expectations, and I have tried to demonstrate some of the features of peripheral organization that resist change — and some reasons why central planning has failed to direct change. Do these suggest that universities are in deep trouble — that they may not be able to cope with the demands of large-scale change that will require central planning and the broadest kind of involvement? Surely such directional shifts will be required if the American research university of the next century is to meet society's expectations for it. Despite the new limits, my own view is optimistic, even though the degree of difficulty will be high.

The first reason for optimism comes from the limits themselves. We know (because Nobel laureate Herbert Simon and others have been telling us) that organizations seldom achieve major economies or directional shifts— even when these would plainly yield important gains—unless the external pressure is intense. As long as things are going along well, successful institutions resist change. We now face that kind of pressure. It can force the consideration of issues that otherwise would rest comfortably under the rug. It can be used by university leaders to direct major institutional reconfiguration.

The second reason is embedded in the message we are being given from the world outside. It is one with which we should be inherently comfortable, because it is resonant with our earlier tradition. The message is nonutilitarian; it emphasizes our obligations to care well for our students, to provide the kind of education that will produce leaders and not followers, and to be a shelter for new ideas and a force for social improvement. We should hear in it an encouragement to reexamine our assumptions, to be prepared to do away with old paradigms—in short, to redesign ourselves in a way that is faithful to first principles.

The third reason is an opportunity to deal imaginatively and constructively with a world that is also being reshaped. Never have our universities lived in a more abruptly changing society. To speak of "academic rigor" by way of appealing to the disciplinary status quo is self-evidently anachronistic now. We need to open up the rigid cages of institutional thought and custom to new cultures, new alignments, and new problems. Fortunately, the new problems are as intellectually exciting and fascinating as any we have ever seen.

What are some of these new opportunities? One will surely be the internationalization of the university. Increasingly, friendly critics of higher education are wondering why—in view of the rapid reformulation of national boundaries, the development of a global economy, and the dramatic change in the very concept of sovereignty—the universities are not more actively becoming "international." The critics often find it difficult, however, to be more specific about what it really means to be an "international university."

Eugene Skolnikoff has thoroughly discussed the present state of affairs elsewhere in this volume. My own quick assessment is that even the best of our universities has not gone very far in this direction. Language and area studies programs are weaker in most places than they were two decades ago. Policy studies, whether on international security or environmental preservation, have a hard time penetrating the academic fabric successfully. Foreign graduate enrollment has grown, but that is regarded in some quarters as a national failure. Foreign undergraduate enrollment is best described as a smattering, fellowship exchange is trivial, and no US university has yet made major, large-scale campus commitments overseas. Thus, although we have, at least by market test, the finest system of higher education in the world, no American university has really become a "world university."

Certainly, some program commitments in this direction are needed: overseas studies centers, expanded fellowship exchange programs, and more focused support of area studies programs are just a few of them. In my judgment, it is at least as much a matter of attitude as of program. The opening of curricula to the full range of sources that have contributed to our own culture has been met by a kind of conservatism that makes its appeal through one of those plausible-sounding claims to academic rigor. But *rigor mortis* is actually more like it. How are we to understand the cultural values and the political traditions of large parts of the world (never mind the diverse ethnic populations that now make up our own society) if we let our students hear only from a single tradition of philosophy or literature? Should we continue to retreat in disorder from charges of "cultural relativism" whenever we suggest that ethnography has value, and that Chinese religions and political economy are important for everyone to know something about? To change both the attitudes and the programs will require major efforts— on the part of universities' friends and partners (including government) as well as on the part of their internal constituencies.

There is another challenge that may be even bigger: a change toward some greater measure of relatedness to the pressing needs of society. There is a certain reactive caution in the academy about this notion; much of it is the result of immunization acquired during the excesses of the 1960s. But that was an aberrant time, in which the revolt was not only antiauthoritarian but anti-intellectual. Now the climate is quite different: the best students are prepared to turn their hands to critical needs, and they thirst for the intellectual tools to make the work go better. As I write, I have been surrounded by twenty Stanford undergraduates who are studying environmental policy at our campus in Washington, D.C. They have internships in agencies or nongovernmental organizations during the day, and return to a center in which they take a seminar course, receive tutorials, and live together. It is hard to know which is more remarkable: their intellectual caliber, the intensity of their commitment, or the ability they have to support one another and get things done together. It has had a transforming effect on my views about experiential education, and the value of merging academic work with practice.

Sometimes it is feared that this merger will lower the standards of the academic enterprise. I suppose in some sense it may, by introducing new material that may force more traditional subjects aside. But it also provides meaning and motivation, induces confidence, and invites full participation. Students simply find more inspiration in applying their developing analytical skills to real problems. Perhaps this is because economically difficult times encourage a more practical orientation. But the problems in which these students interest themselves are desperately important, and provide a chronic rebuke to our academic reluctance to include them in what we do.

Our students ask in some bewilderment why, as the world gets warmer and the cities become more uninhabitable, we are debating whether the addition of such real-world perspective will deduct from our claim to academic excellence.

These big changes are even harder to make than the marginal ones—like which discipline should receive greater emphasis in the sciences, or even whether or not we should add a professional school. But we will find that they refuse to be ignored. How, then, will the governance of universities respond to them over the next decade or two?

THE FUTURE OF INSTITUTIONAL CHANGE

There is no question that the multiplication of knowledge, the skyrocketing cost of doing what we already do, and the thinning support available from societal sources have already created an environment of hard choices. At the same time, these challenges supply an incentive for major change, and, as we have seen, they supply inviting channels for creative institutional efforts. Will universities be able to respond to what amounts to a new world order? How are their mechanisms of governance, weighted with all the difficulties I have described, likely to respond?

Prediction is risky, but I have in mind a scenario that contains three distinct response modes. The first group of institutions will drift into decisions through the familiar model of peripheral control; distributed faculty responses will essentially set the agenda. In a second group, dramatic new coalitions will be formed between unusually effective leaders and their faculties. These institutions will be the first responders. In a third group, change will come about because trustees and administrations recognize — relatively late in the course of the externally-generated crisis—that something must be done. They will take a firm grip, and exert powerful central authority to enforce changes. Because this kind of response is politically possible under conditions of extreme duress, it will occur much later than the second.

This taxonomy of responses, if it is right, suggests a sharp stratification of research universities with respect to their capacity to respond to the new circumstances. Those in the second class—able to form strong coalitions for change by organizational culture, faculty tradition, and/or the quality of leadership —will be the first responders. They may experience initial difficulties, and even some loss of prestige, but in the longer run they will outstrip the others. Trailing them will be the crisis responders, who will suffer not only from some delay but also from the loss of morale that follows any power struggle. Last will be those institutions that cannot or do not sense the urgency, and leave matters in the hands of traditional, distributed forms of decision-making.

What is it about certain institutions that will enable them to be rapid responders? A special relationship between the administration and the faculty will be required, as well as an unusual degree of sensitivity on the part of the governing board in its interaction with both. Each group will have to give up some behaviors that have become habits. For governing boards, caution and incrementalism are well-established—partly because they are generally offered only proposals for marginal change, and partly because their commitment is usually of such limited depth that they find it difficult to undertake deep reconstruction. For the administration, it will mean overcoming a form of isolation that is difficult to avoid, putting in its stead a new level of trust in joint planning processes with the faculty. And for the faculty, it will mean surrendering some important traditions of autonomy and collegial comity.

What is needed, I think, is nothing less than a new "terrain map" of what the institution believes is important. In addition to identifying which areas are suitable for cultivation and which should be left fallow in defining the institution's identity, this exercise *must* include a reexamination of undergraduate education and its relationship to the rest of what goes on in a research university. The conversation about what it means to attend a university college has grown strangely silent; we need to start it up again. How shall we engage undergraduates more effectively in serious scholarly work? How can we create more opportunities for experiential education? Can we do something about the dramatic decline of laboratory instruction in the sciences? Is it possible, in short, to engage a research-oriented faculty more deeply with our students? These are sample questions, meant to illuminate the needs in just one area of what should be a comprehensive inquiry.

The essentiality of professional schools, and the nature of their relationship to their professions; how we prepare graduate students for the teaching portions of their academic careers; how we choose among fields of science; and how we can encourage the formation of new, interdisciplinary programs without freezing them into permanence will surely be among the other questions asked in any deep effort at academic reformation. They will not be answered by academic fiat from the center, nor will they yield to the embedded mechanisms of faculty decision-making. They require a new coalition.

Why will the institutions that develop these coalitions—those that ask hard questions like these and then behave as though they believed their own answers—be the ones that succeed? First, I am convinced that the new economic constraints will be even harsher and more permanent than we now imagine. Second, I believe that although public regard for the universities is still high, there are powerful expectations that these institutions must change —like others in our society. Business as usual will, if these beliefs are correct, be out of the question. The institutions that make the hard choices, that are willing to redefine what is fundamentally important, will eventually distance themselves from the rest, even if they do not take the early lead.

Most efforts to apply evolutionary principles to human institutions fail, but there is one that works. Under severely stringent environmental conditions, a few especially well-adapted designs— often not those that were most successful in earlier and better times—will survive. When things change again, the "line" they represent will radiate and prosper. It will be like that for those universities that can, in this difficult winter of academic discontent, summon the leadership and quality of will to reinvent themselves.

ACKNOWLEDGMENT

The author acknowledges support for the preparation of this article from the Echoing Green Foundation.

ENDNOTES

[1]Derek J. de Solla Price, *Little Science, Big Science. . .and Beyond,* enl. ed. (New York: Columbia University Press, 1986).

[2]Office of Technology Assessment, *Federally Funded Research: Decisions for a Decade* (Washington, D.C.: US Congress, Office of Technology Assessment, 1991). See especially the summary in chap. 1.

[3]Robert M. Rosenzweig, Testimony before President's Council of Advisers on Science and Technology, 24 July 1992.

[4]William F. Massey and Robert Zemske, *Faculty Discretionary time: Departments and the Academic Ratchet,* Pew Higher Education Research Program, Occasional Papers, 1992.

[5]Leon Lederman, "Science: The End of the Frontier?," *Science* (Supplement, January 1991).

[6]Frank Press, "The Dilemma of the Golden Age," *Science, Technology, and Human Values* 13 (3/4) (1988): 224–31.

[7]Donald Kennedy, "The Government, Secrecy, and University Research," *Science* 216 (1982): 365.

[8]*Science* 250 (1989): 746.

[9]Donald Kennedy, Reports to the Academic Council, Stanford University, 1991 and 1992. These documents are available from the Office of the Academic Secretary, Stanford University, Stanford, Calif., 94305.

[10]Henry Rosovsky, 1990–1991 Annual Report to the Faculty of Arts and Sciences, Harvard University, reprinted in the *Harvard Gazette,* 11 October 1991.

[11]The Special Advisory Panel to Stanford University, appointed to evaluate steps Stanford was taking to improve indirect cost accounting, included Joseph E. Connor, Chairman of Price Waterhouse World; Admiral Bob Inman, former Deputy Director of Central Intelligence; Dr. Maxine Singer, President of the Carnegie Institution of Washington; Paul O'Neill, Chairman of Alcoa; and the late Dr. Timothy S. Healy, President of the New York Public Library. In its final report to the university, in which it evaluated the new systems being established on the advice of Arthur Anderson as a result of the federal inquiry, the Panel approved Stanford's response but warned: "Our concern is that the University. . .may have developed an accounting system that is excessive. . . .The accounting tail may well now wag the research dog." At the end of the report, the Panel said: "The precision that seems to be sought by the federal auditors may not be realistically attainable."

Steven Muller # 5

Presidential Leadership

WHERE ARE THE GREAT UNIVERSITY PRESIDENTS of today? Why do we not see the likes of Eliot, Butler, Lowell, Harper, or Hutchins towering over their institutions and raising mighty voices to address society? The most obvious answer, of course, is that the men and women who serve as university presidents today simply lack the greatness of their predecessors. But it is unlikely that the contemporary leadership of universities is much inferior to the leadership of the past. Today's university differs vastly from its predecessor of 50 years ago, and the university presidency today therefore presents a task quite different from that of earlier days. Contemporary university presidents operate under circumstances that differ so comprehensively from those of their predecessors as to defy comparison. A fair appraisal of performance by the incumbents demands an understanding of the revolutionary changes that have transformed the American university, both private and public, over the past half-century.

The single most evident and unarguable aspect of those changes is size. In the 1940s and even into the early 1950s a university—defined as an institution that awards doctorates as well as undergraduate degrees—was not very much larger than a college. Universities might have had several thousand students, several hundred professors, and two or three professional schools, but in many ways they still looked and, to some extent, behaved like large colleges. Everyone knows that, since then, universities have become enormously larger and more diverse. There are now approximately 100 mega-sized research universities throughout

---

Steven Muller is President Emeritus of The Johns Hopkins University.

115

the United States, generally numbering their students in the tens of thousands, faculties and administrative cadres in the thousands, buildings and acreage in the hundreds, and annual budgets in the billion-dollar range. This literal explosion in size took place within only four decades, from the 1950s through the 1980s, but is already accepted and familiar. Its causes—tremendous advances in science and technology, proliferation of highly refined areas of specialization, relentless appetite for ever more access to advanced education—are well understood. Less well understood, however, are a few new key circumstances that, while related to the enormity of growth, also constitute distinctive patterns of evolution of their own. Each of these patterns of evolution by itself represents a significant transformation of the university institution. Each therefore has also reshaped the university presidency, and an evaluation of the performance of that president must take them into account.

EXTERNALLY FUNDED RESEARCH

The first such circumstance is that major research universities in the United States are living far beyond the means of their own resources. The very teaching and research in science and technology for which they are most renowned and respected is precisely that part of their work for which they are themselves utterly unable to pay. External support, primarily from the federal government, pays the bulk of the cost of most university research in science and technology. Without this external support universities would have either to discontinue most of their research and advanced teaching in science and technology or to face bankruptcy in the futile effort to support this work with their own funds. The sums under consideration are in the scores of millions of dollars per year at each of the major research universities and in the hundreds of millions per year at those that are most research intensive and, as a result, also best known and most respected.

This situation has developed, and prevailed increasingly, since the 1950s and is clearly understood within universities, but it appears to be less well understood by the general public. The plain facts are that very few professors in university science and technology departments derive even their salaries wholly from the university that employs them. Almost all of them derive a significant part of their compensation from externally funded research grants or contracts. These professorial salaries, however, are the least of the university's problems were they ever to be fully paid exclusively from university funds. The external grants or contracts for which professors apply may pay part of their compensation, but above all they pay for the acquisition and maintenance of the ever more complex and costly equipment required for both research and teaching. These external grants and contracts also pay compensation for the assistants professors require in their role as principal investigators on a research project, and these assistants are so funded not only to assist the professor but to work as well for their advanced degrees. Stipends and instrumentation are paid for as part of the *direct* cost of externally sponsored grants or contracts. The space occupied by laboratories in which externally funded research is carried on, and the maintenance of that space, are paid as part of the *indirect* cost of externally funded research. Thus, the necessary, complicated, extensive, and expensive university buildings that house departments of science and technology are paid for in large part by the same external grants and contracts that pay those who inhabit them and pay for the equipment they use. It all works, and has indeed worked quite well, for decades; what, then, does it have to do with the university presidency?

For one thing this circumstance has made a congressional lobbyist of the university president. Traditionally the university's chief representative and chief fund-raiser, the president has also become the chief lobbyist with a Congress that determines the budgets of the federal agencies that award the indispensable research grants and contracts on which university science and technology depend. Lobbying makes heavy demands on time and energy. It is not the case that major research university presidents stalk the halls of Congress most of the time, although staff do so on their behalf. It is true, however, that scarcely a week goes by without a briefing and strategy session related to the federal appropriations process and/or the cultivation of relevant members of the Congress. Nor is it coincidence that the Association of American Universities (AAU), which brings the presidents of many major research universities together twice a year, has been transformed from an organization whose primary activity consisted of free-wheeling discussion of common problems, into a tightly organized, well-staffed, and relentlessly active lobbying organization.

There are other factors involved as well. On the matter of indirect cost charges, for instance, the financial interests of the professors who do the research and teaching supported by external grants and contracts are diametrically opposed to the financial interests of the university administration. For university administrators every dollar of indirect cost charges recovered from external sponsors is a precious dollar to be spent on the upkeep of the university's support facilities related to the relevant grant or contract. For the professor or principal investigator, however, every dollar spent for indirect costs reduces the funds available for direct costs, i.e., the salary of the investigator, stipends for research assistants and graduate students, and instruments or equipment. The inevitable resulting tension is aggravated by the professor's knowledge that his or her compensation does not primarily come from the university, prompting him or her to ask, "What do I owe a place that is lucky to have me, and why should I let them rip off *my* research dollars for *their* indirect costs?" The contrary view of university administrators is that the professor "may be brilliant but is also spoiled and totally unrealistic, since he or she simply refuses to recognize that the university loses money on every externally sponsored grant or contract because the full, real indirect costs are never wholly recovered." The heart of the problem, of course, is that—setting aside the exaggerated tone—each point of view is basically correct.

Obviously, such disputes have proven to be survivable over the years, but, nevertheless, they cast a shadow on the relationship between university presidents and some of their most eminent and respected faculty colleagues. There are other more subtle but not wholly insignificant perceptions involved as well. The university president is uneasily aware at almost all times that a huge and absolutely key source of university support is essentially out of his or her control, subject at best to only marginal influence, albeit the result of enormous effort. The faculty also understands this degree of presidential helplessness, and the president knows that the faculty knows. Some presidential humility as a result of this situation may not be a bad thing. A diminution of presidential self-confidence would be. And it is safe to assume that a major university president's public utterance—already constrained by the desire to avoid unnecessary offense to faculty, students, alumni, donors, and the public at large—is still further circumscribed by the need to have the most cordial relations possible with a wide array of members of the United States Congress.

HOLDING COMPANY GOVERNANCE

A second key circumstance involves a transformation of the corporate structure of the university, from a centralized single entity into a holding company. This pattern of evolution during the past few decades was prompted primarily by the arrival of the university's professional schools. True, faculties of law, medicine, and, more recently, engineering had been earlier components of the university and were to some degree separate and autonomous, but the numbers involved—of teachers, students, budget, and space—still permitted close central supervision. Generally, some sense of community also continued to prevail. As the growth of the university exploded, however, and the number as well as the individual size of professional schools increased, each division of the university began more and more to assume a corporate character of its own. This involved the structuring not only of each division's own budget but of its own management as well. The result is a university corporate structure that is essentially decentralized, featuring an array of relatively autonomous academic divisions linked together by a set of shared common support services and some comprehensive policy guidelines. More and more, these corporate entities are also financially autonomous. Their individual budgets tend to be so large as to defy the holding company's financial ability to offer any one of them even short-term, let alone long-term, financial support of any significance. This situation is too well and widely recognized to require further description. It is also easily perceived that a mega-sized university holding company no longer musters much sense of community, inasmuch as virtually no one anywhere within the whole is likely to be familiar with more than that individual's own academic/corporate component.

At least two aspects of the holding company model of university corporate governance, however, newly shape the university presidency in ways that bear some elaboration. The first of these is the fact that the arts and sciences, or liberal arts, no longer constitute the acknowledged and determining core of the university institution. This erosion of the centrality of the liberal arts, the descendant of the faculty of philosophy of the historic Western university, is one of the most significant and disturbing features of the current state of the research university in the United States. All of the implications and consequences of this erosion are as yet neither manifest nor understood, nor is this the occasion to examine them in much greater detail. What is relevant in the present context is that the university organized as a holding company tends to treat its component entities alike, each as a relatively autonomous and self-sufficient unit; that this arrangement works to the disadvantage of the liberal arts component, which is least capable of fiscal self-sufficiency; and that the university president is thus confronted with the choice of either sustaining the liberal arts, at the perceived and therefore objectionable expense of the other components, or of leading an institution lacking in any defined centrality of mission and purpose.

The school of arts and sciences, or liberal arts, is divided within itself, because its physical and natural science departments are largely supported by externally funded research grants and contracts, while its humanities and social science departments are not, which makes for internal inequality and strife. Arts and sciences also remains, in most universities, the academic division that accommodates the majority of the university's undergraduates. Undergraduate education does not pay for itself. A subsidy is required, not so much to add support for the teaching of undergraduates but, rather, to fund the large and expensive complement of counselors and extracurricular services that US undergraduate education requires and of which more will be said. Here, then, is a component of the university which does not function with the relative self-sufficiency of the other divisions within the holding company and which, in addition, is at sixes and sevens with respect to its curriculum. Long regarded as the transmitter of the best of the past to students in the present, it now finds itself facing the charge that its teaching is homocentric, Eurocentric, and rooted in an unjustifiable and insupportable system of values designed by dead white males.

The holding company concept of corporate university governance inhibits the university president from consistently and significantly preferred treatment of this one component, even with respect to presidential time and effort, but most explicitly when it comes to the allocation of fiscal resources. But a president who attempts to treat the liberal arts component simply like all the others confronts an intolerable situation. Not only is there likely to be a faculty-student revolt based on denial of resources, but the poison of confusion about mission and purpose will spread throughout the entire holding company, just as past certainty of mission and purpose served earlier to provide the entire corporation with a guiding and binding rationale.

Ironically, another feature of the holding company pattern of university governance also relates to this presidential dilemma. This second feature consists of the fact that, in a holding company, those individuals in any one of the components relate far more directly and continuously to the chief executive officer (CEO) of the component than to the CEO of the company as a whole. In short, the members of each school, college, or division within the holding company model of the university look to their dean rather than to the university president for leadership. If a component unit lacks adequate leadership, the appropriate response is to select and appoint a new dean but definitely not for the component to be governed directly by the leadership of the holding company itself. Such a pattern of governance substantially removes the university president from interaction with both faculty and students, whose real community is not the whole university but only their own academic division. In effect, therefore, the president no longer has a constituency in which the presidency can take root: the whole institution has become too large, and too decentralized, to serve as a constituency, and each component unit claims its own turf, on which the president trespasses at great risk. The decline of the liberal arts component, in particular, is eroding its traditional role as the core constituency with a special relationship to the university president. Conversely, a presidential effort to exercise leadership in the liberal arts is becoming a perceived violation of the holding company governance rules of the game as well as an invasion of the responsibility and authority of the dean. In summary, the holding company model makes sense for the megauniversity and its cluster of strong professional schools, but it also effectively deprives the university president of significant traditional opportunities to exercise academic leadership.

Yet, some new opportunities also come into play. In the megauniversity holding company pattern academic communication between and among components is difficult to institutionalize. The effort to do so focuses mostly on interdisciplinary centers and institutes, which are often also interdivisional and are specifically designed to foster clusters of collaboration. Even with these efforts the university president and a handful of immediate staff and colleagues are increasingly the only persons in the entire institution who have access to knowledge about what is going on within virtually every component unit. Therefore, the president, assisted by only immediate associates, has the opportunity to pollinate the academic environment by bringing news of innovation from one to other components. In this role as institutional communicator the president is normally perceived as an asset and exercises some degree of academic leadership.

PROFESSIONALIZATION OF ADMINISTRATION

A third circumstance that shapes the university presidency but has not yet been sufficiently understood involves the professionalization of university administration. Obviously, the size of this administration has exploded, in keeping with the overall growth explosion. Just as obviously, the emergence of the holding company model of governance has balkanized the administration just as much as the academic enterprise itself, and each component unit of the university now has its own administrative support force. One might then assume that the holding company's central administration, while larger, of course, than the whole centralized administrative establishment of the university four decades ago, nevertheless can serve as a unified and dedicated source of support to the central leadership headed by the university president. This assumption is in some part correct, but in large part it is also questionable. To at least some degree the coherence of the central administration itself is diluted by the professionalization of its members.

Five or even fewer decades ago college, and even university, administrators were as likely as not to be amateurs, in the sense that alumni or faculty members loyal to the institution would cope with the chores of admission, financial aid, the tasks of the registrar, fund-raising, counseling, and bookkeeping. During roughly the same time span, however, which brought word processors, touch-tone telephones, voice mail, and FAX machines to every office, virtually all significant tasks in university administration took on the status of professional careers, supported by the usual national professional organizations, annual and regional meetings, and professional journals. Just as professors meet, communicate with, and keep track of their colleagues and read the literature of their disciplines, so university administrators now proceed along similar lines in the pursuit of highly specialized and skilled tasks that have become established separate careers. The sophistication and quality of performance have obviously benefited, but the easier fellowship of earlier days and the ability to cross professional lines of specialization have both become less common—again precisely as professional fellowship and discourse across academic disciplinary lines have become more complicated.

As a result of this evolution, the central university administration, which is also too large in numbers to be housed in only one facility, is no more a community than the faculty of one of the component academic units, and its members tend to be preoccupied just as much with their professional careers as their professorial colleagues. As administrators, they too can and do achieve upward mobility by moving from one institution to another. Obviously, many of them also tend often to have closer working relationships with their professional counterparts in the divisions of the university than with other members of the central administration whose assignments vary from their own. As a result, the personal and emotional loyalty of central administration to the university president, whom the majority of central administrators do not necessarily interact with personally any more than other members of the university, is attenuated. Central administration, in other words, represents an essential ingredient in the holding company. model of university governance but at its best offers a high level of professional competence to the presidency rather than personal or political support within the institution.

STUDENTS AS CONSUMERS—AND PATIENTS?

The fourth and last circumstance of the mega-university which is reshaping the presidency involves the changing role of students. Obviously, today's students display the decline in discipline and in respect for authority which has become evident throughout all of US society, and their hugely increased numbers present a new problem as well. Beyond even these substantial changes from the past at least one, or perhaps two, additional factors have become apparent. In the context of the market-driven character of social behavior in the United States students have become substantially more assertive and demanding in their role as consumers of the university's teaching services. In all North American major research universities students pay tuition fees, which in economic terms defines them as the university's customers, or clients. If in commercial terms the adage prevails that "the customer is always right," this clearly clashes with traditional attitudes that characterized students—in the style of Oxford, for example—as *in statu pupillari*. It seems worth noting that the dictionary defines *pupil* as "a person, usually young, who is learning under the close supervision of a teacher" and then traces the origin of the term to Roman and civil law, signifying "an orphaned or emancipated minor under the care of a guardian." This derivation led to the characterization of the old university as standing in loco parentis vis-à-vis its students.

As opposed to the tradition of the student as the most junior member of the academic community and, as a learner, subservient to his seniors, the student as consumer, or customer, has come to represent the payer who calls the tune the piper plays. For centuries it was consistently clear that learning required both effort and talent and that a deficiency of either or both would result in a failure of learning. Today's student as customer is entitled to his or her money's worth and is more and more likely to claim that deficiencies in learning are not at all, or at least not primarily, the consequence of lack of student effort and talent but, rather, the result of inadequate instruction. The self-awareness of students as consumers at a minimum implies for them the movement away from essentially disenfranchised and therefore institutionally passive junior members of the university toward a more active and far less subordinate role. The fact that the length of time students spend in the university remains relatively brief and that their primary concern still focuses on attainment of the credentials that will advance their careers undercuts the degree to which they can organize and promote consumer activism within the institution. Nevertheless, the change in the student role is palpable and increasingly manifest in both word and deed.

Most interesting, however, is the degree to which the concept of the university student as the customer is being coupled with, or even transformed into, the concept of the student as patient. Since the 1960s Americans have become more and more committed to the belief that self-satisfaction represents life's greatest achievement, and that the pursuit of happiness is best defined as the ability to feel good about oneself. At the core of this belief self-respect, self-esteem, and self-satisfaction merge into one composite desire and, more than that, as a natural right to which every American is entitled. Inability to achieve this goal of self-respect and self-satisfaction—viewed as a natural right—has come to be perceived either as social injustice or as an affliction that can be therapeutically addressed, or both. The result, in part, is therefore intense demand that any social action that has the effect of lowering individual self-esteem or denying individual self-satisfaction should be outlawed and is also, in part, an equally intense demand for therapeutic help to relieve individual inability to feel good. The emergence of "politically correct" speech and action in society responds to the first demand. As for the second, the fitness, pharmaceutical, nutrition, entertainment, and counseling industries, in particular, are massively engaged commercially, eclipsing in economic volume the role of religious institutions on the one hand and infringing on the frontiers of medical care on the other.

In this context the university student's right to learn is even more than a paid-for purchase. It is perceived as part of the individual's natural right to achieve self-esteem and self-satisfaction. Academic failure denies this right. As a social institution, and especially one for whose services the student pays, the university thus acquires the responsibility to guarantee student satisfaction. And if instruction alone does not suffice to meet this responsibility, then it is the university's obligation to provide whatever therapeutic treatment is required for the student. And here—*mirabile dictu!*—the American university is well positioned to respond. Unlike its counterparts in most of the rest of the world, the university in the United States, which generally houses some or most of its students, has long found it necessary to engage special staff in large numbers to maintain some degree of order and to address at least the most obvious social needs of the thousands of students who compose the majority of its campus population. The student as consumer activist defies an easy or ready university response because this role runs so directly counter to the student as learner. The widely publicized problems of universities arising from the issue of political correctness to some degree illustrate the university's difficulties with the customer-pupil contradiction, particularly when they involve student efforts to design curricula. The student as patient, requiring therapeutic assistance, is far more acceptable. The roles of student and patient are not self-contradictory, and a response by the university demands only increased, albeit expensive, effort to increase the student-support activities to which the American university is already so heavily committed. There is no inconsistency between assistance to learning and assistance to extracurricular activity as it has evolved in the university over time and the concept that therapy for deficiencies in intellectual development is part of the university's mission.

The university presidency in the United States is also affected by those changes in student attitudes and behavior. That students in large numbers are potentially difficult, sometimes extremely difficult, to deal with is, of course, nothing new. What is novel is, first, that students as the university's customers are exerting their economic power more consistently and effectively than in the past, and, second, that the focus of student pressure is on instructional, and related therapeutic, services. The results are intensified demands on the president's political skills in responding to consistent student pressure, and, in managerial terms, the inability to reduce expenditures for student services even when the total budget must be cut. In fact the rise of those expenditures may represent, unavoidably, a persistent budgetary priority.

CONSENSUS AT RISK

Today's university presidents indeed do not tower over their institutions as their predecessors may have. On the one hand their institutions are much larger. On the other the visibility and authority of the presidency have diminished with the advent of holding company governance and of a professionalized and disaggregated university administration. Not that the men and women who preside over major research universities today lack self-confidence. No one could survive the pressures and tensions to which their assignment exposes them unremittingly without exceptional strength, including a strong and resilient ego. What they lack is authority commensurate to their truly enormous responsibility. One thing the changes in the university have not brought with them is an increase in discipline. On the contrary: not only has the evident decline of respect for authority within US society inevitably included the university, but the decentralization of the university has tended to dilute authority even further. University presidents continue to need to root their authority in consensus, which for authority within the university remains the only accepted source of legitimacy. The holding company pattern of governance in the university is held together only by the fragile bands of consensus, while its counterpart in bureaucracy is anchored in legal authority and in for-profit enterprises by the harsh pressures of the market.

Leadership by consensus is more of an art form than a skill insofar as it derives from the personality of the leading individual, but it is possible only on the basis of a common, inclusively binding idea, which leadership can and must invoke over and over again to maintain or restore both consensus and legitimacy. In the public sphere such a fundamental unifying idea or set of ideas is called ideology. For the American university there is no political ideology, but there is something more than the profit motive which either sustains or destroys commercial corporations. For the university there is the idea of the university itself, an idea that over time has governed and held the allegiance of not only its members but also of its alumni. The university presidency functions effectively as the necessary symbol and implementor of the idea of the university and by appealing to that idea for consensus. Traditionally, the idea of the university has been both sufficiently respected and sufficiently vague to remain useful to the maintenance of consensus and also flexible so as to absorb and include change. The transition to the modern US research mega-university, for example, has already been incorporated into the traditional idea of the university, if not without some difficulty. The openness of the American idea of the university, however, requires constant reiteration and revision of that idea, and this task falls in part to the university presidency. The president needs to appeal to the idea to maintain legitimacy and consensus, and the idea's own continued existence and validity depend on this ongoing presidential iteration.

This is not to imply that university presidents are somehow charged to serve as keepers of the sacred flame of the idea of the university. Presidents rally to the idea of the university only because they have to, in search of consensus. When presidents do this they must hit the right notes in their effort to apply the idea of the university to their specific situation. Each time this happens successfully the idea of the university is apt to take on new shades of meaning, much as the text of a law does each time it is applied to a specific case. Until recently, despite this adaptability to innovation, the idea of the university retained sufficient coherence, when appropriately appealed to, for the maintenance of consensus. At the present, however, this coherence appears to be dissipating. Its evaporation would make the university ungovernable. The centrifugal forces tearing at consensus on the idea of the university are the assault on the validity of the Western tradition; the extreme primacy, both substantively and financially, of research; the vastly lower priority given to teaching; and the drive to convert the university into an instrument of social justice and a therapeutic institution for its students. The performance of university presidents in office today, or tomorrow, depends on the maintenance of an idea of the university sufficiently coherent to rally consensus.

The appearance that today's university presidents are by nature and performance inferior to their "great" predecessors is an illusion. The changes in the institution have in fact been so enormous that it would be easier to assert that those presidents who have achieved long incumbency in the leadership of a major research university must possess a mix of talents of heroic proportion. The fact that they seem now to be dwarfed by their institutions is indeed to their credit, based on the analogy that the captaincy of an aircraft carrier calls for skills far different from the captaincy of a sailing vessel. Yet the task now facing them is harder than that faced by any of their predecessors for many decades. Able to lead only by consensus, they must now try to prevent further crumbling and restore coherence to the idea of the university. That task may prove to be simply impossible, which would doom universities and their presidents to at least a period of failure. To succeed that task will require a radical redirection of the balance between research and teaching in the university. Success, however, will depend on the quality of the new balance, which must preserve and protect the research mission of the university. In the context of a research base for which the university cannot itself pay and which must be reduced as external sponsorship declines; of a holding company pattern of governance which diminishes the central place of the liberal arts within the university; of a professionalized, decentralized administration whose members as individuals are not necessarily committed to the idea of the university; and of students as consumers and patients demanding first priority for a therapeutically enhanced and oriented teaching mission—in this context, a Luddite new version of the idea of the university along the lines of "Teaching über Alles" is not only possible but all too likely.

Much will depend on the men and women who serve as presidents of major US research universities these days. They face a challenge far greater than any raised in past decades: nothing less than the preservation of the university's commitment to human reason and rational inquiry. Contemporary attacks on the validity of the Western tradition involve an explicit attack on reason and science. Teaching as therapy could also involve a temptation to turn away from rational standards for the measurement of performance. Re-emphasis of the teaching mission of the university is overdue and underway; de-emphasis of the research mission is neither desirable nor necessary. University presidents are uniquely placed to respond to the pressure on them by expressing the idea of the university on which they are dependent for the consensus that lends legitimacy to their actions. In the days ahead the men and women who serve as presidents of the major research universities in the United States are likely to be evaluated less in comparison to their predecessors than in terms of the content of the idea of the university they are able to invoke.

Stephen M. Stigler   6

Competition and the Research Universities

Competition is not a goal: it is a means of organizing activity to achieve a goal.[1]

I N BUSINESS, COMPETITION PROMOTES EFFICIENCY, low prices, and diversity of product. In sports, competition encourages the development of skill and the maximum display of athletic prowess. In nature, competition produces the evolution of more diverse and fitter species and the elimination of illness. In higher education, competition fosters complaints of duplication, cries for support, pleas for exemption from laws against collusion, and attempts to restrict new entries. This paradox is heightened by the fact that much of our knowledge of the virtues of competition in business, athletics, and nature is the product of academic research, yet the complaints about the effects of competition upon universities are more likely than not to come from within academia. Indeed, the most audible complaints come from those one might naively suppose would know better, as when the former president of a prestigious eastern university decries the entry of lesser universities into the ranks of schools offering Ph.D.s, or when a professor at an equally prestigious western institution castigates research universities for using young apprentice teachers to improve educational efficiency.

We might ask why competition, which has many friends in universities when treated abstractly for application elsewhere, has so few friends when considered for academia itself. Of course, this

Stephen M. Stigler is Ernest DeWitt Burton Distinguished Service Professor of Statistics at the University of Chicago.

131

phenomenon is far from unique to academia—resistance to competition is found everywhere: business expends huge resources attempting to avoid, diminish, or entirely elude competition; and biological species do not compete except out of necessity. Competition is hard, and if it can be avoided by restricting the competitor, it will, in fact, be a victory. But there are situations peculiar to universities that both help to explain the resistance to competition found there and to show why competition is essential to the universities' enterprise.

VARIETIES OF COMPETITION: INTELLECTUAL COMPETITION

Competition is a rivalry arising when two or more parties seek a goal or resource that not all can possess in equal measure. A discussion of competition and the research universities would seem to presuppose an understanding of who the competitors are —who owns the research university? This is not a simple question. Former Harvard University dean Henry Rosovsky finessed the question in *The University: An Owner's Manual*[2] by addressing the book to a multitude of constituencies: foremost to faculty, administrators, and students; secondarily to trustees, alumni, and donors; but also to federal, state, and local governments and the general public. As attractive as this audience is, and as defensible as it may be for some purposes, it is not helpful for analysis. Here, too, the question will be finessed, but by being too specific rather than too general. For the purpose of discussion, I shall take it as understood that the *faculty* own the university, and that the competition among and within universities is a competition among faculties.

Assigning ownership of the university to the faculty may seem presumptuous, even contrary to laws that vest ultimate authority in a board of trustees or regents. Despite the fact that this is an oversimplification, it can be defended on several grounds. First, the trustees generally play a passive role, setting the ground rules for expenditure levels and assisting in fund-raising, but except in unusual circumstances, trustees of first-class research institutions do not assert control beyond this. Second, the faculty *act* as if they own their universities, even though this active ownership is constrained by the rules imposed by the trustees and the government, and usually vested in academic administrators—presidents, provosts, and deans who serve at the pleasure of the faculty in fact if not in name.

Competition among research universities—or among their faculties—is carried out at several levels and in several arenas, but the goals sought in these arenas enjoy some common characteristics. Sociologist Joseph Ben-David has summarized the general goal sought in competition among universities as *prestige*; an alternative, but no less vague, term would be *reputation*.[3] In the research universities, for their faculties both individually and collectively, the highest value is placed upon the prestige or reputation derived from intellectual accomplishment. The fundamental competition involving our research universities (and the primary focus of this discussion) is the intellectual competition that takes place as these faculties seek to maximize an unusual variety of gain or income. This is the intellectual gain to students (both graduate and undergraduate) and to faculty that is derived from new ideas, whether they be scientific advances or humanistic insights, new understanding of the social or of the natural worlds, discovery of the past, or exploration that will change the future.

Individually, faculty will compete for higher salaries and for such amenities as larger offices, but collectively—as departments, as schools or colleges, and as universities—they compete primarily in the currency of ideas. This is an attractive currency. Indeed, the value some faculty place on the intellectual returns of teaching and research has led them to decline salary offers from outside academia amounting to up to ten-fold increases in extreme cases, choosing instead to pursue rewards that are uncertain as well as unusual.

What makes the intellectual gain from teaching and research in universities unusual is that it requires competition for its recognition and award: it is only through the competition itself that we can tell when we are successful. We may be convinced that an idea is new and important, but we remain insecure until others, particularly those outside our immediate circle, signal their concurrence — especially through a praising citation, but even by a vicious attack. We can, in some circumstances, be absolutely convinced of the correctness of a scientific result. However, until we elicit a reaction from others and see its influence upon their work, we cannot be certain of its importance. We may admire a colleague's fine mind, but the sign that others wish to hire that colleague can extinguish many doubts and uncertainties. This too applies in the recruitment of graduate students, or of junior faculty. In any given instance we may trust our own judgment, but it is only the calibration of this judgment through direct competition with our peers that makes us trust it in general use.

This is not to say that we live in a Hobbesian world of constant intellectual battle —that our insecurity requires every act to face a competitive test. The intellectual competition of research universities differs from ordinary contests in that the goal is general approbation, not a vanquished opponent. This is not a zero-sum game: the act of competition has the curious effect of increasing the resource that is the focus of the competition. The greatest victory is that which attracts the greatest applause from competing peers, and that applause increases with the intensity of the competition. And it is not solely contemporary applause we seek, but that of an educated posterity.

The intellectual competition for new discoveries for ourselves and for our students, for recognition of these new ideas, and for the recruitment of top faculty and graduate students is seldom praised for the fundamental role it plays in organizing our research institutions. It is more likely to have its existence or importance denied, as when a mathematician or a medieval historian asserts the irrelevance of any outside view of his work, or when a chemist or sociologist claims that her only drive is a dispassionate pursuit of the truth. Indeed, the fruits of their labors can be real and lasting, but when successful they are lasting for the same reason that they are undertaken. They achieve the persistent attention of the community.

A benefit of this neglect of the role of intellectual competition is that it is only infrequently the cause of major social friction or national complaint. It may lead to acrimonious debates at scientific meetings, to colleagues refusing to speak to one another, to changes in office, department, or job, but these disputes are well-understood in the academic world and rarely spill over beyond that world. They are a part of the sorting of our goals, of the calibration of our judgments. There is a second variety of academic competition, however, that is a more frequent source of audible pain: the competition for resources within and between universities.

COMPETITION FOR FINANCIAL RESOURCES

For decades it has been a regular—indeed annual—event for a distinguished committee representing a single discipline (for example, mathematics), or a set of disciplines (the sciences or humanities), or even all research universities to meet at great length and after extensive consultation deliver one or both of two predictable pronouncements: *1)* more money is needed or the nation is in a parlous state, and *2)* the universities must restructure their programs and tighten their belts. The perpetual tendency to form these committees in the face of little visible return from their reports is a symptom of a real source of pain, pain caused by the competition for resources within and between universities.

Competition for resources is itself an ordinary phenomenon, and is found in any industry or business firm. In no interesting human endeavor are resources ever sufficient to satisfy all the demands placed upon them. In research universities, such a large premium is placed upon innovation—they exist as research universities for no other reason—that this tendency is more than merely common. It is a valuable part of the fabric of the institutions. To say that competition for resources is a necessary part of university life does not make it painless. Indeed, the problem is exacerbated by a collision between the need to ration scarce resources and collegial norms. These norms encourage the free exchange of ideas across disciplinary boundaries; they permit us to join with faculty in other disciplines within the university in a common enterprise rather than to view our colleagues as threats to our own existence.

In times of plenty, universities expand ("exploit new opportunities"); in financial droughts, they contract ("restructure"). There is a widespread belief that they handle expansion better than contraction, but there is little supporting evidence for this belief. All that can be said with confidence is that the level of complaint is higher in contraction. In any event, research universities are, by all accounts, in an era where sustained expansion is unlikely, and we must be prepared to deal with contraction whether we wish to or not.

SPECIALIZATION, COLLUSION, AND COOPERATION

Specialization is and always has been a fact of life in research universities. No university offers substantive programs in all major fields, at least at a single campus.[4] Few universities support more than a couple of professional schools. No university could conceivably teach—much less study the literature of—more than a handful of the world's five thousand languages. Universities are faced with diminishing resources and, with the expansion of knowledge leading to the creation of expensive new fields, more claims on those resources. Consequently, there must be an increase in specialization at research universities. The question is not whether, but how.

Formally, the answer is simple. Since the publication of Adam Smith's *The Wealth of Nations* in 1776, it has been known that the optimum allocation of resources is such that the marginal rate of return is equal among the different enterprises supported.[5] The intellectual gain expected from an additional dollar spent on a professor of French should equal that spent on a professor of physics. While that formal answer suggests, for example, that universities support their own strengths rather than their weaknesses, it is far from being operational advice. Rates of return are hard enough to determine in industry; in academia matters are even less simple. The long and successful experience of the Guggenheim Fellowship program is encouraging evidence that such comparisons among individual scholars can be made across disciplines. However, even more difficult choices are confronted at an institutional level. The cost of a single physics professor (with laboratory) may be equal to that of a whole (small) department in the humanities. Which should be preferred, and why? The programs cannot be considered in isolation; there are subtle interdependencies among them, and basic (and ever-changing) requirements of disciplinary coverage in what constitutes a university.

In addressing the practical question of where a university should concentrate its resources, there is a tension between two approaches that may sound similar, but are actually antagonistic. On the one hand, we hear complaints of the duplication of efforts, and suggestions that arrangements should be made to reduce these duplications. For example, one state university might be required to leave veterinary science to that of a neighboring state, freeing up resources at the first to cover environmental science. On the other hand, we may hear (but usually only in-house) that at the first state university, veterinary science is weak and should be abandoned to permit concentration on its stronger field, environmental science. Of course, these two routes could lead to the same conclusion, but they are fundamentally different. The first, which in an extreme form could amount to interuniversity collusion, is antagonistic to the intellectual competition that is the basis of our universities' greatness; the second is derived from that same competition. The first could diminish the university; the second could strengthen it.

One topic of debate in recent years was the agreement of several eastern schools to consult, matching the level of merit-based scholarships that they offered to certain newly-admitted undergraduates. These universities claimed that by limiting these awards—by removing them at least partially from the competitive market—they could free resources, resources that they felt would otherwise be consumed in a bidding war, to be used in support of other academic programs. Admitted students would be left to choose among the schools on the basis of the program alone, while the university would be strengthened for all students. They were accused of illegal collusion. It is clear that these limitations amounted to a tax upon the admitted students, perhaps no different (aside from the need for interuniversity consultation) from other taxes that the schools impose, for example, adjusting tuition according to the financial assets of the student's family. It is less clear what the balance of the implications of this practice is for the intellectual competition among these schools. It could be argued that unless universities fully value the presence of meritorious students on their campuses, there will be a lowering of the intellectual competition among them.

Collusion among universities is not simply a legal worry. To the degree that it is effective (an important qualification), any agreement to divide territory, constrain salaries, or restrict scholarships can result in lessened intellectual competition: a diminished incentive to excel; a smaller audience of competing peers to look to for evaluative approval or condemnation; and a slackened alertness and insulation from the challenges of research. It will also tend to produce stagnation by protecting existing fields regardless of their vitality and by lessening the incentive to invent new fields. But if we reject collusion, if we rule out of order any proposal for a national commission to advise on the division of research labor, then a major problem remains, for the decision is thrown back to the universities themselves. While university faculties are the best source of the needed judgments, they have not always proven to be adept at handling this sort of decision.

Of course, collusion is not the same as cooperation. There are many forms of interuniversity cooperation that further intellectual competition, just as there are forms of commercial cooperation that enhance economic competition. The key consideration, however, is whether institutional cooperation encourages intellectual competition. Does it lower costs to all parties and permit the offering of more or stronger programs? Or is "cooperation" only a mask for collusion that limits competition? For example, an interlibrary loan system involving several institutions improves the ability of all to compete by lowering the cost of an important research facility. Other "neighborhood" economies can be pursued on the same basis, with the assurance that if the cooperation serves to permit the flourishing of competing programs at different institutions, then at least the fundamental intellectual competition will be preserved. When cooperation in the name of the elimination of the duplication of programs is suggested, there is the suspicion of collusion.

To date, cooperation has permitted some savings, but it has only slightly ameliorated the tendency toward contraction. In the future, with the development of the computer internet greatly expanding the accessible neighborhood, the prospects for cooperative sharing of resources are immense. We may increasingly expect close collegial relationships to span the globe. Libraries no longer require a close physical proximity in order to be consulted.

It seems plausible that this expanding electronic network will eventually lead to a weakening of our sense of institutional identity and a fundamental change in the intellectual competition that organizes our enterprise. Individual faculty may be in closer contact with collaborating colleagues at other universities (or with graduate students working under their direction in other countries) than with faculty and students in slightly different specialties down the hall. The importance of the geographic unit may be eclipsed by intellectual disciplinary units that are international in scope. For the immediate future, financial resources that are administered by geographically-constrained universities may restrict the scope of any reconfiguration, but in time even that constraint may diminish, leaving the present research universities effectively operating themselves as foundations supporting international, highly specialized, dynamic disciplinary graduate schools.

SOME PRINCIPLES FOR CONTRACTION

If we look to universities for strategies to deal with contraction in the face of diminished resources, it is easier to find examples of ineffective routes than effective ones. For example, the following are some of the ineffective routes that have been followed in recent years: *1)* form a committee consisting of representatives of large or politically unassailable departments and encourage them to suggest the dissolution of smaller units not represented on the committee; *2)* have a small administrative group address the question in insulated privacy and present the result of their deliberation (a Draconian excision of selected programs) as a fait accompli, one made necessary by the financial pressures of the time; or *3)* institute a broad and even across-the-board cut in all programs and departments, with the possible exception of a few that are politically untouchable or have suffered disproportionate cuts in the previous budget. These three routes have all been tried at major research universities in recent years, and all have been found to be seriously wanting. Indeed, in several cases, the resulting dissatisfaction has led to changes of administration and a reversal of policy.

What can be done? In this area it is far easier to recognize egregious error than to suggest a wise course, but past failures suggest some principles for research universities facing contraction. The fundamental role of intellectual competition in organizing our activities ensures that, notwithstanding any claims to the contrary, a university's own faculty is the greatest source of wisdom for the reshaping of its programs. It is sometimes alleged that the rise in faculty power in the governance of research universities in the middle of this century is the passive result of the neglect of responsibility by university administrators. To the contrary, it signals that in these increasingly complex organizations, which have grown immensely in specialization both within and between disciplines, only the faculty (collectively) are sufficiently knowledgeable to decide on major issues. From their intimate involvement with the intellectual competition within their disciplines, faculty are aware of their strengths and shortcomings, and any attempt to move without consultation risks not only dissension but serious error.

However, there are practical difficulties in encouraging a too decentralized decision structure. Faculty not engaged in administration will lack an overview of the institution's problems and the costs of maintaining its strengths, and, as mentioned earlier, a collegial relationship that does not require the public exercise of such judgment is a singular quality of these universities. The implication is that, to the maximum extent possible, the institution should depend upon scholar-administrators, and they must consult with the faculty so that their actions will be in line with faculty consensus. How this is to be accomplished is the hard question. The costs, in time and collegial relationships, suggest that the formality of the consultation be commensurate with the severity of the action. When possible, contraction should be accomplished incrementally, through the selective denial of appointments, where the necessary decisions are made by an administration acting in line with an informally determined (but broad-based) scholarly consensus of the faculty. Admittedly, this is a prescription for slow change, for a determinedly nonsaltationist evolution. When more substantial cuts are needed, pain is unavoidable. It is essential that any excision of units follow a broad discussion among the faculty, where full opportunity is given to the affected units to make their case, and with every attempt made to consider the possible actions in relation to the faculty's perception of the university's specific intellectual goals.

The statement of reasonable general principles is easy compared to dealing with real cases. The seas of academia are not only rough, they are increasingly shallow, and any attempt to implement high principle soon runs aground on hard reality. If a moderate-size professional school is found to be marginal to the institution's central mission, it will be revealed to be making money. If a small language department is thought to be moribund, with but one tenured professor and two graduate students, it will be discovered that the professor is internationally renowned in his specialty and the department's budget is so small that less money would be saved by closing it than would be needed to cover the language course now taught by the professor. If consideration is given to shrinking a chemistry department by cutting a portion of the untenured faculty, the fact that then $3,000,000 in newly purchased laboratory equipment must be scrapped weakens the strongest provostial will. If word leaks out that a dean is considering applying the ax to even a small portion of a long-overstuffed history department, the resulting storm may have that dean thinking of seeking asylum in the US Embassy in Teheran.

The issues involved can be subtle. A well-reasoned judgment should balance two considerations: how central a program is to the university's curricular goals and what is the intellectual quality of the program. Let me cite one pertinent example. When university provosts, deans, or budget committees cast about for targets in desperate times, it is not unusual for them to look at my own field, statistics, particularly if there is no statistician on the committee. At first glance, the case can seem compelling. Invariably the department of statistics is fairly small, with a modest graduate program and little or no undergraduate major program. Furthermore, there are many other departments on campus where some sort of statistics course is, or could be, taught: psychology, economics, mathematics, sociology, and education, to name a few. Surely, if cuts must be made, this is a tempting target! But why then do almost all research universities have statistics departments? It cannot be because of a powerful lobby for statistics, or because of the high national esteem in which statisticians are held.

Statistics departments thrive even in difficult times because they are necessary, even central to the intellectual mission of a modern research university. Not every university requires a research department of statistics, but no university can claim respectability as a teaching institution without a strong program in quantitative reasoning, and statistics is at the core of modern quantitative reasoning. Over the short term, a university can get by teaching statistics in other departments, but in time (often in a very short time) that task is neglected. Statistics is never given high priority by those trained in and hired for teaching other disciplines, and the courses (and students) suffer. Not only does a major component of undergraduate instruction wither, but quantitative research programs in fields of applied science suffer more generally at that university, for want of the collaborative and consultative role an active statistics department can play. Even where statistics courses in other departments continue to thrive, they do so because the programs in the statistics department set a model and provide a competitive spur.

Let me contrast the integral role statistics departments play in research universities with that of computer sciences. Computer sciences is one of the newest branches of applied mathematics, and it has produced exciting and important advances in theories of automata, in data structures, in programming languages, in computer typography, and in artificial intelligence. The best computer sciences departments in the nation are jewels that adorn their campuses. No one can doubt the importance of the computer to our future, but as a field, computer science (beyond the teaching of programming languages) has not yet claimed a basic, central role in the curriculum of our universities. It may someday claim that role, but to date it remains a collection of specialties, where different departments at different universities may contain no overlap beyond the teaching of introductory programming, a function that can be allocated without serious loss to graduate students in mathematics. In particular cases, for example in some universities with engineering schools, computer sciences may be integral to the curriculum, but this is not yet true in the arts and sciences more generally.

Now I expect that this example may be received with skepticism by some nonstatisticians and with outrage by some computer scientists. I believe the argument can be defended, but I only insist on this: arguments of this type must be made in addressing the problems of scarce resources. Some departments will be necessary for all research universities, and some fields will only be pursued where the peculiar local intellectual climate creates a comparative advantage or a special need. The identification of that advantage or need can only follow from a reading of the intellectual competition driving our universities, a reading that must come from our faculties.

Difficult questions arise here. How far can specialization be carried without destroying the character of a university? Which programs are essential to a university? What core must be included if a research university is to be able to provide first-class graduate training in its chosen areas as well as excellent general education in the liberal arts for undergraduates? Surely there are no answers applicable to all universities. It seems safe to say that no major research university is near an objective threshold where one or a small number of changes will prove disastrous, that as our universities are forced to increase their specialization, the diminution in the richness and breadth of their programs will not in the near term be felt with anything like the force of the expected cuts in some graduate programs. But this cannot be true indefinitely.

Even where hard choices are faced with honest determination, change will come slowly. The need for painful, long discussion among the faculty of the university before major cuts are made is a necessary consequence of one of the greatest strengths of these institutions: their ability to provide a stable environment for exploration into unknown intellectual territory. Some areas will be pursued long after they have lost their vitality, but this slow pace is the other side of the universities' relative insulation from transitory fads and their ability to maintain solid traditions that are out of fashion.

A FAILURE OF COMPETITION

Competition for resources within universities produces strains due to the need to protect collegial relationships and to ensure the stability needed to encourage the pursuit of avenues that may not pay off in the short term. Nonetheless, this competition is not a true threat to a university. As resources diminish within reasonable bounds, we can expect the product to diminish roughly in proportion, but no more than that. The fundamental nature of the research university need not be threatened. There is, however, a third major species of competition, the competition of the universities for extramural support, where the same cannot be said. There we find a set of problems that have been increasing in severity over the past two decades, to the point where they do constitute a serious threat to the institutions.

The source of the threat is not the competition for external funds itself—universities are as well-equipped as any business enterprise to recognize and exploit opportunities—nor is the problem specifically the level of support, although major vacillations in government funding over the past decade have created serious dislocations. These in turn have undermined the confidence of those charged with carrying out research (which by its very nature is uncertain in outcome) and of those in the process of making career declarations through their choice of training. The problem is not due to changes in support by private foundations, which, since the desertion of the universities by the Ford Foundation in the late 1970s, have provided a stable and competitive base for many programs. The problem instead stems from the lack of competition among federal funding sources, from the concentration in many research areas of most public support for research in one government agency.

This assertion—that the concentration of government support for university-based research in a small number of agencies is at the root of many of the problems currently faced by research universities—may seem suspect at first. After all, it is a situation that has existed since World War II, at least in the sciences. The past half century is seen even by critics of research universities as a golden age; how could current problems, problems that have only become severe in the past decade or so, be traced to a situation that has existed for a half century? The answer, I would argue, is that a subtle but extremely important change has taken place in recent years in the way that US government agencies have administered their support for basic research. It is not a change due to any political party, and it may be argued that it was an inevitable consequence of the system's success. I shall discuss the change in the context that I am most familiar with, the National Science Foundation's (NSF) support for the physical sciences.

SUPPORT IN THE SCIENCES

In the years following World War II, a remarkable set of agencies was created with the intention of carrying on the efforts that had been organized in the war years to mobilize scientific talent to support the war effort. The first agencies were based in the armed services—the Office of Naval Research was the most important of these—and they pursued the support of basic research in a manner that would never have achieved the blessings of any oversight review inquiring about the relation of the research to the service's narrowly construed mission. In 1952, these agencies were joined by the NSF, and throughout the 1960s and 1970s the NSF gradually took over the major share of the Defense Department agencies' role as the patron of the nation's research in basic science. In the mathematical sciences, the NSF is now clearly the dominant source of extramural support.

These agencies were remarkably successful because of the peculiar way they diffused their concentration of resources. Entrusted with public monies, they nonetheless delegated the responsibility for its expenditure to the scientists themselves. At first sight this seems like a recipe for disaster, with the foxes in charge of the hen house, but there was a very good reason that did not ensue, namely peer review. The system of peer review that was put in place in the 1940s was allowed to work its wonders without serious interruption until the early 1980s. It would not have been effective without the discipline of the first type of competition mentioned above, the intense intellectual competition among scientists. By spreading the responsibility for grant decisions across a broad spectrum of referees—the individuals most knowledgeable about the subjects of the research and the prospective researchers—the effects of the exclusive concentration in a single government agency were lessened, and the pursuit of awards effectively became a competition among a thousand granting agencies. It cannot be said that self-interest was eliminated, but it was at least harnessed and controlled. The government agencies, through their program directors and oversight committees, sat as umpires to ensure that all went according to the rules, and the scientists and the country prospered.

Around 1980 the system began to come under subtle and not-so-subtle political pressures. These pressures are a sign of the success of the enterprise and the value attributed to it by the country, but they have already substantially impaired the system's efficiency, and threaten serious injury to research universities. The most egregious examples of the intrusion of political pressures into the granting process—the congressional earmarking of funds for state projects without any review, for example — are well known. But these examples are less important, even in the aggregate, than the pressures that have worked within the agencies to steer them towards increasing their role in the setting of research agendas.

Over time, the NSF, with the tacit support of the nation's scientists, has accumulated a vast amount of power for the direction of research. As an agency without a serious competitor in the support of research in some areas of the physical sciences and nearly all of the mathematical sciences, it has turned its attention from its client scientists to cultivating the source of its funds—the Congress—and has sought to structure its programs to maximize its appeal to this source. What could be more natural than a funding agency tailoring its mission to appeal to its source of funds? A casualty of this change of focus has been the postwar system of dispersing the concentrated power of the agency through the ingenious peer-review system.

The NSF has found it easier to explain large-scale projects and research centers to Congress than to argue convincingly for the diffuse benefits of a broad-based funding of individual research grants; as a consequence the NSF has promoted large projects. The scientists have to a degree acquiesced in this shift, being told that otherwise it would be impossible to increase support to meet expanded challenges, and that the support for research centers will in fact permit at least a modest growth of funding for other programs. But that has not happened; instead, as might have been predicted, total budgets have not grown in real terms, and, since the highly visible research centers have been enthusiastically sold to Congress, the centers have of necessity been spared the worst of the cuts.

In addition to a concentration of research efforts in research centers, there has been a concentration on centrally-determined projects. Examples might include the insistence that two investigators from two different specified fields must submit a collaborative proposal, that the proposal concentrate on contributions to undergraduate education, that it come from an institution not currently supported in the field, or that it concern work in a specific subfield in biological science. On one view, such initiatives are laudable; the targets are nearly always those an advisory committee could, individually, nod assent to. But the targets of these initiatives are generally areas that have not been supported, or investigated without existing commitments to disciplinary programs. In drawing support away from disciplinary programs, the initiatives undermine divisional strengths and diminish funds available for much of the best university research, as well as reducing competition through their restrictions. These initiatives are not different in kind from those pursued for some time by private foundations, but they differ significantly in that they lack the discipline of competition that exists among the foundations. This tendency toward central coordination has led to a substantial increase in the variability in support, with costs in human capital that are difficult to measure.

Peer review continues to function, but within increasingly narrow constraints (on program, on location), and its effective role as a dispersing agency for centralized power is progressively reduced. Instead of a thousand "granting agencies"— the wide network of young and energetic referees—the research agendas are set increasingly by agency heads, program officers, congressional staff, and advisory committees of perhaps a dozen, where even the more active researchers on the committee cannot help but bring their own limiting perspectives to the table. Whether or not these agencies possess less information about the science involved than was behind the previous awards, there is certainly less variety in their idiosyncrasies. The result for research universities is a decreased incentive to take chances, a decreased incentive for the best scientists to pursue projects that do not fit neatly with federally-directed program goals, and an increased tendency to have everyone march in the same direction.

These developments are understandable, and they may even be inevitable. But if they could be reversed, and a greater measure of informed and varied competition returned to the funding process, science and research universities would be far stronger for it. The history of the period from 1950 to 1980 suggests that the nation would prosper, too. Given current trends, however, there is little reason for optimism. One route —breaking up the NSF into a set of *competing* agencies, with several agencies covering each field—has no realistic prospect, and might entail such substantial increases in bureaucratic cost as to be unworkable. The best realistic hope is to recover the decentralized organization of the 1960s, although that is not the direction in which the political winds now blow.

Present trends are toward concentration in the support of science, concentration through a centrally determined research agenda and concentration at relatively few locations. One possible consequence is that most universities will find budgets for scientific equipment being dramatically reduced. This could lead to a greatly increased emphasis upon theory, at the expense of applied science. Another result may be that the scientific research that is carried out will have a lower expected long-term yield than without such a concentrated agenda. This may not result in an actually lower yield, for progress in the designated directions may well be greater than without constraints, and there will be technological improvements that will make even reduced levels of effort more efficient. But the changes to our research universities promise to be substantial, and troublingly uncertain.

COMPETITION IN TEACHING IN THE RESEARCH UNIVERSITIES

Research universities have been frequently accused of neglecting undergraduate education, of overemphasizing research at the expense of undergraduate teaching.[6] From one perspective, perhaps the most important one, this is an empty accusation. There are thousands of undergraduate institutions in the country where virtually no research is carried out, and a fine education is available, usually at a significantly lower cost than at a research university. And yet, the major research universities remain in demand. Consumers may want more for a lower price, but they are evidently willing to pay at current rates for what they are receiving, whether it be an education or simply reflected prestige. But the question is an interesting one—what does competition in a research environment imply about teaching at these same institutions?

It would appear that there are, nationally, many more good teachers of undergraduates than there are good researchers. Even at top research universities, excellent research scholars are not more numerous than excellent teachers (although both skills often inhabit the same body). Since the research universities are only a small fraction of the schools offering undergraduate instruction, it is not surprising that the competition for researchers is far more vigorous than for teachers. Good teaching is valued, but the scarcer commodity demands the higher price, and stories of one research university raiding another for a faculty member with a reputation only as a teacher are unknown. The fact that teaching ability is not readily visible beyond the limits of the campus is not the reason for the lack of competitive bidding for these faculty; it is a consequence of it. Instead we must conclude that students flock to research universities to seek an undergraduate education precisely because of the successful emphasis upon research. These students may seek only the prestige society accords these institutions, without conscious analysis of how that prestige relates to tangible benefits. Or they (or their parents) may wish to place themselves in an atmosphere where they can expect to benefit from new knowledge, even if, at least in the early years, the immediate source of that knowledge is a teaching assistant working with a research professor rather than the professor directly. But for whatever the reason, prospective undergraduate students are attracted to expensive research universities in large numbers, despite the existence of many other less sought after institutions—institutions similar to the major research universities in size and location, indeed in all characteristics save the emphasis upon research and graduate training.

This does not, of course, mean that undergraduate instruction at research universities is neglected. At some schools, such as the University of Chicago, a large fraction of even introductory courses are taught by senior faculty. Even at those universities where a large proportion of lower division courses are staffed by teaching assistants, they are frequently among the better teachers of those courses. Because undergraduate education provides such an important component of a research university's budget (whether through tuition or as a rationale for state subsidy), it is strongly in the institution's interest, taken here as identical to its faculty's interest, to ensure that those courses are taught well, that where teaching assistants are employed they are carefully selected and supervised.

The situation is somewhat different in graduate education. There the intellectual competition that drives our research universities acts directly as a spur to faculty to dedicate their energies to graduate students. A significant portion of a researcher's reputation is derived from the number and success of his or her students, just as the research successes of a student's major professor are an invaluable enhancement to the national visibility of the student. It is a reciprocal relationship that is celebrated by joint papers, by festschrifts, but most of all by the public pride that is taken in academic kinship.

The value that is placed on graduate education by the faculty of research universities has another benefit: it diminishes the tendencies towards intellectual stagnation that the conservative stability in university research programs might otherwise produce. When a field loses some of its vitality, the need to compete for the best incoming graduate students acts as a powerful incentive to adapt, despite the high costs in human capital.

CONCLUSION

Intellectual competition among the faculties of research universities plays a fundamental role in their organization and their success, and whatever tends to diminish that competition may be expected to diminish our institutions. Competition does not imply a prohibition of cooperation among institutions; rather it encourages associations that enhance the ability of the cooperating institutions to compete. It is important to emphasize that competition does not imply any limit to specialization; indeed, in a time of diminished financial resources, we should expect strong competitive pressures toward increased specialization. It is not obvious how specialized universities can become and still function as universities rather than as technical or professional schools, but universities that do not move toward *some* greater degree of specialization will be condemned to general mediocrity. This move toward specialization must be ultimately guided by the faculty. No other party to the research university—the trustees, a single administrator, or any governmental agency— can be counted on to make the needed informed judgments of disciplinary strengths. Indeed, despite the fundamental health of these universities, the concentration of support and increasing government influence on the shaping of disciplines in some areas constitutes a worrisome trend.

Our universities face pessimistic trends and serious problems today, but how negative a tone is justified? Even Darwin ended his treatise on the much more violent competition in the biological world, the epochal *Origin of Species*, with a poetic note: "There is a grandeur to this view of life, [that] from so simple a beginning endless forms most beautiful and most wonderful have been, and are being evolved."[7] Our more restricted time frame, and the radically different set of forces governing the interaction between our universities and their social environment, do not permit our adopting his lyricism. While we cannot expect our universities to be much more static than their political and social environments, they have already shown themselves to be resilient, and we need not be intellectual Darwinists to believe that with vigilance we will emerge from the present trials changed, but no less strong. The universities' future strength, like their present strength, like the fitness of biological species, will be the product of the competition that organizes their activities.

ENDNOTES

[1]Adapted from G. J. Stigler, "Competition," in the *International Encyclopedia of the Social Sciences,* vol. 3 (New York: Macmillan and the Free Press, 1968), 181– 86.

[2]Henry Rosovsky, *The University: An Owner's Manual* (New York: W. W. Norton, 1990).

[3]See Joseph Ben-David, *American Higher Education: Directions Old and New* (New York: McGraw-Hill, 1972), especially 25– 47.

[4]In the 1982 National Research Council Assessment of Research Doctorate Programs in the United States, thirty-eight major fields were included, and 225 universities were queried on their programs in these fields. The median number of fields included at a single university was 8, the upper quartile 20, about half the maximum.

[5]On this analytical result of Adam Smith's, see G. J. Stigler "Competition," in J. Eatwell, M. Milgate, and P. Newman, eds., *The New Palgrave: A Dictionary of Economics*, vol. 1 (London: Macmillan, 1987), 531–36.

[6]The question is not a new one; for example, it is raised and intelligently discussed by Ben-David, *American Higher Education.*

[7]Charles Darwin, *The Origin of Species* (London: John Murray, 1859; New York: Modern Library Reprint [undated]), 374.

Specialism is the means for advancement in our mobile social structure; yet we must envisage the fact that a society controlled wholly by specialists is not a wisely ordered society. We cannot, however, turn away from specialism. The problem is how to save general education and its values within a system where specialism is necessary.

The very prevalence and power of the demand for special training makes doubly clear the need for a concurrent, balancing force in general education. Specialism enhances the centrifugal forces in society. The business of providing for the needs of society breeds a great diversity of special occupations; and a given specialist does not speak the language of the other specialists. In order to discharge his duties as a citizen adequately, a person must somehow be able to grasp the complexities of life as a whole. Even from the point of view of economic success, specialism has its peculiar limitations. Specializing in a vocation makes for inflexibility in a world of fluid possibilities. Business demands minds capable of adjusting themselves to varying situations and of managing complex human institutions. Given the pace of economic progress, techniques alter speedily; and even the work in which the student has been trained may no longer be useful when he is ready to earn a living or soon after. Our conclusion, then, is that the aim of education should be to prepare an individual to become an expert both in some particular vocation or art and in the general art of the free man and the citizen. Thus the two kinds of education once given separately to different social classes must be given together to all alike.

From *General Education in a Free Society*
Report of the Harvard Committee
1950

Nannerl O. Keohane

7

The Mission of the Research University

U NIVERSITY FACULTIES AND ADMINISTRATORS are notoriously dubious about mission statements. How can something as
pluralistic, as multifaceted, as wondrously complex as a
modern university have a clear-cut mission? The term is redolent of
narrower and more intensely single-minded human ventures such as
crusades or temperance movements. Yet, among modern institutions, those that are keenest on mission statements are businesses.
Dignified statements of institutional goals, embellished with the
corporate logo, are commonly used to encourage the faithful within
the firm and to communicate adherence to worthy purposes to
potential customers. The robust rhetorical tone of such messages
sits poorly with the inherent skepticism and stubborn individualism
of members of a university.

Universities are comprised of large numbers of individuals pursuing many different kinds of purposes. Some of those individuals
(particularly the tenured faculty) enjoy a high degree of autonomy
in defining their goals and measuring success. It is all very well for
presidents or boards to issue hortatory statements; it is much more
difficult to chart a course and arrange the incentive structure of
such a complex institution so as to encourage semiautonomous
actors to converge around common goals.

A mission statement that is sufficiently bland to encompass everyone's conception of their role in the university is of little use to
anyone. A statement that has more substantive content risks threatening or ignoring the goals of some members of the university who
have sufficient power to set their own directions. It is easier to

Nannerl O. Keohane is President of Duke University.

153

celebrate variety than to be selective. To say that there are certain purposes that are definitive of our sorts of institutions, and that these should govern our choices when choices must be made, means taking a stand on some of the key questions we delight in endlessly debating.

Yet, at a time when universities are under attack for failing in our basic purposes and falling away from our historic character, it is of singular importance that we explain clearly and forcefully why our work is crucial, and what it is we are doing that matters so much to the world. It is also a time of internal uncertainty, in which all of us on campus can benefit from a joint discussion of our purposes. We should recognize that there is no single perfect definition; the elegant crafting of abstractions is only one part of this endeavor. The most important aspect is the dialogue, the process, the give-and-take that comes from thinking seriously about what you are doing in the company of others who are engaged in the same enterprise.

In the concluding paragraphs of *Political Parties,* Roberto Michels tells the story of a farmer who, on his deathbed, confided to his sons that there was treasure buried in his fields.[1] The sons could hardly wait till the funeral festivities were over to begin the search. They found no box of buried treasure, but in digging up the fields so assiduously they rendered them more fertile, and the farm increased in value manyfold. We may hope, in the vigorous dialogue of arguing about our mission, to come up with at least a modest statement that we are willing to present to the world. But the real treasure is in the activity, the exercise itself, and the enrichment of common understanding of our purposes.

AN INITIAL STATEMENT OF OUR MISSION

In 1965, on the verge of some especially profound changes in higher education, President James A. Perkins of Cornell University delivered the Stafford Little Lectures at Princeton University on "The University in Transition." He listed as the "three great missions" of the university the acquisition, transmission, and application of knowledge. These were his terms for the familiar goals of research, teaching, and public service.[2]

Perkins pointed out that modern American research universities are a hybrid of two earlier traditions, with a peculiarly American shoot grafted on. The German universities in the third decade of the nineteenth century developed the model of the university dedicated almost solely to research. Founders and reformers of American universities in the latter part of that century combined this with undergraduate collegiate teaching modeled on the universities of Oxford and Cambridge, which had already taken root in American soil. The peculiarly American shoot was first exemplified after the Civil War in the land grant universities, foreshadowed by Franklin and Jefferson, who asserted the practical importance of knowledge "in the nation's service." This hybrid model is still recognizable in our contemporary universities.[3]

use?

Let me broach a core definition based upon this hybrid model. The modern research university is a company of scholars engaged in discovering and sharing knowledge, with a responsibility to see that such knowledge is used to improve the human condition.

I have chosen the terms "discovering" rather than "acquiring" and "sharing" rather than "transmitting" because these metaphors capture more aptly the life of the scholar engaged in research and teaching. The notion of "acquisition" suggests proprietorship, warehousing, and compiling, rather than the searching, journeying, and trial and error that leads finally, when we are successful, to the "Eureka!" experience. "Transmission" implies that the teacher is solely in charge of the object of knowledge, handing it on unchanged to the receptive pupil; whereas teaching, at its best, is a shared experience in which teacher and student strive together towards a clearer explication.

It is important to this definition that the university is a *company* of scholars, a fellowship that provides richly for mutual nourishing in ideas. A university is a community engaged in perpetual self-criticism and self-renewal through conversation and dialogue, an intergenerational partnership in discovery and exploration.[4] Much of what is most distinctive about universities derives from this feature of our lives and work.

We can arrive at such an initial statement of the mission of the university from several different directions, and thus provide a check on our perspective. If we are empirically minded, we can observe what institutions like ours actually do, and attempt to describe it as carefully as we can. If we prefer an etiological or historical approach, we can survey (as Perkins did) the development of our universities and identify the several layers that compose them. Or we can proceed by an Aristotelian method of comparative categorizing, looking around at other human associations that share some but not all features with us, and see what it is that is distinctive to universities.[5]

If we adopt the last of these perspectives, we might conceptualize the research university along a continuum that includes, at one extreme, the solitary hermit-scholar, engaged in wrestling out the meaning of the world or answering one single knotty question. Closer to us would be the research institutes, composed of a number of such scholars engaged in parallel pursuits. Some such institutes engage only in "pure" or basic research, others in applied research devoted to improving the condition of the world often according to the conception of improvement held by some friendly funding source.

Universities include scholars of both basic and applied research. We also have the opportunity and obligation to teach, to replicate ourselves through producing new scholars, and to improve the human condition not only by applied research but by training the new generation of citizens and leaders of society.

Next to us on the other side would be the selective liberal arts colleges, which share our interest in research but have an even greater emphasis on teaching. Then would come institutions devoted solely to teaching, including community colleges, vocational schools, high schools, and seminaries. Anchoring the other end of the continuum would be the private tutor, engaged to teach some skill such as music or Italian to a single pupil.

Somewhere within this set we would need to place more specialized and homogeneous institutions such as monasteries, which are dedicated to conserving a certain kind of knowledge for future generations and to improving the world according to their own conception of improvement. We would need room for philanthropic organizations that are established first of all to improve the human condition, but that engage in teaching or research as an ancillary tactic. And we would have to account for a comparatively new phenomenon: corporate educational centers, which convey not only the arcana of their professions but also basic skills of many kinds to their employees.

The concept of a cluster of cognate institutions, each of which shares some, but not all, of our basic purposes, helps demonstrate what is distinctive about the research university. Most of our concerns about our mission have to do with how these three purposes—research, teaching, and service—are connected, and whether all are still valid for us today. The tensions between teaching and research are the most commonplace of these concerns. It is to these that I will turn in the following section.

RESEARCH AND TEACHING

The functions of discovering and sharing knowledge are intimately related. We obscure this relationship by emphasizing the tensions between research and teaching. Of course, at the pragmatic level of the disposition of professorial time and the deployment of resources, research and teaching often do conflict. Time spent in the laboratory or the library grappling with a research problem competes with time spent elsewhere, including the classroom. Time spent preparing to convey knowledge to undergraduates in terms that will be sensible to them is time not spent describing the results of one's research to informed colleagues. Following up on a graduate seminar over coffee in the common room takes time that might have been spent at the computer writing the next grant proposal.

Yet, it is clear that these activities are not simply opposed to one another. Classroom presentations are enriched by work in the library or the laboratory, which keeps knowledge fresh and pertinent and protects the undergraduates from yellowing pages of brilliant lectures increasingly out of touch with developments in the field. The next grant proposal will be stronger if it follows upon a discussion with graduate students about an especially complex area of current intellectual concern in the discipline.

At an even more fundamental level, the activities of "discovering" and "sharing" knowledge are two ways of defining the same experience. It is true that some kinds of thinking are best done in isolation, and some scholars temperamentally work best alone. But even solitary scholars depend on past experiences of sharing. They must have been taught the rudiments of an exploratory discipline, given a sense of what counts as interesting discoveries and where they are most likely to occur. The solitary scholar is an unusual scholar nowadays. More commonly, scholars are incessantly communicative, through conferences, coauthored journal articles, electronic mail, and joint research projects. Such activities are forms of sharing in discovery.

The discovery or acquisition of knowledge is generally enhanced when it is participatory. This participation can take the form of collaboration, in which the partners bring different strengths and knowledge bases to the enterprise and thus extend each other's reach. Or it can mean competition, in which the work of discovery is spurred by the awareness that others are on the track of the same kind of knowledge. In either case, the presence of others engaged in the same enterprise leads to a dialectic in which the final result is fuller and more complete than anything a single person could have arrived at all alone.[6]

This is all very well, one might reply, but why does sharing in discovery require *teaching,* as opposed to the presence of active and interesting colleagues? How realistic is it to suppose that undergraduates, especially, can be meaningful partners in discovery, that sharing knowledge with them can be anything more than the transmission of what is already known?

According to one fairly common conception of the university, teaching is a distraction from our central mission. It should be minimized, if not eliminated altogether. Derek Bok reports that as he was preparing to become president of Harvard University, a colleague in charge of another prestigious institution suggested that his first bold step might be to eliminate Harvard College. His advisor asserted that "teaching introductory economics to freshmen or European history to sophomores is a waste of talented scholars who should have no responsibilities that divert them from what they do uniquely well," which was, in his view, doing research and training graduate students to do the same.[7]

The higher prestige accorded to research, the availability of more trustworthy interinstitutional metrics for judging whether it is well or poorly done, the comparative rarity of the skills required to do it well, and the undeniable fact that it is often more pleasurable to pursue one's own work at one's own pace rather than to translate it for the uninitiated, combine to give research an undisputed primacy in the self-definition of the university. The oft-noted fact that we think in terms of "teaching *loads*" and "research *opportunities*" is faithfully reflected in the academic reward system, by which professors are lured to new institutions with promises of decreased exposure to undergraduates.

These are formidable supports for the primacy of research. Let us ponder, however, what our institutions would be like if we stopped teaching. Many of us have spent joyful and productive periods on sabbatical at institutes of pure research, and sometimes we think nostalgically that is the way one ought to live throughout one's life. For some scholars this is no doubt true, and for those professionals, the institute devoted solely to research is a proper home. Most of us, however, would eventually miss the robust variety, the give-and-take, the intellectual ferment that comes from the coexistence of people of different ages, at different points along the route to intellectual sophistication, tucked into the same small space and required to interact with one another in sustained and ordered ways.

Almost all of us would accept the importance of graduate teaching to our conception of our mission, productivity, and self-definition in our profession. The threats to even the best research centers are intellectual sterility, a sameness of experience and focus, and the nagging questions about who is listening, who really cares, and how much will what one does matter to the world? With bright and eager graduate students, there is a regular influx of new ideas and new approaches; the evidence that one is engaged in something that makes a difference mounts steadily as one's intellectual progeny move forward in the profession. Graduate students are clearly partners in discovery, sometimes the most effective partners of all.

Why not, then, adopt the model of the German university and separate the professoriate and their apprentice scholars from the novices, letting those who happen to enjoy teaching undergraduates find jobs in colleges instead?

There are several answers to this question, both principled and pragmatic. Liberal arts colleges, and other institutions in our cognate cluster, also educate undergraduates, but universities take a slightly different approach. Colleges offer smaller classes, more exposure to regular faculty, more faculty time spent in informal interactions with undergraduates, and different residential, extracurricular, and counseling facilities. Undergraduates who choose a university, however, can expect a more complex curriculum in many fields, as well as the opportunity to take advanced work in graduate seminars or professional fields. They may also benefit from the presence of graduate students and adjunct professors, and from more extensive library and laboratory facilities. Within our system as a whole, it is educationally and intellectually beneficial to have such options available to undergraduates.

Furthermore, undergraduate teaching can sometimes bring significant rewards. This can be true in any discipline, even the most rigorous, when it is taught so as to enhance the sense of wonder and stimulate curiosity, rather than only to instill accepted methodologies. A fresh perspective can jolt one's stagnant preconceptions and suggest whole new ways of looking at the world. More often than not, graduate students are already too fully initiated into our mysteries, too ready to adopt the latest jargon, too anxious to be accepted as members of the guild, and to ask eccentric, provocative questions. For many of us, therefore, the absence of undergraduates would be a serious loss, however much we might sometimes wish they would behave less like undergraduates.

For others, the difficulty of preparing oneself to enter the mind of the uninitiated outweighs whatever promise there may be of intellectual surprise. As more and more of our undergraduates come to us deficient in some of the basic skills provided in the past by secondary education, teaching introductory material can be onerous. This can make such responsibilities seem only a burden, a pure distraction from one's proper business of research and training graduate students.

Here a more pragmatic answer becomes pertinent: graduate students, however valuable they may be, generally do not come fully funded. Direct support for research is difficult to count on for many scholars; seeking it takes a good deal of time and energy. It can sometimes come with strings attached that deflect us from promising avenues that we might otherwise wish to pursue. Undergraduates, and their parents, support our enterprise with their tuition and fees in the belief that research and graduate training redounds to the better teaching of undergraduates. By accepting the support they give to us, we enter into a bargain with those students and their families. We have an obligation to uphold our end of it.

This rather crass way of putting the matter ignores the fact that no student pays the full costs of a university education; endowment income, gifts from alumni, and corporate, foundation, and government support make up the difference in all cases, even for those who pay the full "ticket price." While this is most obvious in the lower tuition charged at state-supported institutions which enjoy substantial subsidies from the taxpayers, it is also reflected in the generous amounts of financial aid made available by many private universities. Those who enroll in state universities or attend private universities on financial aid have a larger discount, but in every case we are supplementing what a student or family actually pays for with services that are provided without cost to them.

We need to recognize that our responsibility to educate undergraduates does not rest solely on the intellectual enrichment they bring to other members of the university, or on the fact that some of them pay tuition and fees. Educating undergraduates is part of our distinctive contribution to improving the human condition, one of the ways in which we carry out our responsibility to serve society. The most distinctive and effective way we do this is by sharing knowledge with new generations of students, both graduate and undergraduate.

THE OBLIGATIONS OF UNDERGRADUATE EDUCATION

To accept the sharing of knowledge as an element of our mission entails the conviction that society and the human condition are improved by more knowledge rather than less. One of the most distinctive things about the modern university is our sturdy assurance that we (not only our universities, but also our societies) are better off with free trade in what we sometimes call "the marketplace of ideas." This belief may sound innocuous, but there have been human communities deeply suspicious of such a commitment. Even in our post-Enlightenment world there are those who would argue that certain kinds of knowledge are better not pursued, or not communicated.

This should lead us, therefore, to a more direct consideration of what is at stake in educating people, what we take for granted in doing so. Such discussions are of particular importance as we try to explain how we fulfill our obligations to society. Many of the difficulties we face come from dissonant conceptions of what knowledge is all about—what it is supposed to do for its beneficiaries, on campus and outside our walls. Quite a few observers of higher education in America today refer to our "loss of nerve." Part of what they mean is that we fail to justify what we do in terms that are most consonant with our own vision of our purposes.

Undergraduates and their families expect us to provide an education that advances their productive usefulness as members of society. How can we most faithfully keep our side of the bargain with those families and those students? It is, after all, up to us to decide what we will teach. One of the services we might most usefully perform is altering their conception of what they need to know and what counts as an appropriate set of goals for the lives ahead of them.

Our society marks value primarily by monetary benchmarks, judging the worth of a person or an enterprise by how much they earn or will produce. Unlike traditional societies where not only wealth but also family, status, or religious purity mattered to everyone, we have no other measures of worth that are generally accepted, even though specific institutions or enterprises may have their own criteria. As institutions of higher learning in America have increasingly been called upon to defend the worth of what we do, we have described our value in such terms. We have adduced evidence that a baccalaureate degree is highly correlated with earning power across one's lifetime, to persuade our consumers that what we provide is worth the increasingly high prices that we charge.

We should hardly be surprised, therefore, when students major in economics or business not because they are all intellectually intrigued by such fields but because they (or their parents) believe that they will be more likely to garner a high-paying job upon graduation, or press for higher grades because they worry about being accepted at a graduate school that will ensure their professional success. We are sometimes taken aback by such narrow utilitarianism, but if we tell students that we keep our part of the educational bargain by increasing their chances to make a lot of money, they are smart enough to figure out what paths within our institutions are most likely to ensure that goal.

Most of us are idealistic enough to think that the undergraduate years should be years of exploration, risk-taking, and intellectual development, before one settles down to serious professional preparation. We believe that education has multiple purposes, and that students who focus too early and too single-mindedly on their career goals are cheating themselves of many of the most distinctive benefits of the collegiate experience. We must do a better job of explaining our advantages and goals to our consumers. This will mean sharing fuller information about how little graduate and professional schools (apart from medical schools) count on specific preprofessional education; highlighting the successful career paths of alumni with apparently unpragmatic majors such as classics or art history; and reminding students regularly and imaginatively of the importance of service to others and the balance of work, love, and leisure in a good human life.

Such arguments can be persuasive so long as the aura of the university is still powerful enough to give legitimacy to what we say. But the more we accede to or even encourage the prevailing standards of measuring value, the harder it will be for us to stand up to them effectively to protect other values that we believe are important for society to embrace.

We have been hampered in our ability to defend a robust conception of our purposes in undergraduate education by an absence of consensus in the university itself. It is of critical importance that we undertake a thoughtful dialogue about what counts as a strong education in the liberal arts (as well as in other baccalaureate fields such as engineering). Within the past few decades, the burgeoning of knowledge in many fields, the challenges to orthodoxy in the canonical disciplines of Western culture, and the acerbic battles around multiculturalism have caused most faculties to shy away from serious discussion of what one needs to teach or learn. This laissez-faire attitude has allowed us to avoid some internecine conflicts, but it has not served our undergraduates well, and it makes it increasingly hard to justify what we are doing in our colleges and universities.

There are elements in a sound undergraduate education that do not change greatly over time—familiarity with excellent work in several fields of human endeavor, with basic historical facts, and with the approaches and accomplishments of science. We need to be explicit about this in describing what we are doing. Furthermore, we need to take steps to ensure that *all* our students are receiving an education that fits such a model. Students who take their under-graduate degrees in engineering or other more pragmatic disciplines need some significant exposure to such disciplines; students who choose liberal arts degrees ought also to become familiar with at least the rudiments of technological thinking, in order to under-stand some of the most essential components of the modern world in which they will live and work.

Many of our students lack analytical and critical tools, and historical and philosophical depth. It is essential that we teach them how to arrive at critically informed judgments about truth state-ments in a variety of disciplines, and to be suspicious of claims that there is only one single truth, or one viable approach to it. Students are especially vulnerable to shoddy scholarship and to ideological appeals. Shoddy scholarship describes both the approach of the Western culture ideologue—who believes that only the traditional Greco-Judeo-Christian canon is worth teaching, even though it limits our perspective on the world to that of upper-class males, mostly white and European—and the feminist theorist or Afrocentric scholar who teaches that everything in the Western tradition is irretrievably phallocentric or derivative from Egyptian roots.[8]

We need to educate students to participate in a larger human culture, not just confirm their prejudices, whatever those prejudices may be. The essential contributions of pluralism to a good educa-tion are made not only through a variety of disciplines, teachers, and methodologies, but also through working with a variety of colleagues and peers. Anyone learns better in an environment that includes other students who bring a different background and perspective to the same experience or material. Our obligation to educate undergraduates includes assembling a diverse and heteroge-neous student body. This will provide the ferment and creative excitement that is itself part of a good education and will prepare them to participate in a world which promises to be very different from that any of us have experienced.

EDUCATION BEYOND THE UNDERGRADUATE YEARS

One of the most distinctive facets of the university from the early centuries of its development has been the juxtaposition of advanced professional training with baccalaureate education. This double layer of training has become the definitive characteristic of the university in America, and to a large degree throughout the world. Over time, new professional schools such as business, education, and public policy were developed, and graduate studies in the arts and sciences became the basis for a separate school, alongside the other ancient faculties.

Just as the content of education in the liberal arts has evolved significantly over time, so the concept of professional training has been modified as the professions themselves have changed. The greater coherence of professional school faculties, and pressures from associations of practitioners to keep the work relevant and useful, have meant that professional training has been rethought and reorganized much more regularly and systematically than training in the humanities and sciences. The mission of a professional school is easier to define than the mission of an entire university, and the curriculum appropriate to that mission is easier to construe and modify than training in the liberal arts.

We have a good example of such renovative activity in the response by several universities to the ethical problems in business and the professions that have become increasingly apparent in contemporary American society. Our reaction has been to introduce the explicit discussion of ethical dilemmas into our professional schools. We hope that as a result, more professionals in law, business, and medicine will be sensitive to ethical dilemmas in their work and better equipped to deal with them.

Graduate education in the humanities and sciences is less easily susceptible to broad changes, since the direction of the program lies almost entirely with each discipline. The primary purpose of graduate education is to replicate scholarship in that discipline. The strength of disciplinary loyalties and the marks of a successful academic guild—conferences, journals, consistent standards for peer review, a core literature, and agreement on an agenda of the most important problems next to be solved—make clear that this purpose has been served with great effectiveness across the years.

Graduate education derives its quality and resilience from the close symbiosis between master and journeyman scholar. The graduate student comes to be initiated into the profession, to receive the higher mysteries, and be accorded the insignia, so that he or she can move through the ranks of professional success. Only the acknowledged masters of the discipline are able to provide these benefits. In return, the novice scholars support and participate in the work of the masters, as research assistants and coauthors, extending the reach of their research capabilities and bringing prestige both as students and as intellectual heirs. This symbiosis works so well, and is so fully self-perpetuating, that it is hard to bring about significant changes in the format of graduate education. The content of the material changes, sometimes dramatically, as the discipline evolves, but if people elsewhere in the university or in society as a whole believe that other purposes need to be served in graduate education, it is not easy to accomplish them.

A familiar example of such a problem is the recurrent sense that graduate students should be more systematically prepared for teaching. Since many newly-minted Ph.D.s are plunged immediately into a full schedule of teaching undergraduates, both they and their students would be better served if they had more direct preparation for the job. The tasks of a graduate teaching assistant are seldom designed for such a purpose. More often than not, such assignments place them as functionaries in large lecture courses, where their duties are to grade papers, lead discussion sections, and answer questions about the material. The governing motivation of this system is to relieve the professor of much of the detailed work of teaching; the arrangement serves this purpose very nicely. Concerns about the interests of undergraduates and about whether the graduate students themselves derive any useful training from this system have too seldom been seriously addressed.

Conscientious professors sometimes arrange seminars for their teaching assistants, so that they can reflect on their experiences and derive insights about teaching. However, most graduate students have only a vague notion of what is involved in drawing up a set of lectures, devising a syllabus, or taking responsibility for the whole intellectual direction of a course. As a result, the first few years of teaching are very difficult for many novice professors, even though there are some fairly simple changes in graduate education that could provide obvious relief for at least some of these difficulties.

The first steps in reform along these lines are already being taken in several universities, thanks to the recent establishment of centers for teaching and learning. These centers are designed to provide: *1)* mentoring for those who want to improve their skills; *2)* sources of information about new technologies and methods; and *3)* opportunities for experiences such as having a class videotaped or analyzed. This relieves the average professor of graduate students from having to worry directly about training students to be teachers, and gives a cost-effective and centralized location where models of good teaching and training in the skills of undergraduate education can easily be found.

It is easy to forget that apprentice teachers/scholars need training in the ethics of our craft as well. We are more alert to the temptations that will beset the graduates of medical or business schools than those that lie in wait for the members of the professoriate. Understanding the meaning of plagiarism, emphasizing the importance of scrupulous honesty in reporting the results of one's research, and seeing the relevance of concerns about sexual harassment in the scholarly community take specific thought and preparation; we cannot take for granted that such ethical issues are clearly understood by our graduate students.

An opening up of graduate education may also be needed in a parallel direction: in loosening the monopolistic grasp of the disciplines themselves on the training of scholars, and the provision of academic certification and pedigrees. Despite the clear advantages of this system, there are also pitfalls: intellectual arrogance, disputes over turf, and a certain artificiality about the construction of a world that comes in neatly packaged disciplinary boxes. Increasingly, much of the most interesting work done in the university extends across the boundaries of the traditional disciplines, in fields such as political economy, biological chemistry, comparative literature, ecology, public policy, as well as in areas such as medicine and the law, or the environmental impact of business practices.

If graduate training remains too narrowly focused in the traditional disciplines, it will be harder for graduates to take full advantage of such crosscurrents in their own work. Successful scholars need grounding in some systematic approach to the discovery of knowledge, and the disciplines provide this very well. They also need flexibility to work effectively with scholars trained in other fields, to tackle problems that do not lend themselves easily to solution with the tools of any single discipline, and some awareness of where the most valuable cognate fields might lie. Our graduate students will be better served if their training includes exposure to such alternative approaches through interdisciplinary seminars and bibliographies.

As we rethink the organization of graduate and professional training to take into account the growing interdisciplinarity of the discovery and sharing of knowledge, we ought also to consider more broadly our responsibilities to the members of a society increasingly dependent upon knowledge and sophisticated technologies in daily work. Here it may well be time for a bold redefinition of our mission: not just to provide a traditional baccalaureate education followed by graduate and professional training culminating in an advanced degree, but also to serve as resource centers for people at various stages of their lives.

Several of the elements of such a redefinition are already in place. Many of our candidates for a baccalaureate degree today are not of traditional undergraduate age. They return to us to complete a degree, or begin such study for the first time, in the middle decades of their lives. Other middle-aged and older people are satisfying their curiosity, improving their skills, or increasing their earning power by taking courses for pleasure or for specialized professional certification programs of various kinds. Executives and government officials are taking advantage of "mid-career programs" to retool or refresh their approaches to their jobs.

It is reasonable to expect that such "nontraditional" educational patterns will continue to develop rapidly in a society that puts such a premium on access to information and communication. The universities need to think carefully about how to participate in these developments, so that our faculties and facilities will be put to most effective use, rather than either ignoring the importance of this phenomenon or allowing our core mission of discovering and sharing knowledge to be overshadowed by the provision of specific services and techniques that bring short-term economic gains to institutions hard-pressed for resources.

One promising avenue is programs for alumni, who often express the wish for more effective methods of keeping themselves intellectually alive through the "lifelong learning" for which their alma maters supposedly prepared them. Almost every university sponsors alumni seminars or study trips. With the advent of new teaching technologies and more effective organizations for contact with alumni, there are many ways in which we can satisfy such desires more fully. With the clear trends toward earlier retirement and healthier old age, there are many people who have the time and money to travel and want to develop new skills and keep their minds and bodies vigorous in the last decades of their lives. The company of scholars knows no age limits; the intergenerational partnerships that have always characterized the university are susceptible to newly fruitful variations as career and retirement patterns in our society are changing.

THE UNIVERSITY AND THE IMPROVEMENT OF THE HUMAN CONDITION

Our responsibility to our students, of whatever age or level of experience, is clear: they come to us to be educated, and we accept them with the implicit understanding that we will serve that need as best we can. The funds to support this activity come in part from the students and their families, but also more generally from tax-payers, as well as from corporations, foundations, and our alumni. This brings us to the more general question of our responsibility for the improvement of society.

General support for universities, both those that derive almost all their money from public coffers and those that rely more heavily on private funds, is provided diffusely in our society because it is understood that we are performing at least two important func-tions: providing a sound education for the next generation of citizens, and training skilled professionals to perform the tasks that must be done if our society is to flourish. Since we accept such support and enjoy its fruits, we are obliged to carry out our part of the bargain by educating those citizens and professionals to the best of our ability.

Providing such an education is the most obvious way in which we improve the human condition, but there are others. The research done by our faculties adds to our knowledge in every field. In many instances, the research contributes to human welfare in directly utilitarian ways: advances in medical science and in more effective legal systems; in agriculture, architecture, engineering, and ecology; and in enhancing communication, transportation, and urban plan-ning.[9] In other areas, such as art, literature, or history, the benefits of scholarly research are less tangible, but no less important, in expanding our knowledge of the intricate dimensions and potentialities in human life.

We know that research can sometimes lead to results that undermine rather than enhance human welfare; progress, even in scientific research, is never without its costs and detours. But on balance, the research done in our universities makes major contributions to human well-being.

We need to be more confident and bolder in reminding governments and taxpayers about this at a time when the whole purpose and character of universities is being questioned. We need to make more explicit the connections between such specific beneficial outcomes and the more general situation of our universities. It should be made more clearly evident that the so-called "indirect costs" of libraries and laboratory equipment, and other administrative costs (so long as they are carefully and conscientiously derived), are genuine expenses of research. Thus, they are costs that should be borne in part by the society that benefits from them, and not just by the universities themselves through tuition and fees or endowment income.

However, the use of the general term "society" in describing the beneficiary of such activities by the university masks an increasingly serious issue. How do we define the society to whom we are responsible? In the past, such questions have arisen in various forms: pressures from local governments and citizens, preferences of state legislatures, and alumni interests. Today they have taken on a new dimension.

One of the favorite buzzwords on many campuses these days is "internationalization." Universities have always been inveterately international in many ways: since medieval times, scholars have stubbornly refused to be constrained by national boundaries in sharing and discovering knowledge and have been among the most effective forces in breaking down parochialism and xenophobia. As our world has become increasingly interconnected, however, we have become more self-conscious about this dimension of our institutions. The new internationalization is still a vague concept in most instances, intended to emphasize the importance of educating our students to function more effectively as participants and leaders in a multinational world, by providing them with classmates and curricula that give them a sense of countries and cultures other than their own. Admitting more foreign students, strengthening programs for international travel or campuses abroad, encouraging faculty members to develop their ties to colleagues in other countries, increasing support for language and area studies—all these are facets of internationalization as it is usually understood.

In several respects, however, the increasingly international face of the university has created new tensions. The admission of foreign students, whether at the undergraduate or graduate level, raises significant financial issues. Do we see such students as a pure source of funding, or do we apply some of the same standards of equity and socioeconomic diversity that we follow in admitting domestic students? If the latter, where does the money come from, and what happens when there is direct competition for financial aid for domestic and foreign students?

Establishing programs in Japanese, Latin American, or Southeast Asian Studies might seem pure beneficial instances of internationalism, expanding the horizons of our students in an increasingly multinational world. But funding issues are once again important. Who pays for such new programs? The governments or corporations of such countries are one obvious possible source; they have a clear interest in having American leaders better educated in the customs and history of their country. But this can create pressures on the faculty hired with such funds to do research and teach in ways that present primarily positive versions of those countries and their cultures, and discourage critical analysis of their problems and their flaws. There is then a tension with the basic commitment of the university to the pursuit of truth.

Another kind of tension arises because at the same time that we have become increasingly conscious of and explicit about the international dimensions of our mission, we are also defending our public utility in quite specifically and narrowly nationalistic terms. We stress our obligation to train effective citizens and leaders for our own country, not just because it is good to have educated people in the world, but because we want the United States to be healthy and strong. In seeking support from the government and the corporate sector, we emphasize the importance of education in building a strong American economy and allowing us to compete effectively with other nations.[10]

This tension between our developing internationalism and our obligations to our own society has become especially problematic in the admission and training of foreign graduate students, in research funding provided by foreign corporations, and in the sharing of potentially crucial research results with scholars in other countries.[11] It would be nice to be able to treat such issues as transitional phenomena, inevitable by-products of lingering parochialism as we develop closer cross-national linkages and break down historic borders. In the meantime, while we are in the midst of the transition, such issues pose genuine dilemmas for our universities and our polity.

Can we speak of our obligation to improve the human condition without reference to national identity? Or does this mean reneging on our fundamental responsibility to our own country and citizenry? American universities are world-renowned, and the provision of undergraduate and graduate education is one of the areas where our country has a clear competitive edge today. Should we pursue this market superiority by aggressively recruiting students and faculty members from around the world, even though this may sometimes mean excluding citizens of our own country from graduate fellowships or desirable posts? Or should we give priority to the education of our own citizens and the improvement of our own polity, economy, and society? These are thorny questions with no easy answers. They must be discussed openly and explicitly on our campuses and in our governments.

Our national government has become increasingly concerned about the outflow of research ideas and trained personnel from our universities into the economies of competitor countries. There is also concern about the potential military implications of some kinds of knowledge. In the post-Cold War world, this has generated anxiety about the diffusion of technologies for sophisticated weaponry to more and more countries—a situation in which protecting sensitive information becomes more difficult than when it meant primarily the exclusion of Soviet nationals from access to our universities. In this situation, there is a developing sentiment to set limits on the communication of ideas and research findings, and upon the ability of American scholars to seek and accept funding from abroad. Do universities have an obligation to be sure that the results of our research in sensitive fields are available first and foremost to corporate developers and government officials in our own country, so as to enhance American economic strength and protect American military power?

It would be unrealistic for us to ignore the potentially dangerous consequences of a purely open system of information. Too much control would be self-defeating, if it meant denying access for our faculty and graduate students to vigorous open interchange with their colleagues in other countries. The ideal of vigorous open interchange, however, implies that other countries play by the same rules and allow access for our researchers to the same kinds of knowledge. Where knowledge is differentially developed, this may be a requisite with little practical effect. Where cultural attitudes towards sharing knowledge are different from ours, it may be hard to achieve the reciprocal openness we seek.

Such issues assume particular urgency today, for several reasons. In the past, it did not much matter what kind of knowledge was communicated, or to whom, so long as specific military or state secrets were not breached. The level of sophistication of scientific and technological knowledge created by university researchers and the implications of such knowledge for military and industrial power have become significantly greater within the past few decades. These developments are contemporaneous with increasing American concern about international economic competitiveness, at a time when we are no longer a hegemonic power and world creditor. This creates strong pressures to hoard useful knowledge for the benefit of our own society.

Furthermore, our ability to communicate quickly and easily to many different transnational audiences has increased dramatically with the advent of computer networks and the new scholarly habits of electronic communication that have grown up around them. Especially in quantitative and scientific fields, national borders have already become virtually irrelevant to communication.

These developments coincide with a period in which the power of governments to control results has become increasingly significant, because so much of the support for expensive scientific research comes directly from government itself. Withholding funds or placing specific conditions on how research can be carried on if it is to be funded are effective constraints in an era when support costs for the research of a single physical scientist in some fields can be as large as the costs of a small department in the humanities or social sciences, and some of the most sophisticated work in several sciences depends upon funding that is available only from government resources.

The alternative of corporate/university partnerships in research funding is becoming increasingly attractive, as the examples of Silicon Valley in California or Research Triangle Park in North Carolina clearly attest. Corporations direct their support to certain kinds of research rather than to others, but in those areas, enlightened partnerships with business are a strong alternative to government support for university research.

Corporate-sponsored research arrangements for development, marketing, and patenting can create their own complex dilemmas for university researchers and bureaucracies, whether the corporations are foreign or domestic. Proprietary knowledge is sometimes important for corporate success, but it is in principle antithetical to the openness in sharing knowledge that is at the heart of the university's mission. Successful research scientists who develop close relationships with particular corporate funders may become increasingly independent from the university and cease to function effectively as colleagues.

Some of the most successful corporate/university partnerships have occurred when several corporations and universities in a geographic area pool their resources and ideas. This strategy alleviates the disadvantages of special partnerships, and allows both businesses and universities to show leadership in regional economic development as well as to be very productive in applied research. Such developments, comparatively recent and quite promising, demonstrate the advantages of novel resourcefulness in thinking about the best ways to support those aspects of our mission that have to do with the general improvement of the human condition.

CONCLUSION

The modern research university occupies a distinctive niche in both space and time, compounded of equal parts of intense nostalgic localism and a generous sense that members of a university are citizens of the world.

The campus, quadrangles, cloisters, common rooms, and libraries are closely linked with the experiences of discovering and sharing knowledge. They evoke intense memories for members of the university in diaspora and, despite their similarities of form and function from one campus to another, set each university apart as unique in its own fashion. Despite our increasing sense of global connectedness, much of what is most distinctive to the university is clearly localized in specific spaces for inquiry, research, and conversation.

Nonetheless, the university has throughout history been stubbornly cosmopolitan. Scholars are inveterate travelers to conferences, research sites, libraries, and museums. Knowledge in most disciplines is little constrained by language or geography; it is enriched by sharing and by a universalistic perspective. The novel possibilities of electronic communication allow members of universities to do much more easily, cheaply, and effectively what they have always done: exchange ideas along lines of disciplinary interest with almost total disregard for national or institutional affiliation.

Universities also have a distinctive timelessness that provides a generous horizon for our work. We are conscious of our participation in a long heritage of institutions demonstrably similar to ours, reaching back even beyond the medieval European university to the schools and academies of classical times. This sense of history is made palpable in our traditions and ceremonies, our academic processions, colorful regalia, and distinctive feast days— commencements, convocations, and inaugurations. There is a variant of apostolic succession here that gives an assurance of rootedness and continuity even in troubled times.

Yet, universities are also forward-looking, restless, pioneering, attempting to discern and even to control the future. Much of our research is concerned with identifying likely outcomes, adapting the lessons of the past to probable future situations, and equipping people to act more effectively on the basis of well-founded hypotheses about what future options will be like.

The love of learning for its own sake, the fascination with exploration and discovery, is a powerful human impulse, needing no further justification for those who are absorbed in it. Many faculty and students would continue their work virtually unaltered even if they knew that the world would come to a cataclysmic end in the near future. But the basic enterprise of the university as an institution rests also on the faith that there will be time for our efforts to make a difference for good. Education makes little sense unless one believes that there will be a future, and that it is likely to be a better one if people are educated rather than ignorant.

These tensions between parochial and cosmopolitan affiliations, between rootedness in the past and restlessness about the future, and between the love of learning for its own sake and an investment in making the world a better place are close to the heart of the university. However we define our mission, such tensions must be acknowledged if we are to have any hope of presenting our strengths and our character faithfully to the world.

ACKNOWLEDGMENTS

I am indebted to the Rockefeller Foundation and the staff and colleagues at the Retreat and Study Center at Bellagio, Italy, for a fortnight spent in surroundings exceptionally conducive to fruitful contemplation of topics such as this.

ENDNOTES

[1]Roberto Michels, *Political Parties,* pt. VI: 4, trans. Eden and Cedar Paul (New York: Hearst's International Library, 1915), 405.

[2]James A. Perkins, *The University in Transition* (Princeton, N.J.: Princeton University Press, 1966), 7–16.

[3]Harold Perkin, "The Historic Perspective," in Burton R. Clark, ed., *Perspectives on Higher Education: Eight Disciplinary and Comparative Views* (Berkeley, Calif.: University of California Press, 1984), 23–39, provides another good overview of the development of universities, and cites several useful sources.

[4]Jaroslav Pelikan, *The Idea of the University: a Re-examination* (New Haven, Conn. and London: Yale University Press, 1992), includes some especially valuable reflections on this theme; see especially 57–61. See also A. Bartlett Giamatti, *A Free and Ordered Space: the Real World of the University* (New York and London: W. W. Norton & Co., 1976), 33–46.

[5]Charles W. Anderson, *Prescribing the Life of the Mind* (Madison, Wis.: The University of Wisconsin Press, 1993), 41, takes the Aristotelian position that among the "natural associations" created by human beings, there is a need for those that provide "shared methods of deliberative inquiry," of which the modern university is an example. Perkin, "The Historic Perspective," 20, asserts that "all civilized societies need institutions of higher learning to meet their need for esoteric knowledge and its keepers and practitioners."

[6]To paraphrase Aristotle, from *Politics,* trans. Ernest Barker (Oxford: Clarendon Press, 1946), 1281b: Feasts to which many contribute are better than those with a single host. Those who prefer a dinner neatly orchestrated by a single connoisseur to a pot-luck supper may question whether the illustration works as well in culinary enterprises as in intellectual ones, but the basic argument remains persuasive.

[7]Derek Bok, *Higher Learning* (Cambridge, Mass.: Harvard University Press, 1986), 35–36.

[8]Discussions of this topic often generate more heat than light; a useful exception is Charles Taylor, *Multiculturalism and "The Politics of Recognition"* (Princeton, N.J.: Princeton University Press, 1992), especially the Introduction by Amy Gutmann, ed.

[9]Anderson, *Prescribing the Life of the Mind,* 42, speaks of education as the "public purpose of the university," and includes activities such as these in the "cultivation of practical reason" that is part of our educational program. He argues that the university should be "implicated in the affairs of the world" rather than attempting to remain aloof. The university "will scrutinize, and try to improve upon, the practices of the state, business, the arts, medicine, the media, our conceptions of the proper use of arms and the proper stewardship of the earth, and all of this in close collaboration with the practitioners and professionals in these various endeavors." Ibid., 99.

[10]Bok, *Higher Learning,* refers to the growing threat of competition from abroad, and argues that given our economic situation and supply of raw materials, America will have to live by our wits, innovative technology, and imaginative problem solving. "Of all our national assets," he asserts, "a trained intelligence and a capacity for innovation and discovery seem destined to be the most important." Ibid., 5.

[11]Eugene Skolnikoff's essay in this volume provides a good overview of the dilemmas posed in each of these areas.

Educational experiments often take place on a single campus. They are rarely studied or evaluated by other colleges or universities that stand to profit from knowing about them. Inter-institutional cooperation in educational experimentation ought to become more common. It is possible for a group of institutions to plan specific educational reforms jointly, to try out variants of these on individual campuses, to monitor these experiments, and to learn from them. These experiments would then be the common concern of all the institutions involved. Each would have invested funds and manpower resources. Each would have an interest in incorporating into its own programs the results achieved.

Thesis 84

From "The Assembly on University Goals and Governance"
Dædalus 104 (1) (Winter 1975)

8

The Place of Teaching in the Research University

A university is what a college becomes when the faculty loses interest in students.—John Ciardi

R̲ECENT CRITICS OF RESEARCH UNIVERSITIES IN THE United States have pointed out the tensions that exist between teaching and research in these institutions and have suggested that undergraduates, in particular, are being poorly served by the emphasis that universities place on research. Institutional and professional rewards, so their argument goes, are apportioned largely on the basis of research accomplishment rather than teaching effectiveness, with a predictable effect on how faculty members apportion their time. Students, having chosen to attend a research university based on its roster of well-known faculty experts, may find very few of them deeply involved in undergraduate teaching day by day. As a result, it is argued, students may graduate with much less faculty contact than they might have enjoyed at a lesser-known institution where faculty are expected to emphasize commitment to students above research.

Defenders of research universities, on the other hand, point to the advantages of being part of a learning community in which faculty members and students at all levels are actively engaged in the process of discovery, in which cutting-edge courses cover material years away from being part of standard textbooks, in which opportunities exist to participate directly in significant research and scholarly work and to publish results in professional journals even before graduation, in which proximity to experts in

Frank H. T. Rhodes is President of Cornell University.

other fields can provide new insights and new possibilities for collaborative work and a creative approach to knowledge and to life which may be even more valuable, over the long term, than the specific information conveyed.

As with most controversies, the reality is far more complex than either of these generalizations suggest. The diversity of functions and the range of disciplines found within research universities are sources of both tension and strength. The association of professional schools with colleges of arts and sciences in these institutions, for example, makes it possible to establish productive linkages between them so that the basic sciences can inform medicine, economics can inform business, the social sciences can inform law, and so on. Yet issues of funding and "turf" still often limit the interaction between complementary disciplines on the same campus. Similarly, research is often most productive at the boundaries between existing disciplines, but cooperative interdisciplinary research ventures, while more common than they once were, are even now more the exception than the rule. But the challenges of life and of society do not come in neatly packaged disciplinary bundles, and the collective expertise found on research university campuses, while as yet imperfectly harnessed, can be a powerful tool for understanding the complexity that is inherent in most of these questions.

In pursuing those large questions, as research universities are uniquely equipped to do, they are not unmindful of the needs of undergraduates. While the balance may indeed have shifted too far toward research at some institutions, in many others undergraduate education has never ceased to be an activity of primary concern, and in still others it is now being reclaimed. Yet few research universities have come to grips with what exactly their graduates should know and what skills they should possess or have determined how best to apply their strengths as research institutions to maximize the benefits that undergraduates derive from studying there.

UNDERGRADUATE EDUCATION: THE CENTRAL TASK

I believe it is time to state clearly and firmly that, while research and teaching both contribute to the strength and vitality of the US research university, it is undergraduate teaching, and learning, that is the central task. Undergraduate education is fundamental to the existence of the university: it occupies more time, involves more people, consumes more resources, requires more facilities, and generates more revenue than any other activity. Almost everything else universities do depends on it. Other vital functions—graduate education and research, for example—are supported in part by it. Undergraduate education supplies the future generations of research specialists, and it replenishes the supply of teachers. It transmits many of the best aspects of our culture. It prepares the nation's future leaders and voters. It is through undergraduate education that the public encounters the university most directly, and it is on undergraduate education that the health of the research university will stand or fall.

My thesis is that, if research universities are to continue as major forces in American life, they need to give undergraduate education the sustained campus-wide attention it deserves. Approaches will vary from campus to campus, but the questions to be addressed are universal. Let me pose some of them: for example, whose business is the curriculum? Why, everybody's and nobody's. Undergraduate education, more often than not, is the sum of the individual courses of colleges and departments. The curriculum expands as one faculty member is replaced by another or a professor develops a new interest or goes on leave. It grows not by thoughtful review and deliberate selection but, rather, by haphazard accretion. In most universities there is no single graduation requirement; even within the individual colleges and departments the curriculum receives modest and infrequent attention beyond the acknowledged need to teach certain introductory courses with large enrollments as a way to promote a particular major to fill future professional ranks or to justify the number of faculty members and support graduate students.

I believe that at each institution the faculty collectively must determine its educational objectives and design an effective strategy for meeting them. That is easier said than done. We are more devoted to input than output. We shy away from priorities. We are reluctant to suggest that "A" is more valuable or significant than "B" in undergraduate education. The result is that we have replaced requirements by electives, and we have substituted vast numbers of undergraduate courses (a choice from more than 2,000 in most universities) for any critical assessment of their relative merits. Student choice is an essential part of a successful undergraduate experience, but student choice, unguided and uninformed, when the course catalog is an inch thick, can be as bewildering as it is frustrating.

Research universities should and must do better. It is the university that owns the curriculum. It is the university that must reclaim it. Presidents, provosts, deans, and departmental chairs neither can nor should prescribe the curriculum; that is the role of the faculty. But they must be ready to pose the questions to engage the faculty in serious, sustained campus-wide debate. With responsibility for bringing coherence to the curriculum acknowledged and accepted, universities can then consider the next point.

What essential skills and knowledge should be part of every undergraduate's experience? It won't do to argue that the merits of a decentralized system, which are real, outweigh any possible benefit of a coordinated approach to the curriculum. That proposition, at least, must be debated. Nor will it do to argue that to be a specialist—whether a chemist, a psychologist, or an agricultural engineer—requires so much of an undergraduate's time that any discussion of university-wide requirements is pointless.

Are there not common skills that all graduates must master? Are there not shared experiences from which all would benefit? Can the distinctive strengths of the separate colleges not complement one another in a more effective way? Will professional and preprofessional students not gain from closer interaction with those in the liberal arts and sciences, and vice versa?

I believe the purpose of an undergraduate education is to develop a person of judgment, discernment, and balance, with professional competence in some specific area. That will mean that our graduates will not only be well informed but knowledgeable enough to have a sense of relatedness and implication of one area in relation to another. We should strive to produce not only competent engineers, for example, but also engineers who practice their profession with a keen appreciation of the social, economic, and natural environment in which they operate and with a sense of aesthetic scale and human proportion as well as the economic costs and benefits.

We must recapture the curriculum so that it excites rather than exhausts, encourages rather than engorges, and nurtures an outward-looking, generous, and cooperative spirit rather than one of narrow self-preoccupation. We can never guarantee that result, of course: we are a community, not a factory. But we should make that our aim and our expectation.

Let me suggest seven specific attributes that are basic to the balance and breadth our graduates should gain from their undergraduate education. These attributes are crucial to success and fulfillment in any career, indeed in life itself, and so should be goals of every college student's academic career:

- the ability to listen, read, and analyze with comprehension and to write and speak with precision and clarity in the expression of disciplined thought;

- the ability to reason effectively in quantitative and formal terms;

- the ability to engage people of different cultural perspectives;

- an appreciation of the modes of thought and expression of the natural sciences, the social sciences, the humanities, and the arts;

- some sensitivity toward the ideas, values, and goals that have shaped society and some sense of the moral implications of actions and ideas;

- skill in one chosen area of knowledge, with an understanding of its assumptions, foundations, relationships, and implications;

- some active participation in the life of the campus community.

These attributes are not so much a matter of specific courses as of the spirit in which the courses are offered. Our aim should be to present all our subjects, whether twentieth-century Japanese literature or thermodynamics, in a liberal spirit, with a breadth of outlook, a humane dimension, and a concern for their relationships and their implications. Without that, there can be no coherence for our students. Without that, breadth in the curriculum will produce not enlargement of viewpoint but, instead, shallowness and superficiality.

How such understanding is achieved will be a local decision, varying greatly with the aims and resources of each individual institution. That such understanding should be expected seems to me a desirable requirement for all institutions. With it under-graduate education and the culture of the research university will be transformed, not only invigorating teaching but also enriching research.

How can we maximize the effectiveness of teaching? The research universities claim that their students can obtain an outstanding education because of their association with teachers who are also great researchers and scholars. That is undoubtedly true in graduate and professional education. It is frequently, but not invariably, true in undergraduate education. Four things are needed to make it a reality for all students.

First, the cognitive process of learning and the act of teaching need to be studied with the same creativity and professional intensity that we now devote to research. How do students learn? How might we experiment with different styles of learning? What is effective teaching? How and when should we measure it? Whose opinions should we seek—students', faculties', peers', alumni's, employees', or all the above? What can we do to encourage continuous improvement in undergraduate teaching? How does class size affect learning? What support is needed? Are the findings about effective teaching generalizable, or do they vary from discipline to discipline and from place to place?

None of this, of course, will guarantee a successful experience for every student. That will still depend as much on student initiative and motivation as on faculty expertise and commitment. Our task is to insure the greatest opportunity for the encounter to be successful, so that the excitement and challenge of learning will continue for a lifetime.

Second, we must act upon what we learn. It is probable that the answers to some of the questions above will suggest other "delivery systems." We must be ready to adapt, invent, discard, and replace. That does not come easily to universities. The role of the department, the use of teaching assistants, the expectations of the faculty, and the allocation of resources will all need to be reviewed in the light of what we learn. If undergraduate learning is our central task, then the integrity of the institution requires both analysis and action. Neglect and inaction would be a betrayal of the public trust.

Third, effective teaching must be recognized and rewarded, not only by the institution but also by professional societies and the public. All the incentives at present push the other way. From Nobel prizes to salary increases it is research that attracts rewards. Institutions have to create some balance, not by denying or reducing the value and significance of research and scholarship but, instead, by linking them to effective instruction. We need to assure those who devote their creative efforts to teaching that they will be rewarded.

That is not always the case at present, largely because teaching is seen by some as the price to be paid for a career in research. We need to give it equal emphasis, which will involve conscious actions on the part of all of us:

- to devote to teaching the same sustained, imaginative, and rigorous attention devoted to research;

- to respect the integrity of the relationship between professor and student, both in personal and in intellectual terms, so that "hucksterism" or improper advocacy are as unthinkable as abuse or harassment;

- to accept the trust that the transmission of knowledge implies so that fairness, balance, and integrity are exemplified in the way a subject is presented and arguments are handled;

- to establish, for every student and class, clear learning objectives, effective methods, and evaluation of student progress and performance;

- to be scrupulous in personal preparation for class, discussion, laboratory, or other exercise and to provide the same careful preparation and instruction for any student teaching assistants who may be involved;

- to be ready to encourage, help, and mentor faculty colleagues, especially those newly appointed, to become effective teachers and to support the need for effective teaching in departmental discussions;

- to be available for student conferences, office hours, laboratory sessions, and other formal contacts outside the lecture room;

- to take a reasonable interest in the wider issues of student life and campus activities.

None of this will involve substantial change for most faculty members; this is the way they live and work. But it should be universal. A formal statement of some kind involving the elements of a code of professional practice could usefully be drawn up by every faculty governing body. A person committing his or her future to a physician has the assurance that the doctor has taken the Hippocratic Oath, in which the interests of the patient are paramount. Why should students, committing four years, $100,000, and their future livelihood to a university faculty, expect any less commitment?

Behind these details, important as each is, is the larger question of attitude and commitment. We must convince the whole university that teaching matters, that the transaction between student and professor lies at the heart of the university's mission and that it deserves the devoted efforts of us all. Effective teaching is more than the successful transmission of information. University tapes by mail would long ago have replaced faculty members if that were the case. Effective teaching involves the personal engagement of teacher and pupil, the challenge of group discussion, the excitement of team work in research, the cultivation of interests, and the development of outlooks. It is, in current jargon, both cognitive and affective in its components.

And, although the business of the university is intellectual, not moral, teaching has a moral dimension. Universities embody values—freedom of inquiry and expression, individual responsibility, personal respect, dignity, civility, and trust among them— and teaching either reflects and reinforces them or contradicts and undermines them. Moral values are embodied in the assumptions we make, the styles we adopt, and the priorities we establish. Concerns have recently arisen, for example, about integrity as it relates to institutions (indirect costs), individual faculty members (fraud in research), and students (plagiarism and cheating). We need to face these concerns head on, measuring our collective performance against our professed values. And this will provoke heated and healthy debate.

How can we maximize the benefits that the campus community provides to undergraduates? The community in which educational activity takes place has a major influence on its character. A university degree is evidence not only of some level of learning, but also that the recipient has acquired it in the give and take, cut and thrust, doubt and debate, of a university community. It is in these communities that disagreements can take place without those involved being disagreeable, that a difference of opinion is not a misfortune but, rather, an opportunity for further understanding, that one interest or persuasion competes with another and one skill or interest complements and enriches another. Any limitation on freedom of inquiry, however laudable the motives, is inconsistent with the purposes of the university. Isolation and separation have a limiting effect upon the free exchange of ideas, which are the foundation of the university community. That is why any attempt by one group or discipline to impose its own restraints or methods in other, inappropriate, areas restricts the freedom that is vital to the work of the university.

Attention to the campus community has particular relevance now. While the decade-long nationwide numerical decline in the traditional college-age population will reverse by 1995, the largest increase in new students will come from those ethnic and racial groups that typically have been underrepresented in college attendance. In spite of goodwill and serious effort, universities as yet have been no more successful than society at large in creating real community among their members. Self-segregation and mutual suspicion are still the all-too-frequent experience on the campus as well as off it. We must do better; if, with all our resources and expertise, we cannot improve racial and ethnic relations on the campus, the outlook for society is bleak. We need study, experiment, honesty, and patience in addressing what is still one of our most stubborn divisions. If we lack the courage to address this issue, we shall squander our most precious resource: the talents and vigor of our people.

We must also evaluate the role that health care services, counselors, chaplains, coaches, residential halls, tutors, career advisors, student unions, societies, recreational facilities, and cultural programs play in creating the climate of a campus. That such activities and services are valuable is undeniable; the balance they provide to the bookish emphasis of the curriculum is healthy, as are the opportunities they offer for student leadership, teamwork, and cooperation. The emphasis that some place on modes of knowing other than the purely rational—the intuitive and the aesthetic, for example—are useful correctives; the affirmation they provide is an antidote to the prevailing skepticism, cynicism, and relativism of society as a whole.

The remarkable thing is that these programs still seem to have such modest impact that the fraternity party and the six-pack each evening still dominate student culture. We need to take a hard look at this, not to apply an oppressive, heavy hand but, instead, to encourage a culture beyond the classroom which supports the values we profess. We need to ask whether the range and performance of these campus programs support the values and priorities of the institution.

DEPLOYING RESOURCES

If undergraduate learning is the university's most central task, then we must deploy resources—human, financial, physical—and organize the university's structure to reflect this priority. It is not simply the task of instruction but also the excitement of learning which must be served by the way we allocate our time and our efforts. We need to bring to this task the same focused intellectual effort and flair that have produced such remarkable research results. This involves not only decisions at the college and university level but also, and especially, at the departmental level, where most of the action is. Indeed, we need to reassess from time to time the usefulness of departments as vehicles for instruction and research. At least some of the present vigor in the biological sciences has resulted from the merging of what were once separate departments of botany, zoology, genetics, physiology, and biochemistry. Are there other arrangements and groupings that might better serve our needs? Are there new combinations that might provide a useful supplement to existing departments and the divisions and rigidities they sometimes create? Departments arose chiefly because disciplines exist; disciplines arose chiefly as teaching devices. We should not make changes casually, but we need to take a fresh look at our organization from time to time.

What is true of structure is even more true of resources, especially time, facilities, and new appointments. A new faculty appointment represents a major institutional commitment. We need to think very carefully about institutional, as well as departmental, goals in such cases. And we need to do everything we can to support faculty members who wish to develop new skills and new interests as part of these efforts.

The kinds of changes I have described, if adopted, would slowly transform the culture of the research university campus. By far the biggest and most important change would be in the slow emergence of a true community, created from what are now increasingly fragmented and isolated parts. The development of real discourse across the barriers that now divide us would revitalize teaching, enrich scholarship, and produce a new level of excitement and engagement. The atmosphere would reflect the energy, teamwork, friendship, and excitement now found chiefly in small research teams and in a very few of the best liberal arts colleges.

That is a tall order for 1,500 or 2,000 members, not to mention 10,000 or so staff members and 20,000 students, on a typical research university campus. There is, alas, no simple recipe for achieving that kind of community. There are some who question whether an intellectual community can even exist in an age of extreme specialization. But we might at least conduct the experiment. We could make a beginning with a common first-year undergraduate program, incorporating agreed-upon themes not just in courses but also in plays, lectures, films, exhibitions, open houses, and similar ventures.

Knowledge, like perception and experience in general, will always come in fragments. A wise and happy person is able to see things whole, to synthesize, to achieve harmony of understanding and moderation of outlook. That is the aim of education, but it is not the function of the research university to provide canned answers to life's largest questions or majority perspectives or packaged, premature synthesis. The task of the research university is to raise the issues, shelter the debate, provide the tools for discovery and for self-discovery, and convince its members that such a quest is both fulfilling and worthwhile. Research universities stand alone among US institutions of higher education in the resources they bring to that vital task.

Colleges are not very successful in communicating the nature of scientific endeavor or inquiry to those —the great majority— who do not concentrate in the natural sciences. As between the sciences and the humanities, broadly defined, there are large methodological and epistemological differences. So long as the majority of American students situate themselves in nonscientific disciplines, there is an obligation to instruct them in the activity that dominates contemporary culture and yet remains so alien. One problem is to determine what kinds of concrete scientific information would benefit various groups of educated men and women. Another problem is to develop means for instructing undergraduates in certain of the methods and symbolic languages of the natural sciences. Too many colleges and universities have accepted for too long the reality of their students' scientific illiteracy.

Thesis 32

From "The Assembly on University Goals and Governance"
Dædalus 104 (1) (Winter 1975)

Walter E. Massey   *9*

Can the Research University Adapt to a Changing Future?

A MERICAN RESEARCH UNIVERSITIES ARE ONE OF the great success stories of the twentieth century. Starting much later than their counterparts in Europe, especially in Germany, these institutions are now the envy of the world. They have managed to combine the functions of teaching, research, and service in an integrated way that is much different from the traditional European universities.[1] Starting from different models—the undergraduate colleges of the likes of Yale and Harvard; technical schools such as the Massachusetts Institute of Technology (MIT), Cornell, and Rensselaer Polytechnic Institute; public universities such as California, Michigan, Minnesota, and Wisconsin; and universities such as Johns Hopkins and the University of Chicago, which were founded specifically as research institutions—they have evolved to a model that combines research and education in a way that is historically unprecedented.

These institutions have played key roles in the economic and social development of the United States. They have contributed to the founding of many of our great traditional industries and have made the United States highly competitive in new technological areas such as semiconductors and microelectronics and the world leader in industries that depend upon the frontiers of research, such as biotechnology and pharmaceuticals.[2] Moreover, despite obvious failings in many areas, these institutions have educated generations of Americans from backgrounds that cut across all

---

Walter E. Massey is Provost and Senior Vice President for Academic Affairs for the University of California system, and Professor of Physics at the University of California, Santa Cruz.

191

racial, ethnic, and economic groups. The education provided by these institutions has not been confined to US citizens. Thousands of foreign students have passed through their doors, many remaining here to contribute to the welfare of the United States, while others have returned to their native lands and have become important allies and supporters of the United States abroad. The nation's research universities have also successfully combined the teaching of undergraduates with graduate training in a manner that is special, if not unique, to US higher education.

If a story were being written about the history of the American research university and the story ended today, it would certainly end on a note of success, perhaps even of triumph. Yet the story is not ending today. A new chapter is being written, and its ending is not at all certain.

The research community in the United States is perhaps stronger than it has ever been, measured by practically any standard. There are more universities engaged in research, and there are stronger departments and groups in more universities than ever before. More students are attending and graduating with advanced degrees, and discoveries are emanating from our universities at an unprecedented rate. The expectation and belief is that these trends will continue. "Fateful Choices," a report of the Government-University-Industry Research Roundtable (GUIRR), in its introduction states: "The academic research community in the United States is heading toward an era of unparalleled discovery, productivity and excitement in fields as diverse as computing and materials science, high energy physics and psychology, cosmology and neurosciences. University-based research will open new worlds of knowledge and make possible innovations not yet imagined."[3] This vision of the future of the American research university is widely shared among many of its constituents and supporters. Not everyone would agree, however, that this vision can be taken for granted, for it depends on many factors and circumstances that have contributed historically to the strengths of these institutions, and those factors and circumstances may now be changing.

Just as the US research university is enjoying unparalleled success and respect, it is not an exaggeration to say that it is also under a great deal of stress. It is ironic that much of the stress is a result of the successes in research and education which these

institutions have achieved and continue to achieve. Those successes have led to greatly increased expectations on the part of the
public about the ways in which these institutions can and should
contribute to society.

In a post–Cold War environment many of the basic premises for
the support of research in the academic community by the federal
government are being reexamined, and these premises are changing substantially. New paradigms are being sought to build a
consensus for public support of research in academic institutions,
and this has also contributed to the public's increased expectations. Although universities have always been expected to contribute to the national good, both economically and socially, universities are now called upon to contribute in more direct and visible
ways to economic development nationally as well as on a regional
basis. They are seen to be sources of ideas, products, and
processes that will generate new businesses and economic vitality
in their local communities. The paradigm for the 1990s in terms
of economic development is the desire to recreate Silicon Valley
and Route 128 throughout the nation.

Every state has seen the advantage of having "world-class"
research universities within state borders. Also, states increasingly
have been willing to invest their own funds, in conjunction with
federal funds, to improve the quality of graduate education and
research in institutions that once were public comprehensive
universities or state teachers colleges. Research universities are
also being asked to play a greater role in addressing problems—
K-12 education, for example—which are less directly connected
with their traditional areas of expertise. K-12 education has been
recognized as a major national problem, and all sectors of society
are being asked to contribute to the improvement of education in
the schools: businesses, social institutions, and government. So, it
is not surprising that institutions such as the research universities
would be expected to play an even greater role, given that these
institutions train future teachers, generate the knowledge that
students will be expected to learn someday, and develop technologies that might be utilized to improve the quality of K-12
education. Some federal agencies and congressional committees
have even proposed that every research grant should contain a
requirement that university recipients play some significant role in

improving the quality of K-12 education. Furthermore, as Neil Smelser discusses in chapter 2, research universities are now expected to be exemplars in bringing together ethnically and racially diverse groups of people in ways that the broader society has yet to achieve.

At the same time that research universities are expected to contribute more and more in these areas, they are being accused of laxity in other areas. The accusation that universities have mismanaged government funds, especially the indirect costs portion of research grants, has become a cause célèbre over the last few years. Congressional hearings, investigations by government agencies, and articles in the national press (both scientific and popular) have painted an image of universities as being dedicated to "gouging" the federal government for funds that should have gone to support research and education. They are accused of not being sufficiently accountable stewards of the public's resources. Arrogant and indifferent is how the leadership of some of our great research universities are characterized. Many of the current critics of research universities evince disappointment and surprise more than anger in leveling these accusations. Because universities have been held to and have themselves set such very high standards, these instances of improper behavior take on a much wider importance. There is a sense of these institutions having fallen from grace.

Many also continue to be charged with not paying attention to the quality of undergraduate education. While it is conceded that undergraduates receive excellent "preprofessional training" at major research universities, there is concern that many students emerge too narrowly educated, without a broad liberal arts background. The universities respond by stating that research and teaching go hand in hand and that the best teaching results from faculty who are at the cutting edge of their disciplines. This response has not alleviated public skepticism and concern.

The scientific community has been specifically charged with a lack of ability or desire to police itself. Highly publicized cases of scientific fraud and misconduct, no matter how few or sparsely spread, have tarnished the image of the academic scientific community.

How should the US research university and the academic

research community respond to these increased expectations and growing criticisms? How can we insure that the vision of the future painted by the GUIRR will be realized? It will not be easy, given changes in the support base for research. It must be anticipated that resources and funds coming from the federal government will increase at a significantly slower rate than in recent years and that funding will actually decrease in some areas.

There are a number of questions that need to be considered forthrightly if the research community is to be assured of a strong future. I would pose four questions that are exemplary but by no means exhaustive. These are questions that do not admit of definitive answers; they must, however, be reflected on.

• Are there too many research universities?

• Can research universities set their own priorities, their own agendas, while remaining dependent on the federal government for the support of research?

• Can research universities as presently configured and operated produce a new generation of faculty representative of the racial and ethnic diversity of the nation?

• Can we really do more (research and teaching) with less?

Are There Too Many Research Universities?

Many argue that the problems research universities face are exacerbated by the growing imbalance between the number of institutions seeking research support from federal and state governments and the declining base of support. The President's Council of Advisors on Science and Technology (PCAST), in its report "Renewing the Promise: Research-Intensive Universities and the Nation," addresses this issue and notes, "It is unreasonable to expect that the system of research-intensive universities will continue to grow as it did during periods in the 1960s and 1980s." The number of institutions classified as research intensive, using the PCAST definition, has grown over the past two decades. National Science Foundation data show that "the U.S. system of research-intensive universities is roughly three times the size it was thirty years ago: in enrollment and degree production at all levels, in numbers of faculty, and in numbers of research staff." A striking illustration of this growth is that, in 1963, 80 percent of the nation's university-based R&D expenditures were shared by 20 percent of the nation's universities; in 1990, 80 percent of such expenditures were shared by over 45 percent of the nation's universities.[4]

The proposition that there may be too many research universities is not the same as arguing that too much research is being supported. The question in many minds is a matter of balance, whether or not funds are being directed to places where they are most productive. Can the available research funds be used in ways more productive and supportive of the best-quality research? Those who answer yes to such a question point out that many of the best and most respected research faculty members find it extremely difficult to secure funds for their research. More time is spent in writing proposals than ever before. The entire system has thus become less productive. These critics argue that spreading the research thinly in an attempt to achieve a kind of geographic fairness may ultimately lead to mediocrity for all institutions.

Recent Ph.D. graduates, concerned with finding employment, have asserted not that there are too many research universities but, rather, that universities are graduating too many Ph.D.s, given the current and anticipated future job market. A particularly active group, the Young Scientists Network (YSN), has called on federal agencies but also on universities to decrease the production of Ph.D.s in many scientific fields until the job market is able to accommodate those who have already received their degrees.

My own view is that there are neither too many research universities nor too many researchers. As Nicholas Rescher has said: "As best we can tell, the limits of science are economic. We reach them, not because we have exhausted the novelties of nature, but because we have come to the end of our economic tether."[5] Perhaps the more appropriate concern is how we can support and nurture research in universities in an era of stable and perhaps declining resources. At the very least the answer involves modifying the traditional academic model, the model in which every individual investigator is expected to secure funds sufficient to support his or her research, mostly from the federal government.

A greater sharing of resources through the use of research teams and cooperation across departments and among institutions must take place. Cooperation and sharing of resources with nonacademic institutions (e.g., private industry and the national laboratories) can provide other means of support. While this is already happening in many instances, the shift toward more group-oriented research is still controversial within the academic community. The establishment and funding of Science and Technology Centers by the National Science Foundation continues to be hotly debated.

There is a need to reexamine the nature of graduate training. Not every Ph.D. student ought to be led to believe that he or she will be able to follow the career path of his or her mentor or research director. To be prepared to accept a wider set of career options graduate students will need to have a broader set of research and educational experiences in graduate school. Internships in industry and research activities with different mentors in different fields provide some of this broader experience. Institutions will also have to curb their appetites; more specialization accompanied by greater sharing of resources will become necessary. Not every university can or should expect to be fully represented in every sphere of academic research. Adapting to these new expectations will not be easy, but they are necessary.

Can Universities Set Their Own Priorities While Being Dependent on Federal Support?

One of the strengths of the American research university, the use of the appropriate peer community to judge research quality and academic standards, is also one of its weaknesses. The "appropriate peer community," by and large disciplinary and narrowly focused, is professionally based, not institutionally tied, consisting of researchers at all other institutions in the country, and indeed in the world, deemed to be of the same quality. This use of peer judgment for hiring and promotions has meant that the very highest standards are used to identify faculty members worthy of promotions in universities; local parochial considerations have not been the determining factor. This strength of the nation's research university system has also meant, however, that local activities such as teaching and certain "service" activities judged primarily by local standards have not enjoyed as high a priority as commitment to scholarship and research judged by one's peers nationally or internationally.

Federal agencies have supported, encouraged, and reinforced this national system of peer judgment. Research awards are granted through the same system that determines hiring and promotions at major universities. In fact, the ability to garner research funds from a major federal agency has become a surrogate at many universities for local evaluation processes and has come to dominate all other aspects of a faculty member's performance.

There is unlikely to be a significant increase in federal funds in the future; this situation will exacerbate the tension between the touchstone provided by an evaluation by one's national and international peers on the one hand and the need for institutional loyalty and commitment on the other. There will not be sufficient research funds for every deserving researcher to receive an individual grant regularly, and therefore it will not be possible to use federal research support as the predominant criterion for hiring and promotion decisions.

How can universities set their own priorities while they are so dependent on federal support? Although levels of federal funding may not increase significantly in the foreseeable future, federal funding will continue to be overwhelmingly the predominant source of support for academic research. Among all the activities in which faculty engage, excellence in research will continue to be the most easily recognized and appreciated both nationally and internationally. Still, there are signs that the younger generation of academicians may be the source of some change in this area.

In a remarkable document, *America's Academic Future* (1992), a group of National Science Foundation Presidential Young Investigators (PYIs), recognized for their excellence and brilliance in research, offered the following vision for the university for the year 2010:

> We believe strongly that higher education, in general, and our institutions in particular (research universities) must be committed to assuring high quality instruction for all students in all segments of the American education pipeline. It is crucial that growth, change and creativity that are so integral to research become equally

integral to teaching. Thus our vision of higher education in the year 2010 and beyond is *that faculty in all our nation's colleges and universities will be truly recognized for their individual leadership and achievements in support of broad institutional missions involving instructional scholarship, public service and research excellence and for their commitment to provide a quality education for all students at all educational levels.*[6] (Emphasis added)

Can Today's Research Universities Produce the Next Generation of Scientists Who Reflect the Ethnic and Racial Diversity of this Country?

This same group of young PYIs, men and women, minority and majority, also addressed directly the issue of participation in research and faculty careers by underrepresented groups. They pointed out that "the engineering, mathematics and science community cannot expect full support from society if large segments of that society perceive themselves to be unwelcome and excluded."[7] One of the greatest challenges the American research university faces is bringing into its fold, at the highest levels, groups previously underrepresented. The ability to maintain the base of talent required to sustain the level of excellence the nation's research institutions have enjoyed for the last 50 years will be seriously undermined if they do not include groups whose members are increasingly numerous in the society. It is not only that public support for the enterprise may be lost but also that we will not be utilizing the talent pool represented by this growing new population.

California is a case in point, perhaps the most vivid in this regard. In 1992 minorities constituted 46 percent of California's population. By the year 2003 that figure will be more than 50 percent; in other words, the majority of California's population will be minorities. At the University of California minorities now make up over 45 percent of undergraduates, 27 percent of graduate students, and 15 percent of faculty.[8] Although California's configuration and ethnic makeup is not representative of the country as a whole, it does reflect the population in many of our larger urban areas, and it presages the direction of population changes in the country more generally. Educating this new generation of scholars and researchers will require changes in the way faculty are rewarded, the way classes are taught, and the way future scholars become part of the research enterprise.

Such changes imply all of the following: more institutional-based commitment and loyalty as opposed to extra-university peer group affiliation and loyalty; a better integration of teaching into the research practices of faculty; and more group-oriented research activity, to encourage more effective use of resources and more opportunities for minority and female students to work with a variety of researchers with different backgrounds, philosophies, and practices. None of this will be easy, but this is an area in which there are numerous examples of success. Given institutional commitment and a recognition of the historical imperatives for success, substantial gains can be made.

Can We Do More with Less?

There is no other option. The choices available to institutions, and to individuals, are limited. They can choose to do more at a declining level of quality as resources shrink, resulting in a spiraling toward mediocrity or worse. Or they can choose to become more focused, by setting priorities and avoiding inter-university and intra-university duplication.

Many institutions will be able to pursue the latter path quite successfully. Yet for many public institutions, in which the expectations and support base is predicated upon the institution performing, carrying out, and meeting certain mission goals, it will not be as easy to focus, trim down, and specialize. The dilemma for the University of California is unique—how to become smaller in the face of two contrary forces: the state's rapidly increasing population and the spirit of the California Master Plan for Higher Education, which would guarantee a place at the University of California for every qualified California resident wishing to enroll. Trimming down will require doing more with less, carrying out missions and activities in different ways, using resources more efficiently, and cooperating within institutions and across institutions in nearby geographic areas. The public will expect no less—but the public may not be prepared to live with the consequences of such "downsizing."

The term *research university* has been used to describe research-intensive institutions. In many respects that appellation is a misnomer; it fails to capture the full flavor of the spectrum and missions of such institutions. Commitment to scholarship and research is what distinguishes the research university from other types of institutions, but it does not define them. The primary mission of research universities is to educate, and it is this mission that they must focus on as they adapt to changing financial circumstances. As federal funds for research become more constrained, steps must be taken to insure that the available research funds are used in the most productive ways, to increase cooperation across areas, departments, and institutions. But the most important task is to guarantee the continued excellence of the American research university by maintaining its base of research talent. This will entail what I alluded to earlier as the greatest challenge to research universities in the United States—the inclusion, at the highest levels, of groups previously underrepresented. Only by insuring the participation of all segments of society in this enterprise can it be demonstrated that we are responsible stewards of the public's resources and trustworthy repositories for its aspirations.

ENDNOTES

[1] See Burton Clark, *Places of Inquiry* (Berkeley: University of California Press, 1994). Clark demonstrates that in countries like Japan, Germany, and France research has become sharply differentiated from university teaching (i.e., it has become progressively located in business settings, research academies, and nonuniversity centers), and the quality of these institutions has suffered on that account.

[2] It might be noted that in almost every disciplinary area in the natural and life sciences, social sciences, and humanities, research in the United States occupies a position of world advantage and leadership.

[3] Government-University-Industry Research Roundtable, *Fateful Choices—The Future of the U.S. Academic Research Enterprise* (Washington, D.C.: National Academy Press, March 1992), 3.

[4] President's Council of Advisors on Science and Technology, *Renewing the Promise: Research-Intensive Universities and the Nation* (Washington, D.C.: Government Printing Office, December 1992), xii, 5, 8.

[5] *The Sciences* (January–February 1994): 8.

[6] National Science Foundation, *America's Academic Future: A Report of the Presidential Young Investigator Colloquium on U.S. Engineering, Mathemat-

ics, and Science Education for the Year 2010 and Beyond (Washington, D.C.: National Science Foundation, January 1992), 1.

[7]Ibid., 3.

[8]University of California, *Statistical Summary of Students and Staff* (University of California, Fall 1992).

America's Research Universities under Public Scrutiny

ARGUMENTS ABOUT WHAT TO TEACH, TO WHOM, and by whom are standard fare in the history of higher education, but today they are being pressed with an urgency and uncertainty not experienced since the latter half of the nineteenth century, when the precursor to today's research universities was being shaped during the sharply contested shift from religious learning to scientific knowledge as the core purpose of higher education.

Nor is this period the first instance in which research universities have had to redesign their research mission in response to changing priorities by funders. The research system that the Progressives harnessed to their purposes at the turn of the century, or the successive versions that were hastily assembled to advance national security goals during each of the world wars were simpler, smaller, and less expensive than the system before us today. Observers are asking whether the research university system of the late twentieth century has, perhaps, outgrown its available resource base. Buried in this question, of course, are explosive issues for university management and for the rapidly changing relationship between research universities and their primary sponsors—the federal government, private industry, alumni, and tuition-paying parents.

These core issues of the university's teaching and research mission intertwine with a number of less central, though still serious, problems: athletic scandals, sexual harassment, poor teaching, scientific misconduct, fiscal mismanagement, administrative inefficiencies, and litigation of tenure cases, to name those most in public view.

Kenneth Prewitt is Senior Vice President at The Rockefeller Foundation.

This much, then, is certain. The research university system is confronted with a long list of challenges—some serious and others trivial; some central and others marginal; some real and others imagined; some self-inflicted and others imposed from without. These issues pile up, leading many commentators to conclude that "the university is in a state of crises."[1]

Though the term "crises" is much used and abused, its application to the present state of affairs in research universities is apt. A crisis, Webster tells us, is a decisive moment brought about by unusual stress or instability. It is a turning point when it must be decided how to go forward, what to get rid of, or whether different principles are called for.

If we grant the aptness of "crisis" as a description of the present phase in the development of the research university system, we quickly want to know whether our universities can count on the support, the patience, and the understanding of the public. The answer to this question matters; it tells us whether forces external to the university will have to be accommodated as universities work through their current difficulties. Public confidence in the universities is not the only thing that matters, and it does not matter definitively, but it certainly matters.

If the universities lose their credibility with the American people—if they are objects of public suspicion and cynicism—it will be vastly more difficult to reconfigure, and refinance, the universities for the twenty-first century. Reasonable decisions on indirect cost recovery will be harder to come by. Courts will be less sensitive to protecting the confidentiality of the tenure review processes. Local and state authorities will be more likely to intervene when campus disputes threaten public order. To guard against conflicts of interest or misuse of funds, the web of contracts linking campus research with its federal and industrial sponsors will be drawn tighter and more restrictive.

The principle at stake is an obvious one. Every institutional sector in American democracy—the media, the church, the corporate sector, voluntary organizations, labor, the professions—prefers to chart its course and discharge its duties by criteria of its own choosing rather than by those externally imposed. This strong preference for institutional autonomy confronts the equally compelling democratic principle that institutions which have great social power, especially if they draw directly from the public purse, are accountable for how they exercise those powers and spend public monies. In any institutional sector, the autonomy-accountability balance is always under negotiation. Whether the tilt is toward independence and self-direction or toward public control and government regulation depends on many factors. Centrally important, however, is whether a sector is publicly trusted. Holding other factors constant, the greater the public trust, the greater the autonomy.

Research universities have enjoyed an extraordinarily high level of public trust throughout American history. This observation is not meant to deny that there have been troubled periods in the relation of universities to the political society. The Columbia University historian Richard Hofstadter, in *Anti-Intellectualism in American Life,* documented many such periods—ranging from the critique of intellectuals and their institutions by the populist forces in the early decades of the nineteenth century to the skepticism toward "book-learning" by the builders of American business in the later decades of that century, and on into the twentieth century when the patriotism of intellectuals came under suspicion in the 1920s and again in the 1950s.[2] The late 1960s ushered in another troubled period, as the traditional borders which insulated the university from external political strife collapsed under the weight of the massive, student-led antiwar movement.

These periods notwithstanding, across much of the nation's history higher education and especially the leading research universities have enjoyed a public respect not easily matched by other sectors. Higher education accordingly has been granted great discretion in conducting its affairs.

Our concern, however, is less with history than with the present and immediate future. Can the university continue to count on the level of public confidence it has long enjoyed?

Some observers of higher education believe not. Jaroslav Pelikan, Yale University's historian of religion, describes what he calls "the crises of confidence and the crises of credibility."[3] Pelikan is careful to note that the crises are not limited to what is taking place within the university walls but encompass as well the position of the university in relation to the global crises of war, poverty, disease, and environmental damage. He concludes, however, that the university "is in danger of losing credibility."[4]

This judgment is echoed by others, including the prestigious President's Council of Advisors on Science and Technology which issued a report on the research-intensive universities in late 1992, wherein it is categorically asserted that "Public confidence in universities is eroding."[5]

If the university is truly losing the confidence of the public, it will have to position itself differently as it confronts its current challenges. It will have to accommodate interference from various publics who no longer trust the university as it balances its teaching obligations with its research goals, determines the proper demographic composition of the student body, sets the terms of university-industry partnerships, or designs controls to prevent the misuse of public funds.

Those who claim that universities are losing the confidence of the public have argued from anecdotal, not systematic evidence. Perhaps this should not surprise us, for no direct measures of public confidence are available. Indirect measures, however, are available; they do not lend support to the loss of the confidence claims. I will turn to these measures shortly, but first I will look at the context in which the loss of confidence argument has been advanced.

THE UNIVERSITY'S CRITICS

Starting in the mid-1980s, with the publication of the conservative theorist Allan Bloom's, *The Closing of the American Mind: How Higher Education Has Failed Democracy and Impoverished the Souls of Today's Students*, there has been a steady stream of books insisting that the universities are letting the nation down. Their titles and subtitles tell the story: *Killing the Spirit: Higher Education in America; Profscam: Professors and the Demise of Higher Education; The Moral Collapse of the University; Inside American Education: The Decline, the Deception, the Dogmas; Illiberal Education: The Politics of Race and Sex on Campus; In the Company of Scholars: The Struggle for the Soul of Higher Education; Up the University;* and *Impostors in the Temple: American Intellectuals Are Destroying Our Universities and Cheating Our Students of Their Futures.* The beleaguered university administrator—struggling with growing costs, shrinking resources, suspicious government auditors, a faculty divided over whether objective truth exists, and demands from every quarter for more representation—who reads that the university is failing on all fronts, might be excused for leaping to the conclusion that nothing less than public credibility is at stake.

This conclusion is all the more warranted (even though, as we shall see, mistaken) if we consider the audience to which these books critical of the university are addressed. First, we note that this critical literature speaks with the authority of the insider. It is often members of the university community who are confessing to all who will listen that the university stands guilty of fraud and failure.

Why this confessional literature appeared with such vehemence in the 1980s is itself an important question. Certainly, part of the explanation is found in the conditions which it exposes: there is fiscal mismanagement, there is poor teaching, and there are athletic scandals. A broader explanation, which is beyond the scope of this essay, would analyze struggles internal to the university over such serious issues as curricular reform, faculty appointments, research directions, and resource allocations, and then ask why one faction in these struggles has taken its message to the public.

No one who reads this literature could mistake its intended audience. The argument is framed less to engage colleagues in a serious discussion than as a call to arms. Here, for instance, is how a university administrator, himself a distinguished historian, chooses to describe research:

> The argument advanced here can be simply stated. It is that a vast majority of the so-called research turned out in the modern university is essentially worthless. It does not result in any measurable benefit to anything or anybody. It does not push back those omnipresent "frontiers of knowledge" so confidently evoked; it does not *in the main* result in greater health or happiness among the general populace or any particular segment of it. It is busywork on a vast, almost incomprehensible scale. It is dispiriting; it depresses the whole scholarly enterprise. . . .[6]

And here is how a self-described policy intellectual and academic characterizes his university colleagues:

> But today many of these academic intellectuals have betrayed their profession. They have scorn for their students and they disdain

teaching. . . .They are the corrupt priests of America's colleges and universities and, while small in number, their influence is large and pervasive. They are the great pretenders of academe. They pretend to teach, they pretend to do original, important work. They do neither. They are impostors in the temple.[7]

These writings are designed to reach beyond the campus, to enlist, one presumes, a broader public in the anticipated reform of the research university.

From the perspective of this essay, the key question is whether these writings are echoing preexisting public opinion. Are they reflecting and giving voice to a serious public disenchantment with higher education? If instead, however, they are trying to convince the public about the failures of the universities, the question becomes whether their efforts are successful.

PUBLIC CONFIDENCE IN RESEARCH UNIVERSITIES, CIRCA 1990

Beginning in 1972, and continuing to the present, surveys conducted by NORC, a research center affiliated with the University of Chicago, have asked the American public about its confidence in the people responsible for running thirteen major American institutions.[8] Aggregated across twenty years, *Table 1* indicates the rank order, starting with the institutional sector in which the largest number of citizens expressed a great deal of confidence.

TABLE 1. Public Confidence in American Institutions

Institution	Percentage Expressing "Great Deal of Confidence" 1972–1992
Medicine	50%
Scientific Community	40
Education	34
Military	34
US Supreme Court	32
Organized Religion	31
Banks and Financial Institutions	29
Major Companies	26
Press	21
Executive Branch of the Federal Government	19
Television	17
Congress	16
Organized Labor	13

Though there is not in these data a direct measure of public confidence in research universities, a cautious inference is warranted. The institutional sectors with which research universities are most closely linked—medicine, science, and education—rank higher in public esteem than do institutions not so associated. Public opinion, taking that term to mean what it should—the opinion of a cross section of the American public—is not so nuanced and discriminating that it would sharply distinguish between university leaders, on the one hand, and leaders of science, education, and medicine, on the other.[9]

A more specific question can be posed: how did these university-linked sectors fare during the 1980s, the period during which flaws and failures of research universities were aggressively brought to public attention? With one easily explained exception, the institutions held in highest regard in the 1970s were again the institutions held in highest regard in the early 1990s. The exception is the military. Following the extensively televised and acclaimed military success in the Gulf War, the military moved from fourth to first place in public confidence, leaving science second in rank, but dropping medicine from first to third and education from third to fourth.

Rank order aside, what about absolute levels of confidence in these institutional sectors? There could have been an erosion of confidence in science, education, and medicine during the 1980s without altering the overall rank order. In fact, there were small but suggestive changes in the absolute levels of confidence. Fewer Americans held medical leaders in high regard at the end than at the beginning of the decade (a decline of 8 percent). A plausible explanation links the decline to the public's anxieties about the costs of medical care that emerged in the late 1980s. By the same token, public anger about the costs of a college education or charges of scientific misconduct might have led to similar declines in confidence toward leaders in education or science. This, however, was not the case. Leaders in science and education were held in high regard by a *larger* proportion of the American public in 1991 than they were at the beginning of the 1980s (increases of 5 percent in each sector).

Allowing for how indirectly these data measure public confidence in research universities, we can nevertheless conclude that those sectors most closely linked with and dependent upon the nation's research universities have not fallen in public esteem.

We turn to a second, less indirect measure. As noted above, at the heart of many recent critiques of the research university is the charge that faculty have deserted their teaching obligations. Allan Bloom, in *The Closing of the American Mind*, writes:

> These great universities—which can split the atom, find cures for the most terrible diseases, conduct surveys of whole populations and produce massive dictionaries of lost languages— cannot generate a modest program of general education for undergraduate students. This is a parable for our times.[10]

Martin Anderson, a Senior Fellow of the Hoover Institution at Stanford University, describes professors as impostors, and Page Smith, founding Provost of the University of California at Santa Cruz, in *Killing the Spirit*, writes: "The faculties at the elite universities (and, increasingly, at those lesser institutions bent on aping them) are in full flight from teaching."[11]

If professors are impostors, in full flight from teaching, this message has yet to reach the general public. In 1989, the NORC asked a sample of the American public to assess the prestige of 740 occupations, replicating a famous study of occupational prestige first conducted in 1964.[12] This exhaustive study measured public esteem for jobs as varied as beer makers and bankers, aerobics instructors and astronauts, prostitutes and panhandlers.

It is the high prestige occupations which interest us. In 1989, the two most prestigious occupations in the United States were surgeons and physicians. The third most prestigious occupation was the college or university president. At the end of the 1980s, then, those positions presumably most responsible for the alleged failure of the university system were held in extraordinarily high esteem. Further examining the most esteemed occupations in the United States confirms that this is not an aberration in the data. Joining college and university presidents among the very most prestigious occupations are: professor of mathematics (sixth), professor of physics (ninth), professor of biology (eleventh), and professor of psychology (thirteenth). This is not merely a matter of the prestige accorded the physical sciences, for the professor of history is also highly ranked (seventeenth), as is the professor of English (twenty-fifth).

When asked to rate the prestige not of a particular type of professor, but simply "the college professor," the American public could identify only nine nonuniversity occupations to be higher in prestige and 726 occupations to be lower in prestige. College professors are held in higher esteem than architects, engineers, priests, ministers, bankers, directors of large corporations, army colonels, and owners of manufacturing plants.

It is suggestive, not definitive to learn that very few persons in the society are as admired as university administrators and faculty. Obviously, what has been measured is the prestige of occupational titles and not the performance of current incumbents. However, students of public opinion know that such fine distinctions are rarely necessary in interpreting data of this sort. A widespread erosion of confidence in today's university leaders would reveal itself even in indirect measures.

Though the evidence is fragmentary and indirect, those impatient with the argument by anecdote will turn to such data as are available. Were we to have learned that public confidence in the leaders of science and education had declined in recent years or that university presidents and faculty were not viewed as holding prestigious positions, we would be inclined to accept the loss of confidence hypothesis. The pattern points elsewhere. We reach the initial conclusion that the university is not in imminent danger of losing its privileged position in the views of the general public. There is, however, another possibility to consider.

KEY UNIVERSITY CONSTITUENCIES

Public opinion is constituted of more factors than a snapshot of public attitudes at a given moment in time—which is all that has been presented thus far. Studies of opinion formation repeatedly document instances in which the views of the public-at-large reflect views earlier held by influential pockets of opinion. In such cases, the opinions of specialized constituencies or attentive publics gradually spread through the general population, becoming in due time the conventional wisdom. The development of environmental awareness over the last two decades is a case in point.

We have seen that there are disenchanted faculty and administrators whose views of higher education are less supportive, more critical than the public-at-large, and who are forcefully pressing their case in public forums. Is there reason to believe that their judgments are echoed by other key constituencies of the research universities?

There is little doubt that the volume of criticism about selected university practices has increased in recent years among students, parents, and alumni. Our question, however, is whether this criticism is sufficiently deep and broad to lead us back to the possibility that public confidence in research universities has begun to erode. If the nation's leading research universities have lost the confidence of these key groups, we should detect some reluctance on the part of the most gifted and intelligent high school graduates (and their parents) to invest four years (and more than $100,000) in attending research universities. Yet, in the recent period, applications to leading research universities increased over the preceding year more often than they decreased.

More telling, the proportion of those admitted who subsequently matriculate has consistently been higher for the leading private research universities than for selective private colleges. This "yield gap," as it is known, compares colleges widely respected for their teaching programs (including Williams, Wesleyan, Oberlin, Pomona, and Amherst) with research universities among which are those most aggressively charged with dereliction of teaching responsibilities (including Stanford, Harvard, and Yale).[13] Of course, there could be public dismay without public boycott—the antics of major league baseball owners and players are said to have alienated the public, but pennant contenders fill their stadiums. But making do with the measures that are available cautions against concluding that leading research universities are about to lose their most important asset, a steady stream of high quality applicants to their undergraduate colleges, graduate programs, and professional schools.

Moreover, there has not been a decline of support from key university donors. Universities continue to be the favored grantee of the private foundations, attracting a higher proportion of foundation giving than any other sector of the society. The $2 billion in foundation support to higher education in 1992 represented a 38 percent increase from five years earlier. Trustee and alumni giving to universities has steadily increased in recent years, up more than 20 percent over the past five years. A number of leading universities successfully concluded record-breaking capital campaigns in exactly those years when the public had supposedly lost confidence in them. From all sources, giving to higher education was 26 percent higher in 1992 than in 1987. In addition, there have been a number of unprecedented individual gifts, measured in the multiple millions, with every indication that this may be the beginning of sizable bequests from the large private fortunes accumulated in the 1980s. There are anecdotes suggesting scattered instances of alumni who claim they are withdrawing support because of an actual or imagined failure of their alma mater, but conversations with university leaders and development officers indicate that there is no pattern here. Trustees and donors see battles over curricular reform or appointment criteria as squabbles for universities themselves to sort out, not as issues to be debated and decided by a wider public.

INDUSTRIAL LEADERS

Probably no single constituency is as well-placed as are industrial leaders to judge the quality of what is produced by research universities. If graduates have been poorly taught and the research is worthless, America's industrial and corporate leadership would, presumably, begin to disengage.

The opposite is the case. The expansion of university-industrial partnerships in recent years is unprecedented. In less than a decade, industry-sponsored research and development at America's universities and colleges quadrupled, reaching $1.2 billion in 1991. Ten research universities were receiving at least $20 million in industrial-sponsored research. The leader, the Massachusetts Institute of Technology, expects in 1993 to receive nearly 20 percent of its total research budget (approximately $325 million) from private corporations. In the biomedical area, there are more than one hundred arrangements which link research universities with pharmaceutical and other health-related industrial partners. Associations are similarly strong in computers and electronics.

Universities have also been pressed into service on behalf of regional economic development, with many local and state governments attempting to replicate such acclaimed successes as Silicon

Valley, Route 128, or Research Triangle Park. It is estimated that there are now four hundred "technology incubators" which bring together university research, industrial engineering, and public seed funds.

That such ventures have raised contested issues about proprietary research, conflicts of interest, faculty loyalties, or incentives for graduate study is to be expected. Mistakes will be made as the "entrepreneurial university" comes into focus. These mistakes will attract public criticism, as they should, but these criticisms should not be taken as suggesting a generalized "loss of confidence" by the public-at-large and certainly not by the industrial sector. The opposite inference is suggested. The very deepening of the university-industry ties is an indicator of a commitment to and confidence in research universities.

THE SKEPTICAL PUBLIC OFFICIAL

If the critique of universities has not yet generated widespread public disenchantment nor seriously alienated the private sector donor base or the industrial sector, a more complicated picture is unfolding in the public sector. In the federal government and in many state governments, especially those responsible for large public research universities, there is heightened scrutiny of the university.

There is, however, no evidence that this scrutiny is a product of the criticism being voiced from the campus. It is more accurate to see it as reflecting concerns about the high costs of university research at a time of shrinking federal and state budgets. Insofar as examples of fiscal mismanagement fuel this concern, there is a convergence between the message of the universities' critics and the oversight responsibilities of public authorities.

There is more happening than governmental concern with scattered instances of fiscal mismanagement. The question is whether the substantial public investment in the research university is cost-effective. Is the product worth the price? This question, not a general loss of public creditability, leads state legislators to ask about teaching loads and productivity, leads federal auditors to tighten rules on indirect cost recovery, and leads members of Congress to complain about the lag time between basic research and commercial application.

That such questions arise today is not surprising. Massive public funding of the research university system was justified by national security concerns in the aftermath of World War II. A different justification becomes necessary as the nation redefines its economic base and its global responsibilities in the post-Cold War era. A major theme shaping public discourse is, of course, America's competitive position in the international economy. The university, having long claimed that its teaching and research helped make America a powerful force on the world stage, is being asked: "What have you done for us lately?" This question will be asked again and again. It mistakenly will be interpreted in some university quarters as, "Why do they not love us anymore?"

Were loss of credibility the issue, however, we would not expect a concerted effort in government quarters to draw on and redirect the formidable strengths of the research university system. Yet, this is exactly what is happening. In response to pointed comments from congressional leaders, the National Science Foundation, in 1992, considered new arrangements that might more tightly link university-based science with the commercialization of technology. The President's Council of Advisors on Science and Technology noted: "Today the pressure of international competition has introduced a critical time dimension into the system. For the nation's economic interests, the issue is not simply how much new knowledge is being generated but also how fast it is being translated into economically and socially beneficial products and processes."[14] The Clinton Administration's preoccupation with a high-technology industrial policy is being advanced on the assumption that higher education, both in its teaching and research, will be centrally involved. The facts suggest that the heightened government scrutiny of university costs reflect tight public budgets and appropriate concerns about cost-effectiveness rather than some deeper loss of public credibility.

CONCLUSION

This essay finds unpersuasive the assertion that research universities have "lost the public's confidence." If we take the early 1970s as the base point, the level of public confidence in higher education has not measurably declined. Students have continued to apply to our best and most expensive universities in large and even growing numbers. Private giving, though never at the level aspired to by university development offices, has held steady and for some institutions has been unusually generous in recent years. Industrial and corporate leaders are actively seeking partnerships with universities, thereby betting their commercial success on the quality of teaching and research found in university classrooms and laboratories. Federal and state dollars are harder to come by, and their expenditure is more closely watched than in the past, but this reflects budget constraints more than a withdrawal of public confidence. The government is actively seeking to enlist the research university system in rebuilding the American economy.

Might there be, however, a withdrawal of public confidence? Certainly. The road traveled by the nation's health-care providers holds a warning. It was not so many years ago that the health-care sector was widely applauded for its spectacular discoveries and miraculous cures. Expensive, yes, but easily worth it, was the public judgment. Then came scattered concerns about rapidly increasing costs. Gradually, a public argument took shape: perhaps the productivity of the health-care sector was not keeping pace with its ever increasing claims on the Gross Domestic Product. As noted earlier, public confidence in leaders of the medical sector declined in the 1980s. By the early 1990s, political candidates could comfortably campaign on a platform emphasizing far-reaching reform of the medical system. There will be more regulation, less autonomy, in the health-care sector when the dust has settled. It is not out of the question that research universities could travel this same path.

In addition, we should not lose sight of the fact that embedded in the general political climate is a deep public skepticism toward the major institutions of our society. This skepticism, rooted in the events of the late 1960s and early 1970s, led to a sharp drop of confidence in nearly every institutional sector— government, business, labor, media, and organized religion. In the late 1960s, higher education, medicine, and the scientific community suffered an erosion of public confidence along with these other sectors.[15] As previously noted, the rise of public skepticism leveled off in the early 1970s and has remained relatively constant since. Nevertheless, public skepticism toward institutional sectors has become a fact of American political life. No one would be foolish enough to suggest that universities are exempt from this public skepticism. This pressure is not likely to disappear and, indeed, probably will increase. But it misrepresents the facts to generalize from this pressure a significant erosion of public support.

ENDNOTES

[1]Jaroslav Pelikan, *The Idea of the University* (New Haven, Conn.: Yale University Press, 1992), 13. The full sentence reads: "But it does seem fair to say that as Western societies move toward the twenty-first century (and the third millennium) of the Common Era, the university is in a state of crises and is in danger of losing credibility."

[2]Richard Hofstadter, *Anti-Intellectualism in American Life* (New York: Vintage Books, 1962).

[3]Pelikan, *The Idea of the University*, 21.

[4]Ibid., 13.

[5]US Government Printing Office, *Renewing the Promise: Research-Intensive Universities and the Nation* (Washington, D.C.: US Government Printing Office, December 1992).

[6]Page Smith, *Killing the Spirit: Higher Education in America* (New York: Viking Penguin, 1990), 7.

[7]Martin Anderson, *Impostors in the Temple* (New York: Simon and Schuster, 1992), 10.

[8]These measures are calculated from the codebook of the General Social Survey. NORC, University of Chicago, 1992.

[9]The Harris polling organization has also presented the confidence items to a sample of the American public, but Harris has asked about "higher education." "Higher education" consistently receives a higher rating than the NORC item using "education" alone, though the two items follow the same general trend. See Seymour M. Lipset and William Schneider, *The Confidence Gap: Business, Labor, and Government in the Public Mind* (New York: The Free Press, 1983), 45.

[10]Allan Bloom, *The Closing of the American Mind* (New York: Simon and Schuster, 1987), 340.

[11]Smith, *Killing the Spirit: Higher Education in America*, 6.

[12]Data from the NORC/GSS Occupational Prestige Scores were generously made available by the Library of NORC in Chicago, Illinois.

[13]These data were generously made available by the Consortium on Financing Higher Education in Cambridge, Mass.

[14]US Government Printing Office, *Renewing the Promise*, 30.

[15]Lipset and Schneider, *The Confidence Gap*, 3, note this generalized decline in public confidence starting in the mid-1960s and leveling off in the early 1970s: "the public did not lose confidence in different institutions at different times. Rather the data reveal a widespread loss of faith in the leadership of business, government, labor, and other private and public institutions at more or less the same time."

With the growing dependence of higher education on public funding, the risk of leveling increases. Examples of excellence, so important in setting the standards of aspiration for all institutions, become all the more necessary. Difficult as it is politically to favor some institutions rather than others, selective support, public and private, is essential and ought to be fought for. No one ought to underestimate the resistances to this principle; uniform support for all institutions will have ardent defenders.

Thesis 74

From "The Assembly on University Goals and Governance"
Dædalus 104 (1) (Winter 1975)

In Defense of the Research University

W HAT IS THE AMERICAN RESEARCH UNIVERSITY? Why has it been recognized as superior to institutions of higher education elsewhere?

The answer, I believe, is fairly simple. Until recently, the American research university has been the only form of tertiary education which has combined the functions of innovative research with teaching. The former and present Communist countries concentrated scholarship in the academies of science, not the university. Academicians far outrank professors. Germany combines research with teaching, but it has major full-time, very prestigious research institutions, the Max Planck Institutes. In France much of academic investigation goes on in the CNRS, the National Centers for Scientific Research. Most other countries did not take the combination of university-based research and doctoral research training seriously. The US system, initially modeling itself on the nineteenth-century German doctoral seminar, evolved into one that emphasizes combining doctoral training, including classes and research apprenticeship, with the highest-level scholarship.

Students in US graduate schools have received the best formal training while having close collegial contact with leading investigators. The scholars have benefited from their links with the brightest of the next generation, from their ideas and assistance.

Living and working in a highly competitive meritocratic society

Seymour Martin Lipset is Hazel Professor of Public Policy at the Institute of Public Policy, George Mason University, and a Senior Fellow at the Hoover Institution, Stanford University.

and institution, everyone in the upper-level research complex works hard for recognition as the leaders of their fields. And given that the United States has been the least ascriptive society, its scholarly world has been the most achievement oriented—what social class you come from, what schools you attended, count for little, once you begin graduate training. Faculty members are hired by the major universities for their research promise or achievement. They do not have to be graduates of Tokyo or Oxbridge or the Sorbonne to start their scholarly careers at the top in institutional terms.

The competition for status led to national ranking studies, in which faculty have been asked to evaluate universities and departments on scales ranging from excellent to poor. Chicago came out ahead in the first such US survey taken in the mid-1920s, a result that upset the Ivy League schools, particularly Harvard, and emboldened the critics of President A. Lawrence Lowell's emphasis on undergraduate instruction, consciously modeled on Oxbridge. The many subsequent surveys taken since World War II have shown a fair amount of movement within the top 10 to 20 universities. Harvard replaced Chicago at the top, itself to be challenged and overtaken by the two Bay Area giants, Berkeley and Stanford. Most of the "Ivies," particularly Columbia, plus Chicago, declined in general scholarly repute. There is no need to report the changes, except to note that the western state universities did best first in the natural sciences then later in the social sciences, while the old eastern private schools were strongest in the humanities.

The existence of the rankings, plus other indicators of scholarly excellence, such as the number of Nobel Prize winners and members of the National Academy of Science and American Academy of Arts and Sciences and the American Philosophical Society, have provided incentives for competition for "stars." Scholars who are judged to be among the leaders in their field, as indicated by receipt of prizes, status in discipline evaluation studies, citation counts in the *Citation Indexes,* and membership in the honorific academies, are in high demand. The currency of competition has been high salaries, funds for facilities, including large sums for equipment, research, travel, summer pay, and occasionally significant housing supplements, control of graduate student stipends and fellowships, and light teaching loads, in some cases none.

Basically, from World War II on, such competitive orientations turned major parts of the top universities into research institutes that also teach. Much of the personal instruction has been done by teaching assistants and nontenured faculty.

Often the "schools" do not acknowledge the pattern even to themselves. University administrators periodically send the faculty memoranda stressing the importance of teaching. Almost all institutions have teaching awards. Yet these have little effect on tenure decisions in good universities, except marginally. Faculties understand the rules. I recall a colleague at Berkeley who, after hearing the content of a letter on teaching from the dean, publicly noted that, looking over his career, he could report that every important special salary increase or improvement in his situation was brought about by a salary offer from another school, occasioned by his research standing. In effect, he said, the university had repeatedly rewarded him for his research and not given him a nickel for his teaching. This he took as the *real* instructions about how he should budget his time.

On another occasion, while at Stanford, I sat in on a bag lunch with the president, then a well-known and sincerely concerned advocate of emphasis on undergraduate teaching, and three other faculty members, one of whom was a well-known chemist. The president asked him how we were doing against the "competition." The chemist replied, "Not so well"; the major rivals of Stanford in chemistry were Cal Tech and Harvard, and both gave newly recruited professors many millions of dollars to come to the schools, while Stanford could only provide a million or two. I sat with my mouth agape and was later told that the money was transfer costs—money needed to set up a laboratory, bring staff and assistants, and so forth. When Harvard tried to recruit two of my Stanford sociology colleagues, it offered them $500,000 for five years for a research lab and program as well as light teaching loads. Stanford managed to find $250,000 plus a reduction in teaching and held them. Another of my Stanford colleagues, this one in political science, was offered a very large house purchase subsidy.

Universities try to keep some control over salaries, but not perks, in the liberal arts. But professional schools, such as those specializing in business, law, medicine, and even engineering, will hire social scientists at much higher salaries, with more research funds and lighter teaching loads. Hence, some of the leading sociologists and political scientists, not to speak of many economists as well as promising young social scientists, appear on the rosters of professional schools. The stars in African-American and feminist studies, who are in great demand, are extremely well rewarded. One of them, over the course of a few years, moved from Yale to Cornell to Duke to Harvard. Since Harvard has a maximum salary in the liberal arts which is below Duke's, I could not imagine what they did in this situation. I was told by Cambridge friends that the added financial inducements took the form of perks.

The situation is obviously much different in less prestigious universities and the more teaching-oriented colleges. But even these have accommodated the university research culture, as David Riesman emphasized decades ago. They cannot hope to compete with the research elite, the top dozen or so, but many of them try to secure a small group with scholarly distinction to give their campus national visibility, so as to compete with others at levels similar to their own. A number of colleges have special chairs and programs to attract such faculty. Some universities deal with the problem by seeking to develop national eminence and important graduate programs in a few fields, while consciously allowing others to be "second rate."

In any case, higher education in the United States gives infinitely more recognition to research and publication than to teaching. As a system, of course, it is primarily, overwhelmingly, involved in teaching. But it does not esteem such activity. The reason is obvious. Teaching reputations do not carry off campus; research ones do, even among undergraduates. Years ago, while at Berkeley, I served as an advisor to transfer students, those who had started elsewhere. Much to my surprise, a number of them were shifting from small, private schools like Antioch, Oberlin, Reed, and Swarthmore. When I asked them why they would want to give up small classes and personal tutorials to enter the more impersonal University of California system, with its large lecture classes and reliance on teaching assistants, many answered that they preferred listening to the "great men" who wrote the books and articles, which their unknown teachers at the college interpreted. Most college students do not change schools, but I would guess that those who do are among the best.

Much of the discussion of the consequences of the research emphasis focuses on its dysfunctional effects on teaching, on the lack of contact with faculty. I would argue that this focus is wrong. Basically, students, particularly the good ones in the more elite institutions, do not learn from the faculty. The best thing about an education at Harvard and Stanford, two schools I know well, is the quality of the undergraduates. *They teach one another,* as John Henry Newman posited in 1852. They argue about the meaning of what they read, about politics and history, about experiments. What makes these and other schools great educational institutions is that they attract brilliant students, who then find it easy to locate one another. I attended City College in New York (CCNY) in its golden era. Most of its faculty, at least in the departments I took work in, were not very challenging, to put it mildly. But the student body was incredible. They were the cream of the crop of the children of first-generation Jewish immigrants, as well as from other ethnic backgrounds, who were motivated by family and group culture to go to college, one that was cheap. CCNY was called the "proletarian Harvard," and it was—it produced a large number of Ph.D.s as well as Nobel Prize winners and Academy members—not because of its faculty but, rather, its students and their impact on one another.

The research and publication reputations of the faculty are important educationally because they contribute to making colleges centers of student excellence. Their eminence also stimulates undergraduates to appreciate the worth of intellectual achievements, and interaction with research faculty in a kind of apprenticeship relationship does enhance learning. Hence, buying stars, in and of itself, is worthwhile. Good teaching, nay excellent teaching, is needed in schools whose students lack the intellectual background and motivation for learning, much more than in the most highly reputed institutions. Unfortunately, the lesser universities and colleges pay their faculty lower salaries for larger teaching loads, and they receive less status. Much too frequently, boredom overtakes them, they do not keep up with the developments in their fields, and on average they retire much earlier than scholars at the research universities.

These comments do not apply to the group of small elite colleges—Carleton, Colorado College, Grinnell, Oberlin, Swarthmore, Wellesley, Wesleyan, and the like. They have developed and maintained a reputation for teaching excellence, particularly in the humanities and "soft" social sciences. But as David Riesman has noted, even they encourage the research culture, by rewarding faculty for publication eminence more than for teaching distinction.

Beyond whatever effect distinguished research universities have on their students, the US system of higher education, by focusing on achievement and innovation, not on replication and memorization, has created excellent centers of original research, of creativity, which have trained important successor generations. The emphasis on competition, the willingness to find and spend money for research, make the US graduate institutes-schools the best in the world. It would be a tragedy for the country, and intellectualdom generally, if they lost their sources of support.

Is decline in the cards? Not if the United States and its major educational institutions remain focused on competition. Legislatures have been cutting back on the funds for higher education, including the major research centers such as Berkeley. The federal government is trying to reduce its general support, given as overhead for research. Professional schools and science departments are turning to industry for research support, a process that may reduce imaginative work. But universities still want to be number 1, or in the top 5 or 20. Administrators look for ways to reallocate budgets so as to recruit or retain eminence, and so far they have been successful. May the meritocratic research university prosper.

Adrienne Jamieson and Nelson W. Polsby   # 12

The Research University as a Setting for Undergraduate Teaching

C RITICS AND DEFENDERS ALIKE OF THE AMERICAN research university seem more or less agreed on at least one proposition: that the activities of teaching and research are caught in a zero-sum game, in which more of one inescapably means less of the other. It is easy to see how this conclusion might be reached, given the finite resources of time, energy, and money which universities and their inhabitants must manage. And so it is frequently asserted, and conceded, that the best teaching cannot occur in the presence of a strong research program. Sometimes the rhetoric is more heated, and research universities and their faculties are accused, more or less, of defaulting on what is at least an implied contract to give proper instruction to the students in their charge.

We would like to enter a mild dissent to this line of argument and encourage a slightly more complicated way of thinking about learning in a university setting. If learning at the collegiate and postgraduate level were possible only when a student encountered Mark Hopkins at the other end of a—presumably short—log, then of course whenever Mark Hopkins is off the log and doing research the student is out of luck. But consider an alternative.

Suppose that teaching is not only a classroom activity in which faculty transmit a body of existing knowledge to students. Bodies

---

Adrienne Jamieson is Assistant Director of the Institute of Governmental Studies at the University of California, Berkeley. Nelson W. Polsby is Professor of Political Science and Director of the Institute of Governmental Studies at the University of California, Berkeley.

of settled knowledge are probably well served by classroom transmission. But much of what scholars think about and talk about and argue about, especially at research universities, is not settled knowledge at all but, rather, provisional amendments to settled knowledge. The contents of these amendments, and the processes by which they come to be incorporated into an agreed-upon body of knowledge, or rejected, are subject matter that research universities are especially well equipped to teach. Thus, undergraduates in a research setting can become privileged witnesses to the inner workings of real university life—to the formulation and reformulation of problems and to the data gathering, analysis, discussion, and criticism that take place incident to the expansion of knowledge. Students in these circumstances experience and learn from university research as it is conducted day to day by being incorporated into a scholarly community as well as from lectures and reading assignments.

In chapter 7 Nannerl Keohane reminded us that the "solitary scholar is unusual nowadays," that "discovering and sharing" knowledge are parts of the same activity. In our experience the commitment of a nominal amount of research resources and existing infrastructure for the purposes of the undergraduate curriculum can build the kind of scholarly community in which undergraduates as well as graduate students and faculty can participate, one in which research and teaching are closely allied rather than at odds. Our experience in achieving this sort of community at the University of California, Berkeley, may be unique, but we doubt it. We therefore describe some of our recent activities as a way of reminding readers that a great deal more teaching is going on in the research university setting than these universities are getting credit for.

The Institute of Governmental Studies (IGS), founded in 1919, is a center for interdisciplinary research in politics, government, and public policy on the Berkeley campus. Traditionally, research units such as IGS have served at Berkeley as an intellectual home for faculty and graduate students, providing infrastructure, resources, and community helpful to their scholarly work. Faculty affiliated with IGS rely especially on the kinds of resources not always available to traditional academic departments—an in-house library with access not only to printed materials but also to on-line data bases; assistance from professional librarians, re-search staff, and graduate students; and telephones, FAXs, copi-ers, and computers within easy reach. IGS also provides a community of colleagues from a variety of disciplines, who come together explicitly because they share similar intellectual interests. At Berkeley it is not at all unusual for graduate students to participate in this community. A fair number of them have study space in the building, and this is accounted to be an important part of their socialization into academic careers.

Integrating less focused or less committed undergraduates into such a community presents a different sort of challenge. But, since IGS staff also teach undergraduates, it seemed to us natural to extend to our undergraduate students some of the opportunities our graduate students regularly enjoy. Undergraduate students enrolled in advanced courses (in our case a political science class on California politics taught by Bruce Cain and one on Congress taught by Adrienne Jamieson, with 75 to 100 students in each) were assigned ambitious research projects for course credit. These required interaction with faculty and graduate student teaching assistants and dealt with topics not well covered by existing scholarly literature—the kinds of issues we expect students to tackle in graduate seminars. In all of these projects students had to look around for unconventional sources of data and information. They learned to seek out Institute librarians, graduate students, and faculty and, just as important, to collaborate with one another in order to do the work.

Many of the same techniques were used also in a freshman seminar (15 students) taught by Nelson W. Polsby. Here we describe briefly the Congress course. During the fall 1992 semes-ter-long course on Congress, we assigned to each of the students a preselected congressional race then going on somewhere in the United States. Students were asked to describe candidate organiza-tions, strategies, and resources and to relate all these to some aspect of common knowledge about congressional elections which they learned about in lectures and reading assignments. With a few high-profile exceptions, even hotly competitive contests for House seats go largely unnoticed by the major news media. Thus, in short order the usual sources of data (daily newspapers, magazines, books) were exhausted. Students next turned to on-line data bases available through the IGS library, for example, Federal Election Commission data on campaign contributions. Additionally, IGS librarians introduced students to directories that enabled them to track down and interview campaign managers and local political reporters. For this they used IGS telephones and FAX machines. For a week or two in the middle of the semester the Institute took on the look of a newsroom at deadline, with every available phone and computer occupied and a FAX machine constantly churning out communiqués from informants around the country. This temporarily, but not fatally, disturbed the peace of the Institute. In spite of the apparent chaos, faculty and graduate students (at times grudgingly) admitted that they enjoyed the noise. And they were impressed with the results. As the students busied themselves learning a great deal individually, they were also becoming, as a group, an efficient data-gathering machine. The sheer amount of information collected by 75 students can be impressive. Collectively, their inquiries suggested for future exploration a number of leads that congressional scholars had not previously addressed.

There is no question that this approach requires a different allocation of time for faculty members and teaching assistants than traditional lectures and discussion sessions, but it is not as burdensome as we initially feared, in part because the students often taught one another. The results far exceeded our expectations. The students were engaged by the opportunities to collect information no one else had assembled and to use it to expand their knowledge. In their evaluations of the course many of them said that this was the project they were most proud of in their years in college and that being pushed and prodded to approach it as more than just another term paper assignment to be filed away for posterity "changed their lives."

In fact, the student papers in a small way have added to generally available knowledge about congressional elections. Faculty and graduate students have cited their findings in professional articles and grant proposals, and we have received requests for their papers from researchers around the country. A few modest private donations enabled us to provide some of the students who wished to pursue their research further with an opportunity in the spring semester to travel to Washington and interview the new members of Congress whose campaigns they had covered. We plan to publish reports on some of these races in a short volume on Congress for use in courses and contemplate inaugurating an undergraduate research series edited by their faculty supervisors.

Our experience suggests ways in which faculty at research universities can contribute to a reorientation of the research-versus-teaching debate. We argue that research and teaching can coalesce. The fixed resources we devote primarily to research can become assets in our teaching, not only by enriching the content of lectures but also by easing the incorporation of undergraduates into the scholarly community.

This IGS program is merely a variant of the student apprentice-ships that many of our colleagues at Berkeley and elsewhere have used with great success and to the mutual benefit of students and faculty members alike. And, of course, such relationships can develop in nearly any collegiate setting. The added advantage to the student of undertaking apprenticelike activities in the context of a research university is the proximity to models of teamwork in advanced inquiry and access to communications and data-processing equipment that typically only centers of research are likely to have on hand. Students can see for themselves that the growth of knowledge proceeds from diverse activities and influences of scholarly communities, rather than from solitary cogitation alone, and they also learn how scholarly communities go about performing these diverse services in support of the growth of knowledge.

As this educational process unfolds, we expect our students to learn not only the skills that make it possible for them to participate modestly in the creation of new knowledge but also to educate themselves to appreciate the bodies of knowledge to which they are, in a small way, contributing. By seeing the intimate connections between research and preexisting knowledge, students learn the uses of tuning their own minds to a sense of relevance and proportion. By exercising intellectual judgment, they learn to appreciate clear thinking and see how new work is given meaning through its relation to preexisting contexts. They see why intellectual standards are necessary by watching them being applied to the practical tasks of research.

The custom of harnessing research to collegiate teaching by conducting both in the same institutional setting is nowhere in the world more prevalent than in the United States. This institutional arrangement, widespread in the United States and rare elsewhere, almost certainly accounts for the very high quality of the nation's universities. We wonder if it does not also contribute far more than we realize to the high quality of collegiate instruction as well—by giving US undergraduates better access to new knowledge and exposing them to the ways new knowledge is incorporated into the intellectual life of the world in which they must make their way.

Current Criticisms of Research Universities

U NTIL RECENTLY AMERICAN RESEARCH UNIVERSITIES have been hailed as among the most successful institutions in US society, but they have not escaped the public disenchantment with American institutions and professions generally. Currently the criticisms have become more pointed, thoughtful, and informed than in the past. Nevertheless, it is difficult to separate the criticisms specific to universities, especially research universities, from those associated with more general trends in social philosophy and expectations of almost all political and economic institutions.

For example, there has been a big increase in faith in market-oriented solutions to societal problems and disillusionment with the ability of government intervention to improve the functioning of the economy or to achieve societal benefits through the political allocation of public resources. The increasing dependence of the research universities—even, or perhaps especially, the private research universities—on public funding has helped to identify them with the inefficiencies and pathologies attributed to the public sector in general and thus has made them more vulnerable to the public scrutiny and criticism that has beset all public sector institutions.[1] Increasingly, it is being asked why the services provided by universities in research and development (R&D) and graduate education should be subsidized by public funds without any visible or widely accepted method for measuring the societal

Harvey Brooks is Benjamin Peirce Professor of Technology and Public Policy, Emeritus, in the Center for Science and International Affairs at the John F. Kennedy School of Government, Harvard University.

benefits of these services, such as the way revenues and profits of private corporations are said to provide for the rest of the private sector.

At the other end of the political spectrum research universities are increasingly seen as elitist institutions that benefit mainly those sectors of society which are already benefiting preferentially from the existing socioeconomic structure. This criticism is exacerbated by the increasing population of graduate programs, especially in science and engineering, with foreign students who qualify for graduate study more successfully than US citizens from disadvantaged socioeconomic backgrounds. This perspective is further reinforced by a growing belief, not seen since the Great Depression, that science and technology are displacing the jobs of semiskilled workers, both by eliminating these jobs directly and by training scientists and engineers who are employed by our foreign competitors.

All of this is further reinforced by the federal budget deficit and by growing state and local public deficits, which are squeezing discretionary expenditures at all levels of government. This leads politicians to look much harder at all institutions that are beneficiaries of the rapidly diminishing fraction of public expenditures subject to annual appropriations and, therefore, political discretion and accountability.

The general features just outlined form the backdrop against which most of the more specific criticisms of research universities which follow will be outlined and assessed.

Criticism 1
Because universities are organized according to intellectual disciplines, they are unsuitable for addressing societal problems, and their members are accountable only to their disciplinary peers rather than to the university as an institution and its clients, the students and funders.

The organization of knowledge and research into disciplines and ever more narrow subdisciplines has been essential to rapid progress in science, yet, paradoxically, many of the most important new thrusts have come at the interfaces between previously established categories of research. The necessity for specialization is dictated by the impossibility for any one active researcher to keep track of more than a tiny portion of the technical literature at any one time. Improvement in techniques of information retrieval and storage and faster communication are countervailing trends that do enable researchers to transcend some of the boundaries of specialization, and the large number of active researchers also increases the chances that somewhere in the system disciplinary boundaries will be breached if progress is "ripe" for it.

The difficulty is that understanding the challenges of societal problems, which are used to justify public support of research, almost always requires putting together pieces of knowledge from many different disciplines that are not normally in close communication with one another in the course of curiosity-driven research. Hence, the use of science or academic scholarship to illuminate societal problems requires a different set of interconnections among experts than is required for the normal progress of science.

Universities, at least in their Arts and Sciences faculties, are organized primarily to optimize the progress and dissemination of knowledge without reference to its applications to specific societal problems. This affects the whole sociology of universities in that the reference groups for faculty members and graduate students are their disciplinary peers wherever they may be located more than their colleagues within the same institution. If a university, or indeed any research institution, attempts to take on a specific societal problem, it must usually form new coalitions of specialists, which may be only temporary for the particular problem. These coalitions differ from the organization of the university for its normal teaching and research functions and are therefore somewhat problematic. This problem has been extensively discussed in the literature.[2] In the criticism, however, it is often forgotten that universities do not consist only of their Arts and Sciences faculties. They include professional schools that are not necessarily organized by discipline but, rather, by broadly defined societal problems such as health, business management, architecture and design, the law, and various social missions of engineering. Engineering is, in fact, categorized by a mixture of technical tools and social functions. This does not mean that the professional schools are wholly exempt from the influence of the disciplinary culture of the university, which tends to have the greatest prestige and therefore influences the reward systems and communications networks of even the interdisciplinary professions—witness, for example, the basic science departments of medical schools or some of the departmental structures of engineering schools. In the period since World War II, the structure, research agenda, and teaching program of engineering schools has been heavily influenced by "applied science," which exhibits a disciplinary orientation, and has led to what is often seen as an overemphasis on the development and perfection of the tools of engineering analysis at the expense of synthesis and design and training in the social, economic, and political dimensions of engineering practice.

It is also true that one of the important phenomena of the universities in the 1980s was the rapid growth of interdisciplinary centers, sometimes assisted by government programs such as the Engineering Research Centers and Science and Technology Centers initiated by the National Science Foundation (NSF) but often organized on the initiative of the universities themselves. In the 1990s the research university is far more "interdisciplinary" than it was in the 1960s, and public perception has frequently lagged considerably behind reality (I will discuss this further under criticism 3). Despite the complaints of many of the most articulate voices of academic science, applications in the competition for funding of interdisciplinary centers started by government agencies have been, if anything, oversubscribed compared to ordinary investigator-originated project grants. Although this is doubtless in part due to the amounts of money involved, it does indicate a considerable untapped reservoir of potential university initiative in this area.[3] New interdisciplinary areas of research have originated as often in universities as in other research institutions.

Criticism 2
The present career reward system emphasizes research achievement and national reputation through publication to the increasing exclusion of teaching, especially undergraduate teaching, which is the professed mission of even the research universities and also their largest source of revenue.

This is one of the oldest complaints against the research university and one that was actually as common in the 1930s as it is today.

There is little question that it has some validity so far as the reward system is concerned, though how much it results in inferior undergraduate teaching in the research universities is much more controversial. Part of the problem arises from a public perception that research and teaching are competitive, and largely mutually exclusive, activities. This is clearly more true at the beginning undergraduate level than it is at later stages in university education. Indeed, there has been a steady trend toward more opportunities for undergraduate participation in research throughout the university system, including in many colleges that do not have graduate programs. On the other hand, there is little evidence from the market that this is turning undergraduates away from research universities. Quite the contrary.[4] The explanation given for this by critics is that undergraduates select universities on the basis of their research reputation or that of their professors because this reputation is the best assurance of a good job or admission to a preferred graduate or professional school after graduation—possibly a case of market failure due to lack of consumer information.

Another factor that is important in the teaching-versus-research controversy is the lack of consensus standards on what constitutes good teaching or what methods of assessment of teaching are valid. One change from the 1930s is that most universities now include anonymous student evaluations of their teaching in the personnel dossiers of candidates for promotion and tenure. It is less clear how much weight is given to these evaluations in the actual decisions, since many faculty committees are dubious of student popularity as an adequate index of teaching performance. Although there is also much subjectivity in the evaluation of research achievements, there is a greater consensus on standards. Mere counting of publications has fallen out of favor, especially in the leading institutions, and many promotion committees now limit the number of publications that can be submitted for evaluation, encouraging the candidates themselves to submit the best examples of their scholarship and paying more attention to evidence of the impact of the candidate's work on the overall progress of the field. In general, somewhat more weight is placed on teaching evaluations in professional schools than in Arts and Sciences, but even here an outstanding publication record almost always outweighs all but the most egregious deficiencies in teaching or "institutional citizenship."

Criticism 3
There is an inherent mismatch between the university research agenda and the "problems of society," especially the problems perceived by industry to relate to national competitiveness.

This criticism is very closely related to the one concerning dominance of the disciplinary culture and orientation, since understanding the "problems of society" almost always involves cross-disciplinary collaboration. This is a debate that goes on in industrial research and in nonacademic research institutions generally as well as in academia. Most of the technical activities of small and medium-sized firms are heavily interdisciplinary in nature, and this is also true of most of the policy-oriented research and implementation that goes on in government agencies at all levels. Only in the corporate laboratories of large, multinational corporations or large national laboratories in the public sector does disciplinary organization play an important role. It is only in large organizations with a multiplicity of product lines or a diverse range of policy issues to deal with that disciplinary-type organizations are found and that the luxury of disciplinary specialization is regarded as affordable. Even in such organizations there has recently been a significant decline in the importance of and resources devoted to corporate research, accompanied by a shift of technical resources to product divisions or business segments in the private sector.

One could argue, as I have elsewhere,[5] that NSF and academic research correspond roughly on the national scene to corporate research in large corporations. Indeed, the NSF research budget and the total research conducted by academic performers (excluding clinical research in medical schools and crop-oriented research in agricultural schools) constitute roughly the same percentage of total national R&D expenditures (private and public) as does the corporate research in a large multidivisional, multinational corporation. Thus, the present falling from favor of curiosity-driven, investigator-originated research in federal science policy, especially in the Congress, reflects the same change of opinion climate which is occurring in the corporate world.

Some of the recent criticisms of corporate research on isolated campuses in idyllic surroundings, which grew up in the first two decades after World War II, are probably justified,[6] and similar criticisms are applicable to attitudes common in academic research in the 1960s, when it was expanding very rapidly and an unusually large fraction of the Ph.D.s turned out were being recycled into faculty positions in an expanding system of graduate education. During that period the communications between academia and industry broke down, except to some extent in the fields of defense, space, atomic energy, and health, in which federal funding was dominant. The majority of support for research in engineering, for example, with the exception of chemical and civil, was coming from the defense-oriented agencies (Department of Defense [DoD], Atomic Energy Commission [AEC], and National Aeronautics and Space Administration [NASA]), and there was a falling off of interactions between academic and industrial researchers except in these fields also supported in industry by the same federal agencies.

A good deal of the public and political perception of the situation, however, lags behind what has actually been taking place in universities during the decade of the 1980s. There has been a rapid growth in both the number and funding of university-based research centers with close ties to industry (UIRCs) not confined to the traditional areas of government responsibility.[7] Such centers were estimated to number 1,058 in 1990, with aggregate expenditures of nearly $4.3 billion, of which 66.2 percent was devoted to R&D—41 percent basic research, 43.2 percent applied research, and 15.8 percent development. The rest consists largely of training and extension activities. Nearly 60 percent of these centers have been founded since 1980.

Wesley Cohen, Richard Florida, and W. Richard Goe estimate that 12,000 faculty members participate in such centers, and almost 15 percent of all the doctoral-level scientists and engineers (S&E) involved in academic R&D are affiliated with these UIRCs as well as 4 percent of all graduate students. About 8 percent of all S&E Ph.D.s are generated through these centers. More than 16,000 graduate students and 9,000 undergraduates have some connection with these centers each year nationwide, and their subject interests are spread over many fields of potentially applicable science.[8] Sources of financial support for UIRCs as a whole were: 34.1 percent federal, 12.3 percent state, 30.7 percent industry, and 18.0 percent universities themselves. This is to be compared with 57.8 percent federal support for academic R&D as a whole in the same year. Industrial contributions to UIRC budgets constituted 12.3 percent of all industrial R&D expenditures in the United States, and UIRCs accounted for 74 percent of all industrial support for academic R&D. Despite this level of industrial participation, it appears that 72.4 percent of all UIRCs were established at the initiative of academic institutions or personnel, not industry, at least as reported by the center directors to whom the survey questionnaire was directed.

The average number of patents granted to UIRCs per million dollars of R&D expenditure was about half that for industrial R&D in general and considerably greater than that for academic R&D as a whole. The amount of patenting, however, varied a great deal with the general orientation and sources of funding of the centers, with the 40 percent of centers that were "industrially led" (i.e., with industry being their largest single source of funding) generating about three times as many patents per million dollars of R&D expenditure as those that were "federally led."

In short, the 1980s saw something of a revolution in the interaction between universities and industry in a broad range of technical fields of potential industrial interest. Although this blunts some of the traditional criticism of academic research, mainly from conservative critics, as being too divorced from the needs of the economy, it has attracted increasing criticism from the Left as being too close to industry and thus eroding the independence and objectivity of the academic enterprise. (This criticism will be taken up under criticism 8.) Whichever criticism is the more serious, it is clear that much further study remains to be done on just how UIRCs operate, how far and in what ways their "culture" differs from that in the rest of the academic R&D enterprise, and what their contribution is or can be to the improvement of national economic performance and the solution of national societal problems.

Criticism 4
Universities fail to take advantage of modern information technology and cognitive psychology in the design of teaching strategies, leading to a system that is unnecessarily intensive in the use of expensive labor with inadequate measures of value delivered in the form of student learning.

Ever since the 1960s futurologists have been predicting a revolution in educational techniques driven by advances in information technology.[9] But this revolution has failed to live up to expectations, except possibly in the field of military training for the operation of high-tech weaponry and in certain areas critical to public safety such as aircraft navigation and air traffic control. The general structure of university teaching has changed relatively little. Although there has been some shift toward more interactive teaching methods with less exclusive reliance on the lecture method, this has been far from revolutionary, and teaching has remained largely a craft, learned by on-the-job experience, with little input from what has been fundamental research on the learning process and the use of new technology only at the margins. The ratio of senior teachers to students taught has changed very little in three decades, and teaching, particularly at the college level, remains a highly labor-intensive activity. There are wide differences of opinion about the potential of technology for either improving the effectiveness of teaching or reducing the labor intensity of the educational process, especially at the more advanced levels, in which the content and organization of knowledge are constantly changing as a result of the growing volume of research findings in almost all fields, but especially in the natural and social sciences and engineering.

There is still little consensus as to whether the failure to exploit technology is the result of the inadequacies of the technology available and its cost and lack of user-friendliness or whether it is due to the inherent conservatism of educators, partly motivated by the self-protection of a craft guild, not dissimilar to that which has occurred with other craft-oriented occupations such as newspaper publishing.[10] In the latter case the economic advantages of the new technology eventually carried the day, making newspaper production much less labor intensive after a bitter struggle between the organized craft unions and the publishers.

A part of the problem may go back to the lack of agreement on the goals of education and on how its effectiveness can be measured and compared in widely different settings (the same issue that I discussed under criticism 2). Many observers have pointed to how little R&D is devoted to the scientific understanding and improvement of the teaching and learning processes themselves, especially in connection with teaching at the university level. Even where there is considerable individual experimentation by practitioners, there is very little systematic dissemination of successful models or even agreement on what models are successful.[11]

There has probably been more thinking in this area in connection with professional education, for which the goal of effective professional delivery of societal services can be most sharply defined. It is here that the trade-off between the disciplinary organization of the knowledge base and the problem-oriented organization of service delivery in practice has emerged most clearly and where some progress has been made in developing new technology-based tools for coupling the research literature with the demands of practice other than by the classic textbook. This debate has been engaged especially strongly in the field of medical education.[12] In this field, it is pointed out, too much of practice is dependent on totally unrealistic expectations about what an individual practitioner can retain in memory. To quote Lawrence Weed and his colleagues, "Our confidence in our innate human capacity to make judgments as sound and reliable as our collective knowledge theoretically allows is simply unsupported by over 30 years of intensive research in clinical and cognitive psychology."[13] What is required is new computer tools, not to replace memory but to guide the practitioner through an interactive process into the research literature—a process that exploits the superior storage capabilities of the machine in combination with the superior associative and inference capabilities of the human brain. As Herbert Simon has said, "The capacity of the human mind for formulating and solving complex problems is very small compared with the size of the problems whose solution is required for objectively rational behavior in the real world—or even for a reasonable approximation of such objective rationality."[14]

Criticism 5
The tendency of universities is to try to do too many things, to be all things to all people, and to respond to every potential constituency.

This problem was first brought to prominence by Clark Kerr in the 1960s with his famous book on "the multiversity."[15] There are really two different aspects of this problem. One is the tendency of universities to respond to external pressures or funding opportunities with little reference to any coherent plan for or concept of their individual comparative advantages. This includes both the establishment of new interdisciplinary teaching and research programs as well as the delivery of new services to external constituencies, such as manufacturing extension services[16] or the operation of various social service programs, and the tendency to cling to declining fields of knowledge or instruction, as described by Donald Kennedy in this volume. In some ways this criticism is directly contradictory to the first and third criticisms herein, in that it accuses the universities of being too ready to be responsive to external constituencies, whereas the first and third critiques posit a lack of responsiveness and an adherence to an internal agenda. The real basis of criticism, however, articulated by both Kennedy and Stephen Stigler in this volume, is their readiness to take on new tasks and preserve existing programs of declining importance without adequate consideration of the overall opportunity costs to whatever they claim to be their central mission. The problem is compounded by the tendency of the lesser-ranked institutions to imitate the leaders without the resources and infrastructure to do it well, often at the expense of previously socially useful but less prestigious functions that they were fulfilling. The result is too many institutions doing too many things less than adequately, with competition leading to imitation rather than desirable institutional differentiation and division of labor.

This complaint about universities is by no means new. Around 1947 Robert Hutchins, in his last term as chancellor of the University of Chicago, wrote that the university is "peculiarly a prey of centrifugal forces, which are always driving it apart": "this is because no end has yet been discovered and accepted by the American university sufficiently clearly to make sense of its activities, to establish a standard for criticizing them, and to unify those who are carrying them on." Hutchins apparently believed that this was primarily an internal problem—a problem of leadership—arguing that "the administrator's responsibility is to get others to join him in the search for the end and to try to get all constituents to see and accept it when it has been found."[17] In an increasingly pluralistic and ideologically fragmented society, and with institutions increasingly dependent on external resources of support for their activities, this seems to be an impossible task. In this sense the universities are simply mirrors of the surrounding society; the prospects for the kind of leadership which Hutchins envisioned in the late 1940s appear far dimmer today than they did in his time, since the number and variety of constituencies that have to be convinced or placated are far larger than they were then, and the control of necessary resources far more decentralized and diverse.

Several of the authors in this volume suggest that the present perceived crisis of university resources may have beneficial aspects by increasing the pressures both for specialization by individual institutions and cooperation among institutions to design first-rate programs, which none could do well alone. This has, of course, happened in many expensive fields of research such as high-energy physics, radio and optical astronomy, and, increasingly, in molecular biology and the environmental sciences. It is more difficult to achieve, however, in respect to the educational mission of the university, which is still more dependent on geographical proximity than is research, although here is an area in which modern information technology could begin to provide more support for collaborative alliances than was possible in the past. But, by and large, not much has happened yet, and what has happened has tended to be centered in institutions that are more specialized in their goals than universities.

Criticism 6
A system of tenure in place in the higher ranks of the
professoriate erodes accountability, protects mediocrity, and
provides too few incentives for best effort.

Hardly any aspect of universities is more severely criticized or less well understood outside the universities themselves than the system of tenure. This has become rapidly more problematical as the security and permanence of employment in the private sector have eroded during the 1980s. The relative portability of many fringe benefits within the university system through the Teachers Insurance and Annuity Association (TIAA) has also been an aspect of the system which has benefited the security of the majority of university employees even when they do not enjoy the tenure in single institutions which is enjoyed by full professors. Such mobility is much less apparent in periods of contracting resources, however, when tenure becomes a major factor of inflexibility in undertaking new initiatives with new people.

The "tenure problem" has been much exacerbated by new federal laws on age discrimination in employment, which come into full effect in universities for the first time in 1994. Nobody knows how this problem is going to play itself out in the end. There is considerable apprehension that it will close off opportunities for young people in the academic system and reduce new intellectual initiatives and innovative thinking, unless incentives can be devised that are not too costly to make it attractive to professors to elect retirement near the age of 70. Another possible measure may be the experimental replacement of tenure by some form of finite-term renewable contract, although it may be difficult in practice to keep this from being vulnerable to charges of age discrimination in its implementation. This practice is already appearing in some professional schools in professions in which nonacademic employment opportunities are relatively plentiful. Some very high-quality nonacademic research institutions dependent on "soft money" have long had a system of modified tenure subject to availability of funding which has worked quite effectively through the building up of reserves to carry people through temporary lapses in external funding. Yet if the research agendas of the funding agencies in the future consist of a larger proportion of "strategic research" determined by the sponsor rather than the performer, the risks of dependence on soft money may rise to such an extent that the use of modified tenure in such laboratories may no longer be viable, requiring greater reserves than can realistically be raised.

Tenure was originally instituted to protect freedom of thought and speech in academia and thereby to insure the independence as well as loyalty to an ideal of objective truth of the professoriate. It grew up in times when some politicians and conservative university trustees were trying to dismiss faculty who had unorthodox and unwelcome ideas and opinions, particularly in economics and political science. Tenure thus represented a useful practical codification of the concept of academic freedom during the turmoil of the 1930s and, later, during the McCarthy period of the 1950s. Until quite recently, academic freedom seemed to have become sufficiently widely accepted so that public attention turned more to the inflexibilities the tenure system was believed to impose on the academic system and less on the protection of academic freedom which it afforded. Yet with the politicization of some academic disciplines within the universities (as described by Cole, Searle, and Smelser in this volume), the need for tenure, especially among Arts and Sciences faculty, appears to have reemerged as an issue; protection is now required less from external pressures and more from students increasingly willing to use coercive tactics to silence faculty and other academics who express opinions with which they disagree—opinions often labeled unilaterally by the students as racist or ethnocentric or otherwise "politically incorrect."

More fundamentally, the integrity of the notion of tenure depends on general acceptance of the existence of objective standards of intellectual competence and integrity which can be applied independent of a person's political views or preferences. In the view of the "multiculturalists," all intellectual standards are culture based and embody, consciously or unconsciously, a bias in favor of the dominant, or "hegemonic," culture (usually defined as white, male, and middle class). Currently, these issues are more pressing in the humanities and social sciences (in that order) but are showing some signs of emerging even in the natural sciences, in which scientific conclusions about nature are seen as having "downstream" social consequences that disadvantage certain groups or have other distributional implications that make them unacceptable. Examples occur in risk analysis and the role of genetic factors in the susceptibility to disease, cognitive capacities, or behavioral disorders. These issues seem destined to become more pressing as the natural sciences uncover more connections between phenomena at the molecular level and phenomena at the organismic, behavioral, or ecosystem level. The integrity of the tenure system is thus intimately related to the question of the existence of "forbidden" knowledge—knowledge that societies should reject not because it is "untrue" but, rather, because its putative downstream social implications are unacceptable to certain social groups.

Criticism 7
Unbusinesslike practices in the nonintellectual part of the
operation are not subject to market discipline and would and
could not be tolerated in a business required to show a profit.

When the project grant system of supporting research first began, shortly after World War II, it accounted for a relatively small proportion of the costs of research performed by universities. In many cases it was treated as a supplement to what the universities would be doing anyway with internal or private resources, and there was at first considerable variation in the payment of indirect costs, depending in part on whether the research was investigator or sponsor originated. The infrastructure did not have to be much expanded to accommodate the sponsored research. As federal support became a larger and larger fraction of the research budgets of universities, however, the infrastructure had to be expanded, and the universities became more and more dependent on indirect cost payments to support the infrastructure not associated directly with any particular research project but necessary to administer the volume of research which was being performed, even though the separation between what pertained specifically to the research and what pertained to other functions and missions of the university could only be determined by rather arbitrary guidelines and rules of thumb for cost allocation. The payment of the full indirect costs of government-funded research became more and more necessary to the viability of the whole academic enterprise. The workability of the system became more and more dependent on mutual trust between the administrative personnel in the universities and the government agencies that funded their research and, thus, politically vulnerable to infrequent but egregious examples (or alleged examples) of abuse of that trust. Regulations were progressively added to prevent the possibility of each such abuse in the future, with little consideration of their side effects. These regulations became irksome to faculty, who at the same time saw the indirect cost payment taken from their grant budgets, as a tax on their research funds whose benefits to their research were hard to explain. Thus, faculty members were inclined to side against (or at least not actively defend) their own university administrations when politicians or other outsiders questioned the accounting of and magnitude of indirect costs that varied widely among universities for more or less arcane reasons that were hard to explain except to accounting experts. This situation was exacerbated by the fact that much of the money in various categories of the university budget was not fungible because it had come to the university for a designated and restricted purpose, whether from the government or other external donors. It was thus understandable that universities came to be regarded as unbusinesslike.

If, however, this leads to a permanent cap on indirect cost rates, it will force the universities to share a larger fraction of the costs of federal research at a time when the proportion of academic research support already carried by federal sources has shrunk from about 75 percent three decades ago to about 57 percent today. This could well have adverse effects on the educational functions of universities, producing the very opposite effect to rectifying what is already seen as an imbalance, since university subsidization of the indirect costs of federal research can only come at the expense of other nonresearch functions of the academic system.

Criticism 8
Universities tend to adopt more and more of an industry
culture, with their research agenda increasingly driven by
industry and a growing attention to intellectual property
considerations and withholding of the diffusion of new
discoveries for proprietary reasons.

This criticism is essentially the left-wing counterpart of criticism 3. Whereas the increasing movement of public and political opinion toward favoring reliance on market-oriented mechanisms for resource allocation and social discipline has largely prompted criticism of universities for the lack of relevance of their research agendas to the needs of industry and the market, this criticism suggests that universities have already moved much too far toward adopting the culture of the marketplace and expresses the fear that business interests and values and rent-seeking behavior are undermining the distinctive academic culture and its potential contribution to national well-being and social progress, a culture in which the diffusion of knowledge without inhibition was the hallmark.[18]

This erosion commenced in the late 1970s, it is said, with the alteration of the patent policies of the National Institutes of Health (NIH), permitting universities and small companies with NIH support to take out patents resulting from NIH-supported research and to license them to commercial companies, including biotechnology startups. The patent policy of federal agencies has previously differed from agency to agency, with DoD permitting patents and licensing thereof, with a reservation for government end-use, while the Department of Energy and NASA generally required assignment of all patents to the government. Congressional legislation in 1980 and 1984 mandated a uniform patent policy pertaining to all federal agencies, which more or less embodied the new NIH principles, and this led universities to establish much more active policies and special offices to pursue patenting and licensing of inventions arising out of all their research, including that which was federally sponsored.

At the same time, mostly in the 1980s, several federal agencies, including the NSF, established specific programs to encourage collaboration between universities and industry with partial funding by government. The net result of both the changes in patent regulations and federal funding of cooperative projects between universities and industry was the rather rapid growth of university-industry research centers (UIRCs), described in the discussion of criticism 3, and a generally much more receptive attitude toward university-industry cooperation throughout the whole academic research enterprise, strongly encouraged by university administrations because of its potential for new revenue resources, both directly and through royalties.

This trend was led by the rapid growth of the nascent biotechnology industry, largely based on academic discoveries, but spread to many other areas, particularly in solid-state electronics and computer engineering and software. At the same time there was a great deal of variation in the aggressiveness with which different institutions embraced the new orientation and the amount of industrial support they received.[19]

This interest in commercialization of academic research in the 1980s was paralleled by the flurry of both university and government interest in university research and even service delivery related to the solution of societal problems which occurred during the period 1968–1976, with the Great Society programs begun in the Johnson administration, but continued through much of the Nixon and Ford administrations. This was the period of the Research Applied to National Needs (RANN) program of the NSF and the National Institute of Education in the Office of Education, which funded a number of educational research centers in universities aimed at fostering both research and the delivery of experimental educational services or "demonstration programs" (the equivalent of development in the natural sciences). At that time there was considerable questioning whether this was an appropriate role for universities or whether it embroiled them too much in politically controversial areas with strong ideological overtones, compromising their role as disinterested critics of society as well as their fundamental scholarly mission.

In 1970, to deal with these concerns, I proposed in congressional testimony the notion of "buffer institutions."[20] My feeling was that the career lines and reward structures in academia were so different from those required in the effective delivery of social services and "demonstrations" that they would create severe internal strains within the university between parts that differed in their degree of engagement in external service activities, if they were allowed to expand too rapidly. Yet there were also arguments that, if research were to tackle "real-world" societal problems, the researchers would have to have closer contact with deliverers of services whose design should thus be informed by the findings of rigorous academic research. Thus, my proposal was to form intermediary institutions that would actually deliver services on a pilot scale but would have a closer day-to-day relationship with academic researchers than is usually the case for such service deliverers. Rather than form free-standing units within the university itself, I suggested that there be administratively separate institutions with their own career structures and independent governance, but with much more opportunity for interaction and short-term personnel exchanges with the university. An important function of these buffer institutions would be to give both students and faculty easier opportunities for contact with the real world, thereby enabling them to orient their research better to take into account the constraints imposed by implementation but still allowing them to think more boldly and imaginatively than they could if they had the actual responsibility for implementation.

The closest parallel for such buffer institutions at present is probably the teaching hospitals allied with university medical schools. Although such hospitals are not without their problems, they do provide a setting in which medical students and post-graduate interns can learn how to apply their academic knowledge in a realistic setting with real clients. This is something that is generally missing in most other science and engineering fields of near-term applicability and even, for the most part, in the social sciences. The only exception may be agriculture.

Today political and public concern focuses much more on the transition between academic research and industrial operations, but many of the same considerations apply, with the additional complication of proprietary knowledge and trade secrets. Many people consider these elements inappropriate within the university itself because they violate the academic tradition of openness and free criticism.

Of course, the UIRCs studied by Cohen, Florida, and Goe[21] perform many of the functions of buffer institutions, except that they are an integral part of the university and, in practice, limit themselves to applied research, with relatively little development or design, let alone pilot manufacturing operations or marketing or service delivery to clients. There is already growing concern about the degree to which the UIRCs are violating academic norms by necessitating institutional agreements to protect proprietary information or to withhold participation from foreign nationals. The fear is that, if UIRCs were to become much more important than they are now, as many people are proposing, and if they were to move further toward the market, as they might be under pressure to do, there could result a kind of "tipping" phenomenon that would change the whole culture of the university. At the same time, to the extent that they are forced to limit themselves to applied research in order to conform to university norms, they might not create the possibility of close interaction with further downstream operations, which is desirable. The use of buffer institutions would transfer the responsibility for enforcing proprietary rights to a separate organization, which could deal individually with only those who actually participate in its operations. In my view there is a real difference between institutional responsibility in this regard and individual responsibility, which is already handled fairly successfully in consultancies between individual students and faculty members, acting in a part-time individual consulting capacity, and private companies. The buffer institution proposal insures that the external and internal roles of individuals are kept separate while permitting more extensive contact of faculty and students with the world of work outside the university. There would, of course, be many problems to be worked out and much experimentation to be done, but I believe the buffer institution idea would provide a better starting point for dealing with the problems than the present trend toward forming UIRCs internal to the university structure and governance.

ENDNOTES

[1]For a discussion of this secular swing in the climate of opinion, see Harvey Brooks, "Seeking Equity and Efficiency: Public and Private Roles," in Harvey Brooks, Lance Liebman, and Corinne Schelling, eds., *Public-Private Partnership* (Cambridge, Mass.: Ballinger, 1984), 3–29.

²Cf., for example, Daniel Alpert, "Performance and Paralysis: The Organizational Context of the American Research University," *Journal of Higher Education* 56 (3) (May/June 1985): 241–81; David Easton, "The Division, Integration and Transfer of Knowledge," in David Easton and Corinne Schelling, eds., *Divided Knowledge: Across Disciplines, across Cultures*, published for the American Academy of Arts and Sciences (Newbury Park, Calif.: Sage Publications, 1991).

³See also discussion under criticisms 3 and 9 below.

⁴Kenneth Prewitt, "America's Research Universities under Public Scrutiny," in this volume.

⁵Harvey Brooks, "Can Science Be Planned?" *Problems of Science Policy: Seminar at Jouy-en-Josas on Science Policy* (Paris: OECD, 1967).

⁶Richard Florida and Martin Kenney, *The Breakthrough Illusion: Corporate America's Failure to Move from Innovation to Mass Production* (New York: Basic Books, 1990); Harvey Brooks, "Innovation and Competitiveness," in *The Technology Race: Can the U.S. Win?* Proceedings of the J. Herbert Hollomon Memorial Symposium, Center for Technology, Policy and Industrial Development, MIT, 1991.

⁷Wesley Cohen, Richard Florida, and W. Richard Goe, *University-Industry Research Centers in the United States: A Report to the Ford Foundation*, Center for Economic Development, Carnegie-Mellon University, June 1992. The figures quoted in the text are based on a later version of this report, which was kindly provided to the author in draft form by Professor Florida (Wesley Cohen, Richard Florida, and W. Richard Goe, "University-Industry Research Centers in the United States," Center for Economic Development, Carnegie-Mellon University, February 1994). Professor Florida used this version as the basis for a presentation at a meeting of the American Association for the Advancement of Science (AAAS), "The Financing of Research Centers," San Francisco, 22 February 1994.

⁸Harvey Brooks, "Research Universities and the Social Contract for Science," in Lewis M. Branscomb, ed., *Empowering Technology: Implementing a U.S. Strategy* (Cambridge, Mass.: MIT Press, 1993).

⁹Cf. A. G. Oettinger, *Run, Computer, Run* (Cambridge, Mass.: Harvard University Press, 1969).

¹⁰Anthony Smith, *Good Bye Gutenberg: The Newspaper Revolution of the 1980s* (New York: Oxford University Press, 1980).

¹¹Harvey Brooks, "Scientific Literacy and the Future Labour Force," in Torsten Husen and John P. Reeves, eds. *Issues in Science Education: Science Competence in a Social and Ecological Context* (Oxford: Pergamon Press, 1991).

¹²Lawrence L. Weed et al., *Knowledge Coupling: New Premises and New Tools for Medical Care and Education* (New York: Springer-Verlag, 1991); see also Harvey Brooks, "The Relationship between Science and Technology," *Research Policy* (forthcoming).

¹³Weed et al., *Knowledge Coupling*, xvi.

[14]Herbert Simon, *The Sciences of the Artificial*, 2d ed. (Cambridge, Mass.: MIT Press, 1981).

[15]Clark Kerr, *The Uses of the University* (Cambridge, Mass.: Harvard University Press, 1963).

[16]Cf., for example, Gene R. Simons, "Industrial Extension and Innovation," in Branscomb, *Empowering Technology*.

[17]Robert M. Hutchins, "The Administrator," in Robert B. Heywood, ed., *The Works of the Mind* (Chicago: University of Chicago Press, 1947). I am indebted to Professor S. B. Lundstedt of Ohio State University for calling my attention to this reference.

[18]Partha Dasgupta and Paul A. David, *Towards a New Economics of Science*, CEPR Publication no. 320, Center for Economic Policy Research, Stanford University, October 1992.

[19]For a discussion, see Harvey Brooks, "University-Industry Cooperation as Industrial Strategy," in S. B. Lundstedt and T. H. Moss, eds., *Managing Innovation and Change* (Dordrecht, Neth.: Kluwer Academic Publishers, 1989, for the International Institute for Applied Systems Analysis [IIASA]).

[20]Harvey Brooks, testimony in Hearings before the Subcommittee on Science and Astronautics, US House of Representatives, 91st Cong., 2d sess. no. 23, *National Science Policy*, 136–54 (Washington, D.C.: Government Printing Office, 1970).

[21]Cohen, Florida, and Goe, *University-Industry Research Centers*; Brooks, testimony.

William C. Richardson

14

The Appropriate Scale of the Health Sciences Enterprise

$\mathbf{A}$ BRAHAM LINCOLN WAS ONCE ASKED how long a man's legs should be. "Long enough to reach the ground," he said. It is possible to answer the question posed by the title of this essay in a similarly straightforward way. The appropriate scale of the health sciences enterprise in the American research university is, in fact, substantially defined by the marketplace. It is opportunity driven. The appropriate scale is large enough to satisfy the legitimate demands and requirements of education, scientific research, and clinical practice, but not so large as to deform the overall mission and character of the academic institution within which the health sciences center forms one piece of the whole. In other words, the appropriate scale of the health sciences enterprise is big enough to do all of the jobs we have assigned to it, but at a price we are willing to pay.

The price, in part, is the explicit recognition that the rest of the university may see health sciences schools as disregarding or avoiding various academic traditions and university procedures. For example, such a high proportion of medical school revenue derives from the specific research and clinical activities of members of the faculty, and in public universities often from special appropriations, that independence is strongly encouraged. Furthermore, from 1960 to 1990, total US medical school revenues grew at a rate that was approximately twice that of total revenues of all US institutions of higher education.[1] The health sciences center has often been seen as both a political and a financial threat to other university interests.

William C. Richardson is President of The Johns Hopkins University.

Saying that the health sciences should be big enough to carry out its mission, of course, is to fall quickly into tautology, or at least into banality. Needs are infinite and resources are scarce. The first requirement of governance is to choose. The anxieties of many in the academic community only a few short years ago — that the rapid growth of academic health centers would eclipse the traditional academic enterprise in the "core" schools of arts and sciences— are quickly being overtaken by new political and economic realities. If the threat was once uncontrolled growth, it is now underfunded and ill-planned contraction. The solution, if any is to be found, will inevitably lie in the forging of new relations between academic health centers and other academic divisions, including most especially those divisions that have traditionally felt themselves to be engaged in competition for scarce resources with the academic health centers. At the same time, various universities will find themselves coalescing in new forms of collaboration. As in an evolving star, the forces of retrenchment will drive intense new interactions among all the constituent parts of the system.

To some degree, this will be a good thing. It is already compelling greater self-analysis, greater honesty about efficiency, effectiveness, and accountability, and greater creativity in the search for synergies than would be the case in flusher times. There is a point of slow-down, however, beyond which the pain will outweigh any conceivable gain. One of the primary tasks of university leadership for the remainder of the 1990s will be to continue to remind lawmakers and policymakers of the unexcelled contributions that the academic health centers have made. The academic health centers have been pacesetters in biomedical research, in the introduction of cutting-edge technologies and therapies, and— often by virtue of their locations—in the treatment of the indigent.

It is important to recognize the breadth of the resources that the modern research university brings to bear on this array of issues and problems. The school of medicine is at the core of the academic health center, but all of the health professions—nursing, public health, allied health, pharmacy, and dentistry—are increasingly seen (as they should be) to provide crucial contributions to the public's health. Beyond the health professions, though, the university's significant resources include the biological sciences, the information sciences, engineering and the physical sciences as they bear on biomedical research, along with the social and behavioral sciences and the humanities. In an era when death with dignity vies with abortion protests for headline space, the ethicist—housed in a department of philosophy in a school of arts and sciences—may seem no more marginal to the health sciences enterprise than does, say, the organic chemist or the pathologist. The same might be said of the sociologist or the communications theorist who can offer important insights into community-based illness prevention or health promotion campaigns. As the health sciences enterprise comes to be more broadly and more appropriately understood, various parts of the research university will evolve into new, more interesting, and more appropriate relations with each other. The scaling of the health sciences enterprise to the university will be a reciprocal process that may help us to recapture almost forgotten collegial and intellectual values.

One impediment to these developments is the geographic separation of academic health centers from other parts of the university: in some instances the distance may be 100 or more miles, in others, a few blocks. Until recently there have been few incentives for faculty or students to bridge these barriers, and, of course, in the extreme cases there is no practical solution, although digital communications and processing may finally overcome some of the impediments in the years ahead. Nevertheless, where distance permits, there will likely be a greater sense of unity and greater collaboration within the university.

This process must be allowed to occur on a humane and constructive time scale, and not be precipitated by an abrupt withdrawal of massive amounts of federal funds from the health sciences centers or from the research universities themselves. Currently, this threat remains very real and takes a variety of forms. Federal cutbacks of any significant size will likely prove very traumatic, in that mediocrity in our major institutions has become increasingly scarce.[2] American universities, since the 1970s and in response to a variety of pressures as well as opportunities, have divested themselves of many obsolete programs and acted to create new ones in reaction to scientific and intellectual advances.

But the magnitude of the federal deficit and the clear determination in Washington to cap health-care costs as an aggregate percentage of the GNP will make this a difficult case to make for the rest of the decade. A pronounced slowdown in federal research dollars and reimbursements for clinical practice are part of general retrenchment, but also are a reflection of failures to address societal concerns.

The consequences for biomedical research may be profound. Revolutionary advances in molecular biology and genetics are beginning to generate fundamental insights into the origins of various cancers and many other killing and crippling diseases such as Alzheimer's, muscular dystrophy, and cystic fibrosis. This extremely expensive work will require at least several more generations of science to press to successful understanding, much less successful preventive and therapeutic measures. At this immensely tantalizing moment in the history of the life sciences, the resources that the nation is willing to commit to basic health research seem in doubt. Funding from the National Institutes of Health (NIH) for the 1993 fiscal year failed to keep pace with the biomedical research inflation rate. As a consequence, the NIH (together with three new institutes) will fund the lowest number of new grants in a decade.

The prospect of a national health-care system based on managed care, price competition, and with some sort of global cap on spending may well slow what has become a vitally important flow of funds for medical schools—revenue from clinical practice plans.

Far from what might be considered the received view—within much of academia as well as without—it is possible to argue that the nation spends too little, not too much, on biomedical research. Senior vice president and provost for health affairs at the University of Cincinnati Medical Center Donald C. Harrison, for instance, has pointed out that the percentage of the nation's health-care expenditures devoted to research has declined from nearly 5 percent in the 1960s to 3.3 percent in 1990. "In contrast," he writes, "high technology industries that attempt to stay on the cutting edge typically spend from 6 to 12 percent of their total expenditures on research and development."[3]

Granted that it seems an uphill battle in the current budgetary climate, administrators and scientists at the nation's universities must be prepared to state their case for more research dollars. At the least, they should continue to press for an NIH budget that keeps pace in real terms with the biomedical research inflation rate. Members of Congress and officials at the federal research agencies should be reminded continually of what lies so close to being within our grasp —for instance, genetic testing that can identify incipient cases of colon cancer, the nation's second-leading cancer killer, before there are any visible tumors. Where genetic screening and testing are so close at hand, genetic therapy cannot be far behind. It would be very difficult to quantify the opportunities lost in failing to prosecute fully advantages such as this.

This line of reasoning may be applied to the current national debate over health-care costs. It is widely repeated until it has reached the status of incontrovertible myth that spending 14 percent of the nation's GNP on health care is too much. It would be refreshing to hear someone ask: Why? Is $940 billion a year too much to pay for advanced imaging technologies that avert thousands of surgeries a year; for artificial knees and hips that add countless years of productivity and improved quality of life; for innovative (and expensive) medicines such as taxol that offer hope to victims of breast cancer? It is not at all clear that the public will willingly forgo any of these therapies and technologies, or hundreds of others I have not mentioned, in order to reduce the national expenditure by a percentage point or two.

The skewing of the distribution of medical costs in the system has always reduced the visibility of health-care expenditure and, thereby, lessened the political pressure for cost containment. In any one year, 5 percent of the families in the country account for 50 percent of the medical expenditures. In addition, there is a high degree of diffusion by payment source: slightly more than 33 percent is paid by the patient, and the remainder is divided among the federal government, the state and local governments, charity and private industry, and private health insurance.[4]

The claim that health-care spending is too high in this country may largely reflect other criticisms of the system—the unequal degree of access; the total lack of insurance for approximately thirty-five million Americans; inefficient organization of health-care resources coupled with a lack of economic or other regulation; anomalies in prevailing insurance practices such as the refusal to cover preexisting conditions; and the extremely well-publicized costs of some pharmaceutical products which have been developed in part through federal support. There is a line of response to all of this which is highly analogous to that made by Harold T. Shapiro, president of Princeton University, in a recent paper in which he analyzed the claim that the costs of higher education are too high. He notes that there are at least five separable meanings to this assertion that education costs too much: *1)* the prices of inputs (salaries, books, etc.) are too high; *2)* there is waste and inefficiency in the use of resources; *3)* universities' assets are not being deployed toward the right ends; *4)* the "opportunity costs" of higher education are too great as compared with other societal needs; and *5)* the costs of education are not being allocated properly—students and their families are having to bear too much of the costs as opposed to other patrons and users of higher education.[5] All of these observations find direct analogues in the argument over health-care costs, and even more particularly, in the discussion over the allocation of resources to the academic health sciences center.

Like colleges and universities, academic health centers have, in many ways, wound up being targets for criticism because of forces that they experience but over which they have little control. In them critics find ready targets for a frustration that reflects many more intractable problems, such as the cost of inputs, the cost of ever more sophisticated technology, and problems of unequal financial access to the system. And yet, like colleges and universities, academic health centers are indispensable in our society and in our economy. They are indispensable both for research and for education and training. Furthermore, they perform a remarkable degree of unrecognized health services delivery to the poor, for which they have always been insufficiently remunerated.

Overall, the nation's academic health centers provide remarkable amounts of uncompensated care. The 287 Association of American Medical Colleges (AAMC) Council of Teaching Hospitals (COTH) members, representing the largest teaching hospitals in the United States, constitute 6 percent of all hospitals but 26 percent of gross patient revenue. At the same time, the COTH members absorb 28 percent of all medical bad debt expense and 50 percent of all charity care.[6]

Yet, the system is changing more rapidly than ever. If we look back in recent history, the most similar period in terms of stress and uncertainty may have been that immediately following the Johnson landslide victory of 1964, when development of Medicare and Medicaid funding was received with tremendous apprehension by the academic community. As events proved, the new system injected even more money into the academic health centers. Part of the reason these centers have grown so large and occupy so much of our attention is that they have become tremendously adaptable, vigorous, and dynamic. It is premature to be pessimistic, despite the enormous uncertainties posed both by the Clinton Administration's health-care proposals and by the severe sense of constraint in the national agenda that is introduced by the budget deficit.

Indeed, an interesting object lesson is provided by the experience of The Commonwealth Fund when, in 1984, it decided to try to bring about changes in clinical care, education, and biomedical research in the United States by facilitating more cooperation between academic health centers and community hospitals. The Fund believed that in so doing, it could contribute to the viability of academic health centers. The results were surprising. The experiment was (in six to seven of nine grant-supported cases) judged a failure—in large part because the academic health centers (AHCs) were such successes in the 1980s that they outstripped the community institutions with which they were paired. "The health care environment turned out not to be hostile to AHCs as had been predicted," wrote Nancy Kane, Robert J. Blendon, and Susan Koch Madden in a recent analysis.

> By the end of the decade, resources gained by AHCs exceeded all expectations, while many community hospitals bore the brunt of changes in health care payment and delivery systems and were struggling to survive. Strikingly, these gains for AHCs occurred without fundamental changes in missions or strategies. . . .So, despite dire predictions, AHCs were incredibly successful throughout the 1980s, doing just what they had always done. Cooperation was not only unnecessary but in many cases represented a radical shift in a proven and successful strategy.[7]

One senses, however, that the 1990s will prove to be different than the 1980s. The combination of health-care cost reform and federal budget deficits will reduce for academic health centers the dollars that fueled their expansions in the 1960s, 1970s, and 1980s. While sponsored funding of biomedical research has driven and helped to define the strong basic science cast and research orientation of the leading academic health centers, it has declined as a percentage of the budget and has been augmented in the past twenty years by medical faculty members' clinical practice fees. These fees have become a critical revenue source for many institutions, providing approximately 40 percent of the income at medical schools nationwide.[8] At the Johns Hopkins School of Medicine, for instance, the historic shifts in sources of revenue are striking, and parallel the experiences of many other schools. As a *percentage* of expenditures (not in absolute terms), sponsored research in the School of Medicine reached a zenith in about 1970 at 76.5 percent and has fallen steadily since then to about 52 percent (though the growth in actual dollar terms has been substantial). Professional fees, on the other hand, have increased as a percentage of the budget since 1970, rising from 3 percent to 34 percent in 1990—a tenfold increase in twenty years, and even more remarkably, an increase in nominal dollars from $1.03 million to $114.8 million. As Michael Whitcomb, former dean of the University of Washington Medical School, and Daniel Tosteson, dean of Harvard Medical School, have pointed out, while teaching hospitals historically have subsidized the costs of education with patient revenues, faculty practice plans have become increasingly important in the past twenty years to pay expenses that include clinical faculty's, residents', and fellows' salaries, a portion of the undergraduate medical program, and general operating expenses. "In reality, schools of medicine have become heavily dependent upon clinical revenues generated by hospitals and physicians to finance their activities."[9] They further note that this dependency is something of a constraint on efforts to transfer more medical education out of the teaching hospitals and into other settings, such as ambulatory centers and homes.

Everyone associated with the academic health center—faculty, chairpersons, deans, and indeed senior university administrators—would readily concede that this huge increase in clinical fee revenue has not occurred without considerable strain, and perhaps distortions, in the system and on individual faculty clinicians. Viewed from the faculty member's perspective, the competing time demands of managing patient care while leading a research program and at the same time being responsible for graduate and undergraduate medical school curricula is far more demanding than might have been the case thirty years ago, when clinical practice was viewed principally as an element necessary to undertake certain teaching and research activities but not to generate income. As Robert Petersdorf, current president of the AAMC, and Marjorie Wilson, president and chief executive officer of the Educational Commission on Foreign Medical Graduates, stated:

> The increasing dependence on money earned through medical practice has also had a profound effect on the behavior of medical institutions and has resulted in a change in the academic structure of the medical school from a faculty dedicated primarily to teaching and research to one that also has a major obligation to render service. The necessity of caring for patients is unique to medical schools. A business school does not manage, a law faculty does not prosecute, nor does an engineering school build bridges, but a medical faculty does practice medicine.[10]

Another facet of these financial arrangements that will be changing in the coming years is the relationship between teaching hospitals, faculty clinicians, and community practitioners—particularly primary care physicians. The rapid growth of "managed care," that is, various negotiated price agreements for the care of groups of prospective patients among a limited number of providers, will have a profound impact on faculty practice plans.

Currently, much of the direct and indirect cost of postgraduate medical education and other health professions education is included in teaching hospital reimbursement. In addition, hospital and physician charges include a component which cross-subsidizes care for indigent patients, medical education, and biomedical research. Under developing financial arrangements that place the primary emphasis on price competition, the ability of academic health centers to compete while cross-subsidizing these other activities will diminish.

Two related points are worth noting. First, as a group, academic health centers have not been successful in fostering adequate numbers of primary care physicians, nor in providing sufficient attention to care and teaching in out-of-hospital settings. Part of the explanation rests with the funding of education through teaching hospitals and with cross subsidies from faculty specialty groups.

Second, it may be difficult for faculty practice plans to associate fully with one or another managed care organization. While the suggestion of quality conferred by such an association with the plan might seem attractive, there is a potential dark side as well. The success of health plans will not only be achieved by cost-effective clinical management of sick patients, but by avoiding adverse selection—that is, by avoiding attracting to the plan individuals who anticipate needing sophisticated, inherently expensive care which can best be obtained at an academic health center. Thus, the forces at work will provide a tremendous challenge in meeting societal needs while maintaining fiscal viability.

Finally, part of the reason for the enormous pressure on health centers to generate income may lie in the fact that teaching hospitals are, as noted earlier, responsible for more than half of the uncompensated medical care in the country. Indeed, this is an important continuing role, but feasible only if they are organized to do it well and are financially supported by whatever funding mechanisms are adopted in the managed competition health-care reforms now under consideration. The additional costs of training and research must be paid for in a way that allows health centers to price clinical services competitively.

It is in this context that many leading academic health centers are now turning to technology transfer through the commercialization of research discoveries, in an effort to diversify their revenue bases. This activity has been controversial in the past, but is now being pursued under clearer policy guidelines designed to minimize conflicts of allegiance on the part of the faculty members and to manage potential conflicts of interest. A number of health sciences centers are anticipating increases in revenue from the commercialization of their research, especially in molecular biology and its clinical applications.

The academic health center in the context of society's interests in biomedical research, education, and clinical practice is obviously hedged about with uncertainties. It has demonstrated enormous viability throughout its existence, but the decade of the 1990s will be the most trying it has yet faced. Furthermore, rapid financial adjustments could be extraordinarily chaotic.

But what of the academic health center in the context of the research university? Has it become a leviathan, frequently removed geographically as well as culturally and intellectually from the rest, sometimes contributing little to the life of the university from which it historically sprang and by which it is sometimes cited as a point of pride? In many cases, we must concede that this is less caricature than reality. President of the University of Florida John Lombardi refers to the "imploded look, building piled on top of building," of the modern academic health center,[11] in which the architectural separation finds an echo administratively, politically, and intellectually. Yet, as Lombardi and others point out, there are powerful pressures of economics and mutual interest that will drive academic health centers and their home university campuses into tighter collaboration across disciplinary and departmental lines. The Pew Health Professions Commission also has stressed the degree to which professionals in academic health centers must build bridges with their colleagues elsewhere in their home institutions and with institutions in the community. A key concept in the highly managed, more proactive health-care environment of the twenty-first century will be that of teamwork among health professionals. Traditional understandings of scopes of practice will continue to shift. There may be models of community-based health-care delivery, for example, in which nurses, or allied health professionals, are primary gatekeepers to what historically has been medicine. These models may prove, in some cases, less expensive, more accessible, and more effective. Even within the hospital, we may be receptive to more fluidity, more coordination, and better teamwork. This does not, per se, involve the appropriate scaling of the health sciences center to the university, but it does involve the most effective scaling of the various constituents of the health sciences center among and between themselves. Such a readjustment, I suspect, will have consequences that reverberate in larger arenas as well.

Indeed, it is possible that the various constraints of the new era will compel academic health centers to begin doing the right things, albeit for previously unanticipated reasons, such as *1)* a more appropriate balance between primary care and specialization; *2)* greater responsiveness to the needs of the community, including preventive care as applied to populations rather than individuals, and health-care delivery based in various home and community settings rather than in the hospital; and *3)* a conscientious outreach to and integration with other academic departments and divisions within the home university. Let me discuss each of these items in more detail.

Primary care. It has been recently noted that Medicare payments to teaching hospitals for both direct and indirect medical education costs represent "a potential point of powerful leverage for reforming the medical education system—a point of leverage that has never been used."[12] These payments in 1992 amount to $1.6 billion for direct medical education (which includes about $300 million for nursing and allied health) and $3.6 billion for indirect medical education adjustments. This point of leverage has not escaped the Clinton Administration as a potential point of federal expenditure reduction. The Administration proposes to cut $3.3 billion in Medicare payments to teaching hospitals over five years. This would include $1.94 billion in reductions by changes to the indirect medical education adjustment formula, and $1.36 billion in graduate medical education payments. The latter changes would include incentives designed to produce more primary care residents.

As noted earlier, this may help academic health centers begin (or accelerate) doing the right thing. The Pew Health Professions Commission noted in its most recent report that "Medicare funding, in its failure to accommodate training in primary and ambulatory care settings, is out of step with the current health care needs of the public."[13] To the extent that revisions in the Medicare formula can help redirect the deployment of educational resources within the academic health centers toward primary care and away from specialties, they will support a change that should occur both for pedagogical and societal reasons. As the Pew Commission also noted in the same report, while the number of physicians in the United States has more than doubled in the past thirty years, "the ratio of office-based primary care physicians to the population has decreased, with the problem most acute in rural, and inner-city areas. The preponderance of specialist physicians is a factor in the escalating costs of medical care."[14]

A shift in emphasis, then, is not only understandable, it is *desirable*, both to drive and to reinforce changes that would not occur given the status quo ante in the marketplace. Additional emphasis on inducements and incentives is very important as well. However, these beneficial reforms could occur along with a massive hemorrhage of dollars from the medical education system which is much more vulnerable than some federal cost-cutters realize. In turn, that delicate assemblage of constituent parts that is the contemporary research university is much more sensitive to rapid downturns in any of its members than the gross budget figures might suggest to an outside observer. Most research universities have little or no operating margins. Cuts in professional schools may quickly be translated into programmatic cutbacks and loss of educational re-sources for students throughout the institution, including under-graduates in other schools.

Community based care and prevention. Many critics and observ-ers of the health-care system note that emphases must change. Instead of being as heavily focused on illnesses and therapies, typ-ically in acutely ill individuals, the health-care system is expected to begin devoting very significant attention to communities and to prevention. The system will address at-risk behaviors and educate on a public as well as on a personal scale if it is to impact favorably such issues as AIDS, substance abuse, and diseases that have an important behavioral component, such as lung cancers.

Particularly, this may be the case as society becomes responsive to shifting priorities in the health-care system. A system that is oriented toward protecting and improving the productivity of the work force, and toward improving the quality of life for all Amer-icans, will almost inevitably be drawn toward a new community-oriented approach to health services delivery which goes beyond the traditional model of relatively brief encounters with physicians.

Moreover, medicine must be prepared to do more than move its loci of delivery from the hospital to the outpatient setting—a move that is already occurring in the country in response to the econom-ics of health care and advances in technology and therapeutic efficiency. It must also be prepared to go several steps farther, into the neighborhood, the home, or the hospice. A number of academic health centers have been very active in their communities over the years— others less so. The groundwork for this sort of translation across the country, including Johns Hopkins, has been further stimulated in part with help from a number of major foundations. Again, longer-term economic incentives and adequate funding will be essential.

It is important to realize that this geographic outreach is motivated by both altruistic and selfish reasons. Altruistic in the sense that to address the underlying roots of the great health problems of our time, the health professions must be increasingly creative and forth-right in reaching and understanding people where they live. And selfish in that the academic health centers realize a fundamental dependence on—and responsibility to — their home communities.

Each of our institutions has particular histories, circumstances, and missions, tinged indelibly with the native wealth, ambitions, and civic-mindedness of our founders—whether they might be in Los Angeles, New Mexico, New York, or Baltimore. Yet, with the great influx of federal dollars in the past several decades, we have, undeniably, had our heads turned. To some degree we have tended to live in a research-oriented world in which laboratories were interchangeable and home was a jetliner threading its way between scholarly conferences. Toward the end of the 1980s, this world began to shake, even as it had earlier in the mid- to late-1970s. Now that we are well into the 1990s, we realize that simple necessity will bind us more closely than in previous decades to our indigenous resources— our cities, our neighborhoods, our states. We are in a decade of consolidation, if not outright retrenchment, and we will succeed to the extent that we meet demonstrated needs that are of particularly acute concern to our home constituencies.

Academic integration. It is clear that for both intellectual and financial reasons, the academic health center must begin in the 1990s to be integrated with other academic divisions of the university to an unprecedented degree. On the intellectual level, the health-care professional of the future must possess skills, sensitivities, and values that go far beyond the traditional basic and clinical science knowledge base that we have typically demanded. The physician, nurse, pharmacist, allied health and public health professional of the future must be prepared to interact effectively with an aging and more culturally diverse population, in a system where consumers, third-party payers, and the government are all more demanding and more assertive than ever before. The professional of the years 2000 and beyond must understand the economic implications of sophisticated technology and when its use is appropriate. He or she must know how to use computerized data bases and expert systems in a sophisticated way. He or she must have studied and thought deeply about ethics and values, many of which are culturally based, in order to deal appropriately with the psychological and social implications of the increasingly grave decisions that therapeutic advances have placed in the health professional's hands. He or she should be well-grounded in the social and behavioral sciences as they are thrust into community settings and as they attempt to consider community and population-wide implications and messages of their professional practices. In short, he or she should have had solid educations—not only during the collegiate years, but continuing at appropriately higher levels of sophistication in his or her advanced professional years—in many of the traditional disciplines of the arts and sciences.

The intellectual content of the change in the academic health center will drive heightened interactions with the rest of the university in the 1990s and beyond. At Johns Hopkins, for instance, we have already witnessed the merger of the Institute of the History of Medicine in the School of Medicine and the Department of History of Science in the School of Arts and Sciences, and have a joint Department of Biomedical Engineering between medicine and engineering. At Hopkins and elsewhere, this trend will inevitably continue. Perhaps it will be manifest less by formal merger across divisional lines than by sharing of faculty between and among schools, by more joint appointments in which classroom or seminar instruction is as important a component as is laboratory research, by a move toward common (or at least compatible) academic calendars across divisions, by, perhaps more profoundly than anything else, a culture in which *teaching* is recalled as a core value of an academic institution and restored to its place of pride. This is not to imply that the research universities ever stopped taking teaching seriously; it is, however, to acknowledge the fact that in an era of massive research funding, more than one institution found disproportionate rewards in the research enterprise. Now, the pendulum is swinging once again. A serious concern, however, is the source of funding for instructional activities.

One might fairly ask if these sorts of initiatives were not talked about and sometimes actually funded during the 1960s. In fact, some substantial demonstrations and many smaller experiments were undertaken, particularly with respect to the social sciences and humanities in academic health centers. A number of programs or departments became isolated from the university's mainstream departments and faculty were many times not subject to the same degree of rigor. Both the intellectual basis and the financial imperatives of collaboration in the 1990s suggest that more permanent and successful arrangements are in the making.

The heartening thing to all educators should be that, even though this swing of the pendulum is bound to carry pain, it will help nonetheless to recall us to our core academic mission, our own local and historic circumstances, our individual missions. This is true within our geographic and political communities, and it is true for the academic health center within its home academic setting. In the foreseeable future, many academic health centers will experience traumas of a magnitude they have forgotten experiencing. But they have felt them before. The shocks are painful, but they will not be fatal because society needs the academic health center.

If we in the research university community respond deliberately and intelligently, we will have institutions that are drawing on all of their resources in ways they never have before. Our faculties will be livelier and richer intellectually—we will have professors teaching and collaborating across divisional boundaries that were too forbidding to cross before. And both undergraduates and health professional students will receive a richer and more diverse education. We will *still* be regarded as the pacesetters of the world in biomedical research and education. And, like those corporations that have survived the near meltdowns of the late 1980s and the early 1990s, we will be poised for more rapid and more balanced growth once the inevitable recovery comes.

A recent *New Yorker* cartoon showed a doctor holding a patient's X ray to the light and declaring, "Basically, there's nothing wrong with you that what's right with you can't cure." The cure will not be painless, but it will be effective. Driven by many of the wrong reasons, it will force us to accept many of the right conclusions. The cure will result in a more appropriately scaled academic health sciences enterprise. Shrinking budgets will be the immediate cause, but the significant metrics of change will be those of instruction, collegial collaboration, and a more creative use of available resources. Our legs, if you will, may be shorter, and the ground may have tilted, but somehow we will have contrived a way to remain on our feet.

ACKNOWLEDGMENTS

I would like to acknowledge with appreciation the review and comments by the other authors of this volume, and the editorial and research assistance of William R. Sauder, Jonathan Saxton, and C. Alan Lyles.

ENDNOTES

[1]Eli Ginzberg, Miriam Ostow, and Anna B. Dutka, *The Economics of Medical Education* (New York: Josiah Macy, Jr. Foundation, 1993), 31–32; and National Center for Education Statistics, *Digest of Education Statistics 1992*, NCES 92–097 (Washington, D.C.: US Department of Education, 1992), 320.

[2]William C. Richardson, Comments on "The Functions and Resources of the American University of the Twenty-First Century," *Minerva* XX (2) (Summer 1992): 182.

[3]Donald C. Harrison, "Science for the 21st Century: The Coming Biomedical Revolution," in Donald C. Harrison, Marian Osterweis, and Elaine R. Rubin, eds., *Preparing for Science in the 21st Century* (Washington, D.C.: The Association of Academic Health Centers, 1991), 5.

[4]William C. Richardson, "Health Insurance in the USA," in *The Oxford Companion to Medicine* (Oxford and New York: Oxford University Press, 1986), 528 –29.

[5]Harold T. Shapiro, "Notes on the American University in a Changing World," keynote address delivered at The First Richard A. Harvill Conference on Higher Education, The University of Arizona, Tucson, 23 November 1992, 11–12.

[6]"Working paper," School of Medicine, Johns Hopkins University, 18 February 1993, 8.

[7]Nancy Kane, Robert J. Blendon, and Susan Koch Madden, "Tracking the Progress of Academic Health Centers," *Health Affairs* (Summer 1992): 183.

[8]Edward H. O'Neil, *Health Professions Education for the Future: Schools in Service to the Nation* (San Francisco, Calif.: Pew Health Professions Commission, 1993), 72.

[9]Michael E. Whitcomb and Daniel C. Tosteson, "Medical Education in the Context of the Changing American Health Care System," in Edward H. O'Neil and Diane M. Hare, eds., *Perspectives on the Health Professions* (Durham, N.C.: Pew Health Professions Commission, 1990), 52.

[10]Robert G. Petersdorf and Marjorie P. Wilson, "The Four Horsemen of the Apocalypse: Study of Academic Medical Center Governance," *JAMA* 247 (8) (26 February 1982): 1154 –155.

[11]John V. Lombardi, "Science, Doctors, and the University: New Alliances for a Competitive Age," in Harrison, Osterweis, and Rubin, eds., *Preparing for Science in the 21st Century,* 52.

[12]Fitzhugh Mullan, Marc L. Rivo, and Robert M. Politzer, "Doctors, Dollars, and Determination: Making Physician Work-Force Policy," *Health Affairs* (Supplement 1993): 143.

[13]O'Neil, *Health Professions Education for the Future,* 73.

[14]Ibid.

It would be folly to set up a program under which research in the natural sciences and medicine was expanded at the cost of the social sciences, humanities, and other studies so essential to national well-being. This point has been well stated by the Moe Committee as follows:

"As citizens, as good citizens, we therefore think that we must have in mind while examining the question before us—the discovery and development of scientific talent—the needs of the whole national welfare. We could not suggest to you a program which would syphon into science and technology a disproportionately large share of the Nation's highest abilities, without doing harm to the Nation, nor, indeed, without crippling science. * * * Science cannot live by and unto itself alone."

* * * * * * *

"The uses to which high ability in youth can be put are various and, to a large extent, are determined by social pressures and rewards. When aided by selective devices for picking out scientifically talented youth, it is clear that large sums of money for scholarships and fellowships and monetary and other rewards in disproportionate amounts might draw into science too large a percentage of the Nation's high ability, with a result highly detrimental to the Nation and to science. Plans for the discovery and development of scientific talent must be related to the other needs of society for high ability * * *. There is never enough ability at high levels to satisfy all the needs of the Nation; we would not seek to draw into science any more of it than science's proportionate share."

Vannevar Bush

From *Science—The Endless Frontier*
1945

15

Federal Science Policy and Universities: Consequences of Success

T HE US RESEARCH UNIVERSITY IS VIBRANT and conflicted. In laboratories, research buzzes around the clock. Investigators pursue with élan, and mostly with federal funding, the underlying mechanisms of life and disease, the origins and evolution of the universe, new tools for manufacturing, and advanced materials for every product. Yet, crosscutting their extraordinary intellectual vigor—and undercutting their pride about international acclaim for the premier record of American research—faculty in science and engineering feel rising anxieties. The worries range from tight funding, problematic job security, and public taunts regarding the arrogance of scientists and the abuses of technology to unease about how to help national economic competitiveness. In this atmosphere, federal science policy is, as a colloquial expression says, the 800 pound gorilla at major universities.

Every US research university in 1993 is a powerhouse, and more such campuses exist today than a generation ago. For this growth, Uncle Sam deserves much credit: for decades the federal government steadily added resources while universities served the nation's scientific and educational goals. But along the trails of this remarkable growth, forests of mixed motives and unintended results have masked problems that complicate current choices as policymakers confront the consequences of success.

The issue here is how the situation unfolded and how it will change with the pressures caused by slower growth or even cutbacks in federal funding for research. The debate centers on two questions. As cutbacks take place, can an irreversibly less diverse,

Rodney W. Nichols is the Chief Executive Officer of the New York Academy of Sciences.

but still highly competitive, government-university research system produce as much success? As priorities are reset, does the next decade offer a fresh chance for universities to renew healthy autonomy?

Both questions raise the issues of how to define and achieve "autonomy" in a contemporary US research university. If we consider the definition of autonomy—being self-governing or self-ruling, not controlled by others or by outside forces—by some measures this sense of autonomy is still robust. It spans political and intellectual freedoms; these are universally cherished and defended, even when challenged and cracked. It protects against commercial pressures that have grown as financial incentives increase. It encompasses the balancing of a faculty's functions across research, service, and teaching—a balance that is being reevaluated in light of many forces. Autonomy varies over time, across levels of organization, across fields, and with respect to diverse constituencies, markets, and sponsors. All of these are difficult to measure confidently.

In research, the question of autonomy has several angles. To young academic scientists, the potential for autonomy is hearty because a gifted investigator can earn a research grant in the fields emphasized by Washington and chart an independent direction for several years. The fact that only one in four or five grant applications is funded does not detract from the fact that a successful investigator becomes rather independent. To presidents and deans, however, university-wide autonomy in research is often only a shallow slogan because time for thinking is even scarcer than funding for independent efforts. While scientists are mainly loyal to the federal agencies providing their grants, presidents and deans are preoccupied with the shifting administrative terms of federal support.

The research strength provided by federal science funding was enhanced and safeguarded by the university's selective standards for faculty appointments. It was nurtured by national competitions and powerfully reinforced by the integration of research within a demanding system of graduate education. In both public and private institutions, the enterprise has been broadly supported by a physical and human infrastructure of enormous sophistication, including many firms that invent, develop, and service instrumentation. Most of the world envies this pattern. As a consequence, American universities produce superb science by every measure.

However, the sheer growth of federal science funding has engendered a pervasive dependence among our research universities. The government certainly did not aim for this result, but it was caused over time by a constellation of forces. Federal support became less pluralistic as agencies narrowed their research agendas. The government's changing and impatient mission-oriented priorities increasingly overrode investigator-initiated ideas. Washington began to impose heavy administrative burdens ranging from cost-control and safety to affirmative action. Most of all, the present and future cost for much frontier science is so high that only government can finance it. Consequently, the long-running domination of federal finance has eroded the institutional capacity for asserting new directions despite the resilience of universities. This consequence, silently rued by many in the American scientific community, will not be totally reversed, but it could be moderated, as I will argue, by several steps over the next decade.

NATIONAL GOALS AND FEDERAL OUTLOOK

Historically, the federal government had no organized policies about science until World War II. Slow, desultory growth of science in universities occurred during the nineteenth and early twentieth centuries. Academic concerns were primarily practical and local, not theoretical and national. Durable success emerged in fields such as engineering and chemistry. Bold strokes of private initiative helped to build research excellence in fields including medicine and astronomy. Selected federal interventions brilliantly served utilitarian purposes such as agriculture and mining.[1]

World War II revealed the profound powers of the research community, including gifted leaders and laboratories from both universities and industry. Few doubt that the period from 1939 to 1945 was the beginning of a deeply sustained surge of national appreciation of the importance of possessing a broad base of science. Postwar confidence in the likely *uses* of science was justified first and in large part on the ground that new weapons might be needed for national security.

Yet, the national goals for a federal policy about science, originating during the late 1940s, went well beyond the compelling
argument of defense. Indeed, Vannevar Bush's legendary report to
President Roosevelt *began* with the observation that "Progress in
the war against disease depends upon a flow of new scientific
knowledge."[2] To meet such broad goals, presidents and congressional leaders of both parties deftly orchestrated the rising public
conviction that large appropriations were needed for investments in
research. Scientific advisers to Washington were drawn mostly from
universities and, extending their credibility from wartime achievements, framed a convincing case that academe should be the "home
of science."[3] Moreover, the commitment of federal science policy
was almost unconditional in 1960 as the President's Science Advisory Committee observed:

> Both the security and the general welfare of the American people
> urgently require continued, rapid, and sustained growth in the strength
> of American science. . . .The government has one (great) interest. . . .It
> is, quite simply, that university science should be as strong as possible.[4]

Funding increased dramatically: total academic research and
development (R&D) spending rose from a few hundred million
dollars per year in the 1950s to more than $19 billion by 1992.
Federal funds were the engine, accounting for 60 to 70 percent of
the total. While the proportion of federal funds at universities
dropped from about 67 percent in the 1980s to 57 percent in 1992,
overall academic R&D funding nonetheless grew sharply over the
1980s to the present: 3.6 percent annually from 1980 to 1985, and
6.3 percent annually from 1985 to 1992.[5]

New Skepticism

Today, after the Cold War, as national goals outside defense become more pressing, a new skepticism (even from friends of science)
asks whether the continuing claims of research on the public purse
are justified. The questioning resembles a panoramic "audit" of the
results of the post-World War II "contract" between science and
society. Moreover, the social unease and economic recession of
recent years produce dangerous undertows that drag with them
chronic suspicions of intellectuals and newer doubts about the
benefits of technology. While the terms of science's contract with

society for the next generation are being rethought, universities are a visible target. Academic science, a major beneficiary of public resources, is no longer a protected preserve.

Is this skeptical reappraisal a narrow matter of the major research universities being asked to pay the piper? Were Uncle Sam's goals as academic patron primarily to "procure" specific science on a defined timetable in response to an essential public need? If so, proper questions for the audit would long since have been clearer. But Uncle Sam's purpose never was, and surely never appeared to be, that narrowly oriented. In fact, federal science policy unceasingly repeated the broad, national, capability-building purpose of creating a strong base of academic research.

Yet, precisely because the purpose was so expansive and the promise so long-range, unease about accountability—to whom and by whom—gradually became pervasive. Disquiet mounted as federal research spending climbed during the 1980s while other "discretionary" spending declined. Thus, today there is the nagging feeling that some piper must be paid. This has been expressed most vividly in the hours and pages recently devoted to debates about the National Institutes of Health (NIH) and the National Science Foundation (NSF) developing "strategies" for relating research to "national missions."[6] When national needs and moods change, budgets in the billions attract attention.

Many policies affect federal funding for research at universities. The following six themes introduce the impacts of past and ongoing policies.

The Defense Department was the first major sponsor of science in universities and quickly became the most significant.[7] Ample funding was provided for facilities, graduate students, and equipment. Scientific excellence was the standard for awards. Furthermore, the Pentagon had such a light hand in relating scientific interests to long-range military problems that, for most investigators, the research agreements were genuinely based upon mutual interests. Although perceptive leaders in the Pentagon almost always had a military purpose in mind, academic investigators were not troubled by this relevance. The system would not have been feasible without the exceptional consensus, across the nation, elicited by the Cold War era's commitment to high-technology deterrence and by the even broader confidence in the benefits of investment in science.

This era ended, many would say, with the passage of the Mansfield Amendment, which is frequently cited as a watershed in federal science policy.[8] The amendment required a "direct and apparent" relationship between a project in basic science and a specific military requirement. In 1970, Senator Mansfield expressed not only impatience with the Pentagon's role in Vietnam and in foreign policy generally, but also the growing pressures throughout Congress to apply sterner utilitarian standards for "mission-oriented (basic) research," in *all* agencies. By the early 1970s, national science policy was no longer led by defense goals, and was generally less expansive about basic research. From 1960 to 1990, defense funding fell from more than 30 percent to less than 10 percent of the total federal investment in basic science. A price was paid for losing the benefits of defense as an anchor of federal pluralism in research support, especially in the physical and engineering sciences.

Utilitarian pressures on universities were relaxed by the federal government throughout most of the 1950s and 1960s, when federal objectives emphasized scientific excellence and expansion of the research base. Even for the medical arena, NIH set long-range scientific objectives across the broadest frontiers, with near-term applications hardly debated. A large fraction of the most brilliant faculty naturally turned to advising the federal government, often on national security.[9]

Furthermore, with academic science booming as a result of federal support, few universities had any institutional financial incentive to conduct commercially relevant research in collaboration with industry. Most American companies following World War II were so successful and influential that they tended to upgrade their independent corporate research and development. Firms saw little need to foster formal links or joint research projects with academic institutions, and sought only individual consultants from the campuses.

This outlook, running up to the 1980s, resulted in what might be called a mixed R&D economy. There were large and often isolated domains of science and engineering: at universities, in aerospace and defense firms, in commercial electronics, and in other R&D

areas. Communications and mobility between industry and academe became increasingly rare. Most campuses were shifted toward "basic" science and eschewed any concern about comparatively short-run domestic applications. As a matter of policy, universities typically avoided corporate entanglements and, for instance, had little or no experience with what became the rage of the 1980s, to protect intellectual property when industrial funding increased and universities saw potential financial payoffs from inventions.

Since the social and behavioral sciences, along with the humanities, were rarely seen as having any great national or commercial utility, these fields were never the focus of federal science policy. Although the 1960s was an expansive period for the social and behavioral sciences—perhaps because of the confidence about science generally and about managing federal social and economic programs—the funding was modest compared to the scale of the natural sciences. Reviews occasionally were defensive, protecting available funding and responding to attacks and cuts such as those in the early 1980s. One exception to this pattern was the 1988 report by the National Academy of Sciences, which made an eloquent case for the field.[10] Nonetheless, the NSF's support for the social and behavioral sciences and funding by the National Endowment for the Humanities are almost lost in the statistics of either federal science generally or federal support of universities.

Similarly, federal support for the social science-intensive international (or geographical area) studies has been small. These efforts experienced a few booms, many droughts, and occasional fads, hardly the stuff of stable research and graduate education. The Mansfield Amendment scuttled the Defense Department's internationally oriented work in the social sciences, and the State Department has never organized the research program many believe it needs.

International links among researchers in science and engineering slowly renewed as European science recovered from World War II, Asia developed, and many research fields required cooperation on a global basis. In high energy physics, in geophysical sciences and environmental research, and in public health and agricultural fields around the world, the traditional international ethos of science brought the basic research community together for increasingly broad cooperative agreements. Throughout the 1950s and 1960s, new research initiatives were backed by inventive intergovernmental arrangements. Often, foundation funding of pilot efforts paved the way for larger scale, official programs. New, functional benefits of greater interdependence in research projects reinforced the naturally global orientation of the scientific community as individuals, and this trend has been expanding.

In addition, during the post-World War II period, geopolitical demands assured growth in US military exports, which were dependent upon Pentagon-supported R&D. Multinational companies in aircraft and electronics, for example, increasingly saw their markets in global terms. Governmental and corporate staffs were posted abroad, and large-scale R&D efforts were geared to international requirements. Universities were not much involved, except through special defense laboratories.

Science and engineering students from over the world began to seek training in the United States. Talented senior refugees came to the United States during the 1930s and 1940s. Waves of students came from various countries, reflecting political changes every few years: first from Japan, Taiwan, and South Korea; later from Iran and China. By the early 1990s, the total foreign student population was about four hundred thousand—heavily in science and engineering—as American campuses assumed the role of research universities for the world.[11] This result reversed an earlier necessity; many nineteenth- and early twentieth-century American scientists sought their crucial training in Europe.

Until recently, the comparatively easy rise of US universities to world leader may have led campuses to be less concerned with the American public's goals. At the same time, policy has been complacent about the role of universities for US leadership in science, and poorly prepared to resolve the irreducible tensions between global economic competition and international research cooperation.[12]

Facilities and fellowships for research were supported generously during the period from 1950 to 1970, when overall funding grew most rapidly. During the 1970s and 1980s, however, funding for research facilities dropped sharply. As a result, since university executives continued to advocate growth in funding research by their faculty, the campuses (especially the private institutions) became increasingly desperate to finance the construction and modernization of additional laboratories. Campuses sought funds through tax-exempt loans, private capital campaigns, and lobbies for earmarking projects in special congressional appropriations. In some respects, during the 1980s this was a "tragedy of the commons." Every institution tended to concentrate on its own short-term needs, and neither universities collectively nor the government—all aware of the trends—took the lead to craft a coherent balance between funding research operations and assuring adequate research facilities.[13]

This cycle in support for facilities—up and down with little concern for longer-range consequences—is similar to the pattern seen in support for scholarships and fellowships. First, the federal government was interested in increasing the number of doctoral students in science and engineering—notably after Sputnik. Later, it was dedicated to increasing the number of medical students. These cycles in support for human resources tended to last for a decade or less before stringent budgeting—accompanied by inevitable controversies in the projections of needs for scientists and engineers—brought abrupt reductions.

Entitlement has become the bête noire of policy debates about academic science, beginning in the mid-1980s. Comparatively easy money during the 1950s and 1960s led to the expectation that every qualified "basic research" investigator could be supported at a university. Few wanted to recognize the incentives and capacity of faculty members to produce students. Yet, it would be impossible for the federal government to support such an exponentially growing research system. Both executive and legislative analysts are now more realistic. But the painful news has not yet fully sunk in.

As competition in basic research becomes almost cruelly selective, universities see the imperative to assert more forcefully their internal standards on promotion and in their balance between teaching and research. The rest of the research system—especially the industrial base and even a few government agencies—is beginning to come to terms with the rising long-run national needs for competent scientists and engineers throughout many *non*academic jobs. This is especially obvious in the challenges of global economic competition and domestic K-12 science and math educational reform.

Since it is foolish to argue that all who receive advanced scientific and engineering training could or must be supported at universities, temperance is required in producing academic scientists. Nevertheless, for the rest of the 1990s, the country will be coping with the disappointed expectations of extremely qualified people. This harvest of discrepancies surely is one of the most poignant paradoxes among the many consequences of the success of academic science.

Pluralism has been a foundation for, and a high value within, the framework of competitive excellence throughout most of the post-World War II period of federal science policy-making.[14] It inheres in the decentralized system of science, and it receives deep legitimacy from American ideas of political democracy. But in many ways it has recently been deformed to mean that each research campus must do everything—and aim to do everything at a high standard.

An earlier practical meaning of pluralism was that a faculty investigator could go to more than one agency to request support for a good, novel idea. For instance, a physical chemist could go to the Office of Naval Research, or the NSF, or the Department of Energy. This is rarely the case today, because, especially in the wake of the Mansfield Amendment, each agency has trimmed its research interests and tried to separate them from those of other agencies. Another notion of pluralism was that the entire national research enterprise should be highly competitive, with peer reviews in each subfield by each agency to select the best proposals. Although much of this notion certainly was fulfilled in principle, it now applies to only a small fraction of all federal R&D, and to even just a part of academic research.

By the early 1990s, however, another perspective emerged: some argued that we have an excess of pluralism. Too many campuses are trying to be active in every key field, leading to frustration rather than to productive pluralism. At the same time, since so few potential sponsors exist, the enterprise is clogged by overcompetitiveness. Many investigators spend half their time writing and rewriting applications (and reviewing the applications of others), leaving little time for science.

This diagnosis instantly suggests the cure: restore traditional lines of pluralism by renewing commitments to both research across the federal agencies and selectivity for excellence in government and on campus. While formidable, this shift need *not* require greater total funding to produce better results.

THE CAMPUS IN CONTEXT

I have asserted that during the post-World War II era university executives evolved gradually into roles of merely presiding over the spectacular growth of research. By the mid-1960s, the pace and directions were almost always set elsewhere, either in Washington or by entrepreneurial faculty. Senior academic officials agreed with the national inclinations, counted their blessings—sometimes with a tone of braggadocio—and proceeded to build their campuses' capacities to fulfill whatever federal science policy aimed to accomplish.

Across the country, at both public and private campuses, from Harvard, MIT, Cornell, and Hopkins to Michigan, Illinois, Texas, Stanford, and California, the consistent tone was optimism and expansion over the 1960s. The outlook moved to caution and contraction by the early 1990s. Even at small, elite institutions such as Rockefeller, dark budgetary clouds recently threatened to rain on the dedication to excellence.[15]

University Ambitions

Three themes were central, if not always explicit, in statements made over more than thirty years by executives at research universities. One was expanding ambitions that mirrored the Washington outlook for science. Research universities saw themselves as *the* home of science—the best place for stimulating national technical progress and the crucial center of discovery by students and faculty. Accordingly, campuses settled into a mission they defined as essential for *all* national goals in education and research.

This open-ended idea led to a second, operational theme: universities could—even should—respond to any calls to apply knowledge, such as taking on the Job Corps, exploring space, designing new weapons, or building advanced computers. For these aspirations, universities had to plan and manage more centrally, charting long-range aims and assembling expert teams to execute enormous projects through sprawling, decentralized campuses. Along this path, an elastic sense of "service to society" led deans and faculty to absorb and supervise special facilities, join the boards of management of national laboratories, and advise fieldwork in economic development abroad. Most of this was contractual. Few were concerned with the uncertainties of the projects, or the nonacademic character of certain components of the work. Fewer still saw the risks that would emerge when some faculty wished to be an honest critic—"speaking truth to power"—evaluating programs in which colleagues had a great stake.

A third theme naturally emerged in distinctive style: a "corporate attitude." Campuses had to target sales of proposals, negotiate reimbursement of indirect costs, orchestrate capital borrowing to upgrade facilities, launch bidding wars to attract star faculty members, mount financial campaigns with alumni and individual donors, expand revenues at hospitals that served every constituency from the homeless to the affluent, and respond to the growing demands of state government for expansion of economic opportunities. This urgent business occupied any time that research universities might otherwise have devoted to conceiving and pursuing autonomy, and to sticking to what they knew best. Moreover, federal science policy frequently was based upon cheerleading by the government's senior science advisory groups that included academic leaders, most of whom ignored the possibility that rapid expansion would lead to a loss of university independence and selectivity.

Critique and Debate

As university research became big business, it might have been expected that there would be rising contention for shares of the business. Elbowing competition did grow and clever critics took more potshots. Yet, these consequences were not anticipated.

For example, in the encyclopedic 1991 critique from the Congressional Office of Technology Assessment (OTA) about the research community (and, in particular, the ways in which federal research priorities may be set during the 1990s), the OTA suddenly emerged as either a sane and realistic observer of the scene, or as an unsympathetic skeptic about the passivity and drift of both federal and academic science policy.[16] However one views OTA's work, the stance of the study would have been astonishing a generation ago and almost unthinkable even a decade ago. The OTA highlighted the sheer scale of federal research funding, the high rates of growth of academic support in comparison to spending on other national needs, and the evident lack of limits in what academic science wishes to do. Few university deans were pleased to have the OTA starkly underscore their situation and choices.

In light of the growing debate, it was no surprise when House Science Chairman George Brown, a long-standing friend of research, underlined the issues: "Science has promised much more than it can deliver. . . .the scientific community must establish a new contract with policy makers, based not on demands for autonomy and ever-increasing budgets, but on the implementation of an explicit research agenda rooted in (social) goals. . . ."[17] It is still not clear what the implications of this view may be. One daunting challenge in Brown's proposition is to rethink priorities for research—and the role of universities in the national research priorities—in order to both justify investments and build mechanisms of reliable accountability.

In sharp contrast, the American Association for the Advancement of Science (AAAS) president Leon Lederman argued that: "Science in America is in a mood of uncertainty and discouragement. . . .a doubling of the research budget and the education initiative at the level of adding $10 billion to $20 billion. . .would be prudent, long-term investments."[18] The challenge in Lederman's proposition, fundamentally the same as in Brown's, is to show convincingly that long-run research investments are, indeed, "prudent." At the moment, however, economic circumstances—high debt and continuing deficits—push the country toward being more hesitant about seeing academic science as *the* priority for any increases in the federal budget.

Technology Policy

According to the dominant current view, R&D funding must advance the "economic competitiveness" of the country. Although Vannevar Bush certainly would have understood (and supported) this idea, few key scientific officials of the 1950s tried to force such a tight coupling between research and economic applications—between academe and the market.

By early 1993, the Clinton/Gore Administration left little doubt that "technology policy" had become at least as important as "science policy."[19] Indeed, this trend had been emerging for a decade. The shift accelerated with the Bush Administration's somewhat reluctant, but nonetheless novel and constructive, statement in 1990.[20] It was encouraged through the slow birth of an entirely new institution, the Critical Technologies Institute, set up in late 1992 through the NSF at the RAND Corporation, to assist the White House Office of Science and Technology Policy.[21]

The rising concern is to think through both short-range and long-range issues of the linkages between research (often originating with or involving leading universities) and the effectiveness with which American industry applies knowledge in developing products and services.[22] Combining market competition with governmental stimulus leads to hot controversies about what is the best mix. Politics often confounds the economics in any mix. The effects of such technological outlooks are unmistakable as research universities are tugged to do more, with less, toward economic goals while they add a large set of industrial relationships and tacit economic obligations.

Local Interests

There is more to the forces buffeting campuses. Coalitions organized around particular interests frequently cannonade federal and state legislators, influence appropriations, and thrust themselves into the day-to-day operations of research universities.

One vivid example is the "animal rights" movement. These groups, occasionally resorting to virtually terrorist tactics, have disrupted biomedical research while beaming a tempting case to tens of thousands of their members as well as to students, newspapers, and television stations across the country. Some members of Congress have said they receive more mail about the uses (or abuses) of animals in research than about subjects such as arms control, the deficit, or foreign aid. Federal and state agencies have responded to the pressure by tightening regulations, thus raising the costs of essential research in both universities and firms. Yet, a large fraction of biomedical research must, for sound scientific principles as well as for reasons of law and regulation, involve animals. After all, laboratory research is often the crucial route for confirming the safety and effectiveness of medical and surgical advances. And research universities are in the middle.

More broadly, governmental officials at the state and city level are almost desperate about promoting economic development and jobs.[23] Universities face appeals to help in applied projects and "technology transfer." Economic competition— often demanding a measure of secrecy and urgency— complicates the internationally open, cooperative, and long-range character of research. Crisp management of patents and intellectual property rights, along with steering local industrial consortia, have become for some campuses the "vital signs" of research health, and Washington has fostered this outlook.

Furthermore, a few notorious cases of lapses of judgment and outright fraud by scientists have jeopardized the formerly high moral authority of the scientific world. Thus, some observers see diminished public respect for the research universities—although scientists still command esteem—and fear a backlash from federal agencies that would regulate even more the institutional freedoms of intellectual life.[24]

In short, research universities have not reconciled the conflicts among their friends, much less among their enemies. To respond to burning national needs for technology while accommodating broad social concerns about the impacts of that very technological progress, major research campuses must cope with the consequences of the high-tech nation that their success helped to create.

Homogenization and Flattening of Campus Research

Two subtler consequences of research success also may be seen on most campuses. One is the homogenization of the character of the campus. A young investigator sees that a faculty appointment means little more than a partial salary, space, and a license to apply for grants. Any ideas of tradition, or "soul," at campus X is often invisible. Campus X is much like campus Y, aside from geography. Every institution struggles with its responses to external forces such as finance, regulation, and recruitment. Every investigator struggles with the pressures to juggle budgets for a research group, responding to the often idiosyncratic fashions of governmental research interests. The national dispersion and growth of research universities masks a profound leveling, a reduced diversity.

A second consequence is that the driving goal of competitive research determines organizational patterns and loyalties. It is not simply an investigator's financial life-giving tie to a federal funding agency instead of to a university official. It is also the attractiveness of increasingly "flat" collaborations, within large teams, crossing multiple institutional and national boundaries.[25] High energy physics paved this path—as it has so many others—with central facilities and extensive, competitive user groups. A single paper may have hundreds of coauthors from more than a score of institutions, giving results of an experiment requiring years to design and conduct at facilities around the world. Comparable teams have been emerging in the earth sciences, in medical genetics, and in the atmospheric sciences related to global climate change. Even for science policy issues, many nongovernmental organizations and science academies have become clearinghouses, creating "flat" groups that cross the world to undertake assessments.[26]

This trend, however, is not universal. Crucial "little science" continues to flourish, as it always must and will. Yet, the individualized reflexes among scientists—always strong with respect to one-to-one communications, debate, and confirmation—have combined with funding problems simply to overpower much of the institutional advantages of local community, even for participants in small-scale research. Does tenure —the single remaining, and deeply important, source of institutional loyalty for a faculty member— mean less when the most productive scientists know that they could move to tenured positions elsewhere and continue to receive almost all of their support from federal (or nonuniversity) sources? The campus, therefore, increasingly provides for many scientists only the base for a global intellectual life rather than a home for a meaningful institutional life.

NET ASSESSMENT

Two mandatory challenges stand out at the moment in a net assessment of ongoing changes at research universities. One is a retrenchment of the scale of science at many institutions; this creates the opportunity for an essential differentiation of the strengths among independent campuses. A second is adjustment to the reassertion of national needs—mainly for economically useful applications—as the touchstone for federal funding. A third, more practical, but nonetheless essential challenge is how to rebuild the infrastructure of academic facilities and equipment.

Retrenchment and differentiation is the imperative during the mid-1990s for the academic research system. Several universities have already been engaged in this horrific process. Whole departments are threatened, faculty freezes are imposed, and supporting services are being cut. The federal government's budget for the 1994 fiscal year reconfirmed the needs for such trimming. Expected severe controls on the government's reimbursement of "overhead" at research universities—both public and private —will constrain further the critical technical infrastructure required to support the best research.

At each campus, in principle, retrenchment is a time for resetting priorities.[27] This is a new opportunity to renew a few core ideas about what to do, with what comparative advantages, at what scale, for what purposes, in what collaborations, and over what periods of time. This is much easier said than done. Forty years ago, as big-time science began, Einstein ruefully remarked: "If I would be a young man again and had to decide how to make my living, I would not try to become a scientist or scholar or teacher. I would rather choose to be a plumber or a peddler in the hope to find that modest degree of independence still available under present circumstances."[28] There is no reason for us to be that pessimistic with so many talented people and so much investment in research. But to renew optimism, each scientific and engineering community must reassert its priorities.

The essential differentiation of the excellence in research strengths among individual universities will be sensitive, painful, and protracted. Forced by tightening budgets and sharpening national priorities for science, US leadership can be ensured in most fields *if* differentiation occurs. After all, the United States supports more R&D than our leading competitors combined. The recent scattering of support is a response to cries of entitlement, a cave-in to pork-barrel politics, and a way of administering policies that spread the "pain" across the board.[29] Scattering has endangered the vitality of the best groups, and yet has given only partial aid to the medium-rank groups.

The 1990s should restore each institution's commitment to the tradition of funding *individuals* of demonstrated *excellence*.[30] If so, the 1990s will reinvent a meaningful pluralism. To avoid pork-barrel allocations, some federal set-aside of funds could create distinct ways to respond to the understandable ambitions of aspiring centers. Without strong criteria of excellence guiding research choices—at the national, state, and institutional levels—universities will sink into a quicksand of mediocrity akin to that afflicting elementary and secondary schools. For the process of differentiation to work well, federal agencies will need talented leaders with flexible resources. Universities will require faculty creativity as well as forceful top management.

For the country as a whole, the research system merits a different assessment. Academic strategists must participate collectively in a too-long-deferred consultation with industrial and governmental leaders in a brutally realistic assessment of the nation's long-range goals in science. The National Academy of Sciences recently suggested ways of formulating comparative assessments of "leadership."[31] In a sophisticated tutorial summing up years of debate about better connecting research and technology to national goals, the Academy's group proposes a mechanism of field-by-field panels for systematically relating international benchmarks of scientific quality to the federal government's quantitative allocations of resources to all fields of research. This hoary problem will not yield easily to such a monolithic mechanism. One reason is that the federal agencies have independent "missions" that involve science but are not mainly about science, and they defend their overall budgets and R&D in terms of their missions, which are in turn affected by many social and economic criteria. Another reason is that the ultimate decisions on *cross-field* comparisons of scientific quality and potential, and of estimates of the value of major financial commitments or shifts, will almost always depend upon essentially intuitive and political, not professional and technocratic, judgments. But whatever the mechanisms, the point is to put pressure on the research community itself, on all of the institutions carrying out research.

This rethinking should build a process of goal-setting that corrects what a Carnegie Commission report called the "mismatch" between the "inherently long lead times" for research serving major national goals and the "immediate economic and political realities."[32] Retrenchment must *not* become an excuse for permitting, in the biting truth of a Washington aphorism, the "urgent to drive out the important," either on individual campuses or in the national system of academic research. As former Harvard University dean Harvey Brooks has pointed out, "The academic scientific community cannot afford to sit back and become hostage to the dysfunctional performance of parts of the overall science-utilization system over which it believes it has no influence."[33]

Reassertion of national needs, as seen in the federal government's sharply refocused priority on technology, will complicate the tasks for research universities. Some new flexibility in funding for basic and applied research could emerge from the rebalancing of military vis-à-vis civilian appropriations. The Clinton/Gore Administration aims to "reinvest" part of the cuts in defense procurement and standing forces into new civilian activities—and to move the defense/civilian funding split in R&D from 60/40 to 50/50.

But the emerging pattern of other high-technology federal missions has not yet been well-defined. What are optimal longer-range research and development missions for the civilian agencies? For example, the Department of Commerce aims to increase support for its research and technology programs. After being forgotten for almost a generation, Commerce could become for the physical and engineering sciences related to diverse industrial technologies what the Department of Health and Human Services (through the NIH) has been for the life sciences related to medical, chemical, biotechnology, and pharmaceutical industries. As such changing social and economic goals become more prominent criteria in the federal R&D policy calculus, the applied social sciences could also receive added support, such as in shaping and evaluating K-12 educational reform, or analyzing optimal means for technology transfer and diffusion. There could conceivably be significantly enhanced R&D in transportation, communications, housing, and even foreign policy.

What, then, are the implications for research faculty of targeted national priorities steering federal science policy? Some disparage this model with its pejorative implications of a "command planning" paradigm. Yet, new national missions need *not* undercut basic science. Recall, for example, that the "War on Cancer" was strongly utilitarian and widely-supported by the public. As high-level commitments increased the budget of the National Cancer Institute, the Institute's funds largely supported *basic* science in fields pertinent to understanding cancer. Administering successful programs aimed at strongly mission-oriented goals can be accomplished with sensitivity to the independent intuitions and long-term priorities of curiosity-driven individuals at universities and elsewhere. This requires a relaxation of some administrative requirements and an enhancement of the capacity for investigators to change directions.

University research executives must make the case —without being self-serving—for how to achieve *both* quality and relevance in programs. It is perfectly plain to see that science, as Goethe reportedly said, "is to one man the highest thing, a heavenly goddess; and to another, it is a productive and proficient cow, who supplies him with butter." Research conducted in US universities has been, and always can be, both.

Investments in the academic research infrastructure will require decisions that will be fraught with frustration because total capital resources will be limited. New competitive mechanisms will have to be invented to shape choices by reconciling multiple and sometimes conflicting criteria. The criteria span the past excellence of competing investigators and institutions, the future scientific promise of specific projects and facilities, an equitable distribution of funds across the country, and added cost-sharing by nonfederal sources.

One question is how to evolve a *cross-field* consensus on a *process* to winnow out the best ideas, and consolidate whatever limited money is available, for selected, nationally significant initiatives at the leading scientific frontiers. International issues of costly "megascience" will also have to be factored into domestic reviews of priorities for investment in research infrastructure.[34] The new Megascience Forum of the Organization for Economic Cooperation and Development may be a crucial mechanism for both scientific and managerial cooperation, linking national investments with international needs. Good faith work by universities, firms, professional societies, international organizations, and politicians will have to tap the lessons learned from past experience, as with the High Energy Physics Advisory Committee (HEPAC) to the Department of Energy. The trick will be to foster open participation and merit-based cooperation—*without* creating national or global "czars" that choke off the free flow of information or blindly resist unconventional ideas.

For the 1990s, federal science policy will cope with these acutely defined challenges within the same context in which all other national choices are embedded: roughhouse politics, demographic change, and rugged economic trade-offs. In this perplexing context, three directions of outreach should inform campus decisions: *1)* outreach to schools; *2)* outreach across disciplines on campus; and *3)* global outreach. Each proposal runs perilous risks of combining prediction with prescription, and there is optimism in these recommendations about where research universities should go. Furthermore, with the entire system so strained, as Cal Tech physicist and vice provost David Goodstein noted, many do not have "the faintest idea of what (the radically different structure for scientific research and education) will be."[35] Our system is evolving, many specifics remain to be worked out, and the mood is tense.

Links to Schools

One recommendation for outreach concerns the new opportunities for universities to assure that K-12 science and math educational reform will begin to pay off. This is a fundamental issue for the nation, and our major universities no longer can blink it away.

For children entering elementary school during the 1990s, science should be taught more fully and engagingly. In the year 2000, American students should be "first in the world" as many of our state governors urged in 1990. Moreover, the nation's general needs for improved technical skills throughout the work force are becoming ever more apparent. High school graduates, as well as individuals who receive limited post-high school training, will need a better base of science and math; it is crucial and the rationale has been elaborated often.[36]

To assure progress toward this desirable goal, the "science-rich" universities must help the "science-poor" schools. Even at the cost of foregoing some research—which may well be cut anyway—universities should devote more talent to the K-12 years. Both federal and state governments—and university officials—should establish new incentives for faculty activities in elementary and secondary education. These incentives could include direct and competitive grants from the NSF, the Department of Education, and state agencies.

Academic incentives would have to span high-level endorsements by deans and presidents for classroom time in the criteria for considering young faculty for promotion. Undergraduates and graduates might be required to devote a few hours each month to mentoring and tutorial programs in local schools. Such new efforts should not be limited to advice from afar. Faculty should prepare for direct involvement in the classroom, conduct high-leverage courses of teacher-training, and frequently seek exchanges with teachers and students about what works and what does not. All of this will require sustained programs, as patient and probing as any research. Over the next generation, the major universities will benefit directly from such work by creating a much larger cohort of young men and women capable of being outstanding employees throughout the country as well as being science students and faculty. This will both buttress the national science base and strengthen the foundations of economic vitality.

Interdisciplinary Research

A second line of desirable outreach, and my second recommendation, is across fields—what is often called "interdisciplinary" or "systems" studies. Unfortunately, only a very few academic institutions have set patterns of rewards for such research.

During the past generation, for example, materials science and engineering thrived through mixing insights from electronics, chemistry, ceramics, metallurgy, and theoretical and experimental physics—a blend that sparked creativity in what is now called condensed matter physics. The research attracted leaders in both industrial and academic laboratories. The federal government, through the Defense Department, played a major role in these advances which led to rich intellectual discovery and widespread practical application.

For the future, research universities should conceive and nurture comparable initiatives. In the life sciences, for instance, the powerful explanatory tools of molecular biology will have to be reintegrated with clinical investigation and the larger questions of human disease. For meeting other broad social goals—such as modernizing transportation—new engineering approaches will have to be combined fully with economic assessment and social insight. In the environmental sciences—whether at local, national, or global dimensions—chemical, geophysical, and biological research will have to be unified with historical, anthropological, and economic perspectives; the "human-environment science" is a telling example.[37]

Some of this systems-oriented research should be "applied" science, although not all will have that character. Yet, it should not drive out excellent "basic" science in the traditionally defined disciplines. Instead, the point is to welcome — not block—the growing interpenetration of theory and experiment across fields. In seizing new frontiers and clearing fresh paths for technology to serve many industrial goals, universities will be entirely consistent with both the nation's pragmatic original commitment to research and the indisputable future needs for science-based social progress. With Pasteur— who said, "There is only one science: science and the application of science are linked together as a fruit is to the tree"[38]—the point is not to label and suppress work invidiously as "impure" or "applied," but to promote research of productive excellence in ripe, emerging fields.

Internationalization

Universities should reach out globally with new arrangements designed to take advantage of the accelerating process of the internationalization of research. Trends both inside and outside the campus will reinforce global networks. These trends include the rising mobility of talent, the inevitable building of research capacity in many developing countries, and the spectacular reach of modern communications. As noted earlier, compelling internal and professional reasons cultivate the organization of scientists into "flat" coalitions of specialists from institutions in different locations. Often, the resulting decentralized units enhance productivity and efficiency in using scarce resources. All of these powerful contemporary waves push individuals and ideas—across every national boundary—to come together in order to be first-rank in science. Universities should extend their already growing international activities by further high-level encouragement of exchanges of faculty, admission of students, and incentives for investigators to build bridges to research collaborators abroad.

Federal science policy—following the lead of most modern corporate R&D policy—should encourage faculty at the major research universities to form global alliances whenever payoffs appear most likely to result from international partnerships. Federal agencies should score up research applications that involve foreign travel and collaboration. Sometimes the alliances will include individuals from firms as well as from universities.

One practical reason for such outreach grows out of recognizing the past and prospective surge of R&D outside the United States along with the increasing R&D intensity of industrialized economies. Japan now spends 50 percent more than the United States on nondefense R&D as a percentage of the Gross Domestic Product.[39] Only by direct cooperation can US campuses stay in close touch with the best work. The pattern will affect "little science" as well as "big science." It will be an enormous change from the inertial forces emphasizing "national" science, as seen in the historic names of federal agencies and the traditional motives of governmental support.[40]

The triple goals for federal science policy will be: to sustain the intellectual strength of our universities; to contribute openly to the global base of science and education; and to draw freely upon global research and the international pool of talent to serve specific national needs. The hurdles are complex—no one knows yet how to combine competitive excellence at home with greater, authentic cooperation abroad. Many other nations will also be trying to learn how to leap these hurdles.

Major research universities have national obligations that many argue must come first. But is it any longer meaningful to distinguish between a university's roles in domestic and foreign science? In research, as in trade, to be protectionist or insular is to be obsolescent. For the next generation, by taking advantage of global scientific leadership, US research universities can multiply the benefits flowing from the consequences of their past success.

ACKNOWLEDGMENTS

I am indebted to colleagues who offered comments on an initial draft. I thank Stephen Graubard and Jonathan Cole who invited this paper and presided with wisdom and incisiveness as drafts were discussed at an authors' conference in June of 1993. I also thank Jesse Ausubel, Walter Baer, William O. Baker, D. Allan Bromley, William Carey, Daryl Chubin, Edward David, Yaron Ezrahi, Joshua Lederberg, Thomas Malone, John Moore, Thomas Moss, Thomas Ratchford, David Robinson, Frederick Seitz, Bruce Smith, and Robert Sproull. Most of all, I thank Harvey Brooks who has inspired a generation of observers of the trends in science and technology policy and has always showed great generosity in time and spirit by giving cogent suggestions.

ENDNOTES

¹See, for example, A. Hunter Dupree, *Science in the Federal Government* (Cambridge, Mass.: Harvard University Press, 1957); and Bruce L. R. Smith, *American Science Policy Since World War II* (Washington, D.C.: Brookings, 1990).

²Vannevar Bush, *Science—The Endless Frontier,* Summary of the Report, July 1945, reprinted by National Science Foundation, NSF-90-8 (Washington, D.C.: National Science Foundation, 1990).

³Dael L. Wolfle, *The Home of Science: The Role of the University,* Carnegie Commission on Higher Education (New York: McGraw-Hill, 1972); it is informative to compare Wolfle's view with that of another perceptive observer twenty years later: Henry Rosovsky, *The University: An Owner's Manual* (New York: Norton, 1990).

⁴President's Science Advisory Committee, *Scientific Progress, The Universities, and The Federal Government,* November 1960.

⁵National Science Foundation, *National Patterns of R&D Resources: 1992,* NSF-92-330 (Washington, D.C.: National Science Foundation, 1990). Because extensive data are available on federal funding for research at universities, this paper does not include a recapitulation of these trends.

⁶See, for example, *Mission of the National Science Foundation,* Hearing before Subcomittee on Science, Committee on Science, Space, and Technology, US House of Representatives, 3 March 1993 (Washington, D.C.: Government Printing Office, 1993).

⁷See, for example, Genevieve J. Knezo, Congressional Research Service, *Defense Basic Research Priorities: Funding and Policy Issues,* Library of Congress, 24 October 1990.

⁸Rodney W. Nichols, "Mission-Oriented R&D," *Science* 172 (2 April 1971); and Robert A. Frosch, "Relevance, Irrelevance, and General Confusion: Problems in Science Policy," Woods Hole Lecture, 3 January 1983.

⁹For a recent analysis of the roles of consultants to government, see Bruce L. R. Smith, *The Advisers: Scientists in the Policy Process* (Washington, D.C.: Brookings, 1992). For a unique compilation of views from veteran advisers, see William T. Golden, ed., *Science and Technology Advice to the President, Congress, and Judiciary* (Elmsford, N.Y.: Pergamon, 1988).

¹⁰Dean R. Gerstein, R. Duncan Luce, Neil J. Smelser, and Sonja Sperlich, eds., *The Behavioral and Social Sciences* (Washington, D.C.: National Academy Press, 1988).

¹¹Institute for International Education, *Open Doors 1991–92* (New York: Institute for International Education, 1992).

¹²Carnegie Commission on Science, Technology, and Government, *Science and Technology in U.S. International Affairs* (New York: Carnegie Commission on Science, Technology, and Government, January 1992).

[13]For early perspectives see Bruce L. R. Smith and Joseph J. Karlesky, *The State of Academic Science* (New York: Change Magazine Press, 1977); and National Science Board, Office of Science and Technology Policy, and Government-University-Industry Research Roundtable, *Academic Research Facilities: Financing Strategies* (Washington, D.C.: National Academy Press, 1986).

[14]Rodney W. Nichols, "Pluralism in Science and Technology," *Technology in Society,* vol. 8 (Elmsford, N.Y.: Pergamon, 1986); for an enchanting sketch of the profound issues in pluralism, see Isaiah Berlin and R. Jahanbegloo, *Recollections of A Historian of Ideas: Conversations with Isaiah Berlin* (New York: Scribners, 1991).

[15]Internal reports to the President and Board of Trustees of The Rockefeller University, prepared for "retreats" during the 1980s with faculty, officers, and trustees, documented the changing mix of private and public funding. During the 1970s and early 1980s, Rockefeller considered putting a cap on federal funding in order to preserve its independence. By the late 1980s and early 1990s, it was trying to increase its federal funding in order to close the deficit.

[16]US Congress, Office of Technology Assessment, *Federally Funded Research: Decisions For A Decade,* OTA-SET-490 (Washington, D.C.: Government Printing Office, May 1991).

[17]George Brown, "The Objectivity Crisis," *American Journal of Physics* 60 (9) (September 1992); and chairman's Report of the Task Force on Health of Research, Commission on Science, Space and Technology (Washington, D.C.: Government Printing Office, July 1992).

[18]Leon M. Lederman, "The Advancement of Science," *Science* 256 (22 May 1992); and Leon M. Lederman, *Science: The End of the Frontier?* (Washington, D.C.: American Association for the Advancement of Science, January 1991).

[19]William J. Clinton and Albert Gore, *Technology for America's Economic Growth: A New Direction to Build Economic Strength,* White House, 22 February 1993. For a comprehensive review of many issues in the area of changing missions to emphasize technology policy, see Lewis M. Branscomb, ed., *Empowering Technology: Implementing a U.S. Strategy* (Cambridge, Mass.: MIT Press, 1993).

[20]D. Allan Bromley, *The U.S. Technology Policy,* Executive Office of the President, 26 September 1990.

[21]See Department of Defense Authorization Act of FY 1991 [PL 101–510, as amended] creating the Critical Technologies Institute (CTI) as a Federally Funded Research and Development Center with the NSF as sponsor; also see materials from RAND, Washington, D.C., which won competition to start and operate CTI.

[22]See, for example, Nathan Rosenberg and Richard R. Nelson, "American Universities and Technical Advance in Industry," Center for Economic Policy Research, publication no. 342 (Stanford, Calif.: Stanford University, March 1993); and "American Technology Policy," *The Economist,* 25 July 1992.

[23]See, for example, Carnegie Commission on Science, Technology, and Government, *Science, Technology, and the States in America's Third Century* (New York: Carnegie Commission, September 1992), for a lively and practical set of recommendations about improving institutional arrangements, including roles

for universities; and "Universities and Economic Development—Special Issue," *The Bridge,* National Academy of Engineering 22 (3) (Fall 1992).

[24]An enormous literature has emerged during the past decade about "fraud" in science; both the NSF and the NIH, for instance, have organized advisory panels and full-time staff for investigations. See, for example, Howard K. Schachman, "What Is Misconduct in Science?," *Science* 261 (9 July 1993); Lewis M. Branscomb, "Integrity in Science," *American Scientist* 73 (5) (September-October 1985); and Committee on the Conduct of Science, *On Being A Scientist* (Washington, D.C.: National Academy of Science, 1989).

[25]Jesse H. Ausubel and John H. Steele, "Flat Organizations for Earth Science," *Bulletin of the American Meteorological Society* 74 (5) (May 1993).

[26]See, for example, Cesare Maltoni and Irving J. Selikoff, *Scientific Issues of the Next Century: Convocation of World Academies,* Annals of The New York Academy of Sciences, vol. 610; and Carnegie Commission on Science, Technology, and Government, *Facing Toward Governments: Nongovernmental Organizations and Scientific and Technical Advice* (January 1993).

[27]See, for example, the views of two independent groups of observers: President's Council of Advisors on Science and Technology, *Renewing The Promise: Research-Intensive Universities and the Nation,* White House, December 1992; and Government-University-Industry Research Roundtable, *Fateful Choices: The Future of the U.S. Academic Research Enterprise* (Washington, D.C.: National Academy Press, 1992).

[28]Albert Einstein, cited in *Reporter,* 18 November 1954.

[29]Frederick Seitz, "The Threat of 'Pork-Barrel' Science," *The World and I,* January 1993; and see, for example, "House Panel Will Examine Pork-Barrel Projects," *Chronicle of Higher Education,* 17 February 1993.

[30]See, for example, Joshua Lederberg, "Does Scientific Progress Come from Projects or People?," *Current Contents* 48 (27 November 1989).

[31]Committee on Science, Engineering and Public Policy, *Science, Technology, and the Federal Government: National Goals for A New Era* (New York: National Academy Press, 1993). Also see reactions to the report in *The Scientist* 7 (15) (26 July 1993): 1.

[32]Carnegie Commission on Science, Technology, and Government, *Enabling The Future: Linking Science and Technology to Societal Goals* (New York: Carnegie Commission, September 1992).

[33]Harvey Brooks, "Research Universities and the Social Contract for Science," in Branscomb, ed., *Empowering Technology: Implementing a U.S. Strategy.*

[34]President's Council of Advisors on Science and Technology, *Megaprojects In The Sciences,* White House, December 1992.

[35]David L. Goodstein, "Scientific Elites and Scientific Illiterates," *Engineering and Science* (Spring 1993).

[36]For a comprehensive recent review of the national scene, see Carnegie Commission on Science, Technology, and Government, *In The National Interest: The Federal Government in Reform of K-12 Math and Science Education,* September 1991.

[37]See, for example, Paul C. Stern, "A Second Environmental Science," *Science* 260 (25 June 1993); and the broader review of potential interdisciplinary themes in Carnegie Commission on Science, Technology, and Government, *International Environmental Research and Assessment*, July 1992.

[38]Originally in *Revue Scientifique*, Paris, 1871; and cited in National Science Foundation, *Only One Science*, NSB-80-1 (Washington, D.C.: National Science Foundation, 1981).

[39]Data on international comparisons of R&D funding, and of the global distribution of scientists and engineers, are available from the National Science Foundation and other sources; in addition, US firms (and universities) must take account of the developing world—magnets for booming investment in plant as well as for added R&D savvy—as summarized in "U.S. Firms Turn To The Developing World," *Wall Street Journal*, 4 August 1993.

[40]Possibilities for global work on the environment, and for even broader partnerships in every field involving developing countries, were documented in Carnegie Commission on Science, Technology, and Government, *International Environmental Research and Assessment: Proposals For Better Organization*, July 1992, and *Partnerships For Global Development: The Clearing Horizon*, December 1992.

Robert M. Rosenzweig

16

Governing the Modern University

T WO PERSONAL ANECDOTES SUPPLY A CONVENIENT context for these observations about the problem of governance in the modern university. The first concerns a conversation with Kingman Brewster many years ago, when he was still president of Yale University. I wondered why a friend who had recently left Yale for another position had decided to go. "Well," said Brewster, "he wanted to be a vice president, and we just don't do that sort of thing at Yale. Harvard has vice presidents, but they run that place like an insurance company." That is, I believe, the purest expression of academic disdain for administration I have encountered in thirty years of university life. An extreme case, perhaps, but it is, I believe, indicative of a broadly held view, especially prevalent among faculty. Faculty may tolerate administration and those who do it, but the notion that the university is actually better off if it is well governed and well managed is tolerable only in the Jeffersonian sense: that government is best which governs least.

The second episode took place not long ago, during a meeting with a group of management consultants engaged by a large university to examine its administrative organization and processes. It was the end of a long day, and the consultants had come together to compare notes. The meeting quickly became a recital, one after another, of inefficiencies and redundancies that they had uncovered which, supposedly, would never be countenanced in any well-run business. How, they wondered, could an organiza-

---

Robert M. Rosenzweig is President Emeritus of the Association of American Universities.

tion that took in and spent nearly a billion dollars a year, survive in such a state?

Even recognizing that what they were saying had considerable merit, my defensive hackles rose. At last I asked them to think for a moment about which US social institutions had been the most successful in the last 40 years. Surely, it was not US business, which not only could not compete abroad but had also lost a large share of its own domestic market, the largest in the world. It certainly was not our political institutions, which seemed less and less able either to lead or to respond. In truth, the answer is that the university has been the most successful of the nation's domestic institutions, enormously important at home and widely admired and imitated abroad. That being the case, I said, one really had to ask whether its success had come about in spite of or because of the arrangements that look so peculiar when seen through a lens that focuses primarily on efficiency. If the latter, then the cost of fixing all of the inefficiencies might be more than society should be asked to bear.

While my outburst served its immediate rhetorical purpose, it was too glib a response to their concerns, and I have thought about it a great deal since that day. The answer is still not clear to me. It seems likely that the independence conferred on faculty members to pursue their own interests has been an important element in the results that have been achieved and that it is difficult and perhaps counterproductive to impose administrative discipline in a context of programmatic autonomy. It is surely true, however, that there is a large self-serving component to that standard justification for management inefficiencies. Indeed, it is not at all clear whether there is a large element of plain snobbery, of the kind that Kingman Brewster expressed, behind the traditional academic antimanagement bias.

Two things, however, are clear: first, the financial constraints that all universities now face make it inevitable that what the rest of the world believes to be inefficient and wasteful will not be tolerated in institutions whose existence depends on public support; and, second, just as some changes in the external environment make greater institutional self-discipline necessary, other changes have made it harder to impose than ever before. The result is a real challenge to the governance systems of these institutions. I think it likely that those universities that find internal political arrangements that blend fiscal discipline and programmatic independence—liberty and order, as it were—will prosper, and those that do not will in various ways become less good.

It will not be easy to pull it off. In universities, as elsewhere, management systems follow the reality of political relationships. The central reality of the university political system is the substantial autonomy of the tenured faculty who, individually and collectively, are responsible for the university's main work— indeed, its reason for being—which is teaching and research. Budget processes, accounting systems, personnel policies, control mechanisms, all of the standard apparatus of management, reflect that reality in a university.

So, too, do the main political arrangements. The university is held in trust by a lay board of trustees. They are absentee landlords, remote from the actual work of the institution, and, if they insist on being an active force in the governance of the institution, that is usually seen as a sign of a deep political dysfunction. The president of the university, the board's principal agent of governance, is perhaps the weakest chief executive of any significant organization. He or she has little or nothing to do with the main personnel decisions, those having to do with faculty. Virtually no one outside the immediate presidential office and a few senior officials is beholden to the president in a meaningful way. The president issues few orders, has no real political constituency, and has few powers beyond those of persuasion. The typical university president is a more potent person off campus than on.

It is extremely difficult for people outside the university, even quite sophisticated people, to grasp the reality of university governance, and, when something goes publicly and embarrassingly wrong in a university, there is not likely to be much sympathy for the difficulties under which its administrators labor. They are, after all, largely self-imposed. Until recently, that is, for the way in which universities have grown since World War II has made them even less manageable institutions than they once were, and the forces currently operating move in the same direction. At the very least the nature of these forces makes a clash between traditional academic notions of governance and management and the demands of a new external environment inevitable. It also makes an accommodation between the two very important and very hard to manage. A brief description of some of the more important of them will make that clearer.

The scale of the university has grown enormously in every dimension: enrollment; faculty size; number of schools, programs, and departments; budget; administration; research volume; and so on. As in the Pentagon, it is impossible for anyone in a modern university to be confident that plans agreed to in principle are being implemented in practice or that information systems exist which adequately monitor the daily flow of events. When, for example, Stanford University was asked whether the yacht it owned was being charged against its indirect cost rate, top university administrators first denied that it was. They were not disingenuous, only uninformed by a system that was not able to keep track of and retrieve information about so remote a transaction as the gift to the athletic department which had bestowed the yacht on the university.

The role played by the federal government since World War II has transformed university administration and governance. When I arrived at Stanford in 1962, for example, as associate dean of the Graduate Division, my responsibilities included managing the graduate financial aid budget, caring for several small internal research grant programs, and reading and approving every research grant and contract proposal leaving the university for their conformity with university and governmental policies. It did not seem at the time terribly burdensome; there were, after all, many fewer proposals and even fewer policies. Such an assignment would be inconceivable now. Those same chores, along with a laundry list of others, are now done by a small army of administrators, who undoubtedly feel pressed by the volume of work that crosses their desks.

Government policies have in many ways removed from universities control over policies that were once wholly within local jurisdictions. To mention but a few, control over hiring, firing, and conditions of labor are now subject to myriad restrictions imposed by National Labor Relations Board jurisdiction, affirmative action laws, and retirement laws; enrollment policies and practices are affected by the rules governing financial aid programs; restrictions on the way human and animal subjects are used in research ended what many faculty believed at the time of their imposition was a part of their freedom as faculty investigators. I can recall quite vividly the outraged indignation over the loss of academic freedom which members of Stanford's Psychology Department were able to muster when they first learned that new government regulations required review of experiments using deception, a common feature of psychology experiments, and required also that subjects, including students in their classes, who had previously been conscripted as experimental subjects give informed consent to their participation. And even intercollegiate athletic programs have been changed dramatically by sex bias laws. If, for example, there comes to be a national championship tournament in football, it will be against the better judgment of most university presidents, but their academic judgment will be overridden by growing financial pressures caused, in part, by the requirements of federally mandated gender equity.

The list could obviously be lengthened considerably. More to the point, however, each of these incursions of the government into university policy is the result of successful efforts on the part of some interest group, and each of them has empowered constituencies inside the university and restricted institutional control over its own processes. All of these specific regulatory initiatives may be necessary and good; the point is that they have made the university, as an entity, vastly more difficult to govern and to manage.

Partly in response to the accumulated requirements of government, university administration has become more professionalized. It is hard to find a significant administrative role on campus which does not have at least some of the accoutrements of a profession—specialized training, some kind of credentialing body, and, most of all, its own national organization. The last is especially important. On most campuses, for example, the financial aid administrator is a mid-level functionary who is not really thought of as a policymaker. In Washington, however, the national organization of financial aid officers is a powerful player in the making of national financial aid policy, much more powerful in the actual writing of legislation and regulations than the organizations that represent university presidents. It is not only possible, but it actually happens, that financial aid officers in Washington press policies that would be rejected if they had to be approved on campus.

I was involved in an incident of that kind involving the national organization of bookstore operators. At issue was proposed legislation changing the taxation of unrelated business income, a subject of great importance to universities. The bookstore operators, through hired Washington counsel, were pressing a position that would have been extremely damaging to the larger interests of the universities. It took an extraordinary effort on the part of a number of presidents to bring the bookstores into line. Faculty members, it seems, are no longer the only independent operators on university campuses.

It is easiest to see this change in a simple quantitative measure. In 1962, when I first had occasion to do a count, there were about 20 organizations with offices in Washington representing some aspect of higher education. By no means did all of those engage in lobbying on behalf of their members. In the mid-1980s, when I again had reason to count, the number had grown to close to 200, not counting the Washington offices of individual universities established to look out for their separate interests. To list all of those organizations would be to see the modern university laid out in all of its centrifugal glory.

One recently retired university president made this point with feeling in an interview: "When I became president, or even when I became provost, I used to walk around the administration building which was newly built, and it was built for the purpose of containing the administration. And for a couple of years it did, before the administration outgrew it. Then I knew everybody. Well, that became just impossible. There were legions of people, and when you talked to them they had their own language, their own professional criteria and so on. They were still loyal to the institution, just as a professor of economics or history or medicine was loyal to the institution. But there was also that other world out there which had become incredibly complex and with which, of course, by the time I left they were all, in touch electronically. So that it was a world that was not out there; it was, Goddamn it, in their office all the time."

The growth of professional education has changed the map of

universities and altered relationships between the center and the constituent units. The strength of a professional field lies in its connection to the profession for which it is training future employees. Law, medicine, and business are the most obvious examples of how strong professions reinforce the claims of professional schools for special treatment on campus. In contrast, education on most campuses is among the weakest of the professional schools, a condition that accurately reflects the weakness of its external constituency. Faculty are, of course, paid more in the strong schools because the relatively permeable boundaries between professional and faculty employment create a market that has no counterpart in other academic fields. Specialized accrediting agencies, usually consisting of academic and professional members, constitute a pressure on university administrations to allocate resources preferentially to their member professional schools using the threat of disaccreditation. Professional schools frequently demand greater autonomy in fund-raising and, in the process, may weaken the ability of the institution to shape its fund-raising efforts to broader university priorities.

None of this is meant to deny the contributions of professional education to the modern university. Strong professional schools are almost as distinctive a mark of the strong university as are strong Ph.D. programs—a fact that, in itself, says much about the way in which universities have changed. For present purposes, however, it is important simply to note that one effect of the change has been to weaken further the capacity of central decision-making entities.

We seem to be entering a period of greater directiveness in research funding. The apparent triumph of industrial policy as advocated by the Clinton administration is already showing its effects in governmental research funding. Increasingly, universities and scientists are being asked not simply "What have you done for us lately?" but "What, specifically, do you propose to do for us now?"

I do not wish to overstate this point. It has always been the case that the direction of scholarship has been influenced by the interests of the patrons of scholarship. In the years following World War II, however, the direction of science in the United States, funded largely by the federal government, has been the product of interaction between fairly broad governmental goals and the opinion of scientists about which scientific directions are most promising and which scientists are most likely to produce good science. Since the scientists involved in this process have been mostly university faculty, there has been every chance that the results would be consistent with university values and habits of work.

The new dispensation appears to be one in which, increasingly, the government will set fairly specific economic targets and then support those science and technology efforts that are deemed most likely to produce the specific desired results. All universities have large infrastructures, including faculties, built over the last several generations on the assumption that outside funding would be available to pay for them. If the nature of the work for which funders are willing to pay changes, and if the changes are in a direction that is inconsistent with the institution's traditional conception of its role, then an enormous, perhaps irresistible, pressure to yield is put upon institutional decision makers. This seems about to happen.

Last in this catalog of forces bearing on institutional political and management systems are the issues of race and ethnicity which have bedeviled US society but from which universities were long isolated through their own policies of exclusion. These issues are now integral parts of university life, and they constitute a continuing challenge to many of the assumptions that have long been held to govern academic institutions, beginning with standards for admission of students and appointment of faculty and including the purposes and content of the curriculum, the organization and content of the academic disciplines (including the creation of new ones built around issues of race, ethnicity, and gender), and what utterances constitute unacceptable harassment and therefore lose their protected status as free speech under university disciplinary codes. Core institutional values have come under challenge, a circumstance that always complicates the task of governing.

If all of these forces had come to bear on a university system that was financially healthy, they would be hard enough to deal with. But the opposite is the case. It is now necessary to face the possibility—I would say the probability—that the steady growth of funding which has marked most of the last forty years has come to an end; that what has become the normal experience for virtually everyone now in the university system was in fact an aberration, not to be repeated for the foreseeable future. The lubricant of easy money, always so attractive to political leaders, will not be available to those who lead universities.

Universities have never been easy places to govern or manage. The very words are enough to excite opposition on most campuses. Perhaps that is the way it should be. A healthy suspicion of governing and of those who do it is certainly part of American tradition, and university people partake of that tradition in full measure. But, just as excessive suspicion of politicians can lead to paralysis in government, its counterpart on campus may prevent institutions from meeting the challenges they now face. As the foregoing suggests, those challenges come in many forms. They would be daunting individually; in the aggregate they constitute a major threat to the kind of university which has served so well in the last half of this century.

There are no easy answers to the political and managerial problems faced by universities, just as there are none to the comparable set of problems faced by the nation's political institutions. There is, however, a great deal of experience in both arenas to suggest that hard and divisive problems cannot be dealt with in the absence of strong, risk-taking executive leadership. It is now quite clear that the United States Congress, without a strong lead from the president, is not capable of generating an agenda for action and mobilizing the majorities needed to implement it. The forces of separatism, constituency interest, and self-interest work too strongly in the other direction. Exactly the same is true of university faculties. Both bodies are indispensable participants in the policy-making process, but neither can perform its role properly unless a strong executive is willing to lay out the facts of the case candidly, set an agenda for dealing with it, and insist that a program for doing so be agreed to.

It should be said that these have been hard times for political leaders and for university leaders. In both arenas constituents have preferred to believe that their problems are temporary, that they are of someone else's making, not their own, and that those who tell them otherwise should move on to some other form of employment. Any rewards for courage have been left for history to bestow. But as we are learning again, presidents of the United States have one enormous advantage, which, if shrewdly and forcefully exercised, can change the nature of public discourse and action. That is the power to set the agenda and to define the terms of the debate that follows. University presidents have the same opportunity, and if they choose to use it, they, too, can produce the kind of coherence and focus which governance has lacked for too long and so badly needs now.

I am not here expressing a judgment on the performance of incumbent leaders. As I have suggested, they can muster only limited resources to deal with seemingly limitless problems. As a result, in a period of fragmentation, conflict, and challenged legitimacy, there has been a tendency for leaders to manage issues rather than confront them, to react to today's problems rather than seek agreement on overarching principles that might guide an approach to the future. How expansive can a university's reach be when resources are constrained? If it cannot sustain its present activities without sacrificing quality, what principles should guide the necessary retraction? To what degree can a university respond to demands for short-term payoff on the investment in its faculty's research without losing the very character that has made academic research such a valuable contributor to society? When resources are limited, how can an institution strike a sustainable balance among its principal missions: undergraduate teaching and graduate and professional education and scholarship?

These are large and vexing questions. They are urgent questions because of the change in the financial condition of universities and the heavy demands of a society that has come to depend on them. There is no hope of managing universities successfully unless those who lead them put their own approaches out in public and then engage in the debate that is bound to follow. As always, management follows politics, and as always in a free political system, liberty and order cannot coexist without leaders to point the way.

Francis X. Sutton

17

The Distinction and Durability of American Research Universities

MANY KNOWLEDGEABLE AMERICANS THINK THAT the golden age of research universities in the United States was in the past and worry earnestly about the future of these institutions. This is a bit surprising, since most of the world continues to gaze on them and the research they produce with admiration and envy. Kenneth Prewitt provides evidence in chapter 10 that the nation's research universities are in no crisis of falling or lost prestige among the US public. Americans' pride and respect for these universities often swell into claims that they are the best in the world.

These universities retain worldwide prestige in a time when Americans seem as much disposed to doubt or deplore the quality of other of the nation's institutions as to hold them up for emulation. The collapse of the Communist adversary may have brought a triumphant reassertion of free markets and democracy as the true paths to prosperity and general felicity, but this triumph has not stilled doubts about the capacity of the United States to meet international competition in the open world we have helped foster. It is now fashionable for nations all around the world to worry about the quality of their "human resources" as the most important determinant of their future successes. The United States has joined in these concerns with characteristically loud and vigorous self-criticism. We produce studies like the National Adult Literacy Survey which somehow display almost half the adult population in parlous incapacity, and we bravely set

Francis X. Sutton is Secretary-Member of the Chancellor's Commission on the Future of Aga Khan University and a retired officer of the Ford Foundation.

309

nearly impossible "National Goals for Education" to remove our worst deficiencies by the end of the century. We are accustomed to embarrassing comparisons of our schoolchildren with Asian schoolchildren and are even a bit surprised when the Organization for Economic Cooperation and Development (OECD) tells us we are not doing so badly among the rich countries.[1]

Dissatisfaction with US education may be less pronounced at the college and university levels than at lower levels, but there is periodic scolding, and cries of alarm are sounded about the quality of our higher education, such as the recent declaration sponsored by four foundations that "higher expectations for higher education" should be "an American imperative."[2] Amid so much deploring, one must suppose that the respect for US research universities rests on exceptional qualities that most education in the country, and at least a great deal of higher education abroad, do not possess.

Whence these distinctive qualities? Have the research universities done so well simply because the United States has been so rich and powerful, or is it because of distinctive characteristics of US culture and society which are weaker or missing elsewhere? Such an inquiry clearly must look abroad to international comparisons, and it must begin from familiar features of US higher education. It is not the sort of inquiry that is likely to be of much help with immediate policy problems facing these universities; indeed, a certain detachment from responsible policy-making is necessary to it. But it may help us know how seriously we should take the worries within and about these universities that whatever has made them great can no longer be counted on. In short, it may have something to say about their durability and their longer-term futures.

SOURCES OF ACADEMIC DISTINCTION: EDUCATING LEADERS

There are two ways in which universities in the modern world have attained distinction. The first, and historically prior, has been in educating (or "forming," as the French nicely say) the leadership of nations. The second is by attaining and exemplifying intellectual superiority and creativity, as the label "research universities" asserts to be their distinctive merit. A convergence of these two modes of distinction has, of course, been normal. Oxford and Cambridge have historically been sites for the education of aristocratic elites, political leaders, and higher civil servants. As meritocracy has grown, they have become channels for selection and elevation of the talented to join in leading a modern Britain. Across the globe Tokyo and Kyoto universities have been similarly, and perhaps even more particularly, devoted to preparing a rigorously selected elite for national leadership. But these institutions have also been homes of distinguished research and scholarship. Similarly, the *grandes écoles* and the old Sorbonne have had dual distinctions in France in educating national elites and intellectual eminence. The German universities, as the historic progenitors of the "research" university, have had a more dispersed and less differentiated pattern but have likewise combined their pursuit of learning and discovery with education of the country's elites. The United States has been peculiar in its radical democracy and mistrust of government, which has given a distinctive cultural character to the national state, inhibited the development of an elite higher civil service, and left a less clear role for universities in selecting and preparing the governmental leadership of the country.

In contrast to most of the world, the United States does not have a university or set of universities established and supported by the federal government (excluding the service academies and institutions in the District of Columbia). For much of US history higher education was principally private, and, as public higher education grew, it was dispersed across a large country under the responsibility of state governments. Also in contrast with the practice of other nations—and in particular to the European nations, whose practice spread across the world through imperialism or plain cultural prestige—*the federal government in this country has not set standards for academic degrees*, and until recent decades it did not attempt to regulate the practice of higher education in any significant way. Such academic standard setting as has occurred has been at the state level and through regional accrediting bodies and has been more concerned with minimal than uniform standards. The result has been the very wide spectrum of quality which has been characteristic of US higher education, with some institutions and their degrees being recog-

nized as much better than others. There has been a certain
courteous reticence in flaunting distinctions, but in fact there has
been a lively competition, within regions and increasingly at the
national level, for prestige and recognition. This pattern of higher
education has fitted a large country in which the role of national
government was for a long time quite limited, in which employment has been primarily private, and in which the principal
function of higher education was indeed education, not research
and scholarship or forms of public service.

Other countries have large private sectors in higher education.
Japan and the Philippines have long been prominent examples,
and in recent decades private higher education has grown remarkably in such Latin American countries as Brazil and Colombia.
But the dominant pattern when modern universities came to be
established outside the European world was set by the public
national universities, oriented above all to public employment and
upholding uniform national standards. These patterns were reinforced with the emergence of newly independent states constituting a "Third World" after 1950; these new states exhibited a
jealous concern for national control of their institutions and a
corresponding mistrust of private higher education.

Universities in the United States have had to distinguish themselves amid the populous array of institutions of higher education
in which they grew up. They have been identified by their
embracing character, incorporating undergraduate "colleges," in
the US sense, along with professional schools at both first-degree
and more advanced levels. One can think of cases of enterprising
"universities" that have taken on the name when they added a
liberal arts program to a professional school or two, without
venturing to claim a role in the advancement of knowledge.
Normally in this century, to be a university in the United States
has meant some sort of conscientious commitment to the advancement of research and scholarship. The universities that have called
themselves research universities (or been so labeled in the Carnegie
Foundation for the Advancement of Teaching's effort to classify
US higher education) have undertaken major commitments to
research utilizing public and private resources.[3]

The omnivorous character of the American university was
deplored by older critics such as Abraham Flexner but came to be

accepted by latter-day rationalizers such as Clark Kerr. It is now quite standard and stands in some contrast with the nature of universities over much of the rest of the world. The provision of various forms of professional education in universities—for law, medicine, dentistry, engineering of many sorts, and so on—is, of course, effectively universal and not peculiar to universities in the United States. But the incorporation of a liberal arts college, devoted in good part to education that is regarded elsewhere as pre-university schooling, is one of their distinguishing features. The scale and depth of commitment to research and scholarship which has grown up in the research universities, particularly since World War II, may be another.

Research university is a proud label. But it is not clear that it is because they are research universities that the leading American universities are so much admired, envied, and sought after at home and abroad. The luster and lure of degrees from Harvard or Berkeley have an immediacy of appeal against which eminence in research and scholarship does not easily shine forth. Obviously, the nation's research universities are, and in most cases have for a long time been, places that have educated the leaders of US society in diverse professional fields, from the professors, clergymen, lawyers, and doctors of many generations past to the more recent businessmen and -women emerging from Master of Business Administration (MBA) programs. The graduate schools, academic and professional, which are essential components of leading universities, afford coveted paths to rewarding careers in the United States and abroad. Like leading institutions in other countries, the US research universities unmistakably hold some of their prestige because they provide paths to rewarding careers and high status. Either being private or having the quasi-private independence that leading public universities have maintained,[4] these institutions have been in a position to maintain selective admissions and to control the size of their graduate and professional schools.

The four-year undergraduate liberal arts colleges that have been peculiar features of universities in the United States were once thought by presidents of Chicago, Johns Hopkins, Michigan, or Stanford to be destined to disappear from the US research university.[5] On the contrary, they have proven to be exceptionally hardy, often winning flattering attention as the hearts of their universities. One reason is that these colleges have been recognized and sought after as stepping-stones to lofty prospects in US society. The well-to-do have long sent their offspring as undergraduates to Ivy League universities with this expectation.

The advantages of such an education in the decades before World War II may have been more social than intellectual, but they were nonetheless real, and the residential "collegiate culture" set an envied pattern, which was widely sought after and gradually opened to poorer sorts on a selective basis through scholarships and financial aid. The advantages of passing through a selective college, particularly after the arrival of mass higher education in the 1960s and 1970s, have evidently been appreciated; students and their families have been willing to pay handsomely for these advantages, and both universities and liberal arts colleges have been anxious to maintain their ranking among their selective competitors. The *Harvard College Gazette* proudly headlined recently, "Poll Ranks Harvard Top US University,"[6] not because of its numbers of Nobelists but, rather, because it came out first among universities in the *US News & World Report* ranking of some 1,371 four-year colleges in the United States. Princeton came second in this ranking, and its president, Harold Shapiro, puts teaching undergraduates first in his current strategic planning document: "Princeton remains distinctive among major research universities in its exceptional commitment to teaching—especially at the undergraduate level."[7]

The major research universities have not had a monopoly on selective undergraduate liberal education, but they evidently continue to have strong motivations to maintain and strengthen the position they have in it. The reasons for this devotion to undergraduates clearly go beyond a lust for fee-paying students. They lie, on the one hand, in the social functions of these universities in forming as much of a national elite as Americans dare allow themselves and, on the other, in the idea of a university as devoted to the unbounded advancement of knowledge, "seeking truth," as Neil Rudenstine has recently put it, "in all its forms and formulations."[8] The United States has had elite private schools, but they have not had the centrality in forming national leadership which the lycées, gymnasiums, and public schools of

Europe have had. A common, binding experience for people who disperse after college into diverse trades and professions has had to be sought a little farther up the educational ladder. What that experience ought to be is a perpetual challenge, but it clearly must go beyond specialized preparation for the later world of work. The resources it needs to draw on are as broad as the scope of human knowledge, and the affiliation of undergraduate colleges with graduate schools of arts and sciences is natural. Graduate professional education may increasingly be the high road to success, but it cannot provide the basis for a common sense of status and belonging that the undergraduate liberal college does. The endemic tensions between research and teaching would be greatly eased if the research universities were not so attached to their colleges, but they could not let go of them without losing a principal source of their strength.

Being a selective funnel for the talented and ambitious, those who aspire to high station and rewards, thus appears to explain in part the distinction of US research universities; it may be as important in this regard as eminence in research and scholarship. For some of the graduate schools of research universities, strong research programs are clearly needed to maintain their attractiveness as graduate schools. But it is not clear that this is so for law or business schools, and there is a dangerous tendency toward inverse relationships between eminence in research and commitment to undergraduate liberal instruction. To call these universities research universities may not be to denote their essential character but only to emphasize one of their less obviously invidious characteristics.

THE DEMAND FOR HIGHER EDUCATION AND THE APPEAL OF
SELECTIVE UNIVERSITIES

The possibility of maintaining some institutions as places in which a superior, or ostensibly superior, higher education is provided to a limited number of choice students is unquestionably a critical feature of the US system of higher education. The education these institutions provide is more expensive than that available in less selective and prestigious institutions, and it is, with exceptions, not free. The tuition charges have been very large by international standards; indeed, they recently looked "exorbitant" to the *Economist*, even though they notoriously cover less than half the cost per student. The research universities are a large part of this selective sector of US higher education and a sizable fraction of the whole. Roger Geiger has calculated that they train practically all the Ph.D.s and medical doctors for the country and provide about 30 percent of the bachelor's degrees.[9] The account I have given of the characteristics of these universities has stressed their autonomy and their acceptance as highly respected national institutions. The importance of these characteristics, to the universities themselves and to US society, stands out sharply when one considers the factors that influence higher education in the world today.

The appetite for higher education is now nearly universal and nearly insatiable. In poor and rich countries it strains public and private resources and leads to questionable budgetary allocations and public policy. Political leaders are deterred by the eagerness for higher education from restraining its growth even when it is clear that the flow of graduates far surpasses their prospects of finding employment. These problems have long seemed peculiar to poor, developing countries and have been blamed on ill-suited imported forms of education. But there is reason now to believe that no country, however rich, can fully escape such problems, though they may be mitigated.

The troubles that have afflicted higher education in countries such as India and Egypt have long been at least vaguely known internationally. The spread of Western higher education to such countries followed Western European models in being publicly funded for the most part and essentially free to students. The opportunities that were opened to university graduates were large and seductive and the demand correspondingly intense. Colonial governments could be insensitive to demands for the expansion of higher education beyond the scale of reasonable expectations for employing graduates. But even they could sometimes not quell demand (as India and Egypt found), and independent nationalist governments have been helpless against the pressures, with the result that higher education in most parts of the Third World has been expanded disproportionately to the opportunities for university-level employment and, despite regular scolding from the

World Bank, at the expense of public expenditures for other kinds of education and other fields. (In 1988, for example, the Egyptian government spent one-third of its education budget on 680,000 university students, while the remaining two-thirds had to suffice for the 11 million students in Egyptian schools.)

Differences in quality and facilities between universities have been difficult to sustain in the Third World, where European models of uniform standards for degrees predominate, along with egalitarian values that discourage the growth of private higher education or significant fee paying in public institutions. There have been some exceptions, cases in which selective institutions of high quality (like the Indian Institutes of Technology) have managed to flourish, but generally limited resources have been spread too thinly over too many institutions and students, with a resulting painful decline marked by student unrest and disorder. A columnist in the Pakistani daily *Dawn* recently declared that, across the South Asian countries, "the system of higher education has collapsed," and it is easy to encounter educators and public officials in these countries who passionately agree.[10]

Small, poor, underdeveloped countries can quickly educate enough graduates to fill the few thousand or tens of thousands of jobs in their economies which might require such degrees. This has been done in some African countries, where the cost of maintaining a university student for a year was at least 10 times the per capita gross domestic product (GDP)—as against about 1 per capita GDP in a rich, developed country—with predictably disastrous consequences. But one does not have to go to Africa south of the Sahara to encounter despairing observations about the state of higher education. The recent actions of French university students sent tremors through much of Europe. The students "descended into the street" waving banners complaining of "*Facultés asphyxiés, chômeurs assurés.*" There were too many students for the seats in the dilapidated lecture halls and for the overburdened professors. And like their counterparts in the Third World, they knew they would soon be among the multitudes of the unemployed. Italians, with their universities in a similar state, were supplied by their media with abundant, worried accounts of these demonstrations. In 1993 the *Frankfurter Allgemeine* warned that the German universities and higher technical schools would soon contain two million students; the lecture halls were already overflowing, and the professors could not keep up with the rising tide of students.[11] It feared that German students might see their universities the way French students saw theirs, as "holding pens for the unemployed." Worse, the German universities are, in principle, all of the same rank; unlike in France, there are no *grandes écoles* for the chosen few, and all of the German universities could in one general ruin become storage places for the unemployed.[12]

The French protests and German anxiety are rooted in the situation that poor nations have long faced. Equality of opportunity is accepted as a proper claim for all, male or female and of whatever origin. European political leaders are under pressure everywhere to provide opportunities for those who seek a higher education, and the tradition of free higher education for all who have completed the appropriate secondary school has put a terrific strain on national budgets. The expansionist, egalitarian pressures arising in the late 1960s came as the older faith that more university-trained talent was a prime key to economic growth was eroding. Governments have been unable or unwilling to continue the increases in expenditures which that faith inspired. Since uniform standards in facilities, staffing, admissions, and degree requirements have been maintained for most universities in most countries, the trend has been toward diminished or clearly bad quality for the whole array, while the yield of graduates has been great enough to make unemployment a commonly feared prospect.

There is no reason to suppose that the United States can avoid running out of career opportunities for graduates of higher education or that its political leaders will be able to stop responding to popular pressure for supplying places in higher education. Indeed, there are those who think that the disparity between opportunities and aspirations is endemic, and no mere cyclical pain. Exasperated undergraduates are not yet marching in protest up Pennsylvania Avenue or down Broadway. But only a brave prophet would assure us that such demonstrations will not occur on this side of the Atlantic, even given a national tradition that makes the costs of higher education a private responsibility. Widespread disillusionment with the rewards that Americans can expect after the efforts and sacrifices of winning degrees would have multiple and unpredictable consequences. The *Economist* believes there is currently under way "nothing less than a populist backlash against academia" which encourages critical assaults on the universities by politicians in Europe and America.[13]

The effects on the US research universities of popular disillusionment with the possibilities of advancement through higher education would certainly be cushioned if it was recognized that graduates of the research institutions enjoy better prospects than graduates of other higher-education institutions. In the "climacteric" of the late 1960s there were strong leveling pressures, which in Europe brought both expansion, leading to present overcrowding, and also democratic changes in the constitutions of universities. In the United States the research universities were shaken by the campus revolts of the late 1960s, but they avoided structural changes like the ones that, for example, the German universities underwent, and they kept control of the size and selection of their student bodies. The critical condition for this insulation from leveling pressures has evidently been the legitimacy of their autonomy and differential character, whether as private or public institutions.

Whether there now exist serious threats to the values in US society which legitimize selective and expensive institutions educating disproportionately large fractions of US leadership is a question that probably admits a negative answer. There is a great deal of evidence in many countries that uncertain or discouraging career prospects at any level and quality of education produce a drive toward higher qualifications. An inflation of educational qualifications for jobs occurs at least as much because of increased competition as because of better performance by those with higher qualifications. The large increases in the holders of university degrees which the expansion of US higher education has brought in the last decades has certainly produced such a sharpened competition and made a striving after higher qualifications seem attractive. The readiness in recent decades of families and students to pay the costs of selective higher education, even as these rose very sharply, indicates that many Americans continue to value the possibility of gambling on the gains from more selective education. As long as such readiness exists, the legitimacy of elite universities is bolstered by continuing demand for the advantages they promise. If the relative advantage of degrees from research universities should disappear, the situation would of course be different. But this seems most improbable, even for bachelor's degrees. Americans remembering easier times are now distressed to hear of whole groups of B.A.s and B.S.s emerging from universities as distinguished as Yale or Michigan and drifting, taking up unsuitable employment or finding none at all if they do not go on to graduate study. But if there were a gloomy future for the colleges of the research universities, it is unlikely that there would be as much effort to strengthen them as is now being made.

In one important respect the research universities bumped a ceiling as early as 1970. The sudden change about that time from a confident sense of need for more Ph.D.s in the country to the spectacle (or fear) of glut signaled that a limitation was being reached on the demand for a product from these universities which was organically related to their research function. Upper bounds on the demand for Ph.D.s and, correspondingly, on opportunities for graduate students came from, first, the scale and rate of growth of higher education generally and, second, the demand for research both within and outside the universities. The assessment of demands has been full of uncertainties, but clearly Ph.D.s in many fields have been regularly oversupplied, and there has been a general disposition since the 1970s for the leading universities to hold steady or reduce the scale of their Ph.D. programs. (One of the evident sources of renewed attention to undergraduate colleges lay in this restraint on further development of graduate study and research.) How serious these limitations may prove to be for the research universities may perhaps best be assessed after a more frontal consideration of their roles qua institutions of research and scholarship.

THE VOCATION FOR RESEARCH IN THE RESEARCH UNIVERSITIES

Making a university stand on two legs of distinction is an awkward metaphor because the legs are never quite equal: either the intellectual side or the human selection and development side is stronger, and those who establish university policy are constantly busy making appropriate adjustments. The rise of a US collegiate culture in the 1920s initiated a counterbalancing increase in research and scholarship in the nation's leading universities. We are apparently now in a period in which the balance is shifting the other way; the demands for more attention to teaching at least suggest that this is so. Whatever the balance at any particular time, there are intrinsic reasons why these "legs" go together. Any elite institution must have a basis of intellectual authority to buttress its claim to respect. There can, of course, be different sorts of elites—great scientists are not usually great political leaders—but dispositions toward mutual respect between different elites contribute to the coherence of societies. The history of the world shows numerous cases in which the political authority of illiterate warriors had to be coupled with the authority of those who, like the Islamic ulema or the medieval Christian clergy, could master texts. But since the Renaissance the spread of literacy and classical education provided common experience and prestigious accomplishments for aristocracy, clergy, and some fortunate members of the lower ranks of society. The institutions that provided these marks of proper cultivation to the higher ranks could not be inferior in intellectual pretensions, however weak they may at times have been. Hence the necessary effort to make the modern universities that educate elites into leading places of research and scholarship. Yale between the two world wars might in fact have been, as Hutchins famously charged, a "finishing school for boys," but it was also moving vigorously to distinction as a research university.

The period between the end of World War II and the late 1960s, and in particular the decade after Sputnik went up in October 1957 and sent the United States into paroxysms of anxious effort, is now celebrated in retrospect as a great flourishing of the American universities as research universities. It was the time when the famous "social contract" between the federal government and the universities was formed, and unprecedented resources flowed to the universities from the public purse. Whereas before World War II university research had been largely, as Geiger labeled it, "a privately funded research system,"[14] public support came to dwarf foundation and other private support after the war. Performance responded to opportunity, and universities in the United States became fountains of research and scholarship. It was in this great efflorescence that the particular prominence of research within the universities became pronounced; the old leaders among the research universities felt their research vocation more central, and new aspirants sought to take on that vocation. The universities were especially entrusted with responsibilities for basic research, distant or divorced from immediate utility, and conflicts over the legitimacy of what they were doing were blessedly infrequent.

The floraison of research in US universities in the 1950s and 1960s depended on more than Cold War anxieties. In retrospect, this was a period in which there was an extraordinary faith in the potentials of scientific investigation and the role of universities as homes of that enterprise. The origins of the faith cannot occupy us here; they lay partly in spectacular wartime applications of science but also had deeper and longer roots. It was an international faith, but with special forms and intensities in the United States. The positivistic streak in the US heritage which appeared in Progressivism at an earlier time was still alive after World War II (though it was doubted and opposed as it had been before). Faith that unbiased, empirical study of problems would lead to solutions was not confined to the natural sciences; it also gave confidence to social scientists and to academic and philanthropic leaders that they could show the way to social policies that would benefit all. When two leading authorities on foundations surveyed their field in 1946, they depicted the major foundations as engaged in "methodical . . . undramatic research looking to the future" rather than "aggressive, immediate action."[15] The label research foundations came to be applied to the big foundations that sought not to deal with "symptoms" but, rather, to probe for "causes," and they honored that label in the kind of programs they funded. More than research was supported, but the Carnegie, Ford, and Rockefeller foundations' faith in the promise of academic inquiry made them major supporters of the social sciences and the newly developing area studies within American universities. Looking back decades later, when the ideal of a value-free social science seems naive or quaintly dated, when foundations are seen not as neutral searchers for the common good but, instead, as being committed to either a liberal or conservative agenda, when the ambition to make American universities places of expertise in remote foreign areas arouses qualms of conscience about "orientalism" or worse, the 1950s appear as a simple time of unperturbed faith. Of course, they were hardly so; denunciations of "empirical social science" were heard then in congressional committees, and suspicions of disloyalty shadowed foreign interests there too. Still, there prevailed a sufficiently general confidence in what universities and the intellectual inquiry they nurtured could do that government, private donors, and the general public happily invested confidence and treasure in them.

This enthusiasm for universities and faith in what they could do was quite universal through the 1950s and the early 1960s. It was promoted around the world by UNESCO, the United Nations Educational, Scientific, and Cultural Organization, prophet of manpower planning and human resource development, as well as by eager governments. The conception that there were various sorts of "gaps" between the United States and other countries which could be narrowed by higher education and research filled popular and learned literatures of the time. The United States was looked to as a model and leader, and it was indeed exemplary at least in the strength of its faith. Sputnik came at a time when there were other stimuli to the expansion of universities and their research activities. The diffuse anxiety over US competencies which it provoked stimulated no narrowly focused remedies but, rather, a broad strengthening of basic research and an effort to promote educational excellence in the universities. In doing so, it joined with the aspirations of academic leaders who wanted to build not merely large but also intellectually distinguished universities. The enthusiasm of university presidents for the area studies centers promoted under the National Defense Education Act (NDEA) is a striking example. A movement had been under way, encouraged by Ford and other foundations, to deparochialize American universities with non-Western area studies. The passionate attachment of universities to these centers was displayed when later attempts to eliminate funding that was trivial by Washington standards was bitterly and repeatedly fought by an aroused academic community; these internationalizing programs had clearly responded to a salient aspiration of universities.[16] Sputnik also gave a rationale for a strong entry of the federal government into activities that had previously been left to private funders and the states. When Daniel Patrick Moynihan recalled in a 1975 piece for

Dædalus what happened in those years, he wryly emphasized the way demands for opportunity and equity through federal student aid overtook the original purposes and conceptions of the National Defense Education Act.[17] He saw, too, how the new federal role in higher education brought a democratizing spread of the array of research universities away from concentration on East Coast leaders by its encouragement of new aspirants elsewhere; the accent was on leveling, not on peaks of excellence.

When *Dædalus* surveyed US higher education in 1975, Clark Kerr said it had been passed through a "climacteric" and wrote ominously that "seldom has so great an American institution passed so quickly from its Golden Age to its Age of Survival."[18] The climacteric of the late 1960s swept around the world, shaking universities almost everywhere. US research universities seem to have gone through it, and the "Age of Survival" Kerr thought they were enduring, with less damage than came to universities elsewhere, protected as they have been by their autonomy and acceptance as being legitimately different from others. But the great cultural changes that came in the late 1960s had aspects and consequences beyond those we have already noticed and which bear directly on the intellectual climate affecting universities.

The "New Spirit" that came in the late 1960s brought an elevation of egalitarian and antiauthoritarian values, and not only in ethical senses. It encouraged and rationalized resistance to intellectual along with other forms of authority, and it challenged the symbols that lent dignity to institutions. The corresponding individual freedom became for a time an antinomianism in thought and behavior which had its climactic expression in the campus revolts in the United States, in *les événements* in France, and in violence on German and Japanese campuses and elsewhere.

More lastingly, these altered values presented challenges to the very conception of an authoritative institution as the social repository of valid knowledge. The conception that knowledge and cultural heritages are different, and differently valued, across societies and between groups within them challenges the pretension of a "Western," "elitist" university to declare for all what is valid and worthwhile. The contrast is stark between such a conception and the usual claim that science is good science only when its validity does not depend on who discovers or presents it.

These relativistic views also contrast with the older US faith that properly professional academic experts can come to unbiased conclusions even on human and social issues hard to reduce to rigorous scientific investigation. The impacts of this "postmodern," or "culturally relativistic," skepticism on different branches or sectors of knowledge have been quite different. While in obvious ways the New Spirit has been antiscientific, its most conspicuous effects have not been in the physical or biological sciences but, rather, in the social sciences and the humanities.[19]

Some think that Thomas Kuhn showed in the 1960s that there is no scientific knowledge independent of the social position of the knower. But such exaggerated interpretations of Kuhn's views seem to affect very little the actual practice of the sciences in the universities. They have had more consequence in the social sciences, in which old beliefs in unbiased inquiry have been abandoned, and in the humanities, in which postmodernist skepticism and relativism are flourishing remarkably. One would expect such divergent trends to sharpen academic quarrels, and they seem to have done so in such fields as psychology, psychiatry, and anthropology.[20] In any event, there is a challenge in this divergence to Neil Rudenstine's ideal of a university "seeking truth in all its forms and formulations" while keeping comity among its seekers.

It should be emphasized once again that the intellectual currents that have come with the New Spirit are not peculiarly American but, rather, thoroughly international. The theoretical methods of structuralism and deconstruction are, after all, mostly European imports in this country, and in the now-globalized world nearly all countries are eager importers of the prevailing intellectual fashions. In each cultural setting special uses are made of the international currency. In Turkey, for example, we read of Islamic conservatives using postmodernist arguments in their continuing struggle against Western science and Kemalist secularism. In the United States the effects of the New Spirit have no doubt been distinctively American in ways we do not always easily see. The internal effects within the university world have been accompanied by shifting attitudes in US society toward research and research universities. I have already recalled the description of major US foundations as research foundations. The large general-

purpose foundations would not respond to such a name nowadays, nor would the support of basic, academic research stand out
as a principal focus of their programs. They have shifted away in
recent decades from policies that once set the development of an
academic field or profession as an essential step toward one of
their social and philanthropic objectives. Observers of foundations have detected a movement in their policy and practice since,
say, 1970, from the older support of academic fields first to policy
studies and then increasingly to exemplary, or pilot "action,"
programs (a similar movement has been seen by observers in
Europe). A gradual withering of the strong and intimate relationship between major foundations and leading research universities
which existed until well along in the 1960s has accompanied this
shift. There have, of course, been several reasons for this, not least
among them a growing disparity between university budgets and
foundation resources, particularly through the 1970s. But the fact
that foundations seeking in diverse ways to advance the general
welfare look more to means other than academic research suggests
a loss of confidence in such research in one significant sector of US
society.

There are many similar sorts of evidence of public moods to
worry the leaders of the research universities. The assaults from
Washington on the integrity of scientific researchers or university
accounting for public funds may be less disturbing than a loss of
faith in the intrinsic merit of pursuing the "endless frontier"
wherever it may be or a questioning of the critical role of research
in human progress. The old reverential regard for universities
rested on a dual faith in the essential roles of highly educated
people and of the advancement of knowledge for the betterment
of the human condition. They were, no doubt, uncritically
exaggerated faiths, but the pleasures of basking in them have not
been easily abandoned. Loud rejections of these faiths are heard
nowadays, as, for example when the readers of *Science* are told, in
response to a proud recital of the contributions of medical
research, that "academic health centers . . . are . . . fiscal black
holes into which society can pour endless resources and often get
little in return," the great challenges to health in the United States
now having "little to do with the agenda of the academic medical
centers."[21] The particular merits of such charges are of less interest

here than that they seem to appear more freely and at a time when there is widespread disgruntlement over the constraints on research funding. Rodney Nichols, in this volume, tells of a 1991 study by the Congressional Office of Technology Assessment which complained of "the evident lack of limits on what academic science wishes to do"; he says, "The stance of this study would have been astonishing a generation ago and almost unthinkable even a decade ago." Nichols goes on to underscore the sharpness of public-academic differences by contrasting a call from Congressman George Brown, a longtime friend of academic science, for research agendas more closely related to social goals, with Leon Ledermann's call, as president of American Association for the Advancement of Science, for a doubling of public funding for science.

Despite criticisms and skepticism over recent decades, the funding of scientific research in the major research universities has not suffered grievously. The period immediately after the cultural upheavals in the late 1960s did, in fact, produce a notable decline in the federal funding of academic scientific research (except for biomedical research), but the loss was recouped by the late 1970s, and increased funding continued through the 1980s.[22] The current distress over highly qualified but unfunded researchers comes after a period of remarkable expansion. Although it may provoke the uncertainty and discouragement that Ledermann has deplored, it hardly presents a basic threat to the vocation of the research universities. A public mood more critical of science and more skeptical of its beneficence may keep a ceiling on the growth of academic science and strengthen the demands for more attention to teaching, without disturbing resolutions such as Princeton's to "maintain some independent capacity to support a greater amount of research and scholarship of the highest quality even if external funding is not available."[23]

It is important that the ideal of a common commitment to ideals of unfettered inquiry seems to persist in the research universities without discrimination by fields. However disturbed some parts of the social sciences and humanities may be by the new skepticisms, relativisms, and resistances to authoritative doctrine, there is also the academic ideology of disciplined and critical inquiry which provides a binding sense of shared purpose. There is also in these American universities the common enterprise of providing a liberal education for undergraduates, to constrain either absorption in specialization or in some "alternative" culture. It is still too soon to say confidently how the effects of the New Spirit, present since 1970, will work out across the divisions and perturbations the universities now show. But there are some speculations about the future which can be offered in closing.

THE FUTURE OF RESEARCH UNIVERSITIES IN THE UNITED STATES

The depiction of the nation's research universities which I have given has set them in an international context, more to point up their distinctive characteristics than to stress any international influences or interests affecting them. These are, first of all, American universities, with a key role in providing US leadership and intellectual resources. But they are also parts of the wider world in most of what they do—in the universality of scientific knowledge they cultivate and many of the values that guide them; in the international, or non-US focus of whole fields of knowledge; in the cosmopolitan interests of faculty and students; and in the international origins of many of them. Since World War II life everywhere has been profoundly influenced by a globalization affecting more than just communications and commerce. The world has become one in adhering to ideals of universal human rights and dignity; there has been a great leveling felt by peoples and nations everywhere. However imperfectly applied, these ideals have changed both the internal character of the United States and how it relates to the world outside. The universities have been affected by the nation's economic and military strength in this new world but very strongly, too, by the moral and cultural appreciations it has brought.

It seems unquestionable that a great part of the turbulence and divisions that have appeared in US research universities since the 1960s has come from sharing in the worldwide movements toward equality, with the related assaults on authority and the rising voices from those previously unheard. The campus revolts of the late 1960s were our form of a linked series of social explosions around the world. They were transitory, but the values they expressed and the effects they brought were not. The movements toward equality of access, respect, and attention which had dramatic expression in those exciting times have gone forward in efforts to open the universities to yet more women and minorities, in admissions and faculty positions and in what is studied and taught. The American universities, as I noted earlier, had also been eagerly trying to be more international since World War II, expanding their studies of the non-Western world, engaging in foreign aid projects, and receiving increasing numbers of foreign students. Much of this internationalizing was done to serve the US national interest in some instrumental way. But it was also a response to a widening appreciation for different peoples and cultures, often ones remote from direct US experience.

Respect for the basic worth of all peoples and cultures can readily be put to political and ideological uses, as we have seen frequently in "Third World" and other campus movements here and abroad. It also provides a moral basis for intellectual movements that are ideologically challenging to established orthodoxies. The passion invested in many multicultural subjects seems hard to account for in purely intellectual terms. Similarly, it is puzzling that satisfaction can be found in the skepticism expressed in postmodern reductions of different bodies of theory and fact to merely alternate "discourses" with no differential pertinence to reality, unless destruction of somebody's authority is being sought. The assault on the "Western rationalistic tradition" which John Searle describes thus would appear to be grounded in antiauthoritarian polemic.

If these are correct perceptions, the current divergence in US research universities between the sciences, on the one hand, and the humanities and the social sciences, on the other, is due to no intrinsic differences between the branches of learning but, rather, to ideological pressures that may or may not persist. The fact that we are increasingly and irrevocably engaged with the wider world promises continuing awareness of differences and inequities that stir ideological passions. The rather bleak state of higher education around the world also seems to be persisting and is likely to generate ideological movements of colorful sorts. Many of these movements dwell on invidious distinctions in a world cruelly exposed to displays of great differences in wealth and modes of behavior. The United States is particularly exposed to such reactions by its prominence and the appeal of the life-styles it exhibits. It must, in embracing international interests, expect to find some of them unsettling.

Fortunately, there are strong motivations that continue to press US higher education, and the research universities in particular, toward more international vocations. Some of these are quite pragmatic, springing from recognition of the growing US engagement in the competitive international world. Others are more ideological or purely intellectual, continuing the enthusiastic thrust of earlier decades which brought Indian philosophy and African languages into US course catalogs. This opening to other cultures has certainly not been free from tensions and conflict, as the quarrels over the canon show. But the challenge of recognizing and grasping the full range and diversity of human experience is an inescapable one for a university that purports to be seriously responsive to our globalized time. If American universities in the coming 21st century achieve the internationalization they commonly proclaim as their goal, they must achieve a synoptic command of the variety of human experience much beyond anything achieved so far.

The challenge is a formidable one, not simply because a great breadth of knowledge must be brought into some coherent order but also because new types of education must be developed which flow from new understanding and appreciation. It has sometimes been thought presumptuous that Western universities should attempt to understand the whole world; the 1960s radicals called institutes of area studies "institutes of applied imperialism" or worse. But clearly the choice for a large and powerful nation like the United States is not between attending to home or international interests but, rather, between instrumental or sympathetic engagement with the world at large. The latter has some of the hazards that multiculturalism has made familiar in American universities. But it also has the potential of enveloping cultural differences that preoccupy students and teachers within their own national bounds and which have contributed to recent intellectual confusion in a much wider, intellectually challenging, and less emotionally charged set of cultural differences. It may be that the internationalization of the universities is the only satisfactory way to deal with the social and cultural variety they now face and to bring it to coherent intellectual expression.

Research universities in the United States would seem to be especially well equipped to pursue this internationalization. They can use their commitment to the advancement of knowledge as a discipline to guide them through distorting passions. Moreover, their clinging to undergraduate liberal education as essential to their character imposes an obligation not to leave what they master as mere specialist learning but, instead, to bring it to coherent synthesis, worthy of the education of global citizens. If they can meet such challenges, the future of these universities looks secure.

ENDNOTES

[1]See *New York Times*, 9 December 1993, 1.

[2]The report, by a panel of 16, including several members of national distinction, was so entitled and subtitled; it was sponsored by the Hewlett, Johnson (Racine), Lilly, and Pew foundations. Available from the Johnson Foundation, PO Box 2029, Ravine, WI 53400. See *New York Times,* 5 December 1993, 46.

[3]See Roger L. Geiger, *Research and Relevant Knowledge: American Research Universities since World War II* (Oxford: Oxford University Press, 1993), 339 n. 1, for a reference to the Carnegie study and his own definitions of research universities.

[4]See comments on this point in *Privatization of Higher Education: International Trends and Issues* (proceedings from a conference of the International Council for Educational Development, Princeton University, 1988), 40. Drawing on a conference paper by Clark Kerr, Geiger argues that major state universities "are not subject to the direct control of state or politician . . . [and] many . . . are even guaranteed legal autonomy by the constitution of their state." "As a result they are 'substantially privatized' in that their governance and financing are 'more private than public.'"

[5]See Roger L. Geiger, *To Advance Knowledge: The Growth of American Research Universities* (Oxford: Oxford University Press, 1986), 115ff, with abundant references.

[6](Fall 1993) 1 (2): 1.

[7]*Princeton University: Continuing to Look Ahead* (report of the president, November 1993), 7.

[8]In *Harvard: The Years Ahead* (report to the Board of Overseers); summary reprinted in *Harvard Magazine,* November–December 1993, 77.

[9]Geiger, *Research and Relevant Knowledge,* vii.

[10]Eqbal Ahmed, "A South Asian Dialogue," *Dawn* (Karachi), 21 November 1993, 15.

[11]22 November 1993, 14.

[12]A recent account of the German universities with particular attention to their roles in graduate education and research may be found in the chapters by Claudius Gellert (1–116), in Burton R. Clark, ed., *The Research Foundations of Graduate Education: Germany, Britain, France, United States, Japan* (Berkeley: University of California Press, 1993).

[13]25 December 1993–7 January 1994, 72. Older politicians were inhibited by a faith that universities were critical contributors to national progress. They have now had a couple of decades of experts' criticisms of that faith, as, for example, in Burton R. Clark's 1977 judgment: "The Italians experienced an 'economic miracle' between the early 1950s and the late 1960s; yet there is no evidence that the rapid economic growth of that period involved in any way trained minds prepared by higher education" (*Academic Power in Italy* [Chicago: University of Chicago Press, 1977], 115).

[14]Chapter 5, pp. 174–245, of *To Advance Knowledge,* his study of the research universities to 1940, is so entitled.

[15]Shelby Harrison and F. Emerson Andrews, *American Foundations for Social Welfare* (New York: Russell Sage Foundation, 1946), 88.

[16]It is ironic that language and area studies became a part of NDEA in the first place almost by the accident of James Bryant Conant's personal influence on President Eisenhower. See Barbara Barksdale Clowse, *Brainpower for the Cold War: The Sputnik Crisis and the National Defense Education Act of 1958* (Westport, Conn.: Greenwood Press, 1981), 56–57.

[17]Daniel Patrick Moynihan, "The Politics of Higher Education," *Dædalus* 104 (1) (Winter 1975): 128–47.

[18](Winter 1975): 1.

[19]There was indeed quick and tangible evidence of an antiscientific spirit from 1968. I remember asking a leading participant what happened to the reform efforts on mathematics instruction which the National Science Foundation promoted in the post-Sputnik enthusiasms of the 1960s and were lost from view a decade or so later. "Oh! we were dead after 1968" was the answer.

[20]A single current issue of *Science* (10 December 1993, 1639–42) had news stories about the "biology-culture gap" (or chasm) in anthropology and of a bitter clash between neuroscientists and psychologists and social scientists.

[21]A letter to *Science* (3 December 1993, 1497) from a former governor of Colorado, Richard D. Lamm, who wrote from within the bosom of academia, at a Center for Public Policy and Contemporary Issues at the University of Denver.

[22]The record is summarized by Harvey Brooks in "Research Universities and the Social Contract for Science," in Lewis Branscomb, ed., *Energy Technology: Implementing a U.S. Strategy* (Cambridge, Mass.: MIT Press, 1993). There are also interesting specifics in Geiger, *Research and Relevant Knowledge,* 320ff.

[23]Geiger, *Research and Relevant Knowledge,* 9.

Eugene B. Skolnikoff   # 18

Knowledge without Borders? Internationalization of the Research Universities

THE CHANGING ENVIRONMENT FOR THE RESEARCH UNIVERSITIES

AMERICA'S RESEARCH UNIVERSITIES PLAY a major role in the nation's affairs, perhaps a larger role within American society than institutions of higher education in other countries. That role has deep roots, but its significance for the international position of the nation dates, in large measure, to World War II.

The allocation of substantial public funds to support science and technology in the universities was the most visible development following the war, but all fields of scholarship were affected, both by the general stimulus resulting from federal funding and, most importantly, from the new role of the United States in world affairs. The universities grew and prospered with the development of entirely new patterns of support and interaction with the federal government and with the society at large. International activities and research in many fields became important aspects of university scholarship, with a steadily growing foreign-student enrollment in most major research universities.

By the 1990s, however, many domestic and international developments have altered the environment for the universities. Some of those developments have come about gradually as a result of a natural process of economic growth, scientific advance, and political evolution; others were sudden and unexpected, most strikingly the precipitous end of the Cold War. Many have had important

Eugene B. Skolnikoff is Professor of Political Science at the Massachusetts Institute of Technology.

effects that influence — or should influence — the place of international activities and education in universities.

One of the most evident, but gradual, elements of evolution since World War II has been the intensified integration of societies and economies on the international scene, a development that was itself stimulated by the technological products of research and development (R&D). This integration has been accompanied by significant change in the patterns of relations among nations brought about, inter alia, by the rise of multinational industry, easier and more extensive communication across borders, increased dependence within any country on developments and decisions in others, and growth of issues and technologies with global dimensions. With this new level of interdependence has come a host of major international issues in economic, environmental, and security areas, and a wholly new level of interaction in science-and-technology-related issues across national borders.

The education of American students, to be able to function effectively in this new integrated world, has become a major charge on American universities, especially on those that are themselves significant participants in the international community. The research universities—with an important role in the training of future national leaders for the public and private sectors both in the United States and abroad—now have a central responsibility to prepare their students adequately for the global environment in which they will participate throughout their professional careers.

Along with the rise of interdependence, the level of competence in science and technology has risen markedly in most industrialized and many developing countries, resulting in the erosion of the postwar scientific and technological dominance of the United States. Quality research is widespread, and nations once dependent on the United States for the latest developments in science or technology now contribute from their own laboratories. All nations must now monitor developments on a global basis in order to stay competitive.

The most obvious sudden change with significant implications for research universities has been the end of the Cold War. Among other important effects, it has diminished the security rationale for defense R&D—the largest share of US government R&D funding (approximately $43 billion out of $75 billion of federal funds in the proposed budget for the 1993 fiscal year).[1]

The diminished security threat has given way to major growth in international economic competition, particularly in technology-related fields. The once-dominant American international trade position has resulted in negative trade balances, even in high-technology products which had been considered the hallmarks of the US comparative advantage.[2] As a result, the climate for US policies regarding science and technology has been markedly altered. The economic challenge has become the dominant concern, with a growing demand for visible economic returns to the nation for investment in R&D. The "social contract" (an implicit agreement between the government and the scientific community in the universities at the end of the war) that promised unspecified future security and economic benefits in return for general support for science now is giving way to closer control of the use of government funds and to expectations of short-term benefits.

The funding for defense-related R&D is not likely to fall sharply, but it will certainly become a smaller portion of the whole, and will be under pressure to demonstrate an economic as well as a security contribution. Meanwhile, new R&D and other science and technology-related programs directly tied to economic goals will be added, and existing programs will be recast to emphasize economic objectives.[3] Budgetary and economic constraints, however, will make it quite unlikely that funding for R&D will keep pace with inflation, especially funding for basic research which does not have rapid economic returns. Those constraints will also be likely to result in more regulations affecting the conduct of science and technology such as conflict of interest rules, ceilings on overhead reimbursements, attempts to control access to the results of research, and increased oversight of the conduct of research.

The challenge of technological competitiveness will also no doubt lead to an increase of industrial support for university R&D as a proportion of total R&D support, especially as American industry decentralizes its own research, moving away from large, central in-house laboratories. Such a development will raise to greater prominence a variety of issues such as how and by whom research objectives are determined, who owns intellectual property rights, and the extent of foreign industry access to university research.

The emergence of global-scale issues, the spread of scientific and technological competence, and the rising cost of research equipment and facilities have come together to increase the need and incentives for international cooperation in the conduct of R&D. International cooperation is typically not a preferred option for American scientists (except in those fields where there is no choice), notwithstanding the universal nature of science and the many international interactions of university scientists and engineers. Nor do the policies and funding procedures of the US government encourage it: cooperation with others, for example, is typically sought only after projects are well along. Little allowance is made for the extra initial costs of arranging a cooperative project, and the United States has often reneged on projects after agreement, thus earning a reputation as an unreliable partner.[4] The existence of these and other disincentives to international cooperation is usually little appreciated, except by those trying to arrange such cooperation.

The presumption of a closer relationship than in the past between the laboratory and the commercial marketplace is another substantial shift in the environment. Shorter product cycles, increased science dependence of some technologies, and entrepreneurial activity of faculty and students in many fields suggest a closer, more immediate tie between the conduct of science and its market potential. The actual relationship is complex and varies among fields and technologies. Though the promise of quicker economic returns has been a spur to the support of science in the universities and to the transfer of knowledge to the commercial marketplace, it also has raised the level of concern about possible conflicts of interest for research faculty and about the costs to competitiveness of maintaining open research laboratories.

Added to the overall picture is the changing demographic situation in the United States that is resulting in both a reduced pool of eligible students born in the United States who might become engineers and scientists and an increased proportion of college-age Americans that come from disadvantaged educational backgrounds. The past weakness of K-12 education in many parts of the United States has had a significant negative effect on the preparation of Americans for, and their interest in, higher education in science and engineering. The demographic trends coupled with the weakness in early education mean that the research universities and industry are likely to be increasingly dependent on students and trained workers from abroad who elect to remain in the country.

Notwithstanding these changes, many of which raise very serious problems for American research universities, the universities remain the envy of the world. Scientists, industrialists, and students flock here from other countries to study, to carry out research, to exchange knowledge, and increasingly to sponsor research. The persistence of that reputation is not a foregone conclusion, however, and the changing international and domestic conditions will require both the universities and the government to adopt new policies and attitudes.

MAJOR ISSUES

Given this background, what are the key issues that must be confronted? There are three categories of issues—not mutually exclusive —that dominate the subject and that pose significant challenges for the nation and for the universities themselves: internationalization of the curriculum; economic competition and the flow of knowledge; and the number and role of foreign students.[5]

These will be taken up in turn, but first a discussion is necessary of what is (or ought to be) the appropriate relationship between these universities and the nation, and in particular what responsibilities the universities have to respond to government policies and goals. Should the universities be considered independent institutions and, therefore, not accountable to the government (except in a fiduciary sense for the funding they receive), or should they be considered an instrument of the government, and hence of public policy? This is a question of underlying principle that arises frequently and is critical to understanding several aspects of the international roles of the university.

The Responsibilities of the Research Universities to the Nation

With over $10 billion of federal funds expended in 1991 for R&D at universities and colleges in the expectation of serving national purposes, and $6.5 billion of that going to fifty institutions, the instrumental view would seem to have considerable justification.[6] In this view, the universities should be considered simply as an instrument for achieving policy purposes, an attitude that often carries with it the assumption of their availability to serve the nation's immediate economic, security, or other goals. If the universities do not accept this responsibility, they should not be eligible to receive large funds from the public treasury. Discussions of the research universities' relationship to both the nation's economic needs and foreign economic competitors are often couched in that framework.

The universities, by and large, resist such a view, arguing that it is only through maintaining their independence and the freedom to determine their own agenda that they can adequately perform their fundamental roles in education and research. It is these roles, not the solution of near-term policy problems, that they consider to be their primary contributions to the nation's needs and long-term goals.

Both perspectives assume an important societal responsibility for universities. The research universities in particular are an integral part of the nation's education and research system. They seek public funds for proposed research and respond to invitations to undertake tasks identified by public sector agencies. They have benefited from the receipt of substantial public funds. In this respect, research universities have an implied responsibility to the nation dictated by their origins, by the receipt of public support, and by their many forms of participation in the society.

The two perspectives need not conflict, as long as it is generally accepted that the central responsibility of the universities to society is to perform their roles in education and research as well as they are able.[7] In that conception, the universities are legitimately elements for the achievement of public policy goals, but they can only perform well when they have the independence to chart their intellectual pursuits. Other, more instrumental commitments to government or society at large, such as special programs to serve national security or industrial needs, are appropriate, but only under the umbrella of the primary commitment to the quality of education and research.

Internationalization of the Curriculum

The most general of the major issues stemming from internationalization that is confronting the research universities concerns their capacity and will to meet the changes required in the training and education of students, changes mandated by the altered environment. There are many dimensions to those changes, but perhaps the single most important is the need for internationalization of the undergraduate curriculum and experience. It is the undergraduate years that will play the largest role in influencing students' attitudes toward, and preparation for, the global society within which they will have to function.

A list of relevant innovations introduced in many universities in recent years appears impressive. New courses dealing with foreign cultures and international relationships have been initiated, area research centers have flourished, junior-year abroad programs have become common, Third World economic and social development has become a standard subject of scholarship, and growing attention has been given to "global" issues, such as climate change, energy dependence, and the implications of worldwide communications networks. Several major universities have established campuses abroad with a quality of instruction equal to that of the home campus, and most research universities have encouraged substantial foreign student enrollment at the undergraduate level to leaven a largely American student body. The evident international nature of economic competition has not only placed greater focus on the university's role in issues of the national economy, but has demonstrated the need for educating students more effectively for the supranational environment that they will be entering upon graduation. Several major university presidents have made "internationalization" of their universities a key aspect of their incumbency.[8]

These are all important changes and serious commitments on the part of administrators. Yet, an observer is left with considerable disquiet as to whether these changes penetrate deeply into the curriculum, and whether the result has been the genuine internationalization of the university. The repeated calls by presidents, provosts, and deans of the need for greater commitment to internationalization is itself evidence of limited progress, and bears out the concern that the universities and the education they provide continue to be far more parochial than the times demand. Are the structural difficulties and the specialization of the faculty so great that the conservative nature of all institutions, and particularly universities, will inevitably frustrate the needed evolution? The 1991 report by Craufurd Goodwin and Michael Nacht, scholars of international affairs at Duke University and the University of Maryland respectively, of faculty and administration attitudes toward international activities, based on interviews at thirty-seven institutions, does not give grounds for much optimism.[9]

The impediments to substantial change are numerous. Probably the most important is the disciplinary basis for professional rewards in universities. Hiring, promotion, and tenure decisions all depend upon performance at the frontiers of a discipline, as defined by scholars in the field. For those disciplines for which geography is irrelevant, particularly the sciences and engineering, there is little incentive for a faculty member to be concerned about internationalization either of the field or, more generally, of the entire curriculum. In fact, there is a disincentive: a major career price may be paid if substantial time is diverted from discipline-defined research in order to serve international goals.

In scientific and technological fields, in fact, the problem appears to be even more serious because of the enormous expansion in the material that must be covered (or that it is believed must be covered) in the time available. It is a telling observation that the Massachusetts Institute of Technology (MIT), in the process of extending its professional engineering curriculum to five years, will use the extra time almost wholly for additional technical courses.[10] The original hope of some was to add courses that dealt with the political and social setting of technology, including international aspects; but somehow there did not prove to be enough space in the curriculum.

The persistence of parochial attitudes among US faculty is a further problem, notwithstanding the acknowledged international spread of scholarly competence and the recognition that the United States no longer dominates scholarship in many fields as it did since World War II. Goodwin and Nacht report much continued evidence of this parochialism, and are further supported by a government study that shows how limited is the use of foreign data sources by American scientists and engineers.[11]

The disciplinary structure of universities creates another difficulty with a long history: the inconvenient fact that the world's problems do not conform to that structure. The need for multidisciplinary approaches to public issues is well understood, but the record of research universities in attempting to apply their knowledge to understanding those issues and recommending policy alternatives has been decidedly mixed. This is particularly evident when it has been necessary to cross disciplinary lines between the natural and social sciences. International policy issues are no exception; in fact, the need for participation of a broad range of disciplines is typically even greater for international than for "domestic" issues. Many universities are attempting to organize to be able to study international issues effectively, but the impediments are severe.

Will these impediments doom efforts to enhance further the international dimensions of the university? Not necessarily, but they do make it clear that success will not be achieved without a struggle. The scholarly and educational justifications for internationalization are not likely, on their own, to result in effective progress. At the very least, a clear and strong commitment on the part of university administrators, as well as support from trustees, industry, and government are necessary. A commitment on the part of the faculty is essential, especially for those fields in which disciplinary rewards do not recognize international accomplishment. That commitment is commonly present in rhetoric, but often becomes frayed when practical issues of resources, promotion, and scholarly recognition are encountered.

Economic Competition and the Flow of Knowledge

The second major category of issues that universities must confront arises from the growing significance of international economic competition which the nation's scientific and technological resources, prominently including those in the universities, are expected to address. That expectation raises implications for the universities that are not easy to sort out, that often have little theoretical or empirical underpinning, and that are not infrequently of contradictory import. The conditions required for effective transfer of knowledge from the university to industry, for example, are surprisingly little understood in depth, but that does not deter strong assertions about the dangers of foreign access to university research.

The single issue that has received the most political prominence is whether the unimpeded flow of ideas and knowledge across borders, viewed by the scientific community as an essential condition for maximum progress in science, results in an unacceptable assistance to foreign economies, or whether it is in fact essential for the maximum rate of productivity increase in the American economy.

The question would not arise if industry in the United States continued to dominate high-technology trade as it did for most of the postwar years. That trade balance, however, has fallen essentially to zero; it went negative at the end of the 1980s, but recovered somewhat in the early 1990s.[12] The problem arises, therefore, because in this competitive, technologically-dynamic global economy, American industry has not fared as well, with some exceptions, as might once have been expected, and finds itself under severe challenge from foreign industry.[13] The reasons for poor performance are complex and disputed, going well beyond questions of access to new knowledge. They relate to management competence, time horizons for investment and performance, industrial structure, availability and cost of capital, training of the work force, government policy, and a host of other matters, including in particular the adeptness of industry at translating the ideas of the laboratory into commercial products.[14]

The universities are far from blameless. They bear responsibility for fostering the often outdated attitudes and behaviors of industrial and financial managers; for developing the ideas that have contributed to structural rigidities in industry, or failing to develop alternatives to them; and in particular for emphasizing engineering science and disciplinary accomplishment in teaching and research, while relegating manufacturing design and production to second-class status.

But, how should these deficiencies affect today's policy toward the international flow of knowledge? Whatever the cause of the relatively weak performance of the American industry, does it mean that unfettered movement of knowledge across borders is contrary to the national interest?[15] If foreign industry will always win the race to market, as some have asserted, then equal access to knowledge will necessarily work to the disadvantage of the United States. Should information from university research laboratories then be distributed initially only to American companies?[16]

Such a policy would not only be unwise on grounds of principle and practicality, but counterproductive. Restricting the flow of information in substantial ways would be likely to cause greater damage to American universities and industry than it would to the country's foreign competitors (to say nothing of the political and institutional reactions that would follow). Promoting restrictions on access to university research indicates a lack of appreciation of the research and education process—of the innumerable discussions, seminars, classes, theses defenses, and electronic-mail messages that take place within and among universities, usually long before actual publication of a research paper. It is hard to imagine substantial restrictions that would not result in interference with the critical ability to exchange information, so essential for the research enterprise in the United States.[17]

Moreover, in this technologically-competitive world, research excellence can no longer be guaranteed within the borders of any nation. The diffusion of competence in science and technology means that even if the United States is the preeminent technological nation in breadth of endeavor, it is not necessarily the leader in any given field and has equivalent or superior competitors in many. As a result, it is now essential for the health of science and technology in the United States, as it was not in the immediate postwar years, for American researchers to have access to and to keep abreast of research throughout the world.

That goal requires general acceptance of the principle of open exchange of knowledge, implying that American university laboratories advocate and practice unfettered information exchange, with the expectation that others will follow the same rules. There is no doubt that maintaining that stance of openness can help America's economic competitors. But it is of direct benefit to American industry as well—in maintaining immediate knowledge of developments abroad—and would be of greater value if American industry were better able to translate knowledge rapidly into products for the marketplace.

Proposals to restrict the flow of information from the universities received a great deal of attention in the 1980s when the Department of Defense sought to impose strict controls on foreign access. Two National Academy of Sciences studies effectively demonstrated why open research laboratories were in the US national interest and why controls would be counterproductive for the nation's security.[18] Today, similar proposals based on economic concerns would equally damage the very source of new research and innovative ideas critical to future productivity growth.

At this level of generality, most observers knowledgeable about the actual workings of R&D in the universities would probably agree with the desirability of unrestricted access to research information. Several difficult issues arise when specific situations are examined, however, issues that blur the edges of the general principles and, to some observers, call them into question.

One problem is that dependence on the open exchange of knowledge to keep abreast of developments wherever they take place requires that Americans have access to research abroad, actively seek information, and be in a position to use it once acquired. In fact, science and engineering students are not typically equipped by their education to engage effectively in the international exchange of knowledge, especially at the more applied end of the spectrum where results are not always reported in English. Furthermore, too many, especially in engineering, maintain a "traditional" not-invented-here attitude that leads them to devote little effort to gaining access to relevant information from other countries.[19]

A question of much greater political consequence is whether it is possible to achieve truly equal or reciprocal access to knowledge between two nations with quite asymmetrical research structures, as between the United States and Japan. The asymmetry grows out of the difference in the locale at which most research, especially basic research, is carried out in the two countries. In the United States, the preponderance of basic research is performed in open university laboratories; in Japan there is proportionally less basic research and most of what there is—at least the more interesting work—is typically found in industry. Japanese industry, as industry in all countries, does not freely divulge information it considers proprietary. The result is that while the laboratories of American universities are open to visitors from abroad, the roughly equivalent laboratories in Japan are often shielded by proprietary barriers.

Japan is gradually evolving toward sponsoring more research in its universities, increasing its support of basic research overall, and initiating large multinational research programs that will be fully open to all participants. But those are developments for the future that have little effect on the current imbalance. Moreover, Japan has assiduously sought to gain knowledge from other countries by sending students, postdoctoral scholars, and visitors to American universities; joining industrial liaison programs; sponsoring research; and establishing laboratories close to the major research centers in the United States. In these activities as well, there is a very large asymmetry between the two countries.

Given this situation, it is fitting for American universities to make serious efforts to encourage faculty to insist on an expectation of equivalence in their dealings with all foreign scientists and corporations. This does not always happen easily; too many faculty still believe they do not have much to learn from other countries, and would rather share their own latest work.[20] There is no obvious way of mandating reciprocity in the exchange of knowledge; it is a matter of behavior at the level of the individual scientist. But scientists can be sensitized to the broader significance of the issue beyond their own scientific interests. It is a small step, not likely to satisfy critics, but a useful step nonetheless.

Does the existence of asymmetry with Japan mean that open access to American university research results in excessive transfer of technology to Japanese industry? Critics of ties between American universities and Japanese government and industry certainly believe that to be the case.[21] A judgment on the question must depend on an understanding of the conditions under which the transfer of knowledge between universities and industry in fact takes place, and which are the most effective channels for that transfer.

A general and reasonable rule of thumb is that the most successful transfer of knowledge is achieved through the movement of people who carry with them not only the knowledge that appears in published form, but also the embedded knowledge sometimes thought of as "know-how."[22] The transfer of technology within a company, between companies, across borders, or between any two entities is well understood to be most effectively carried out, other things being equal, through the actual transfer of people who have the pertinent knowledge.

In the same way, the most effective transfer of knowledge from the university to industry comes about through the movement of people — the university students who enter industry after graduation. Thus, the predominant transfer of knowledge from American universities occurs via students, most of whom are American and enter American industry.[23]

A second important route for the transfer of knowledge is the industrial consulting of faculty. Widespread data on consulting ties are not generally available, but a recent survey of the MIT faculty showed that less than 20 percent of faculty consulting was with foreign-based industry.[24] If the MIT experience is typical, there is little need for concern about consulting as a route for transfer of knowledge to foreign industry.

Visits by representatives of foreign industry or government are another potential avenue of knowledge transfer. Anyone involved in attempting to transfer technology from industrial to developing countries, or even within a company from the research laboratory to manufacturing, knows how hard a task that is. Yet, it is often assumed by critics of the universities that a visitor to a research laboratory, no matter how short or long the visit, will leave with the latest results of that laboratory fully assimilated and able to be passed on back home.

Of course, that is nonsense, but it would be equally foolish to assert that there are no conditions under which a well-prepared visitor can learn a great deal even in a brief visit. Longer visits by postdoctoral students, visiting research associates, and visiting professors, on the other hand, will more naturally result in effective knowledge transfer, for in those cases the visit is presumably part of an intellectual collaboration that is intended to involve a genuine exchange of knowledge, benefiting both.

An increasingly common activity of American research universities that is arousing concern about the inappropriate transfer of technology is the operation of industrial liaison programs that include foreign corporate membership. The programs typically provide "facilitated" access to research under way at the university through such activities as brief visits, special symposia, and distribution of publications, in return for a fee that covers costs and some income to the university. The programs can be lightning rods for criticism since they have been accused of "selling" the products of research that may well have been funded by the government.

In fact, liaison programs generally do not provide economically-relevant information to members in advance of its general availability to the scientific community, to nonmembers, or to any others who seek it. The purpose of membership is to make knowledge more easily available, not to restrict its distribution. In fact, the substantial gap between university research and commercial application, even in new high-technology fields, means that companies will typically use liaison programs as a general window on the state of a research field rather than as a means of obtaining specific information.

Most of the contacts made through liaison programs involve only brief visits or attendance at symposia, so that there is little reason to accept the charge that member companies are receiving special access not available to others. Foreign companies that do not have the advantage of proximity or cultural familiarity with American mores typically find the programs a less daunting way of obtaining a general picture of research activities. In fact, based on the MIT survey previously cited, faculty contacts with American corporations are more numerous outside the liaison program structure than they are through the program. The same survey also indicated that contacts with visitors from other countries have provided significant information about *foreign* technological developments, with useful information flowing in to campus research projects (and on to American corporations).[25]

The willingness of the universities to accept more general support from foreign sources has also become a focus of criticism. The limitations of public funding for research and education at a time of increasing costs have led many universities to mount aggressive fund-raising activities. The result is a continuing search for new funding sources, with foreign support appearing to be both attractive and feasible. With varying success, universities have been able to raise funds for the support of research, for professorial chairs, and sometimes for buildings and other special purposes from foreign corporations and, occasionally, governments.

To date, these funds represent but a small portion of the research and endowment funds of any university. MIT, which has been one of the more successful in raising funds from abroad, received research support totaling $8 million in 1991 from foreign industry ($5.8 million of that from Japan) which was 20 percent of the total research support from industry that year. However, those funds made up only 3 percent of the total campus research budget.[26] On a national basis, the research support from foreign sources at research universities is probably considerably less than 3 percent.

Two concerns are raised by this research support from abroad. One is that these funds might bias the research objectives of American faculty toward the interests of foreign industry, rather than those of American industry or government. The argument is not specious, for there is an inevitable interaction between the establishment of research objectives and the goals of the funders of the research. The effect varies with field and with how fundamental the subject is. In more basic subjects, the research agenda is determined largely by the frontier of knowledge of the discipline and thus determined largely by the scientists working in the field. In subjects closer to application, the interests of the funders will necessarily influence the proposals made to them, and thus will affect the research that gets done. The proportionally small scale of funding from foreign industrial concerns makes this issue of relatively minor importance.

The other concern is more serious, at least in its political implications. Some universities and other research institutions have been willing to negotiate special intellectual property arrangements with companies in return for major research support.[27] When the company is foreign-based, the question is raised whether the intellectual resources of the faculty and their concurrent US government-sponsored research have been "bought" by a foreign corporation in a way that will benefit that corporation abroad. This is a legitimate question, but it is less of a problem than it appears. Rarely is funding from foreign corporations substantial enough for this to be an issue. Even if the foreign company has first priority on licenses, the research, if it is at a university, always is (or always should be) published without delay, open to colleagues during progress, and accessible to industry and for the education of students.

Nevertheless, even if relatively rare, the magnitude of individual agreements brings attention to the issue, and affects the political environment for all research universities, not just those that have negotiated the agreements. Of particular sensitivity is the possibility that the agreements give privileged access to federally-funded research when such research is commingled with that supported by the foreign corporation. Extreme care is required to ensure that the terms of those arrangements conform not only to legal restrictions, but also to the norms of open access to research and the free flow of information.

These concerns would be of much greater importance if foreign research support were to become a substantially larger proportion of the total support. What proportion ought to raise alarm is a matter of judgment, but it is an idle speculation since support of research from abroad is unlikely to increase substantially relative to support from domestic sources.

Number and Role of Foreign Students

Notwithstanding the growing strength of science and technology in other countries, the quality of American research universities continues to make them attractive to students from all over the world. In the years 1991-1992, there were some 399,000 international students (exclusive of refugees) attending US universities, a 33 percent increase from the decade of the 1980s.[28] Approximately 50 percent of those students studied engineering and the sciences, including the social sciences. However, at the graduate level, constituting roughly half of all the foreign students in the United States, more than 60 percent are in engineering and the sciences. The proportion of graduate students from abroad in some leading American research universities is on the order of 25 to 33 percent, higher (sometimes much higher) in those fields which have declined in interest for American students (for example, nuclear engineering). More than 50 percent of foreign students choose to stay in the United States after graduation and have become valuable, in some cases critical, sources of trained manpower for American industry and universities.[29]

The appropriate proportion of foreign students that should be admitted to the research universities at both the undergraduate and graduate levels has been a source of debate within the universities for many years, with significant variations of policy among the universities and among the disciplines within a university. In fact, the universities have come to depend on foreign-born staff, especially in science and engineering, proportionally even more than American industry. A national survey of department heads in 1986 found that about 10 percent of all faculty in science and engineering were noncitizens, and many more were naturalized citizens.[30] In 1985, 47 percent of junior faculty positions (under thirty-five years of age) on engineering faculties across the country were held by noncitizens. At MIT, some 17 percent of assistant professors are not citizens or permanent residents; about 30 percent of all faculty members were born abroad.[31]

This situation poses many issues for the research universities and for the nation at large. Three stand out as the most serious, politically and academically: *1)* the effect on the nation's competitive economic position; *2)* the effect on the quality of education and research in the universities; and *3)* the effect on the countries of origin of the students—the "brain drain" issue.

Foreign Students and Competitiveness. Education undoubtedly constitutes the most effective form of the transfer of knowledge; that is its fundamental purpose. As noted earlier, universities are in effect training future competition if foreign students in economically significant fields return home after graduation to staff industrial firms. That is unavoidable. The question is whether the interests of the United States are served by the open admission of foreign students, especially for graduate study, at the country's premier research institutions. Even if the answer to that question is positive, there remain subsidiary issues about free access of students to economically-promising fields or research projects, and whether there may be other costs for American society, such as reduced opportunities for minorities.

The issues of the education of foreign students are similar to those arising with regard to access to university research. The research universities strive for excellence in their teaching and research; it is in that way that they best serve the nation's interests. The applicants from abroad, typically more numerous at the graduate level than domestic applicants, are usually of high caliber. The result is that in admissions based dominantly on a criterion of quality, there is likely to be a substantial proportion of foreign students admitted.

In dynamic, economically-exciting scientific fields that have strong attraction for Americans, such as molecular biology or materials science, the average quality of both domestic and foreign pools of potential students is so high that it is possible for a department to favor American applicants without diminishing the quality of entering students. Several departments at MIT, for example, set caps on the proportion of foreign students admitted. In fields in which the American pool is small, however, admission on the basis of quality results in large numbers of foreign students. The most disturbing aspect of this latter situation is not the number of high-quality foreign students, but the diminishing pool of interested and qualified Americans.

Given the importance of foreign students to US higher education and industry, there seems little question that the presence of foreign graduate students is decidedly favorable to the US economy. Are the proportions of foreign students at the graduate level too high? Perhaps, though the criteria to make such a judgment are not at all clear. But, if the proportions are too high, the sensible cure is to increase the number of American students who desire and are able to study science and technology, not to cut down on the number of foreign students who want to come. Industrial and academic leadership in the United States should be concerned about what the effect on the US economy would be if the number of students from abroad wanting to study in the United States were to decrease. Several countries are making strenuous efforts to entice their science and technology-trained nationals back, apparently with some success. A more widespread shift away from the United States would be sorely felt in the competitive economic domain that stimulated questions about the "high" proportion of foreign students to begin with.

The general conclusion that there is substantial economic value to the universities and the nation from the presence of foreign students does not settle the subsidiary issues that arise. In particular, the argument is sometimes made that foreign students, though they may be admitted without restriction, should not be permitted to work on and receive financial support from publicly-funded research projects that are particularly relevant to commercial interests or considered to be crucial to the nation's economic future, such as microelectronics, materials science, and molecular biology. Several government agencies have threatened (informally) to impose such restrictions in their research grants.

This issue falls in a gray area where important principles may conflict, and where formal university policies may not reflect the informal laboratory or faculty practices. Most major universities would resist federal rules that would exclude certain categories of students from federally-funded research projects, arguing inter alia that the restrictions violate deeply-held values of the open nature of the university and that the valuation of students on racial, ethnic, or religious grounds is unacceptable. The government should not ask the university to be its agent in such a policy, and the universities should not accept that responsibility.

However, it is also a matter of academic principle that it is the prerogative of individual faculty to select students to work on their research projects. The knowledge that a funding agency strongly disapproves of the employment of foreign nationals is bound to affect scientists receiving funds from that agency, some of whom may even agree with the policy. In that situation, the exclusion of certain nationalities from areas of research may well be unavoidable, even if it constitutes tacit discrimination and in practice may not be in the best interests of a research project.

There is also a question of financial aid for foreign students. Foreign student participation in research projects funded by the US government means under present practices that those students are receiving support for their graduate education from the federal government on an identical basis with students who are American citizens. The pattern of graduate student support in the sciences and engineering is largely determined by the tight linking of research and education in the universities, so that taking part in a research project is an essential element in any student's graduate education.[32]

The denial of support for foreign students from government-funded projects would prevent these students from participating in those projects, leaving few alternatives open to them since projects sponsored by industrial or foundation sources are rarely numerous enough. Such a policy would thus effectively keep foreign students from receiving a graduate education in the sciences in the United States. Opportunities for Americans might be increased by default, but because of the smaller number of qualified Americans in many fields, the result would be a decrease in the quality of research in most fields in the major universities, a substantial reduction in the number of foreign students, and a serious curtailment of the research and educational value of the universities for the nation.

A more limited policy would be to deny foreign student support only in fields considered by the government to be "economically-sensitive." This would have fewer repercussions on overall numbers of foreign students, but would inject a degree of formal government intervention that universities would undoubtedly find repugnant. Informally, however, there is little doubt that individual faculty or laboratories are sensitive to the preferences of government funders, or to the possibility of unwanted political attention from the Congress.

The argument has also been made that when government-funded research fellowships are given to foreign students, minority American students are in effect being denied the funding that would make it possible for them to attend the university.[33] The availability of funding for the university training of minorities is a serious problem for the United States, but placing minority students in competition with foreign students mixes quite disparate national purposes. Foreign students are funded as a by-product of the research enterprise in the United States which must emphasize quality to serve the purposes for which public money is provided. Refusing foreign students in favor of minority students, independent of quality, would be damaging to the research enterprise. It is essential that other means be found to enable minorities to participate fully in research in science and technology, but not at the expense of the vitality of that enterprise.

Foreign Students and the Quality of Education and Research. At the undergraduate level, the presence of foreign students is important to the internationalization of the educational experience. They help to provide a setting where American students can learn to interact with foreign cultures and differing ethnic and racial groups, an aspect of a college education that is increasingly important in preparation for careers in a globally-integrated world. Foreign students also contribute significantly to the intellectual life of the university. They usually approach issues in research, education, and current affairs with different ideas and perspectives. And, of course, there are the benefits to the economy when foreign students stay after graduation and become essential contributors to American industry and education.

If foreign students return home, the fact that they spent their formative professional years in the United States can provide a variety of benefits for the nation in research collaboration, business relationships, and political support. The benefits cannot be uniformly realized or predictable — occasionally graduates of American universities have become rabid foes of the United States—but it is instructive to recall how important the education of future foreign elites was considered to be during the Cold War. The United States is probably the only major industrial country that makes little effort to induce students from abroad to come to study in the expectation that their experience would bring future political and economic benefits. It is an advantage the nation realizes without extra effort, simply because of the reputation of an American university education.

Undergraduate foreign students do not come, however, without incurring costs. Some prefer to live, or are encouraged to live, in campus ghettos, so that interaction with American students is minimal. Financial aid can also be a problem. For undergraduates from abroad, universities usually make financial aid available on roughly the same basis as for American students (for most leading universities the financial aid decision is— or is claimed to be — completely separate from the admission decision). Data from 1990 and 1991 shows that the primary source of funding for foreign undergraduates is personal or family resources that support about 80 percent of foreign students.[34] The next largest source of funds is the American college or university, providing for 6.5 percent of the students. For those latter funds, which are from private or other scholarship resources of the universities, American students are in effect in competition with foreign students. Because of the shortage of dollar resources for many foreign students and/or the difficulty of determining need, foreign students may actually be receiving higher average awards.[35] There is nothing improper in this, but to the extent that it is common, it implies that American universities may be subsidizing foreign undergraduates to a greater extent than American students.

Presumably, most universities have made conscious decisions about the proportion of undergraduates from abroad they will accept, recognizing the added financial costs and other possible problems, but balancing that against the importance to undergraduate education of a nationally, ethnically, and racially mixed undergraduate student body. The "proper" proportion is an uncertain and arbitrary number, but the presence of foreign undergraduates is typically highly valued by the leadership of the research universities.

There is a potentially serious educational cost of a different kind at the undergraduate level due to the teaching role filled by foreign graduate students. The dominance of research qualifications in the selection of graduate students means that many, and in some fields most, of the teaching assistants (TAs) who bear a considerable share of the responsibility for teaching in large undergraduate courses are likely to be foreign born. It is evident, though the evidence is primarily anecdotal, that there are problems with the extensive use of foreign TAs, often stemming from their inadequate command of the English language. The problems this can raise for the quality of undergraduate education are obvious.[36]

At the graduate level, it has been alleged that for some departments in some universities, students are accepted from abroad only to maintain a rationale for the continued existence of a department and to provide a basis for seeking research funds to keep the faculty of that department engaged in funded research.[37] The charge cannot be fairly evaluated here, but certainly there is a relation between the size of the faculty and research budgets on the one hand, and the number of students admitted to a department on the other. Whether the numbers admitted are inappropriate cannot be asserted as an abstract judgment, but is an issue that must be of concern to all universities in restrictive budget times.

Brain Drain. As American society and universities became increasingly attractive to citizens of other countries after the war, a steadily growing number of students, especially from developing countries, have come to American universities and have stayed in the country after graduation. The issues associated with this migration of talent or "brain drain" have been a continuing source of controversy because of the effects on the countries from which the individuals came. Some have argued that the universities have a responsibility to ensure that the students return home after graduation, or at least a responsibility to tailor an educational program suitable for the situation of that home country.

Most research universities make little provision for adjusting their educational program to the needs of developing countries. This is especially so in the most popular fields of engineering and science where the quality of the curriculum depends on close interaction with the cutting edge of research, a relationship that cannot be altered by fiat. In fields in which issues of particular concern to development form important parts of the research agenda, such as urban studies, political science, and civil engineering, relevant courses and research opportunities can be offered. But, in the majority of fields at a research university, the domestic needs of developing countries are not directly addressed. This increases the likelihood that students from those countries will be dissatisfied if they return home after completing a degree. In effect, the advanced curriculum of the research universities is providing an added incentive for those from developing countries to stay in the United States. But the students typically come because of that advanced curriculum, and not to learn about their own problems.

Universities cannot be indifferent to the issue, but neither is it their role to restrict admissions, control students after graduation, or compromise their educational objectives because of the possible effects on other countries. It is clear, however, that this is an important economic and foreign policy issue for the United States, and a domestic issue for the countries of origin. As mentioned earlier, some countries are making new efforts to create the conditions at home that will lure their former nationals back. This is a sensible step for those countries, for it is only by finding ways to make effective use of the training received in the United States that the economic advantages to the home nation can be realized.

The US government is not an innocent party or indifferent to the brain drain; immigration legislation actually encourages individuals with skills to remain in the United States. If the brain drain were to dry up, the US economy would suffer unless successful steps had already been taken to increase the supply of American students moving into the fields in which foreign students are making such a large contribution.

CODA

As we move into the twenty-first century, the international roles of the American research universities in both education and research are likely to be (or ought to be) more important to both the nation and the world than they have been in the latter half of the twentieth century. It is essential that the nation recognize the nature of those roles, their significance to the country, and the policies that are required to assist the universities in meeting them effectively. It is equally essential that the universities respond to the many implications of the fundamentally more international world in which they and the nation are embedded. The universities must do a better job of relating education and scholarship to the rest of the world; they must move from the parochial attitudes that are still prevalent, and develop curricula and programs for students that better prepare them for the world in which they will have to live and perform.

The support required for this within the university is not just hortatory; university administrators have to demonstrate the will to commit scarce resources, to overrule other initiatives that ignore, neglect, or conflict with goals of internationalization, and to create an environment for faculty and students that responds to more than discipline-based incentives and rewards.

The task is not an easy one, nor is it assured of success. As Goodwin and Nacht observed, "The internationalization of US colleges and universities that is required for the 1990s is far more profound than that accomplished in earlier decades."[38] It is an essential task, and one in which the research universities must be both leaders and exemplars of the internationalization required throughout American society.

ENDNOTES

[1]American Association for the Advancement of Science, *AAAS Report XVII: Research and Development FY 1993* (Washington, D.C.: American Association for the Advancement of Science, 1992), 50.

[2]National Science Foundation, *International Science and Technology Data Update: 1991*, Survey of Science Resources Series, NSF 91-309 (Washington, D.C.: National Science Foundation, 1991), 118; Organization for Economic Cooperation and Development, *OECD in Figures: Supplement to the OECD Observer* 176 (June/July 1992): 56–57.

[3]The technology-policy plans of the Clinton/Gore Administration promised to raise civilian R&D to 50 percent of the budget from the 1993 level of 40 percent, and included a variety of programs intended to contribute to the economy, for example, promoting cooperation with industry for precompetitive technology, supporting manufacturing research and outreach centers, and diverting weapons funding at the National Laboratories to cost-shared commercial development with industry. "Technology for America's Economic Growth, A New Direction to Build Economic Strength" (Washington, D.C.: The White House, 22 February 1993).

[4]Eugene B. Skolnikoff, "Problems in the U.S. Government Organization and Policy Process for International Cooperation in Science and Technology," in Mitchel B. Wallerstein, ed., *Scientific and Technological Cooperation Among Industrialized Countries* (Washington, D.C.: National Academy Press, 1984), 29–43. Alexander Keynan, "The U.S. As a Partner in Scientific and Technological Cooperation: Some Perspectives From Across the Atlantic," Carnegie Commission on Science, Technology, and Government, June 1991.

⁵In this analysis, it is important to note that my starting bias is that greater internationalization of the universities is essential for the nation, for the progress of science, and for the education of students. In a brief paper, not all the reasons for that position can be explored in depth; some assertions have to be taken as matters of faith or conviction, rather than fully justified in the text. It should be recognized that my views to a considerable extent have been formed by the situation at MIT and my experience at that university.

⁶National Science Foundation, *Selected Data on Academic Science and Engineering R&D Expenditures: Fiscal Year 1991*, Surveys of Science Resources Series, NSF 92–329 (Washington, D.C.: National Science Foundation, 1992), 7, 19. The analysis of this chapter refers primarily to the research universities that are major international institutions and that receive the largest share of government funding.

⁷There are other, often controversial, elements that define the university's responsibility to the society in which it functions, and define what some would consider to be the more fundamental functions of institutions of higher education that transcend national borders or temporal societal problems. An extended discussion would be inappropriate in this paper; this general assertion of responsibility is sufficient for our purposes.

⁸MIT, Michigan, and Harvard presidents have all spoken to this effect; I believe others have as well.

⁹See the excellent survey and discussion of its results in Craufurd D. Goodwin and Michael Nacht, *Missing the Boat: The Failure to Internationalize American Higher Education* (New York: Cambridge University Press, 1991).

¹⁰A four-year degree remains, but the first professional degree will now be considered the Master's degree, awarded after five years.

¹¹Goodwin and Nacht, *Missing the Boat*, 28 –36; a General Accounting Office (GAO) study in 1992 showed how inadequate was the collection or use of foreign technological information in the United States. General Accounting Office, *Foreign Technology: Federal Processes for Collection and Dissemination*, Report to the Chairman, Subcommittee on Defense Industry and Technology, Committee on Armed Services, US Senate, GAO/NSIAD-92–101.

¹²Organization for Economic Cooperation and Development, *OECD in Figures*, 56 –57.

¹³The casual use of "American" and "foreign" industry masks the blurring of the distinction between these terms. It is a source of dispute what meaning they should have, but the use here signifies where the headquarters is located, a measure still thought to be significant. See Robert B. Reich, "Who is Us?," *Harvard Business Review* (January/February 1990) and Laura D. Tyson, "They Are Not Us," *The American Prospect* (Winter 1991).

¹⁴A major report on this set of issues, *Made in America* (Cambridge, Mass.: MIT Press, 1989), was published by the MIT Commission on Industrial Productivity (chaired by Professor Michael Dertouzos) in 1989.

¹⁵A faculty study at MIT, completed in 1991, discussed the broad range of issues and principles involved in MIT's international relationships. See Eugene Skolnikoff et al., "The International Relationships of MIT in a Technologically Competitive World," Report of a Faculty Study Group, Cambridge, Mass., May 1991.

[16]That restriction has been specifically put forward by Senator Shelby (D-Alabama) who proposed on 17 February 1993 a prohibition on the sharing of information with representatives of foreign corporations or their American subsidiaries before publication of NSF or NIH-funded research. He withdrew the proposal on the promise that hearings would be held on the subject.

[17]These ideas, easily accepted in the research community, are frequently challenged as naive in the more cynical milieu of Washington. The gulf between the academy and the political community in the acceptance of principles such as these, considered in the universities to be both necessary and realistic, is often uncomfortably wide, with potentially serious consequences.

[18]*Scientific Communication and National Security* (the Corson Report) (Washington, D.C.: National Academy Press, 1982); *Balancing the National Interest: U.S. National Security Export Controls and Global Economic Competition* (the Allen Report) (Washington, D.C.: National Academy Press, 1987).

[19]Goodwin and Nacht, *Missing the Boat*, 29–36; General Accounting Office, *Foreign Technology*.

[20]Goodwin and Nacht, *Missing the Boat*, 29–31.

[21]Committee on Government Operations, "Is Science for Sale?: Transferring Technology from Universities to Foreign Corporations," Twenty-Eighth Report by the Committee on Government Operations, US House of Representatives, 16 October 1992; Stephanie Epstein, *Buying the American Mind: Japan's Quest for U.S. Ideas in Science, Economic Policy and the Schools* (Washington, D.C.: The Center for Public Integrity, 1991).

[22]That is one of the reasons that the licensing of inventions (at MIT at least) that result from university research is preponderantly to companies in reasonable proximity to the university campus rather than at distant points in the United States or overseas.

[23]Since there are substantial numbers of foreign students, particularly at the graduate level, this raises the obvious policy question of how many foreign students are being trained, in what fields, and where they go upon graduation.

[24]D. Eleanor Westney, "Report on MIT Survey of Faculty International Relations, Prepared for Provost's Committee on MIT's International Relations," 1992, 28.

[25]Ibid., 29.

[26]Skolnikoff et al., "The International Relationships of MIT," 14.

[27]A recent example is a contract for $300 million over ten years between the Scripps Research Institute (not a university) in La Jolla, California and the Sandoz Pharmaceuticals Corp., a Swiss-based concern. Philip J. Hilts, "Health Chief Assails a Research Deal," *New York Times*, 12 March 1993.

[28]Institute of International Education, *Open Doors, 1990/91* (New York: Institute of International Education, 1991), 1. Unless otherwise noted, the data on foreign students in the United States comes from this report and its companion, *Profiles: 1980–1990*.

[29]National Academy of Engineering, *Foreign and Foreign-Born Engineers in the U.S.* (Washington, D.C.: National Academy of Science, 1988), 3. National Re-

search Council, *Summary Report 1989: Doctorate Recipients from U.S. Universities* (Washington, D.C.: National Academy of Science, 1990), 46. The data on the rate at which international students stay in (and American students depart from) the United States are weak, but available information suggests that there has been no change in the rate over the past decade. There is anecdotal evidence that a few countries, notably Taiwan and Korea, have become better able to attract their former nationals back in recent years by providing a more congenial and productive climate for their work, but this effect may have been counteracted by an increased likelihood that students from other countries (such as China) will stay. See Michael Finn and Sheldon Clark, "Estimating Emigration of Foreign-Born Scientists and Engineers in the U.S.," unpublished, Labor and Policy Studies Program, Oak Ridge Associated Universities, January 1988; and Stephen K. Yoder, "Reverse Brain Drain Helps Asia But Robs US of Scarce Talents," *Wall Street Journal*, 18 April 1989.

[30]National Science Board, *Report of the NSB Committee on Foreign Involvement in U.S. Universities*, NSB 89–80 (Washington, D.C.: National Science Foundation, 1989), 10; National Academy of Engineering, *Foreign and Foreign-Born Engineers*, 76.

[31]Skolnikoff et al., "The International Relationships of MIT," 11.

[32]Nearly 40 percent of foreign graduate students in 1990 and 1991 were supported by their US college or university, presumably through research or teaching assistantships. Institute of International Education, *Open Doors*, 73.

[33]HR 4595, introduced by Representative Paul Henry (R-Michigan), 26 March 1992, "To Encourage Institutions of Higher Education to Use Federal R&D Funding for the Support of American Students, and for Other Purposes."

[34]Institute of International Education, *Open Doors*, 73.

[35]That is the situation at MIT.

[36]Elinor G. Barber and Robert P. Morgan, *Boon or Bane: Foreign Graduate Students in U.S. Engineering Programs* (New York: Institute for International Education, 1988), 14–18; Richard Saltus, "Language Barriers: Students on US Campuses Frustrated By Teachers with Rudimentary English," *Boston Globe*, 12 March 1993.

[37]John Deutch, "The Foreign Policy of U.S. Universities," *Science* 253 (2 August 1991): 492. It has also been alleged that some universities—presumably not the leading research universities—seek undergraduates from abroad primarily to increase tuition income.

[38]Goodwin and Nacht, *Missing the Boat*, 114.

The Research University: Notes toward a New History

T HE HISTORY OF THE AMERICAN RESEARCH UNIVERSITY in the 20th century waits to be written. It cannot be written so long as certain of the myths now common about higher education in the United States remain unchallenged and so long as it is conceived to be essentially the tale of a handful of prestigious institutions predominantly located in the eastern corridor extending from Cambridge to Baltimore, in the West from Berkeley and Palo Alto to Los Angeles and San Diego, and in the Middle West in a universe that embraces Chicago, Ann Arbor, and Madison.

Institutions in these places, however important, are in fact part of a much larger galaxy, whose visibility even today is only dimly perceived. In scanting whole regions, the South, the Southwest, and the Northwest, but more important, in neglecting to consider how political, economic, and social change have conspired to make even the most traditional (and purportedly ancient) of these institutions something very different from what they were at the beginning of World War II, violence is done to the story of the evolution of US higher education in this century.

It is obvious, for example, that the intrusion of the federal government into higher education since the end of World War II, in wholly unprecedented ways and in every part of the system, has greatly influenced the size and character of student populations, both undergraduate and graduate, making for an expansion of the professoriate to a size almost inconceivable when the United States dropped its atom bombs over Japan. Federal involvement

Stephen R. Graubard is Professor of History at Brown University and the Editor of Dædalus.

has also operated to create university administrations, sometimes pejoratively dismissed as bureaucracies, of a kind never previously imagined. All sorts of new functions have accrued to higher educational institutions, especially perhaps those with national reputations, not to speak of the much smaller number that can claim some kind of international visibility.

A system seeking and securing federal subvention on a scale inconceivable before 1945 is by that fact alone increasingly subject to public scrutiny, by Congress, of course, but also by numerous executive agencies and by the so-called mass media. When, in addition, federal courts are increasingly led to intervene to regulate universities, the external controls on higher education are necessarily different from those that existed before. The very substantial financial costs incurred in complying with federal regulations create the need for new funds but also for new personnel, thus establishing novel forms of dependency.

It is a truism that the federal government is today the sole support of any number of research activities, principally in the physical and biological sciences, and that many of these would not continue in the absence of, or in the case of severe reductions in, federal financial aid. A fact less commonly noted is that the transformation of the major universities in the United States, and not only their expansion in size, is linked to economic and social developments in the larger society, particularly in the new and more influential American middle class spread across the country, living in comfort, with very substantial discretionary income, which it is prepared to use to benefit its children but also to endow US colleges and universities in ways literally unheard of in any other society.

The distinctive features of US higher education are still underappreciated. There is too little understanding of how Americans came to develop a university system in the decades after the Civil War which was fundamentally different from what had existed before and only in very superficial ways resembled anything that existed in Europe. How did this come to pass? Through acknowledging in the first instance that universities could be made useful—that there was no need to imitate what existed at the time in Europe—and that this purpose could be achieved by serving the nation's principal economic interests, not least those represented by agriculture. In time, industry became another claimant on the university, with its corporate cadres increasingly trained in universities in engineering, business, and other programs deemed useful to US enterprise.

For this to happen, it was essential that Americans propagate the simple principle that all knowledge could be "privileged," that there were no subjects peculiarly suited to university study. Through the workings of the Morrill Act, but, more important, through the determination to prove themselves useful in wholly new ways, the nation's colleges and universities sought to provide instruction intended to appeal to men and women, in unprecedented numbers, preparing them for occupations and professions fundamentally different from the ones their parents and grandparents had pursued. The nation after the Civil War, seeing itself as a renewed society, invented new kinds of universities.

The tolerance for innovation allowed agriculture, for example, to be made a university subject, rendered "scientific," rationalized, given new theoretical and practical dimensions, offering solutions to problems that had confounded the early pioneers who had settled on a perpetually moving American frontier. New discoveries waited to be made; they were expected to create greater annual yields, crops more resistant to blight, more fertile soils. In time they would create incomparable new wealth, giving the nation new standing among those who came to recognize how much profit might be made from the export of agricultural produce.

The concept of "service," as much as that of "research," in its uniquely American formulations, took hold, particularly in those institutions that relied on public funding. To serve the farmers of Wisconsin, for example, became a respected task, whether achieved through "extension service"—another US educational innovation—or through more traditional teaching methods. The dark premonitions of Ricardo and Malthus, with their exaggerated early 19th-century fears of population outrunning food supply, retreated before an optimism that led agronomists and economists to see the potential for vastly expanded agricultural output, increased by more rapid and efficient transit on land and sea, with new methods of storage and refrigeration creating a supply never previously imagined.

In a rapidly changing industrial society committed to the creation and sale of all manner of new products, the applied sciences, generally embraced under the all-encompassing term *engineering*, gained respectability. While an apprenticeship system had once sufficed to create a work force able to handle the complex tasks associated with road, bridge, and canal construction in a vast and largely untamed wilderness, the building of railroads and the exploitation of mineral resources called for instruction that came to be centered increasingly in the universities of the country. Later in the century, when the discovery of oil and the problems associated with its extraction became preoccupying, new geological and technological research opportunities were perceived and seized upon by universities whose national and foreign reputations were negligible.

If the industrial revolution, in its late 19th- and early 20th-century manifestations, called for scientific, technological, and managerial skills of a kind not previously demanded, these were provided by universities and institutes ready to give instruction in the requisite subjects. The United States, a vast continental society fundamentally different from the nation-states of Western Europe, could not rely on a handful of higher educational institutions to offer such professional training. The instruction had to be made available in many places, and these did not simply replicate one another, with all concentrating on the same basic technologies. The inventions of a generation of "tinkerers," who collectively caused a major revolution in transport, energy, and communications, were now exploited by higher educational institutions prepared to give new definitions to the old term *teaching* but also to the new and increasingly significant terms *research* and *service*.

The higher educational system that evolved was not simply that of Europe translated to a new continent. While many who have written about this period have chosen to dwell on how Harvard, Yale, Princeton, and Columbia were changed, what the creation of Johns Hopkins, Chicago, and Stanford meant for higher education, the story cannot be told in so narrow a frame. If all knowledge was privileged, as has been argued, and if institutions defined their teaching and research opportunities differently, few saw the need to imitate the medieval or modern universities of Europe. While Oxford and Berlin had their admirers in the United

States, of course, they, like any number of others across the Atlantic, did not provide the template congenial to those who constructed or reconstructed the universities of post–Civil War America. Cornell never believed it was Tübingen or Heidelberg on Lake Cayuga. For Cornell "home economics" was a university subject; veterinary medicine was as much a science as physics; instruction in the classics, history, and political science and in French, Sanskrit, Spanish, and Chinese were all available, often offered to minuscule numbers of students. The American university began to resemble a vast emporium, with all manner of products calculated to appeal to social strata whose members had not previously imagined the university was intended for them or their children.

By the beginning of the twentieth century the American university had become popular, thronged by students, men and women, in unprecedented numbers. By the strict standards of Europe— those of Germany, the United Kingdom, or France, for example— many American institutions that called themselves universities would never have merited that title abroad. A substantial number, in the opinion of those educated in Europe, were essentially "finishing schools," providing a kind of basic education, particularly at the undergraduate level, which secondary schools in Europe offered. Even so sympathetic an observer as Lord Bryce, one of the first to understand the dimensions of the revolution that had taken place in the United States, who lauded the higher educational developments almost too effusively, knew that only a handful of the nation's institutions were playing in the same university league as those of Europe. The student population, though vastly larger than that of Europe, did not arrive with an equivalent preparation; the faculties, however animated and committed to their teaching, were only rarely able to claim scholarly credentials comparable to those common to professors in the best European universities.

Still, things were changing even in this regard, as Bryce noted in the last edition of his classic work, *The American Commonwealth,* first published in 1888, which, reissued with an additional chapter on higher education, appeared just before World War I. Bryce, deploring the corruption of US politics and less than wholly beguiled by its capitalism, was enthusiastic about its universities, which were giving the nation a new purpose, a new moral sense. These institutions, rich and becoming richer—a comment that could not have been made before the Civil War, when the gifts of devoted alumni were minimal and when state legislatures were stingy in their appropriations—were led by responsible and dedicated men, whose vision and integrity guaranteed growth and improvement.

While Bryce recognized the novelty of the US system, he never considered in sufficient detail why it would never come to resemble that of Europe. For many reasons he did not take seriously enough the observations made almost a century earlier by his great French predecessor Alexis de Tocqueville. The European, who more than any other understood the society he had visited, yet who never saw a college campus—there was not very much to see in the early 1830s at Harvard or Yale—asked the most penetrating questions about the nature of US culture. Tocqueville wondered whether Americans would not in time produce a "democratic art" and a "democratic science" as unique and distinct as the polity they had so assiduously created. Acknowledging the need for a new political science to interpret a society neither monarchical nor aristocratic in the European sense, Tocqueville asked implicitly and explicitly what elements of the older European culture would survive and prosper in the United States. Would its learning prove to be distinctive, and not only because of the society's continuing preoccupation with utility? Would the society ever come to respect theory? Would it ever become preoccupied with beauty?

Bryce saw what private philanthropy and state legislative appropriations were doing to create US universities, incomparably rich in their facilities and ambitions. It was impossible for him to see that, before the twentieth century was half-spent, another force would enter the arena; the federal government would become both funder-in-chief for many crucial university activities but also, and inevitably, regulator-in-chief. With the arrival of a national political interest, politics of a quite new kind would intrude into higher education. Bryce understood the power of public opinion. As the disciple of Tocqueville and of A. V. Dicey, who had written brilliantly on the subject and who was Bryce's traveling companion on his first American journey, he never underestimated its influence. He had seen how public opinion operated in individual state legislatures, holding California, for example, hostage to a "know-nothing" opinion that impeded the growth of that state's university, in contrast to conditions that obtained at critical junctures in Wisconsin or Michigan. Public universities could not fail to be influenced by politics.

Knowing what individual state legislatures were capable of doing to give new attention to public education at both the secondary and the university levels, Bryce recognized the key role of the politician. When secondary public school education, particularly in the more recently and sparsely settled states of the West, became more generally available, the results would be many. Academic standards would almost certainly improve; the pressures to enter university for young and ambitious men and women would grow. Many of the newer state universities would then be in a position to abandon their preparatory programs, essentially remedial in nature, which they felt obliged to offer as long as high school instruction was so obviously primitive (or unavailable) in many localities. In the new conditions, at least in the more enlightened states, universities would be able to admit students better equipped to pursue a more rigorous and adult regimen of studies. Whether this would also affect university student culture in the United States, on which Bryce had much to say, was less certain. The pursuit of honors degrees in Europe, in universities such as Oxford or Cambridge, had no equivalent in much of the United States either in public or private universities. Still, implicit in Bryce was the proposition that university improvement depended on better schooling, which stemmed from deliberate political action.

Bryce, as a pre–World War I European, was still thinking of the "civilizing" function of universities, creating cultivated and attentive publics committed to rational discourse, prepared to advance new fields of learning, accepting of the benefits of contemporary scholarship. If US politics had become too harsh and venal, too intimately related to an economic order both cruel and unjust, these deficiencies might be alleviated or moderated by an education that was neither pedantic nor traditional, that gave a certain primacy to the values of citizenship. Again, Bryce saw a role for the university which he acquired in substantial part from his own experience and which he heard discussed by many of his American academic friends. Bryce, in 1914, knew the academic scene in the United States as few others did.

He knew, for example, that the old eastern private colleges and universities had become substantially less hidebound, more open to innovation and experiment. If Harvard had led, mostly through the influence of its long-serving president, Charles Eliot, the others were not very far behind, which is not to suggest that all the old schools meekly followed prescriptions set out in Cambridge for curricular reform. On issues as controversial as compulsory chapel attendance, a Latin requirement, and the elective system more generally, the old Ivy League colleges differed markedly. All, however, saw the need to admit a greater number of undergraduate students, to appeal to "old money," which had not always recognized the need for university training, while seeking out also the children of those whose fortunes had been made more recently.

Eliot, in his inaugural address in 1869, not fearing to be thought "elitist," spoke of the need to admit the children of the rich, the obviously advantaged, who in many instances were destined to hold high and responsible places, but he saw the need to search also for the talented sons of those less prosperous. Because many of their families would be unable to meet university expenses, they would require scholarship aid. Eliot, the good Yankee, intended to provide it, but he expected the debt to be repaid, not in equivalent dollars but, instead, in generous benefactions to help others who would come after them. In 1869 it was still possible for a Harvard president to speak of a dual reward for philanthropy, in heaven but also on earth, in the Harvard Yard.

While other of the Ivy League institutions might be more concerned to achieve the first objective—to draw in the well-born children of the rich—all knew that their hopes for a larger undergraduate student population depended on their being able to establish close relations with feeder schools, those that would regularly send them good students, whose recommendations in respect to character and promise could be relied on. For many of the private colleges and universities in the East, this led them to form links with private preparatory day schools but also with the still extant 18th-century academies and the greatly expanded group of boarding schools, established more recently, intended to keep the Protestant children of the well-to-do protected against an urban population, increasingly immigrant and thought to be dangerous. The old private colleges of the East became "popular" in ways that would have astonished their pre–Civil War presidents, who had overseen communities of a few hundred young adolescents.

In the decades after the Civil War and continuing until World War II, a new undergraduate culture emerged, with certain common features through the country, particularly evident in the more prominent public and private colleges and universities. This was the age of the Greek-letter societies, fraternities and sororities, clubs, secret and open, all involving some principle of exclusion. It was also the age of undergraduate competitive sports; football dominated almost everywhere, and the construction of great stadia became as important as the creation of new libraries. Indeed, the two, though marching to different tunes, expressed the ambition of suddenly expanded institutions of higher learning to be centers of both play and study. If football and crew became salient competitive sports on the more prosperous campuses of the East, appealing often to their private school student clienteles, the high school boys of other regions were no less avid about playing football and often scarcely less enthusiastic about baseball and basketball. Alumni associations thrived, as much on the pleasures of Saturday afternoons at the stadium as on the pre- and post-game parties they generated. A new "school spirit" quickly insinuated itself, as much at State U as at Yale.

If the student bodies in particular institutions showed considerable homogeneity, not least in their religious beliefs but also in their social and economic behavior and comportment, this was not thought to be a serious impediment to the faculty engaged to teach them, mostly through lectures, whose own scholarship and research did not ultimately depend on the student responses they elicited. If there was active competition among a few universities to recruit the most renowned faculty, to buy their services with the promise of greater remuneration and, even more, of greater kudos, this was all a much more limited enterprise before 1914 than is sometimes imagined. New universities found it difficult to recruit from those already established; chairs were often left vacant in these institutions until the time they might be filled by a new generation of scholars. In all too many instances, "old boys," former undergraduates, remained to gain their doctorates and then to serve their departments, rising very slowly to their appointed summits as full professors.

In a society in which many were becoming exceedingly rich and in which alumni, particularly in a pre–income tax age, were prepared to share their wealth, imitating in a more modest fashion the extraordinary bequests of the very rich, the Carnegies and Rockefellers, private university campuses grew, with libraries, sports stadia, museums, laboratories, and classroom buildings showing the opulence (and sometimes the frugality) which reflected the values and taste of successful alumni. The state universities, not wishing to be left behind, showed an equal concern to provide for their students and faculty, and state pride guaranteed that this situation existed in many places in the Middle and Far West, the preferred turf of the great public universities.

The life of the research scholar differed from that of the more conventional university professor principally in the amount of attention given to library and laboratory research, the writing and refereeing of learned articles for professional journals, the educational needs of graduate students, and participation in the activities of a professional society. By 1914 larger universities provided instruction in a myriad of subjects, broken down by discipline, fragmented in ways that certain Europeans thought were positively anti-intellectual. The complaints of British academics with respect to German scholarship were now beginning to be sounded with respect to what the Americans were doing. The whole system, however, depended on an ample supply of students. Whether the university was state supported, allowing every high school student to enter, though the principle of the revolving door might expel him or her within a year, or whether the "Gentleman C" and "gut courses" guaranteed survival in the more fashionable private institutions, student culture separated undergraduates from their professors even where tea and cakes were intended to cement relations. The two lived in isolated worlds, but neither could do without the other.

The higher educational galaxies were growing in number, and

several were gaining in influence. Not only regional but also social, gender, religious, and racial characteristics distinguished them; each tended to move in its own specific orbit, defining its teaching and, where appropriate, research obligations differently. The well-endowed private universities of the East were not much in competition with one another, either for students or faculties. Few actively and persistently searched for students or faculty from other regions of the country, though some might from time to time be so recruited. In their commitments to research they differed greatly. A few, even before World War I, made research a principal concern in their appointment of faculty in specific departments; others were more reluctant to do so. While many faculty and alumni preferred to think more of Yale College than of Yale University, finding even the name a betrayal of sorts, others thought Harvard the prototype worth imitating, less provincial, less dominated by an old-type teaching ethic. At Princeton the battles fought by Woodrow Wilson had little to do with professional research, though very much to do with dining clubs, the nature of the preceptorial system, and the location of the graduate school. If Princeton's library was no longer open only an hour a week, on Saturdays, as it had been in 1870, principally for the exchange of books, few described it as a "research library," and even fewer used it as such in 1914.

The history of US higher education during World War I, the 1920s, and the 1930s remains remarkably unstudied. Even an institution such as Harvard, with all of its contemporary prestige, has not had its post–World War I historian. Samuel Eliot Morison's tercentenary history is far more complete for the 17th, 18th, and 19th centuries than for the first 36 years of the 20th. No one—not even James Bryant Conant's very accomplished recent biographer—has described the Harvard that Conant first knew as president. It is remarkable that there is still no adequate modern history of Columbia, of all that Nicholas Murray Butler, who served as president from 1902 to 1945 and who followed the much shorter though scarcely less significant administration of Seth Low, did to make Columbia a major research university. The story of the University of Chicago, as William Rainey Harper, its first president created it and as it came to be transformed in the decades before an even more charismatic leader, Robert Maynard Hutchins, took the helm coincidental with the beginning of the most serious world economic depression of modern times, is still too little analyzed. Even the story of the remarkable growth of the University of Wisconsin, admirably told by Merle Curti in a work of great erudition and detail, does not adequately explain why and how a professorial vocation came to be created so very rapidly, what a succession of presidents, beginning with Charles van Hise shortly after the turn of the century, did to create undergraduate and graduate degree programs and professional schools of very considerable distinction.

If insufficient attention has been given to the many accomplishments of what may now appear to have been a heroic generation of presidential leaders at Michigan, Stanford, Yale, or the University of California, the fault is not to be ascribed simply to the contemporary tendency to denigrate distinguished individuals, to be suspicious of hagiography. Something much more basic happened to transfer power in many spheres from presidents and boards of trustees to professors and legislators and, most important, to an even greater power, that of public opinion. We do not know nearly enough about how the major US professions, established in the late 19th and early 20th centuries, were altered by world wars I and II, by the civil rights movement and the fighting in Vietnam, not to speak of a bloodless decades-long ideological battle with the Soviet Union. We know remarkably little about the academic profession, specifically, and not much more about the medical or the legal. Yet in each instance the universities had a substantial role in forming these professions, in providing them with the ethos thought to be significant in shaping them.

Scholarship flourished in a handful of universities at the start of the twentieth century as it had not previously done, but it is good to put the matter into perspective. If a few were able to boast remarkable individuals of great erudition and individual departments truly ground-breaking in their research, there were many more who did little that attracted substantial attention abroad or, for that matter, nationally. With someone as cool and detached as James Conant, the situation at Harvard, for example, in the 1930s must have been crystal clear. He could not fail to note how few of his faculty could lay claim to an international reputation. As a scientist, he must have seen that the Nobel Peace Prize, more than the Nobel Prize in Physics, Chemistry, or Medicine, was the one that Americans seemed to win. The scholarship celebrated in 1936, at the time of Harvard's tercentenary, carried American as well as European markings; that was indisputable. Yet in those fields that Conant, a scientist of substantial accomplishments, knew best, the US contribution, while growing, was inferior to what Europe produced. Thorstein Veblen, decades earlier, had seen that the world war, with its decimation of the most talented youth of Europe, would give an advantage to the United States, and it had done so, but it had not given the nation primacy in fields of scholarship in which international judgment was possible. In many nonscientific disciplines, as Conant must have come to recognize very early, the research was negligible, parochial; there was no international competition to contend with, and habit governed what individuals chose to do.

It is not surprising that during the Depression years Conant, like the presidents of other major research universities, was wary of spending money. Instead, he settled on schemes that would save the university money or at least carry no additional costs. It was a good time, for example, to reorganize the system of faculty appointment, to rationalize and improve it. Looking at men who stayed on year after year in nontenured faculty positions, Conant, after consultation, agreed to end the system. "Up or out" became the new principle of faculty promotion and selection. Believing that permanent appointments should be based on meritocratic criteria, and knowing that this was not always the case in many departments, he introduced a new ad hoc committee system, which in effect required that every permanent professorial appointment be approved by a committee of disinterested experts, scholars from other institutions, joined by professors from Harvard departments other than the one making the specific recommendation for the appointment. The selection of faculty members, which had passed very largely to the individual departments, presidents and deans having lost much of their earlier influence in such matters, would now be even more disinterested, objective, and professional.

Conant understood that, if quality were to be maintained, he could not simply depend on the votes of a department in which academic politics often dictated professorial choice, in which a difficult or astute chairman, with his own personal preferences, could in effect veto the choice of others or create such havoc within the department as to achieve the same purpose. There was no possibility of a president ever again being able, in the manner of Eliot, to press for specific faculty, to pretend that he knew and understood their scholarship. In the new era of specialization all the president could hope to retain was a veto on appointments, judiciously and rarely used, in accord with fixed practices based on extensive consultation.

If Conant wished to build on what his predecessors had done, and if others in other research universities hoped to do the same, none in the 1930s dwelled on what was lost by their institutions remaining largely white male preserves, in which the opportunities for professional appointments of Jews, Catholics, blacks, and others were so limited as to be virtually nil. These were not issues that preoccupied the heads of institutions—presidents, deans, or professors—during the Depression or in the four years of war that followed. During the 1930s, when opportunities arose to appoint refugee scholars, some with substantial reputations in Europe who had been forced to flee Hitler or had come even earlier, the financial resources of most colleges and universities were thought to preclude such appointments. When so many US-trained Ph.D.s were without employ or obliged to do relatively menial scud work in so-called para-academic institutions, there was no possibility of doing much for a group of men, however gifted, who had recently made their escape from nazism or fascism.

An equally important story, insufficiently documented or told, has to do with how the colleges and universities fared during the war itself. That their traditional student bodies largely disappeared, that most able-bodied young men over age 18 either volunteered or were conscripted into one or another of the military services, and that this created enormous financial problems for many institutions of higher education is widely acknowledged. Budgets had to be reduced and every kind of economy practiced. While the company of adolescent boys under 18 and the large complement of adolescent girls and adult women, together with those exempted from military service for physical and other reasons, was probably sufficient to sustain some well-endowed institutions for a time, other sources of revenue had to be sought. Many discovered them in the military, in the willingness of the armed services to use the facilities of colleges and universities for their own training programs, often with their own staffs. Where so many of the junior faculty were absent, on military leave, and where senior faculty, though in obviously smaller number, took on other kinds of "war service," salaries were a less heavy charge. Still, economies had to be made, and how all this affected library, museum, and laboratory budgets and what it did to scholarly research more generally has not been much reflected on.

Indeed, an argument can be made that more attention has been given to certain of the spectacular scientific developments that occurred off the university campuses, often involving highly classified research, than anything that took place in the major colleges and universities. The country's scientific and technological accomplishment, as reflected in the successful manufacture and delivery of an atomic bomb over Japan, has been told many times and is the story best known, if only by its constant repetition. The role of the research universities in all this has been amply documented, revealing how often the site of a crucial experiment might be the secret installations at Los Alamos or the only scarcely less secret facilities in Chicago. So, too, the story of the development of radar, the discovery of penicillin and the sulfa drugs, of all that was done to create new and more sophisticated military weapons, offensive and defensive, often requiring collaboration with the country's principal allies, is only slightly less known. We know a great deal also about World War II intelligence, about all that the Office of Strategic Services, for example, did to hasten the defeat of the country's principal enemies and how it proposed to pacify them.

What, then, do we not know? We know, by comparison, very little about how the war affected the millions who served abroad in every kind of battle zone, the many other millions who served at home, and the much larger number who remained at home, excluded from military service by reason of age, sex, physical disability, or the like. It is extraordinary that we know so little about the research that proceeded during the war on the university campuses of the country. What great books were written during this period? How, if at all, do they reflect the circumstances of the war? Does Gunnar Myrdal's *The American Dilemma*, for example, qualify as a war book? Would it have had the same emphases had the threat of war and the war itself not intruded at every point in its composition? Where, indeed, did the prominent Swedish social scientist, selected by the Carnegie Corporation for his presumed objectivity—an American could not be expected to show the same dispassion on the issue of race in a riven America—find his collaborators? Many were white scholars; others were black. Where had they been trained? Were they part of the US research community? Were they as important in their own way as those who wrote about war and peace, urban government, nutrition, public health, rural decay? Where did they fit into a research company that included scientists who understood the ways in which Einstein's theories had transformed physics?

Such questions are asked because the real nature of the US research enterprise is so rarely explored in any depth. The conditions that create learning, indeed the conditions that create a learned profession, a professoriate, to take only one of many, are too rarely examined. Who, for instance, understands how much the US research university, and the many others that would not have once thought to denominate themselves as such, are in their present form the unique creations of World War II, the extraordinary optimism that attended the end of that tragic conflict, and the exaggerated self-confidence and utopian visions it helped generate in the United States? Nineteen forty-five was a seminal year for the country and the world, but its dimensions are still not adequately understood. Since the era that opened at that time ended only in 1989—the true terminal date of the twentieth century—it becomes important to reflect, however briefly, on what 1945 represented. What did prominent and successful academics think at the time? What were they saying? How did they view the world?

It may come as a surprise to some that the two 1945 texts chosen to illustrate academic opinion in that fateful year were commissioned by two presidents, one the president of Harvard, the other of the United States. Each in its own way expresses the enthusiasm and confidence of a society that has emerged from an ordeal and believes itself to be superior but recognizes that it cannot rest on its laurels. The first, the report of a committee of senior professors at Harvard who had not gone off to war, who remained behind as civilian teachers in Cambridge, is colloquially known as the Redbook, a reference not to its radical politics but, rather, to its somewhat discrete cover. "General Education in a Free Society," commissioned by President Conant in the spring of 1943, when he was working in Los Alamos on a project that no member of his committee could even imagine, is sometimes thought to be a proposal for the reform of the Harvard undergraduate curriculum. It is certainly that, but no one who has read more than a few pages of the book can doubt that this may be the least consequential of its findings, as given to the Harvard community in the summer of 1945.

So, too, with the second document, "Science: The Endless Frontier," sometimes thought to be important mostly for its influence in creating the National Science Foundation (NSF). While such a body is explicitly called for, Vannevar Bush, another of the secret Los Alamos scientific group that created the atomic bomb, had no need to write at such length, or involve so many of his distinguished colleagues who had no knowledge of what was going on at Los Alamos if this had been his sole purpose. The report merits reading precisely because it answers what the now dead president, Franklin Roosevelt, asked for. Roosevelt, in his letter of November 17, 1944, requesting a report, said: "New frontiers of the mind are before us, and if they are pioneered with the same vision, boldness, and drive with which we have waged this war we can create a fuller and more fruitful employment and a fuller and more fruitful life." The president had not asked for a report on what the nation needed to do for science; he asked for something considerably larger. Harry Truman, his successor, who received the report, needed only to look at its table of contents to realize that it dealt as much with disease as with national security, as much with jobs as with scientific and industrial research. It was a collaborative effort, the work of humanists as well as of social scientists and natural scientists.

What message is common to the two reports? That the obligation of the society is to nurture ability, to raise the competence of the average. Both dwelled on wasted talent, of those who failed to finish school, who never accomplished what they might in other circumstances have done. The general education report, asking why algebra was meaningless to half of all 14-year-olds, spoke of intelligence depending on "habit and outlook which in turn go back to earliest opportunity." Democracy, the report went on to say, "is not only opportunity for the able": "It is equally betterment for the average, both the immediate betterment which can be gained in a single generation and the slower groundswell of betterment which works through generations. Hence the task of the high school is not merely to speed the bright boy to the top. It is at least as much (so far as numbers are concerned, far more) so to widen the horizons of ordinary students that they and, still more, their children will encounter fewer of the obstacles that cramp achievement." The report emphasized the diversity of US society and insisted that education would not be "adequate until it catches the image more exactly." One of the most important of the book's sections dealt with the impact of social change.

"Science: The Endless Frontier" stressed many of the same points. While it accepted that the "responsibility for the creation of new scientific knowledge rests on the small body of men and women who understand the fundamental laws of nature and are skilled in the techniques of scientific research," it argued that "it would be folly to set up a program under which research in the natural sciences and medicine was expanded at the cost of the social sciences, humanities, and other studies so essential to national well-being." While higher educational opportunity in the United States might be more available than in any other country, this did not prevent Bush and his colleagues from saying: "Higher education in this country is largely for those who have the means. If those who have the means coincided entirely with those persons who have the talent we should not be squandering a part of our higher education on those undeserving of it, nor neglecting great talent among those who fail to attend college for economic reasons. There are talented individuals in every segment of the population, but with few exceptions those without the means of buying higher education go without it. Here is a tremendous waste of the greatest resource of the nation—the intelligence of its citizens."

While there is reason to say that Vannevar Bush merits the distinction of being the "father" of the National Science Foundation, for doing as much as any other individual to bring the federal government to consider making substantially larger appropriations for research—a very simple graph gave eloquent testimony to how little the federal government was involved in supporting research before the war—no one, to my knowledge, has called him the father of the GI Bill of Rights. Yet, that single piece of federal legislation, perhaps as much as any other act passed in this century, changed US higher education. In embodying the major principles that made Bush and Conant anxious to provide educational opportunity to many more individuals, creating a student population that in less than a decade dwarfed any that existed before World War II, it was the opening shot in a revolution that has continued to this day, creating problems but also fundamentally changing America's colleges and universities. The GI Bill, in allowing many millions of adult men and women to enroll in US higher education institutions, did more than simply provide admission to numerous colleges and professional and graduate schools. It allowed individuals to attend institutions they would not have previously gone to, to pursue careers they would not have considered. It did as much to transform the US academic profession, for example, as any other single act of government.

This has not been sufficiently recognized. A new academic profession was created which served a vastly expanded body of students, exceeding in size and social complexity any that Lord Bryce could have imagined. With the beginnings of the Cold War, and given the enormous reputation that university-educated men had acquired through their scientific and technological work during World War II, the universities were invited to add yet new fields to an already burgeoning research agenda. If unprecedented federal funds were made available for scientific, defense, and health research—reflecting the priorities set in the federal government—the universities could not simply be transformed into scientific and technical institutes. It was not because a member of Vannevar Bush's many task forces had said that "science cannot live by and unto itself alone" that money poured in for other studies as well. The impulse to do research on cities and poverty at one moment, on arms control and defense policy at another, but also on matters that fell into the domain of the humanities, guaranteed that many in the professional class would now wish to see themselves as researchers, profiting from the private and public grants that would allow them to do research abroad, travel widely, attend conferences, and show themselves to be scholars as well as teachers.

Much of what has happened in and around these institutions in the last half-century has been described in the essays in this volume. It would be useless to repeat or embellish what others have said. Still, it may be useful to mention developments that others have not focused on. If, to return to the very first sentence of this essay, it is correct to say that "the history of the American research university in the twentieth century waits to be written," some outline, however brief, of that history must be attempted. If, in the first decades of this century through World War II, the research university galaxy in the United States remained relatively small, if it showed characteristics that had evolved essentially in the last decades of the nineteenth century, as described by Lord Bryce, that was no longer the case by the late 1960s and is even less so today.

In short, James Conant, returning to Harvard today, or Vannevar Bush, returning to MIT, would recognize the institutions but would realize at once how much has changed. It is not simply that the physical plants have grown—they have, of course—but both institutions, and those that once bore a very large resemblance to them, are today preoccupied with issues, subject to pressures, and committed to purposes that did not exist or were not salient until quite recently.

A second revolution, quite as important as the one that followed the Civil War, has taken place in the last decades. Someone who knew New York University, the University of Texas, Indiana University, the University of Florida, Duke University, Boston University, Georgetown University, Stanford University, Brown University, and any number of others before 1945, would be astonished by the changes that have taken place. To put the matter most simply, research has become very conspicuous in all these institutions and in hundreds of others in ways that would have seemed almost inconceivable half a century ago. With all the differences that still distinguish Harvard from Yale, and both from Columbia, Pennsylvania, Princeton, and Chicago—and they remain considerable—they are substantially less than those observable four decades ago, at a time still vivid to older professors who remain active in these institutions today. The same, no less emphatically, needs to be said for all the major prewar public research universities, including Wisconsin, Michigan, and California: they are not what they once were, and it is not simply that they have grown larger.

Without wishing to make it appear that all have become federal grant universities—that all are equally dependent on governmental contracts for defense, health, and environmental and other researches that their faculties have been encouraged to undertake—it is a fact that federal subventions have given all these and a host of other institutions substantial new income, allowing for expansion, particularly in the natural and social sciences, but encouraging growth in other areas as well. In the humanities, even after the creation of the National Endowment for the Humanities (NEH), the growth has depended largely on private giving but also on the willingness of universities to use their own funds to make additional appointments, to act, in effect, as patrons of the humanities. Alumni and others, making large contributions to private universities and, increasingly, to public universities, have created resources for instruction and research beyond any imagined by those who led these institutions in the pre–World War II years. A fund drive at Harvard in the 1960s, which aimed to raise $82 million, an unheard-of sum at the time, is today rivaled by one that seeks several billion dollars. Inflation does not explain the change; ambition does.

In distinguished institutions such as the University of Michigan the social sciences were only beginning to be developed in the period before World War II. Much of their growth since, not only in fields like psychology and sociology, has depended on federal research grants as well as on the willingness of foundations, the state legislature, and federal agencies to encourage certain kinds of inquiry and to provide funds to allow students to pursue graduate study and, ultimately, to become researchers. The importance of the Cold War for the natural sciences—physics, chemistry, astronomy, biology, geology, engineering, and medicine—has frequently been discussed. The importance of the rivalry with the Soviet Union for the social sciences has also been examined. In creating wholly new disciplines collectively embraced by the term *area studies,* in which the Soviet Union always figured most prominently, but also in providing funds for arms control and defense policy research, the alarms raised in Washington by Sputnik and the growth of Soviet military capability gave a large impetus to many new kinds of social scientific inquiry. For a time, when Lyndon Johnson's "war on poverty" seemed more than a cliché invented for political gain, there were funds also for research on urban problems and on the poor, not yet denominated an "underclass."

It was not the federal government alone which made the US public and private universities more conscious of the world in something other than its American and West European dimensions. The need to offer instruction in languages once thought exotic—Chinese, Japanese, Russian, Arabic—did not immediately create large cadres of competent linguists, and it was understandable that a major East Asian historian complained of the dearth of US linguistic competence in respect to a country called Vietnam, where such ability might have mattered, but some progress was registered, even in regions scarcely known to Americans before World War II. Research, however rudimentary, began in areas previously closed to scholarly inquiry. Why? The research was thought to be useful.

Under these conditions research could not fail to take on an importance it had never previously enjoyed. While the first of the academic revolutions, that of the mid- and late 19th and early 20th centuries took place in response to domestic needs, those of the mid- and late 20th century were responses in very substantial part to what were perceived to be new and threatening international hazards. Domestic considerations still played a role, of course. It was not at all strange that an aging population, with many no longer as persuaded of the truths of religions that promised immortality, should wish for medical researches that would prolong the only lives they expected to enjoy. Nor was it at all strange that the achievements of medicine, registered during the war, should be seen as only the first act in a drama that would continue to play. Medical research expenses grew exponentially, not only in the hospitals of the country but also in all the major medical schools. The extraordinary nineteenth-century promise of Johns Hopkins Medical School, moving toward its centennial celebrations, and the others that followed its example in reforming their medical and public health curricula, making research a more integral part of their activity, seemed to be wholly fulfilled in the very ambitious research proposals made by physicians and scientists in response to the promise of generous and NSF and National Institutes of Health (NIH) support.

It was in the physical and biological sciences, as much as in those that could be specifically called medical, that the most conspicuous research changes occurred. Again, what had been achieved during World War II certainly played a substantial role in giving prestige to all such research, and indeed in legitimating it. The discoveries of the postwar years, in DNA but also in space, in high-energy physics but also in molecular chemistry and biology—and the fragmentation of all these disciplines into ever smaller units—made education in them a more complex matter, requiring even greater diligence and industry. In the natural sciences specialization took on new forms; laboratories took on new appearances. It was not only expensive equipment that characterized the post–World War II university science laboratories but also, increasingly, the presence of a small army of graduate students and postdoctoral scholars who congregated there, knowing what close collaboration with a talented mentor could mean for a successful career. Funding for new fellowships and research, at certain intervals, seemed relatively easy to secure. At other times the federal purse seemed less open for certain kinds of scientific research; other demands weighed more heavily with politicians. In a federal system MIT had to accept that, in competition for a research grant with the University of Florida, it would not always win.

This, then, was the new research university order created by federal subvention. The financial resources were clearly unmatched; there was no precedent for such vast appropriations. Universities that had once thought of themselves principally or only as teaching institutions decided to enter the game. Those marginally involved before World War II became substantially more engaged. The few major prewar research universities in the United States, profiting from an academic culture they had already embraced, however tentatively, became major players. When the University of California realized that its resources exceeded those of many nation-states of Western Europe, including a number known to be exceedingly prosperous, and after it took in the full dimensions of the changes in its economy produced by the war, the idea of becoming something more than a California institution, however distinguished, took hold. The University of California, like many other institutions, did not in a single moment of sudden illumination aspire to become national. Still, such an ambition insinuated itself.

The California Master Plan, intended to create a new kind of higher educational system in the state, the creation of the early 1960s, was both Baedeker and Bible, in the words of Berkeley historian Sheldon Rothblatt. Understanding why and how California acquired its reputation as the most innovative state in the nation, Rothblatt wrote of its "silicon valleys, service sectors and diversified economy mixing agriculture and industry," allowing California to emerge "as the first and perhaps most advanced example of a 'postindustrial society.'" There was no longer any need for the University of California to look to the University of Michigan as its model; it had itself become the model for others. If Harvard, in the East, was in some measure influencing Yale and Princeton to change their ways, to make research more central to their educational enterprise, Berkeley and UCLA had a comparable influence on Stanford. All were now in much closer touch, competing for able faculty in the sciences, particularly, but in many other disciplines as well. Berkeley, taking Harvard to be number one as a research university, had no desire to remain the Avis of higher education. It would challenge Harvard for faculty talent. The whole world was thought to be waiting for a call from Cambridge or Berkeley. There was much self-delusion in such aspirations, but before the Berkeley disturbances of the 1960s it seemed reasonable to imagine that a distinguished scholar from Paris or Oxford might indeed prefer the splendor of the classical Roman architecture and skies of California to the long, dreary winters of northern Europe.

While few in fact came from abroad, particularly after Western Europe became more prosperous and the elevated salaries and benefits of US research university faculty did not greatly exceed those of Germany or France, a greater number came from the United Kingdom, where the opportunities seemed more restricted, even before the arrival of Prime Minister Margaret Thatcher. The more important movement of faculty, however, occurred within the country, from one research university to another. Where there were so many more institutional and professorial players, where the stakes were so very high, where a university might seek to distinguish itself in an area not already claimed by another, and where regionalism seemed to be declining before a much expanding national culture, which could not fail to touch scholarship and research, the move from Madison to Cambridge, Ann Arbor to Los Angeles, Chicago to New York, and between any number of less celebrated centers of learning became common. In an expanding higher educational universe such transfers were easy; they required no repudiation of loyalties, these being more attached to a specific discipline than to any single university. Those who were desired were research scholars. It was less common for noted teachers to be recruited; they were less known and also less coveted.

This situation continued for a number of decades. When it finally ended, in good part because of economic recession, but also because the numbers recruited in a relatively short period filled even the greatly expanded complement of professorships in both old and new fields, the research university in the United States had changed dramatically. There were many more of them, and, though the most eminent might not imagine themselves to be challenged by the new arrivals, they were. If lawyers were four times more numerous in the 1980s than they had been in the 1940s, it was not only because the country had become more litigious. Law was a very profitable employ, and many universities were able to add to their law faculties, at relatively modest expense, to satisfy the growing demand for places. If there were many more excellent medical schools, with their professors engaged in significant research, it was because ample funds were available for such inquiry. If a university such as Indiana vastly expanded its horizons and chose to make itself a center of East European studies, providing instruction in the languages, histories, and economies of the region, it was not simply because Herman Wells was its exceptionally gifted president, a leader in the 19th-century mold. If urban universities, once required to cater to the less well-off, saw new possibilities for themselves, if they imagined they were now in a position to compete with others, this could be achieved most easily by presenting themselves as incomparable centers of research.

To buy a whole department could be a relatively cheap matter, though never in the natural sciences. To buy a single professor, a name likely to resonate through the country, and to do so with some regularity, was not a terribly expensive undertaking. It was substantially less easy to find fellowship funds from private individuals to support indigent but able students, in the way Charles Eliot had done at Harvard late in the nineteenth century. Few, in fact, were able to do so, not least because wealthy alumni (and others) much preferred to seek their immortality through having buildings named after them. Many of the new private research universities catered to the children of the middle class, who came in good part because they believed that the instruction would be better than any they might find in the new public research universities. Again, the postwar story about the creation of these public research universities has not been told. What part of the new higher educational system of New York, for example, is owing very largely to initiatives taken by a single governor, Nelson Rockefeller? Did the State University of New York develop in the way that it did, at Stony Brook and Buffalo, to name its "flagships," because private universities in the state were unwilling to educate at a certain price and in certain disciplines? Who imitated whom, and why? Was research emphasized in these new universities because the times demanded such effort?

To ask such questions is to inquire also about how research universities in the United States, particularly those with adequate or large endowments, came to accept their responsibility to admit black students in unprecedented number and, indeed, to search for students from other disadvantaged minorities. It is to inquire about how they soon came to compete for such students, and others, and what this did to change the character of their student populations, both undergraduate and graduate. It is to ask why many of the course offerings, which are unbelievably abundant, were never even considered by the greatest number of the undergraduates who came to these distinguished universities, said to be the best in the country. Science, in any form, was an inconceivable option even for students thought to have had a superior schooling. For many, science was something to be gotten over, a modest requirement that needed to be met. In these circumstances instruction given in the humanities and in the softer social sciences—the new economics was thought to be too theoretical and complex for any but the mathematically gifted— became the staple subjects of what still passed for education in the liberal arts. Many who looked at these standard undergraduate offerings took delight that an earlier geographic and cultural provincialism had been lost; some worried about the new provincialism that had taken over. Did the first compensate for the second?

In the universe of the post–World War II research university, professors were remunerated as they had not previously been. Students received financial aid from the federal government, states, and university scholarship funds in amounts that had never before been considered. If tuition fees had escalated, both in private and public institutions, costs that educational institutions were obliged to bear were blamed. Imposing very real hardships on many, and creating a great deal of bustle among those in the country who believed that too many of the tenured professors were idle, that too much of what they taught was useless, the reputation that attached to all institutions of higher learning in the early 1990s was not what it had been in the early 1960s. The "multiversity" of Clark Kerr was less esteemed in the day of President Clinton than it had been in the time of Kennedy or Johnson.

But it was not only the large private or public research universities that had changed. All the institutions that made up once segregated galaxies had been fundamentally transformed. The women's colleges, for example, losing certain kinds of students to the newly created Ivy League coeducational universities, were obliged to find a new reason for being. Many discovered it in their claim to offer a kind of instruction uniquely suited to women who wished to go on to the professions, now increasingly open to them. Something of the same argument was made by the smaller coeducational liberal arts colleges, which insisted that they, more than the larger universities, remained loyal to their teaching role, confusing it with no other, and that they were admirably suited to prepare men and women for the professional schools they would choose to enter. The black colleges, making something of the same argument, knew that many of the most talented of their prospective students were being siphoned away to the more prominent research universities concerned with recruiting able black students. Many of the Catholic universities became more secular, appointing non-Catholics to faculty positions, vying for research funds, and claiming to be doing what they had always done, providing a basic education to those who searched for rigor. In all the major research universities, but in many others as well, women entered the professorial ranks in numbers that would have been almost unthinkable immediately after World War II.

In short, the system of higher education in the United States, and not only its research universities, is passing through a time of very great transition. While some insist that it is troubled, unable to adjust to the demands increasingly made on it, reluctant to accommodate its several paymasters, old and new, including parents, others see these persistent claims to its being in "crisis" as highly exaggerated. While curricula have indeed been expanded, with new subjects figuring much in the way they always have, it is not at all obvious that the changes have made the institutions more parochial, as some are inclined to say. Still, there is reason to worry. In many fields the research of a few years ago is no longer adequately supported. Grade inflation, however attractive to some students, does not appear to have made the academic life more agreeable or more compelling a professional option for those able to consider others. Many disciplines, particularly in the sciences, rely on foreign students to a troubling extent. US-born students do not appear to seek out the arduous disciplines that call for persistent study over many years.

Still, a close examination of the accomplishments of many of the major research universities, now significantly expanded in number, suggests that ambition has not fled, that the wish to innovate, found new fields, and offer new options remains unabated. Whether or not some of them can legitimately claim to be the best in the world, in any meaningful sense of the term, ought to be seen as a matter of little moment. No one claimed such distinction for US research universities in 1939; it would not be a great tragedy if such hyperbole, associated with a time of extraordinary hubris, ceased to figure. What must be seen, however, is that the system, as it developed in the last one hundred and fifty years as well as more recently, was very largely influenced by domestic pressures of one kind or other, as often political as economic, and that this is still the case today. Under these circumstances the American political and social systems, and the specific values that govern action, and not only by those who exercise power in Washington, are crucial elements in an equation that seeks to explain why US culture is as it is, why intellectual life takes the form it does, and why Tocqueville, perhaps as much as any other commentator, knew that the American democracy might take many roads. He was not sanguine, which did not mean that he despaired.

The dreams of Vannevar Bush, and of others who were considering the country after World War II, have been realized in many respects. In other regards they remain very substantially unfulfilled. US schooling was not very good when James Conant and other of his colleagues studied it. It is not very good today. The affluence of the society influences what is taught in the universities, how students react to such teaching, what they choose to study, and what ardor they show. It also determines to a very great extent who goes where and who has no chance to attend at all. It is easy to argue that a new research agenda waits to be fashioned, one more suited to these post–Cold War times. It is more difficult to know what that agenda should be and how it can respond to the racial, ethnic, and religious differences that divide the society on fundamental political, social, and economic issues. Those differences will not be quickly resolved, and they cannot fail to affect the intellectual enterprise of the nation's colleges and universities. There may be a need for a third "revolution" in US higher education, but to call for it is neither to describe its major contours nor to mobilize the energies that will be required to secure significant change. The two other educational revolutions in the United States were made in a time of optimism and hope. Both are in very short supply today.

Yet if it is acknowledged that many of the intellectual revolutions of our time have been university based, that in respect to the computer as to telecommunications more generally, the role of the university has been absolutely crucial, there may be a better understanding of why and how whole disciplines have been altered by the US example. It is in no way surprising that the concept of an "industrial park," for example, originated in the United States and that such parks were invariably located near major research universities. That they are today being copied elsewhere, in Japan as well as in the United Kingdom, at institutions no less venerable than Oxford, suggests why US higher educational inventiveness is so widely recognized. More important, certainly, is the fact that US scholarship in many disciplines, both theoretical and applied, provides a measuring rod today by which others abroad locate and define their own achievements. This has all happened since the end of World War II. Little precedent for such foreign emulation existed before 1945, and it was almost unimaginable a century ago.

American concerns with learning are said to be part of the country's democratic tradition. Whether this will lead it to attend to its very grave problems in primary and secondary education in the next decades remains to be seen. So, too, whether tolerance for new styles of learning, in novel fields and disciplines, will in fact continue, serving to generate new understanding in the social sciences and the humanities as much as in the natural sciences, is a challenge that the greatly expanded universe of research universities will almost certainly be required to meet. The earlier higher-educational revolutions created a unique set of institutions, committed to research and service of a kind others abroad never contemplated with equal fervor. Whether anything of comparable boldness will be tried again, serving other no less important purposes, and what these are likely to be are all unanswerable questions. No one alive in 1865 prophesied the American university of 1888; no one in 1945 foresaw the events of 1968 or, indeed, those of 1989. Who can imagine what opportunities will be perceived and acted on by any part of a higher educational system as various as the one that now exists in the United States? Which institutions are likely to profit from the nation's continuing political appeal to prove themselves useful? How will they show themselves committed to what are perceived to be the requirements of contemporary democracy?

Index

AAMC. *See* Association of American Medical Colleges

academia, 133, 136, 236, 248, 256; backlash against, 319; communications with industry, 237; cultural diversity in, 38; freedom of thought and speech in, 244; principles of, 140

academic health center (AHC), 254, 258, 259; ability to compete, 261–62; contributions of, 254, 258, 265, 326; funding of, 259–62, 264; place within the university, 254–55, 262–63, 266–68. *See also* biomedical research

academic research, 236, 249, 275, 326; commercialization of, 248; criticism of, 238; federal funding for, 198, 246; investments in, 290, 308; peer reviews in, 280; retrenchment in, 287

"academic rigor," 109

academic science, 234, 276, 279, 280, 327

accountability, 205

administration, 10, 16, 96, 140, 302; academic disdain for, 246, 299; changes made by, 111, 112, 139, 305; criteria of choice, 8, 107; divisions in, 53; financial interests of, 118; professionalization of, 122–24, 127, 129, 303; size of, 304

admissions, 235, 313; need-blind, 4, 235; of foreign students, 171, 172, 293, 350–55, 356; of minorities, 42, 44, 52, 329; role of merit in, 13, 14, 350; standards in, 306, 318; of women, 44, 329. *See also* financial aid

affirmative action, 4, 52, 273; debates about, 39–40, 56; and hiring practices, 73, 302

African Americans. *See* blacks

Aga Khan University, 309

age discrimination, 243

agricultural schools, 236

agriculture, 169, 249, 273, 363, 384

Ahearne, John F. viii

AIDS, 265

allocation of fiscal resources, 121, 258

alumni, 46, 119, 132, 168, 371; allegiance of, 128, 369; career paths of, 163; gifts from, 161; role of, 6, 9, 11, 43, 123, 169, 170, 184, 203

Alzheimer's disease, 256

ambivalence, 37, 42; in the diversifying process, 47–53; of faculty, 25, 42, 53; of students, 49–52, 53

American Academy of Arts and Sciences, viii, ix, 220

American Association for the Advancement of Science, 95, 283, 327

American Commonwealth (Bryce), 365

American Council of Learned Societies, 69

American Dilemma (Myrdal), 376

American Philosophical Society, 220

America's Academic Future (NSF), 198

Amherst College, 212

Anderson, Martin, 210

animal rights, 43, 102, 284

anti-intellectualism, 46, 110

Anti-Intellectualism in American Life (Hofstadter), 205

Antioch College, 222

391

applied mathematics, 142
applied research, 156, 174, 237, 250, 289
applied science, 141, 147, 234, 293, 364
appropriations, federal, 117, 366
Apter, David E., viii
area studies programs, 109, 171, 323, 339
argumentum ad hominem, 66, 75
artificial intelligence, 142
arts and sciences, 142, 254, 267, 315; faculties of, 104, 233, 244; graduate studies in, 165, 235; place within the university, 4, 9, 120, 180; relation to health sciences, 254–55
Asian Americans, 42
assimilation, 44
Association of American Medical Colleges (AAMC), 258, 261
Association of American Universities, 89, 117, 299
atmospheric sciences, 286
Atomic Energy Commission (AEC), 237
autonomy, 305; of the faculty, vii, 112, 153, 283, 300, 301; of the university, 106, 204–5, 216, 272, 282, 316, 319, 324

bachelor's degrees, 162, 168, 316, 320
Bailyn, Bernard, viii
Barber, Elinor, viii, 33
basic research, 31, 156, 323, 335, 344; expenditures in, 237, 256; federal funding of, 28, 88, 144, 279, 289; restrictions on, 102, 276; utility of, 214, 276, 277, 322
basic science, 180, 234, 277, 293; federal support of, 88; knowledge base of, 266; relationship to military, 276; resources for, 89, 289
behavioral sciences, 266, 277
Bell, Daniel, viii
Ben-David, Joseph, 133
Berkeley. *See* University of California, Berkeley

Berkeley, George, 60, 81
bidding wars, 282
"big science," 294
biological sciences, 146, 188, 254, 325
biomedical activities, 30, 213
biomedical research, 284; federal funding of, 256, 327; role of academic health-care centers in, 254–55, 259, 261–62, 268
biomedical sciences, 89, 95
biotechnology, 191, 247, 248, 289
biotechnology incubator companies, 31, 32
black population, 37
blacks, 14, 42, 44, 374
Blendon, Robert J., 259
Bloom, Allan, 206, 210
Bok, Derek, 26, 158
Boston University, 380
"brain drain" issue, 344, 346, 350, 355, 356. *See also* federal government
breast cancer, 257
Brewster, Kingman, 299, 300
Brooks, Harvey, ix, 289, 294
Browder, Felix, viii
Brown, George, 283, 327
Brown University, 361, 380
Bryce, James, 365–68, 379, 380
"buffer institutions," 248–50
Bush, Vannevar, 28, 29, 274, 283, 377–80, 389
Bush Administration, 284
Butler, Nicholas Murray, 2, 115, 371

Cain, Bruce, 227
California Institute of Technology (Cal Tech), 107, 221, 291
California Master Plan for Higher Education, 200, 384
Cal Tech. *See* California Institute of Technology
Cambridge University, 86, 155, 311, 367
Carleton College, 224
Carnegie Commission, 288
Carnegie Corporation of New York, 376

Carnegie Foundation, 322. *See also* Carnegie Corporation
Carnegie Foundation for the Advancement of Teaching, 312
CCNY. *See* City College of New York
certification programs, 168
chancellors, 10, 107, 241
"cheap science," 96
Citation Indexes, 220
City College of New York (CCNY), 223
civil liberties, 38
civil rights movement, 3, 37, 372
Civil War, 68, 155, 366, 380; development of university system following, 362–63, 365, 369
class, 72
clinical practice, 253
Clinton, William, 387
Clinton Administration, 215, 259, 264, 283, 289, 305
Closing of the American Mind (Bloom), 206, 210
"cognitive map," 107
Cohen, Wesley, 237, 249
Cold War, 275, 353, 379, 381; anxieties about, 322; end of, 333, 334; post–Cold War years, 30, 172, 193, 215, 274, 389
Cole, Jonathan R., vii, ix, 107, 294
collaboration, 158, 267, 287, 383; among departments, 122, 236, 254–55, 263; between universities, 29, 268; between universities and industry, 247, 276, 346, 353; international, 286, 293–94, 353
collegiality, 42, 43, 92
collusion, 131, 135, 137, 138
colon cancer, 257
Colorado College, 224
Colorado River Basin, 90
Columbia University, viii, 1, 31, 107, 205, 220, 364, 371, 380; closing of departments at, 8–9, 97; growth rate, 3–4; School of Library Service, 8, 10, 97
Commonwealth Fund, 259
community colleges, 156
competition, 146, 147–51, 158, 272, 279, 282, 284, 285, 319; among universities, 44, 133, 137–38, 150, 220, 241, 312, 369, 371; effects of, 24, 133–34, 148–49, 171, 224; in health care, 256, 261; intellectual, 132, 134, 139, 142, 145, 150; international, 215, 278, 309, 335, 337, 339, 341, 350, 354, 373; for resources, 7–8, 134–35, 143–47, 234, 254, 353, 383; universities' resistance to, 131–32
computer sciences, 142
Conant, James Bryant, 1, 371, 372–74, 377, 379, 380, 389
Congress. *See* US Congress
congressional hearings, 194
congressional leaders, 215, 274
congressional legislation, 247
Congressional Office of Technology Assessment (OTA), 282, 283, 327
congressional scholars, 228
congressional testimony, 248
Connor, W. Robert, viii
conservatism, 94, 95, 97, 109, 239
constituency interest, 307
contraction, 138, 139, 140, 254
cooperation, 135, 290, 294; between departments, 197; between industry and universities, 248; between universities, 138, 150, 242; international, 277, 278, 336
Cornell University, 154, 179, 191, 222, 281, 365
corporate educational centers, 156
correspondence criterion, 64, 65
correspondence theory of truth, 17, 22, 60, 63–65, 77
cost-control, 273
"cost disease," 106
Council of Teaching Hospitals (COTH), 258
credibility, 204, 205, 207, 215
Critical Technologies Institute, 284
criticism, 93, 103, 226, 249, 346; of health care, 257; of higher education, vii; literary, 68; of universities, viii, 195, 212, 214, 231–50, 258, 327, 347; of Western Rationalistic Tradition, 59
curriculum, 1, 48, 70, 72, 92, 93, 98,

curriculum (*cont'd*)
99, 121, 126, 142, 160, 187, 357;
debates about, 4, 39, 55, 77, 306;
diversification of, 4, 39, 74, 94,
109, 170, 337, 338–40, 388;
importance of coherence in, 27,
181–83; internationalization of,
337, 338–40, 355–56; of
professional schools, 165, 260,
383; undergraduate, 226, 377. *See
also* engineering; graduate schools;
medical school; natural sciences
Curti, Merle, 372
cystic fibrosis, 256

Dædalus (journal), viii, ix, 324, 361
Darwin, Charles, 98, 150
Darwinism, 49
Dawn (journal), 317
dean, 7, 97, 100, 104, 105, 132, 133,
141, 221, 260, 272, 283, 289, 292,
302, 339; role of, 11, 121, 122,
182, 281, 373, 374; term of
service, 91
deconstruction, 49, 325
deconstructionists, 76
defense funding, 276
deficit. *See* federal deficit
Department of Commerce, 289
Department of Defense (DoD), 102,
277, 343; funding of research, 237,
275; role in scientific research, 144,
247, 292. *See also* basic science
Department of Education, 291
Department of Energy, 247, 280, 290
Department of Health and Human
Services, 289
Depression, the (1930s), 232, 374
Derrida, Jacques, 71, 72, 76, 77, 79
de Solla Price, Derek J., 3, 87
Dicey, A. V., 366
differentiation, 287, 288
digital communications, 255
direct costs, 117, 118, 261, 263
disciplinary boundaries, viii, 55;
crossing of, 123, 135, 180, 233,
263, 268, 341
discipline evaluation studies, 220
disciplines, academic, 9, 16, 55, 68,
69, 86, 92, 107, 123, 136, 141,

157, 160, 164, 175, 184, 187, 194,
227, 232, 233, 267, 291, 293, 340,
341, 348, 349, 357, 370, 373, 384,
386, 388, 390; choosing among,
90, 92, 95, 96, 99, 111;
competition, 135, 139, 180;
direction of, 17, 93, 163, 165;
evolution of, 22, 71, 76, 139, 150,
166, 167, 188, 383, 389;
formation of, 4, 73, 74–75, 167,
306, 381; loyalty to, 92, 98, 105,
385; politicization of, 244; survival
of, 94–95, 97
discrimination, 15
disquotational theory, 63–65
diversification, 37, 46, 53. *See also*
curriculum; graduate students
diversity, 38, 40–45, 180, 285;
cultural, 14, 15, 37–38, 48, 199; of
faculty, vii, 4; of student body, vii,
4
doctoral candidates, 44, 104
DoD. *See* Department of Defense
Dole-Bayh Bill, 30
Duke University, 153, 222, 339, 380

earth sciences, 286
Economist, 316, 319
Educational Commission on Foreign
Medical School Graduates, 261
efficiency, 300
egalitarianism, 15, 40, 42
electronic communication, 173, 175.
See also internet
elementary education, 291. *See also*
K-12 education
elementary school, 288, 291
Elements (Euclid), 58
Eliot, Charles, 1, 115, 368, 374, 386
elitism, 20
endowment, 31, 161, 170, 347
engineering, 37, 77, 107, 169, 199,
222, 233, 254, 261, 271, 336, 363;
computer, 248; curriculum, 234;
funding for, 31, 214, 237, 352;
growth of, 273, 276, 279, 292,
364; and industry, 289, 342;
internationalization of, 232, 277,
278, 340, 344, 349, 355; teaching

of, 94, 119, 142, 163, 164, 239, 267, 313
Engineering Research Centers, 234
enrollment, 109, 302, 333
entitlement, 14, 15, 279, 287; of faculty, 100, 101, 104; of groups, 40, 42
environmental science, 136, 242, 292
ethnicity, 72
European Enlightenment, 59, 161
experiential education, 110, 112

fascism, 374
"Fateful Choices" (GUIRR), 192
federal cutbacks, 255, 271
federal deficit, 88, 232, 255, 259, 284
Federal Election Commission, 228
federal government, 132, 208, 257, 302, 311, 356; brain drain, 172; criticism of universities, 214, 346; financial aid for students, 4, 303, 324, 352, 387; involvement in university policy, 2, 216, 289, 291, 292, 303, 323, 333, 337, 341, 361, 366, 382. *See also* federal research support
federal research support, 5, 28–30, 95, 102–3, 106, 110, 116, 193–96, 203, 224, 248, 271–79, 287–88, 305, 321, 362, 379; diminished, vii, 246, 271; and health care, 257; increase in, 96; and university policy, 197–98, 245, 272. *See also* basic research; biomedical research; research and development
federal science policy, 236, 271–94
feeder schools, 368
financial aid, 106, 123, 302; and admissions, 4, 14, 303, 304, 354; availability of, 161, 314; federal, 4, 324, 362, 387; for foreign students, 171, 352–54
Finn, David, viii
first principles, 108
fixed costs, 10. *See also* direct costs; indirect costs
Flexner, Abraham, 312
Florida, Richard, 237, 249
Ford Administration, 248

Ford Foundation, 144, 309, 322, 323
foreign industry, 346, 347
foreign policy, 276, 289, 356
foreign students, 278, 356; admission of, 192, 232, 329, 337, 339, 349, 350–51; financial aid for, 171, 352, 353, 354. *See also* admissions; graduate students
Foucault, Michel, 72
Frankfurter Allgemeine Zeitung (newspaper), 317
Franklin, Benjamin, 27
fraternities, 46, 47, 188, 369
freedom, 42, 48, 324; academic, 38, 41, 45, 91, 106, 187, 244, 303, 338; intellectual, 272, 285; research, 101; of thought, 21, 186
free exchange of ideas, 187
free speech, 14, 15, 16, 22, 244, 306
Frege, Gottlob, 61
Freudianism, 49
fund-raising, 99, 117, 123, 132, 305, 347

Gardner, Howard, viii
GDP. *See* Gross Domestic Product
Geiger, Roger, 316, 321
gender, 72
genetic fallacy, 66, 75
George Mason University, 219
Georgetown University, 380
German doctoral seminar, 219
German university, 33, 155, 159, 311, 319, 324
Giamatti, A. Bartlett, 25
GI Bill of Rights, 379
GNP. *See* Gross National Product
Goe, W. Richard, 237, 249
Goethe, Johann Wolfgang von, 290
Goodstein, David, 291
Goodwin, Craufurd, 339, 340, 357
Gossett, Philip, viii
governance, 6, 9, 99, 111, 249, 250, 300; by administrators, 42, 85–86, 254, 308; corporate models of, 1, 119–22, 124, 127, 129; by faculty, 7, 10, 42, 85–86, 139; problems of, vii, 2, 5, 299, 301–2
governing board, 112
government. *See* federal government

Government-University-Industry Research Roundtable (GUIRR), 192, 195
grade inflation, 388
graduate education, 149, 172, 181, 193, 237, 308, 315; federal funding of, 231, 352; format of, 166, 167, 184, 272; in humanities and social sciences, 165, 277; support for, 25, 118, 181
graduate schools, 162, 235, 315; curricula, 197; financial resources, 139, 224; student preparation for, 163
graduate students, 25, 46, 47, 48, 118, 138, 140, 159, 161, 173, 226, 227, 228, 233; demand for, 134, 181, 320, 361; diversification of, 53, 199; education of, 26, 28, 133, 149, 157, 158, 165, 197, 370, 383; foreign, 109, 172, 351, 354; role in research, 237, 275; teaching by, 27, 112–13, 142, 160, 166–67, 292, 354
grandes écoles, 311, 318
Graubard, Stephen R., viii, ix, 294
Great Society programs, 248
Grinnell College, 224
Gross Domestic Product (GDP), 216, 294, 317
Gross National Product (GNP), 255, 257
group conflict, 43
Guggenheim Fellowship program, 136
GUIRR. *See* Government-University-Industry Research Roundtable
Gulf War, 209

Habermas, Jurgen, 72
Harper, William Rainey, 115, 371
Harrison, Donald C., 256
Harvard College Gazette, 314
Harvard University, 3, 26, 104, 132, 212, 220, 221, 222, 223, 231, 260, 281, 289, 299, 313, 366, 368, 371, 372, 373, 376, 377, 380, 381, 384, 386; Medical School, 260; undergraduate education at, 27, 158, 191
"hate speech," 16, 41

health care, 216, 259, 266. *See also* competition; criticism; federal research support
health-care costs, 255, 257, 258. *See also* reform
health-care reforms, 262, 265
health-care system, 256, 265
health professions, 254, 265
health sciences, 3, 4, 253, 254, 255. *See also* mission
health sciences center, 253, 255, 258, 262, 263
Heidegger, Martin, 76
High Energy Physics Advisory Committee, 290
higher education, ix, 20, 56, 72, 109, 189, 192, 205, 219, 253, 314, 316, 318, 324, 336; changes in, 2, 5, 71, 90, 330; conceptions of, 69, 82, 323; crisis within, viii, 43, 208, 212, 310; debates in, 55, 60, 258; decline of, 1, 89, 162, 216, 329; environment of, vii, 131, 351; funding of, 30, 213, 218; growth of, 317, 320; history of, 203, 311, 312; pluralism in, 99, 107; role of, 44, 49, 198–99, 215, 222, 224, 304, 315, 319, 333
high schools, 156
Hippocratic Oath, 186
hiring policies, 44, 198, 306. *See also* minorities
Hise, Charles van, 372
Hispanics, 42, 44
Hitler, Adolph, 374
Hofstadter, Richard, 205
holding company, 119–24, 127, 129
Holton, Gerald, viii
Hoover Institution, 210, 219
humanities, 46, 107, 135, 136, 174, 183, 220, 255, 329; curricular debates in, 16, 55–56, 70, 244, 325, 327, 390; educational mission of, 69, 71, 72, 75–76, 165, 387; funding for, 120, 277, 378, 379–81; teaching of, 224, 267
human resources, 279, 309
Hume, David, 59, 60
Hutchins, Robert Maynard, 1, 115, 241, 242, 321, 372

IGS. *See* Institute of Governmental Studies
immigrants, 37
Indiana University, 380, 385
Indian Institutes of Technology, 317
indirect costs, 106, 186, 204, 214, 246; funding for, 89, 103, 117, 118, 170, 194, 245, 282, 302; of medical education, 261, 263
industrial liaison programs, 346, 347
industrial research, 236
industry, 135, 136, 191, 236, 247, 257, 273, 284, 341, 343, 363, 384; foreign, 335, 342, 344–45, 347–48, 349, 351, 353; partnerships with universities, 2, 30–32, 174, 206, 214, 237, 248, 276, 277, 336; sponsorship of R&D, 197, 203, 213, 224, 238
information revolution, 4. *See also* electronic communication
information technology, 239. *See also* electronic communication
innovation, 94
Institute of Governmental Studies (IGS), 226–29
intellectualism, 46
intellectual property rights, 277, 285, 335, 348
interdisciplinarity, 168, 226, 292
interdisciplinary programs, 93, 94, 113, 122, 234, 241
internationalism, 171
internationalization: of curricula, 170–71, 337, 338–41, 353; of research, 293; of research universities, 109, 330–31, 333, 357. *See also* curriculum; engineering
internet, 138. *See also* electronic communication; information technology
intersubjectivity, 68, 70
Irish Catholic Americans, 37
Ivy League, 220, 314, 368, 387

Jamieson, Adrienne, ix, 227
Jews, 37, 72, 374
Job Corps, 281
John F. Kennedy School of Government, 231

Johns Hopkins University, The, 115, 191, 253, 265, 267, 281, 313, 364; School of Medicine, 260, 267, 382
Johnson, Lyndon, 258, 382, 387
Johnson Administration, 248

K-12 education, 193–94
Kane, Nancy, 259
Kant, Immanuel, 60
Kaysen, Carl, viii
Keller, Morton, viii
Kelley, William, viii
Kennan, Elizabeth T., viii
Kennedy, Donald, ix, 241
Kennedy, John F., 387
Keohane, Nannerl, ix, 226
Kerr, Clark, 241, 313, 324, 387
Kevles, Daniel J., viii
Killing the Spirit (Smith), 210
knowledge base, 5, 158, 240, 266. *See also* basic science
Kuhn, Thomas, 71, 78, 79, 325
Kyoto University, 311

land grant universities, 155
leadership, 2, 93, 107, 194, 199, 254, 288, 294, 311; administrative, 86, 121–22, 242, 351; presidential, 115, 123, 127, 129, 307; quality of, 112; university, 90, 91, 101
Lederman, Leon, 95, 283, 327
liberal arts, 122, 222, 312; education in, 142, 163, 164, 165, 194, 387; place of, in the research university, 120–21, 129, 182
liberal arts colleges, 38, 313, 314; emphasis on teaching at, 156, 159, 189
liberal education, 48, 49, 314, 328, 331
liberalism, 40
libraries, 138, 157, 160, 175, 226; and university budgets, 87, 89, 170
Liebman, Lance, viii
life sciences, 86, 256, 289, 292
Lincoln, Abraham, 253
"linear thinking," 59
Lipset, Seymour Martin, ix
"little science," 286, 294
Locke, John, 62
"logocentrism," 59

Lombardi, John, 262–63
Los Alamos, 375, 377
Low, Seth, 371
Lowell, A. Lawrence, 115, 220
lung cancer, 265

Madden, Susan Koch, 259
Malthus, Thomas, 363
Mamet, David, 17, 18, 21, 22
"managed care," 261
managed competition, 262
Mansfield Amendment, 276, 277, 280
"marketplace of ideas," 161
Marxism, 49, 72, 74
Massachusetts Institute of Technology (MIT), 191, 213, 281, 333, 340, 346, 347, 349, 350, 380, 383
Massey, Walter E., ix
Master of Business Administration (MBA), 313
mathematical sciences, 144, 145
Max Planck Institutes, 219
McDonnell Foundation, James S., ix
media, 30, 43, 204, 216, 227, 362. *See also* national press
Medicaid, 258
medical education, 240
medical research, 326
medical school, 163, 254; curricula, 167, 261; research in, 236, 253; revenue, 256, 260. *See also* university medical schools
medical science, 169
Medicare, 258, 263, 264
"megascience," 290
Megascience Forum, 290
mega-university, 115, 199, 122, 124, 128
Mellon Foundation, Andrew W., ix
meritocracy, 1, 22, 41, 311; as opposed to entitlement, 14, 15, 40, 42; traditional values of, vii, 13, 38
Meyerson, Martin, viii
Michels, Roberto, 154
microelectronics, 191
Middle Ages, 59, 75, 170
minorities, 41, 50–53, 71, 199, 200, 329, 350, 353, 386; and university

hiring and admissions policies, viii, 39, 40, 44, 92, 93. *See also* admissions
mission: of Columbia University, 8–9; of faculty, 48; of federal agencies, 144, 146, 273, 275, 276, 288, 289; of health sciences, 254, 259, 266, 268; intellectual, 39, 69, 126, 141, 248; multiculturalist, viii, 45; research, 23, 32, 47, 91, 130, 199, 203, 281; of research universities, vii, 1, 56, 120, 121, 140, 153, 154, 155, 157, 158, 159, 165, 168, 171, 174, 176, 201, 241, 245; teaching, 23, 25, 47, 91, 129, 161, 186; of University of California, 200
mission statement, 86, 153
MIT. *See* Massachusetts Institute of Technology
mobility, 40, 49, 123
modern science, 17
monasteries, 156
Moore, Sally F., viii
Morison, Samuel Eliot, 371
Morrill Act, 363
Moynihan, Daniel Patrick, 323
Muller, Steven, ix
multiculturalism, 14, 37, 39, 56, 163, 330. *See also* social sciences
muscular dystrophy, 256
Myrdal, Gunnar, 376

Nacht, Michael, 339, 340, 357
NASA. *See* National Aeronautics and Space Administration
National Academy of Sciences, 95, 220, 277, 288, 343
National Adult Literacy Survey, 309
National Aeronautics and Space Administration (NASA), 237, 247
National Cancer Institute, 289
National Centers for Scientific Research (CNRS), 219
National Defense Education Act (NDEA), 323, 324
National Endowment for the Humanities (NEH), 75, 277, 381
"National Goals for Education," 310
National Heart, Lung, and Blood Institute, 102

National Institute of Education, 248
National Institutes of Health (NIH), 247, 256, 275, 276, 289, 383
National Labor Relations Board, 302
national press, 194, 208. *See also* media
national ranking studies, 220
national science base, 292
National Science Foundation (NSF), 147, 195, 197, 198, 215, 234, 247, 275, 280, 284, 291, 383; creation of, 377–78; support of research, 144–46, 236, 277
national security, 273
Native Americans, 44
natural sciences, 61, 77, 183, 220, 248, 322; curricula, 244–45, 341; funding for, 120, 277, research in, 239
nazism, 374
NEH. *See* National Endowment for the Humanities
new areas of knowledge, 5, 10, 136
New Federalism, 89
Newman, John Henry, 223
"New Spirit," 324, 325, 328
Newtonian Mechanics, 71
New Yorker, 268
New York University, 380
Nichols, Rodney W., ix, 327
Nietzsche, Friedrich Wilhelm, 59, 71, 72, 76, 79
NIH. *See* National Institutes of Health
Nixon Administration, 248
Nobelists, 314
Nobel Prize, 2, 108, 185, 220, 223, 373
nonacademic research institutions, 236, 243
NORC, 208, 210. *See also* University of Chicago
NSF. *See* National Science Foundation
null, 14, 16, 23; cognitive, 17; ownership of, 11, 18, 19, 20, 21, 22
null hypothesis, 12, 13, 14, 15, 16

Oakley, Francis, viii
Oberlin College, 212, 222, 224

objectivity, 58, 68, 70, 238; attacks on, 11, 55, 56, 69; belief in, 22, 74, 75; standards of, 72
OECD. *See* Organization for Economic Cooperation and Development
Office of Education, 248
Office of Naval Research, 144, 280
Office of Strategic Services, 375
Oleanna (Mamet), 17, 21
on-line data bases, 227, 228. *See also* electronic communication
Organization for Economic Cooperation and Development (OECD), 290, 310
organized skepticism, 13, 22, 32
Origin of Species (Darwin), 150
Orlen, Joel, viii
OTA. *See* Congressional Office of Technology Assessment
Oxbridge, 220
Oxford University, 124, 155, 311, 364, 367, 390

paradigms, 108, 193, 289
parochialism, 170, 172, 340
Pasteur, Louis, 293
patents, 238, 247, 285
PCAST. *See* President's Council of Advisers on Science and Technology
pedagogy, 27
peer judgment, 197, 198
peer review, 91, 145, 146, 147, 165, 280. *See also* academic research
Pelikan, Jaroslav, 205
Pentagon, 275, 276, 278, 302
Perkins, James A., 154, 155, 156
Petersdorf, Robert, 261
Pew Health Professions Commission, 263, 264
pharmaceuticals, 191, 257, 289
Ph.D. programs, 4, 305
Ph.D.s, 131, 196, 316, 320
philanthropic organizations, 156
philosophical relativism, 4, 49
philosophy of language, 61, 62
physical sciences, 107, 254, 289, 325; funding for, 120, 144, 145, 276; prestige of, 210

plagiarism, 167, 186
Planck, Max, 87
Plato, 74
pluralism, 45, 164; of higher
    education, 99, 107; in research
    support, 276, 280, 288
political correctness, 13, 17, 41, 45,
    125, 126
Political Parties (Michels), 154
polity, 42, 43, 45, 172
Polsby, Nelson W., ix, 227
Pomona College, 212
positivism, 16
postdoctoral students, 196, 223, 305,
    320, 344, 346, 374, 383; funding
    for, 25; training of, 131, 166, 197,
    237, 316
postmodernism, 56, 68, 77, 82, 325
postwar period, 5, 28, 342, 343
presidency, 124
president, 10, 25, 86, 88, 91, 93,
    119, 131, 154, 158, 210, 211, 221,
    253, 258, 262, 274, 292, 299, 303,
    304, 323, 368, 369, 371, 372, 376,
    385; role of, 7, 11, 97, 100, 104,
    107, 116, 117, 128, 132, 153, 182,
    272, 301, 308, 339, 373, 374
Presidential Young Investigators
    (PYIs), 198, 199
President's Council of Advisers on
    Science and Technology (PCAST),
    89, 195, 206, 215
President's Science Advisory
    Committee, 274
prestige, 47, 166; cultural, 311;
    occupational, 210–11; in research,
    24, 158; of research universities,
    38, 85, 112, 133, 148, 234, 309,
    312, 313
Prewitt, Kenneth, viii, ix, 309
primary care physicians, 261, 263,
    264
Princeton University, 97, 107, 154,
    258, 314, 327, 364, 371, 380, 384
priorities, 197, 198, 203, 272, 273,
    283, 290; establishment of, 86, 87,
    107, 186, 195, 200, 282, 287; in
    health-care systems, 265; resistance
    to, 96, 181

productivity, 90, 214, 257, 265, 293,
    343
professional schools, 46, 112, 115,
    150, 163, 212, 222, 235, 243, 313;
    relationship to research universities,
    107, 111, 119, 122, 136, 140, 165,
    180, 224, 233, 264, 305, 312. *See
    also* curriculum
professions, 37, 112, 204, 243, 303,
    305, 313, 315, 326; changes in,
    165; education in, 104
professoriate, 17, 26, 105, 159, 167,
    243, 244, 361, 376
Progressives, 203
Progressivism, 322
provost, 7, 10, 11, 256
public service, 154, 191, 199, 312
pure research, 156, 159
PYIs. *See* Presidential Young
    Investigators

quotas, 37
quota systems, 14

R&D. *See* research and development
race, 72
racial tensions, 37
racism, 12, 15, 52
RAND Corporation, 284
rationality, 57, 58, 59, 67, 68, 69,
    78, 80, 240; challenge to, 11, 13,
    55, 56, 73; critics of, 17, 70, 76;
    traditional values of, vii, 22, 66, 72
Ravitch, Diane, viii
"realism," 56, 60, 61, 73, 76, 80, 81
reality, 59, 62, 71, 81; conceptions
    of, 55, 57, 69; correspondence to,
    79; independently existing, 58, 60,
    61, 66, 72, 76, 78, 80; nature of,
    56, 70; relationship to language,
    65
Redbook (report), 377
"redundancy theory of truth," 64
Reed College, 222
reform, 70, 166, 208, 264; curricular,
    52, 73, 74, 207, 213, 368, 377; in
    elementary and secondary school
    education, 279, 289, 291; health-
    care cost, 259

regents, 86, 99, 132
"relativism," 75, 110, 188, 325, 327.
    See also philosophical relativism
Relativity Theory, 71
Renaissance, 59, 75, 321
"Renewing the Promise: Research-
    Intensive Universities and the
    Nation," 195
Rensselaer Polytechnic Institute, 191
reputation, 133
Rescher, Nicholas, 196
research. *See* academic research;
    applied research; basic research;
    biomedical research; medical
    research; pure research; scientific
    research; university-based research
research and development (R&D),
    213, 240, 280, 283, 288, 293, 294,
    334, 335, 336, 343; expenditures,
    196, 236–37, 256, 274, 337;
    federal support, 231, 238, 278,
    287, 289. *See also* industry
Research Applied to National Needs
    (RANN), 248
research assistants, 117, 118, 227
research centers, 146
research grants, 117, 120, 193, 194,
    302, 351
research hypothesis, 12
research institutes, 33
research mission, 129, 130, 203
Research Triangle Park, 174, 214
resource allocation, 8, 11, 86, 184,
    207, 231, 288, 305
resource centers, 168
retrenchment, 286, 287, 288. *See also*
    academic research
reward system, 13
Rhodes, Frank H. T., ix
Ricardo, David, 363
Richardson, William C., ix
Riesman, David, 222, 224
Rockefeller, Nelson, 386
Rockefeller Foundation, 176, 203,
    322
Rockefeller University, 281
Roosevelt, Franklin, 377
Rorty, Richard, 71, 72, 76–79
Rosenblith, Walter A., viii

Rosenzweig, Robert M., viii, ix
Rosovsky, Henry, 104, 105, 132
Rota, Gian-Carlo, viii
Rothblatt, Sheldon, 384
Rudenstine, Neil, 314, 325

Said, Edward, viii
scholarship, vii, 17, 219, 311, 312,
    320, 327, 356; commitment to,
    198, 201, 313; criteria of, 16;
    direction of, 305, 321, 333, 329;
    eminence of, 315; instructional,
    199; traditional, 75
science. *See* academic science; applied
    science; atmospheric sciences; basic
    science; behavioral sciences, "big
    science"; biological sciences;
    biomedical sciences; "cheap
    science"; computer sciences; earth
    sciences; environmental science;
    health sciences; life sciences; "little
    science"; mathematical sciences;
    medical science; modern science;
    natural sciences; physical sciences;
    science and technology; "science
    boom"; social sciences; veterinary
    science
Science (journal), 326
science and technology, 32, 116, 232,
    270, 333; funding for, 30, 117,
    306; international competence in,
    334–35, 343, 349, 351, 353
Science and Technology Centers, 197,
    234
"science boom," 88
"Science: The Endless Frontier"
    (Bush), 377, 378
scientific misconduct, 203, 209
scientific research, 23, 147, 253, 291;
    funding for, 4, 5, 29, 96, 173, 327;
    progress in, 170. *See also*
    Department of Defense
Searle, John R., ix, 11, 244, 329
secondary education, 160, 291, 367,
    390. *See also* reform
secondary schools, 288, 318
selectivity, 282
semiconductors, 191
seminaries, 156

senescence, 94, 98
separatism, 307
sexism, 20
sexual harassment, 20, 167, 203
"sexual preference revolution," 37
Shakespeare, William, 68
Shapiro, Harold T., 257, 314
Silicon Valley, 174, 193, 213–14
Simon, Herbert, 108, 240
Singer, Maxine, viii
Skolnikoff, Eugene B., ix, 109
Sloan Foundation, Alfred P., ix
Smelser, Neil J., viii, ix, 15, 194, 244
Smith, Adam, 136
Smith, Page, 210
"social contract," 321, 335
social sciences, 12, 16, 46, 55, 77,
    95, 107, 174, 180, 183, 220, 224,
    249, 255, 266, 323, 329, 390;
    disciplinary lines in, 341;
    foundations of, 17, 94, 322;
    funding for, 120, 289, 381;
    multiculturalism in, 244, 349;
    research in, 239, 267, 277, 378;
    skepticism of, 325, 327, 387. *See
    also* graduate education
Socrates, 58
Sorbonne, 220, 311
sororities, 46, 47, 369
specialization, 150, 233, 236; in
    medicine, 263; need for, 135–36,
    139, 142–43, 197, 232, 242;
    professional, 123; in research
    universities, 116, 189, 339
speech codes, 13, 16
Spinosa, Charles, 82
Sputnik, 90, 279, 321, 323, 382
Stafford Little Lectures, 154
Stanford University, 3, 85, 86, 93,
    95, 96, 97, 101, 102, 105, 106,
    220, 221, 281, 302, 303, 313, 364,
    372, 380, 384; Hoover Institution,
    210, 219; indirect cost abuses at,
    89, 103; minorities at, 92;
    undergraduate instruction at, 93,
    110, 212, 223
State Department, 277
state teachers colleges, 193
State University of New York, 386
Stigler, Stephen M., ix, 241

Strategic Plan, 86
Street Corner Society (Whyte), 50
structuralism, 325
Structure of Scientific Revolutions
    (Kuhn), 78
student body, 16, 17, 105, 164, 319,
    354. *See also* diversity
Sutton, Francis X., ix
Swarthmore College, 222, 224

taxol, 257
Teachers Insurance and Annuity
    Association (TIAA), 243
teaching assistants, 149, 166, 227,
    228; instruction by, 184–85, 221–
    22, 354–55
teaching hospitals, 249, 258, 260,
    261, 263, 264
teaching loads, 100, 105, 214, 221,
    222, 223
technical schools, 191, 317
"technology transfer," 285, 289
Teitelbaum, Michael, viii, ix
tenure, 7, 14, 18, 21, 66, 86, 91, 96,
    98, 100, 105, 203, 204, 245, 286,
    340; history of, 243, 244; review
    process, 104, 235; and teaching,
    11, 20, 26, 28, 221
"term of art," 18, 19
Thatcher, Margaret, 384
Thier, Samuel, viii
Third World, 316, 317, 329, 339
Tocqueville, Alexis de, 366, 389
Tosteson, Daniel, 260
Truman, Harry, 377
trustees, 86, 90, 98, 102, 132, 301,
    372; role of, 6, 11, 99, 111, 150,
    244; support of, 103, 212–13, 341
tuition, 101, 124, 149, 161, 170,
    203, 315, 387; escalating costs, 26,
    138

UCLA. *See* University of California,
    Los Angeles
UIRCs. *See* university-industry
    research centers
undergraduate education, 101, 102,
    107, 120, 164, 167, 168, 184, 354,
    355; history of, 49; quality of, 112,

146, 148–49, 161, 163, 172, 180–
82, 188, 194, 314, 331
undergraduate instruction, 220, 221
undergraduate students, viii, 27, 46,
47, 53, 133, 158, 159, 166, 180,
199, 222, 265, 292, 318, 354, 368,
370, 386; education of, 23, 25–26,
28, 89, 110, 112, 120, 142, 148–
49, 157, 160, 161–64, 179, 182,
186, 192, 194, 210, 220, 221, 226,
229, 230, 235, 237, 268, 314;
foreign, 109; quality of, 48, 137,
223, 227, 361. *See also* Harvard
University
United Nations Educational,
Scientific, and Cultural
Organization (UNESCO), 323
universalism, 15, 41, 42
universality, 69
University: An Owner's Manual
(Rosovsky), 132
university-based research, 192, 219;
foreign industry access to, 335,
341; funding, 31, 215, 248
university-industry research centers
(UIRCs): development of, 237–38,
248; role of, 249–50
university medical schools, 249
University of California, 191, 200,
222, 281, 372, 383, 384; early
years, 381; minority representation
at, 199
University of California, Berkeley, 2,
37, 55, 97, 220, 221, 222, 224,
226, 227, 229, 313, 384
University of California, Los Angeles
(UCLA), 384
University of California, Santa Cruz,
191, 210
University of Chicago, 3, 131, 200,
241, 313, 364, 371, 380; NORC,
208; undergraduate instruction at,
149, 191
University of Cincinnati, 256
University of Florida, 262, 380, 383
University of Illinois, 281
University of Maryland, 339
University of Michigan, 107, 191,
281, 313, 320, 372, 381, 384
University of Minnesota, 191

University of Pennsylvania, 380
University of Texas, 281, 380
University of Tokyo, 220, 311
University of Washington, 260;
Medical School, 260
University of Wisconsin, 191, 372,
381
university presidency, 5; holding
company model and, 120–22; past
and present, 115–18, 127–30;
student impact on, 126–27;
university administration and, 122–
23
US Congress, 88, 100, 117, 214, 227,
229, 284, 307, 353, 362; as source
of research funds, 30, 119, 145–
46, 236, 256, 276; public
confidence in, 208
U.S. News & World Report, 107, 314

Veblen, Thorstein, 373
veterinary science, 136
Vietnam, 276, 372, 382
"visiting committees," 96
vocational schools, 156
Voltaire, 59
von Neumann Whitman, Marina, viii

Wealth of Nations (Smith), 136
Weed, Lawrence, 240
Wellesley College, 224
Wells, Herman, 385
Wesleyan University, 212, 224
Western Rationalistic Tradition, 11,
63, 65, 72, 73, 80; attacks on, 66,
71, 75, 76–79, 329; conception
and features of, 57–61, 67, 68;
relation to the university, 69–70
Whitcomb, Michael, 260
White House Office of Science and
Technology Policy, 284
Whyte, William Foote, 50
Williams College, 212
Wilson, Marjorie, 261
Wilson, Woodrow, 371
women's movement, 37
World Bank, 317
World War I, 365, 367, 371, 372
World War II, 220, 237, 245, 314,
333, 334, 340, 361, 375, 379, 382,

World War II *(co*
   389; effect on t
   387, 388; impa
   university, 273,   , ⌐02,
   369, 376, 380, 381, 383, 390;
   post–World War II years, 87, 144,
   215, 221, 234, 274, 276, 278, 280,
   281, 305, 313, 321, 322, 328, 329
world wars, 203, 231

Yale University, 25, 97, 205, 222,
   299, 364, 366, 369, 371, 372, 380,

esearch
           , ⌐1; undergraduate
   ...truction at, 191, 212
"yield gap," 212
Young Scientists Network (YSN),
   196

Zuckerman, Harriet, ix

Library of Congress Cataloging-in-Publication Data

The Research university in a time of discontent / edited by Jonathan R. Cole,
Elinor G. Barber, Stephen R. Graubard.
   p.   cm.
   Expanded version of Dædalus, v. 122, no. 4, proceedings of the American
Academy of Arts and Sciences.
   Includes index.
   ISBN 0-8018-4957-8 (alk. paper). — ISBN 0-8018-4958-6 (pbk. : alk. paper)
   1. Education, Higher—United States—Aims and objectives. 2. Research—United
States. 3. Research institutes—United States. I. Cole, Jonathan R. II. Barber,
Elinor G. III. Graubard, Stephen Richards. IV. American Academy of Arts and
Sciences.
LA227.4.R47   1994
   378.73—dc20   94-19837
                                                                    CIP